797,885 Books

are available to read at

Forgotten Books

www.ForgottenBooks.com

Forgotten Books' App
Available for mobile, tablet & eReader

English
Français
Deutsche
Italiano
Español
Português

www.forgottenbooks.com

Mythology Photography **Fiction**
Fishing Christianity **Art** Cooking
Essays **Buddhism** Freemasonry
Medicine **Biology** Music **Ancient Egypt** Evolution Carpentry Physics
Dance Geology **Mathematics** Fitness
Shakespeare **Folklore** Yoga Marketing
Confidence Immortality Biographies
Poetry **Psychology** Witchcraft
Electronics Chemistry History **Law**
Accounting **Philosophy** Anthropology
Alchemy Drama Quantum Mechanics
Atheism Sexual Health **Ancient History**
Entrepreneurship Languages Sport
Paleontology Needlework Islam
Metaphysics Investment Archaeology
Parenting Statistics Criminology
Motivational

THE LIBRARY
OF THE
NEW YORK STATE SCHOOL
OF
INDUSTRIAL AND LABOR
RELATIONS

AT
CORNELL UNIVERSITY

NATIONAL HEALTH INSURANCE.

HANDBOOK

FOR THE USE OF

INSURANCE COMMITTEES IN SCOTLAND.

(1st October 1915.)

EDINBURGH:
PRINTED UNDER THE AUTHORITY OF HIS MAJESTY'S
STATIONERY OFFICE
By MORRISON & GIBB, LIMITED, TANFIELD.

To be purchased, either directly or through any Bookseller, from
H.M. STATIONERY OFFICE (SCOTTISH BRANCH),
23 FORTH STREET, EDINBURGH; or
WYMAN & SONS, LIMITED, 29 BREAMS BUILDINGS,
FETTER LANE, LONDON, E.C., and 54 ST. MARY STREET, CARDIFF; or
E. PONSONBY, LIMITED, 116 GRAFTON STREET, DUBLIN;
or from the Agencies in the British Colonies and Dependencies,
the United States of America, and other Foreign Countries, of
T. FISHER UNWIN, LONDON, W.C.

1915.
Price One Shilling.

CONTENTS.

                                                                  PAGE

INTRODUCTION—GENERAL SCHEME OF ADMINISTRATION OF THE NATIONAL INSURANCE ACTS . . . v
    Central Authorities.
    Local Administration.
    Special Committees.

CHAPTER I.—CONSTITUTION, PROCEDURE, POWERS AND DUTIES OF INSURANCE COMMITTEES 1
    Constitution :—
        Introductory ; Insurance Committee Areas ; Composition of Insurance Committees ; Representatives of Insured Persons, County and Town Councils, Medical Practitioners, and the Commissioners ; Combination of Committees.
    Procedure :—
        Standing Orders ; Offices.
    Powers and Duties :—
        Administration of Benefits ; Miscellaneous.

CHAPTER II.—CONSTITUTION, PROCEDURE, POWERS AND DUTIES OF SUB-COMMITTEES OF INSURANCE COMMITTEES . . 25
    Sub-Committees :—
        Medical Service Sub-Committee ; Pharmaceutical Service Sub-Committee ; Joint Services Sub-Committee ; General.
    District Insurance Committees.

CHAPTER III.—LOCAL MEDICAL COMMITTEES, PANEL COMMITTEES, AND PHARMACEUTICAL COMMITTEES   35

CHAPTER IV.—MEDICAL BENEFIT . . . 45
        General ; Arrangements with Practitioners and Institutions ; Arrangements with Chemists and Pharmacists ; Register ; Arrangements in reference to Insured Persons ; Complaints.

CHAPTER V.—SANATORIUM BENEFIT 83
    Arrangements with persons and Local Authorities, including arrangements with Medical Practitioners :—
        General ; Institutional Treatment ; Dispensary Treatment ; Domiciliary Treatment.
    Expenses of Sanatorium Benefit and miscellaneous administrative questions :—
        Financial basis ; Recommendation for Sanatorium Benefit ; Expenses of Conveyance.
    Extension of Sanatorium Benefit to Dependants.

	PAGE
CHAPTER VI.—DEPOSIT CONTRIBUTORS	102

Contributions; Refunds; Rules; Medical and Sanatorium Benefits; Sickness and Disablement Benefits; Maternity Benefit; Administrative Procedure.

CHAPTER VII.—FINANCE AND ACCOUNTING OF INSURANCE COMMITTEES	128

Medical Benefit Income :—
    General Medical Benefit Fund; Medical Benefit Fund Account; Central Medical Benefit Fund; Special Income.
Sanatorium Benefit Income :—
    General Sanatorium Benefit Fund; Central Sanatorium Benefit Fund.
Administration Income.
General Purposes Income.
Transfer between Funds.
Expenditure and Accounting :—
    General; General Cash Book; Ledger Accounts; Current Account with the Commissioners; Medical Benefit Fund; Panel Service Fund; Practitioners Fund; Drug Fund; Institutions Fund; Special Arrangements Fund; Temporary Residents Fund; Special Transactions; Sanatorium Benefit Fund; Administration Fund; Deposit Contributors Benefits Account; General Purposes Fund; Alternative Forms of Accounts; Bank Account.

CHAPTER VIII.—GENERAL	156

Administration.
Contracts.

APPENDIX I.	LIST OF ACTS AND PRINCIPAL REGULATIONS AND ORDERS	157
APPENDIX II. (A.)	CONSTITUTION OF INSURANCE COMMITTEES	159
(B.)	ELECTORAL DIVISIONS AND VOTES FOR APPOINTMENT OF DRUG ACCOUNTS COMMITTEE	160
APPENDIX III.	MODEL RULES FOR ADMINISTRATION OF MEDICAL BENEFIT	161
APPENDIX IV.	LIST OF LOCAL MEDICAL COMMITTEES RECOGNISED BY THE COMMISSIONERS	165
APPENDIX V.	LIST OF PANEL COMMITTEES WITH MEMBERSHIP, QUORUM, AND SECRETARIES	165
APPENDIX VI.	LIST OF PHARMACEUTICAL COMMITTEES WITH MEMBERSHIP, QUORUM, AND SECRETARIES	167
APPENDIX VII.	AGREEMENT BETWEEN MEDICAL PRACTITIONER AND INSURANCE COMMITTEE	169
APPENDIX VIII.	PROCEDURE IN INQUIRIES AS TO RANGE OF MEDICAL SERVICE	173
APPENDIX IX.	MEDICAL RECORD CARD	175

		PAGE
APPENDIX X.	MEMORANDUM DEALING WITH NEW SYSTEM OF MEDICAL CERTIFICATION OF INCAPACITY OF INSURED PERSONS FOR WORK (MEMORANDUM 211 I.C.)	177
APPENDIX XI.	INSURANCE COMMITTEE AREAS FOR WHICH THE POST OFFICE MEDICAL SYSTEM HAS BEEN APPROVED UNDER SECTION 15 (4) OF THE 1911 ACT.	195
APPENDIX XII.	AGREEMENT BETWEEN PERSON UNDERTAKING TO SUPPLY DRUGS AND APPLIANCES AND INSURANCE COMMITTEE	195
APPENDIX XIII.	MEDICAL CARD	200
APPENDIX XIV.	LIST OF SANATORIA IN SCOTLAND APPROVED BY THE LOCAL GOVERNMENT BOARD FOR SCOTLAND FOR THE INSTITUTIONAL TREATMENT OF TUBERCULOSIS UNDER THE NATIONAL INSURANCE ACTS	204
APPENDIX XV.	MODEL SCHEME OF ARRANGEMENTS FOR THE DOMICILIARY TREATMENT OF TUBERCULOSIS, WITH RELATIVE CIRCULAR	209
APPENDIX XVI.	LETTER OF THE CHANCELLOR OF THE EXCHEQUER TO MR. HENRY HOBHOUSE REGARDING FINANCIAL ARRANGEMENTS FOR DEFRAYING THE COST OF SCHEMES FOR TREATMENT OF TUBERCULOSIS	216
APPENDIX XVII.	MODEL RULES FOR DEPOSIT CONTRIBUTORS	217
APPENDIX XVIII.	DIAGRAM ILLUSTRATING THE SYSTEM OF MEDICAL BENEFIT FINANCE . opposite	220
APPENDIX XIX.	SCHEME FOR THE DISTRIBUTION OF THE PARLIAMENTARY GRANT IN AID OF MILEAGE IN SPARSELY POPULATED DISTRICTS IN SCOTLAND, EXCLUSIVE OF THE HIGHLANDS AND ISLANDS, FOR THE YEAR 1914	221
APPENDIX XX.	COMMISSIONERS AND OFFICIALS	222
APPENDIX XXI.	(A) INSURANCE COMMITTEES IN SCOTLAND, WITH NAMES AND ADDRESSES OF CLERKS AND TELEPHONE NUMBERS; (B) ADDRESSES OF INSURANCE COMMITTEES IN ENGLAND, IRELAND, AND WALES	224
APPENDIX XXII.	REFERENCE CIPHERS OF INSURANCE COMMITTEES (UNITED KINGDOM)	231
APPENDIX XXIII.	FAIR WAGES CLAUSE IN CONTRACTS	233
APPENDIX XXIV.	INSURANCE COMMITTEES CONTRACTING WITH MEMBERS (CIRCULAR No. 427)	235
APPENDIX XXV.	ADMISSION OF PRESS TO MEETINGS OF INSURANCE COMMITTEES (CIRCULAR No. 382)	236
INDEX		237

INTRODUCTION.

This Handbook is intended primarily for the assistance of members of Insurance Committees, and does not profess to be an exhaustive or technical exposition of the powers and duties of the Committee. Detailed information and authority for administrative purposes should be obtained from the National Insurance Acts, 1911–1915, and the Regulations and Orders made in pursuance thereof. A list of the Acts and the principal Regulations and Orders forms Appendix I. hereto.

The general scheme of administration of the National Insurance Acts in Scotland in so far as relating to National Health Insurance is briefly summarised in this introduction in order that the position of Insurance Committees which is dealt with in detail in the subsequent chapters of the Handbook may be seen in true perspective.

Unemployment insurance which is administered through the Board of Trade and the Labour Exchanges controlled by that Department is not dealt with.

The following is the general scheme of administration of National Health Insurance :—

I. Central Authorities.

1. *The Treasury*—
    (a) Appointment of Commissioners and Joint Committee.
    (b) Appointment and direction of Auditors of Insurance Committee and Approved Society transactions.
    (c) Appointment of Valuers of Approved Societies.
    (d) Approval of Staff of Commissioners.
    (e) Control of Payment of State contributions to cost of benefits and administration thereof and control of Special State grants in aid of benefits and administration thereof.
    (f) Consent to Orders under Sec. 78 of 1911 Act to remove difficulties, and Special Orders to bring classes of persons within scope of the Act (Sec. 1 (2) of 1911 Act).
    (g) Making of Regulations—
        (1) defining duties of Joint Committee (Sec. 83).
        (2) prescribing conditions for investment by the National Debt Commissioners of sums in the several funds available for investment (Sec. 54 (3) of 1911 Act).

(h) Consent to Regulations under Sec. 56 (1) of 1911 Act as to transactions between Commissioners and Approved Societies.

2. *Joint Committee*—
   (a) Financial adjustments between funds of the several countries.
   (b) Preparation of schemes for the administration of Government Grants and their apportionment between the several countries.
   (c) Making of Regulations common to the several countries.
   (d) Making of Special Orders.
   (e) Approval of International Approved Societies.

The Chairman of the Joint Committee is the Minister responsible to Parliament in matters relating to National Health Insurance.

3. *Commissioners*—
   (a) Carrying the Act into effect in Scotland (Sec. 80 (1)).
   (b) Making of Regulations, Orders, and Special Orders.
   (c) Management of the Scottish National Health Insurance Fund.
   (d) Supervision of payment of contributions.
   (e) Approval of rules of Approved Societies and powers of control of mismanagement.
   (f) Co-ordination of financial relations between Approved Societies and Insurance Committees, and distribution of Special State Grants.
   (g) Approval of office arrangements and staffing of Insurance Committees.
   (h) Determination of questions of liability to insurance or right to become a voluntary contributor subject to appeal to the Sheriff and Court of Session.
   (i) Determination without right of appeal of questions of rate of contribution.
   (j) Determination of disputes between an insured person and an Approved Society or Insurance Committee, or between two Societies or two Committees, or a Society and a Committee, or a Committee and a panel practitioner or chemist.
   (k) Determination of questions arising in regard to transfer from one Approved Society to another.

4. *Local Government Board for Scotland*—
   (a) Administration of capital grant for Sanatoria (Sec. 64 (1) of 1911 Act).
   (b) Assisting the co-operation of local authorities for the provision of Sanatoria, etc. (Sec. 64 (3) of 1911 Act).
   (c) Approval of sanatoria and institutions for treatment under Sanatorium Benefit.

(d) Approval of manner of treatment under Sanatorium Benefit otherwise than in an approved institution.
(e) Determination of what diseases are to be treated under Sanatorium Benefit (with approval of Treasury) (Sec. 8 (1) (b) of 1911 Act).
(f) Consultation with Commissioners as to form of reports by Insurance Committees on the health of insured persons.

The Board also administer the Special Maintenance Grant voted in terms of the Hobhouse * letter for the relief of Local Authorities who are treating tuberculosis under a general scheme approved by the Board.

5. *Other Authorities to whom certain duties are entrusted are—*
   (1) Secretary for Scotland (Secs. 63 (6), 80 (3), and 80 (4) of 1911 Act).
   (2) Registrar of Friendly Societies (Secs. 72 and 75 of 1911 Act).
   (3) Comptroller and Auditor-General—audit under direction of Treasury of Scottish National Health Insurance Fund.
   (4) Board of Trade—formation of Seamen's National Insurance Society (Sec. 48 of 1911 Act).
   (5) Commissioners of Inland Revenue—preparation and issue of stamps and regulations applying provisions of Stamp Duties Management Acts.
   (6) Post Office—sale of stamps and issue of forms.
   (7) Admiralty and Army Council—administration by arrangement with Approved Society of Maternity Benefit of sailors and soldiers and of Navy and Army Fund benefits (Sec. 46 (2) (iii.) and (3) (f) of 1911 Act).
   (8) The Highlands and Islands (Medical Service) Board—improvement of medical service, including nursing in Highlands and Islands (Highlands and Islands (Medical Service) Grant Act, 1913).

II. LOCAL ADMINISTRATION.

1. *Approved Societies—*
   (a) Maternity Benefit for all members.
   (b) Sickness and Disablement and additional benefits (except those of nature of Medical Benefit), for all members who are not members of the Military or Naval Forces of the Crown.

2. *Insurance Committees—*
   (a) Sickness, Disablement, and Maternity Benefit for all Deposit Contributors.

* *See* paragraphs 345 and 347.

(b) Medical and Sanatorium Benefit for all insured persons resident in the area of the Committee except—
  (1) Members of Military and Naval Forces of the Crown.
  (2) Members of the Seamen's National Insurance Society.
3. *Seamen's National Insurance Society—*
  All benefits of members, but may arrange for Medical or Sanatorium Benefit through Insurance Committees.
4. *Navy and Army Insurance Fund—*
  (a) Maternity Benefit of all soldiers and sailors who are not members of an Approved Society, administered by the Admiralty and Army Council either directly or through Insurance Committees.
  (b) All benefits of discharged sailors and soldiers whose state of health precludes admission to an Approved Society.
  All persons entitled to benefits out of the fund are deemed to reside in England, and the fund is managed by the National Health Insurance Commission (England).

III. SPECIAL COMMITTEES.

1. *Advisory and Joint Advisory Committees—*
  Consulted by the Commissioners and Joint Committee in connection with the making and altering of Regulations (Sec. 58 of 1911 Act).
2. *Local Medical Committee—*
  Consulted by Insurance Committee on all general questions affecting the administration of Medical Benefit (Sec. 62 of 1911 Act).
3. *Panel Committee—*
  Medium of conveyance to the Insurance Committee of the opinions and wishes of panel practitioners in its area (Sec. 32 of 1913 Act).
4. *Pharmaceutical Committee—*
  Consulted by Insurance Committee on all general questions affecting the supply of drugs, medicines, and appliances to insured persons in the area (Sec. 33 (1) of 1913 Act).
5. *Association of Insurance Committees in Scotland—*
  (Sec. 31 (3) of 1913 Act.)

CHAPTER I.

CONSTITUTION, PROCEDURE, POWERS AND DUTIES OF INSURANCE COMMITTEES.

SECTION (I.)—CONSTITUTION.

(i.) Introductory.

(1) The local administration of the National Insurance Acts is entrusted, with certain exceptions, to bodies called "Insurance Committees," which are established for the purpose under Section 59 of the National Insurance Act, 1911, and to the Societies approved under the Acts, subject in both cases to the central control in matters so provided in the Acts of the National Health Insurance Commission (Scotland) and the National Health Insurance Joint Committee.

(2) Insurance Committees are bodies corporate with perpetual succession and a common seal. They have power to sue and be sued and to acquire and hold land for the purposes of the Act (subject in every case to the consent of the Commissioners) (Sec. 30 of the 1913 Act).

(ii.) Insurance Committee Areas.

(3) Section 59 of the Act of 1911 as applied to Scotland by Section 80, requires that an Insurance Committee shall be set up for—
  (1) every county, excepting (a) Clackmannan and Kinross, and (b) Elgin and Nairn, in which two instances the counties are to be regarded as a single county; and
  (2) every burgh containing a population of 20,000 or upwards, according to the census of 1911, including the burghs of Dumfries and Maxwelltown, which are to be regarded as a single burgh.

All burghs other than those falling under (b) are included in the appropriate counties, and in those cases where they were not represented on the County Councils they have been given such representation for the purposes of the Act, under an order issued by the Secretary for Scotland on 25th May 1912 (Sec. 80 (4) of 1911 Act).

(iii.) NUMBER OF MEMBERS OF INSURANCE COMMITTEES.

(4) The number of members of each of the 56 Insurance Committees in Scotland has been determined by the Scottish Insurance Commissioners, subject to the following limits laid down by the Act of 1911, viz. the minimum is 25 where the population within the area of the Committee is less than 40,000 and 40 where the population is 40,000 and upwards, and the maximum is 80. Where a Committee contains less than forty members, its composition may be varied by the Commissioners, but no alteration may be made in the proportion of the members appointed by insured persons and by a County or Town Council, or in the number of members possessing a medical qualification (Sections 59 (2) and 80 (6) of 1911 Act). The membership of no Committee was fixed as low as 25, owing to the fact that with a Committee of that size it would not be possible for the Commissioners to include among the persons appointed by them two women as required by the Statute.

(5) In determining the number of members of the respective Committees, the Commissioners in general adopted population as the basis; but in the case of counties other circumstances were given weight, such as the density of the population, the means of communication, and the geographical conditions of the county generally. A proportionately higher membership was therefore allowed in counties containing a widely scattered population than in counties where the area is smaller, the population more compact, and the difficulty of securing attendance at meetings less.

(6) The number of members determined for each Committee is given in Appendix II. (A).

(iv.) COMPOSITION OF INSURANCE COMMITTEES.

(7) The composition of Insurance Committees consisting of forty members or more, is as follows:—

(a) Three-fifths of the members represent insured persons resident in the county or burgh who are members of Approved Societies and who are Deposit Contributors, in proportion as nearly as may be to their respective numbers.

(b) One-fifth are appointed by the Council of the county or burgh.

(c) Two members are elected, either by an Association of duly qualified medical practitioners resident in the county or burgh which has been formed for that purpose, or, if no such Association has been formed, by such practitioners.

(d) One, two, or three (according to the size of the Committee) medical practitioners are appointed by the Council of the county or burgh.

(e) The remaining members are appointed by the Commissioners.
(Sec. 59 (2), Act of 1911.)

(8) The exact composition of each Insurance Committee in Scotland can be seen from the Table in Appendix II. (A).

(v.) REPRESENTATIVES OF INSURED PERSONS.

(9) The representatives of insured persons on Insurance Committees are appointed or elected under regulations made in pursuance of Section 59 (2) (a) and proviso (i.) of the Act of 1911 (Appointment of Representatives of Insured Persons on Insurance Committees Regulations (Scotland), 1913, and Amendment Regulations, 1914 and 1914 (No. 2)). The representation is apportioned between Deposit Contributors and Approved Society members in proportion to their respective numbers resident in the area. The basis of the scheme of apportionment between Approved Societies is to give each Society a right—itself to appoint or to vote with other Societies—measured by its membership in the area. The carrying out of the election is entrusted by the regulations to the Clerk to the Committee.

(10) The Clerk to the Committee must appoint in writing some fit person to be his deputy The deputy so appointed may exercise any powers and do anything which the Clerk is authorised or required to exercise or to do under the Regulations. If the Clerk is unable to act and no deputy appointed by him is available the Commissioners may appoint one (No. 32 of 1913 Regulations).

Count of Insured Persons.

(11) Triennially, in 1916, 1919, and so on, on a date in February specified in the Regulations, the Clerk ascertains by counting the index slips in his index register—
    (a) The number of Deposit Contributors resident in the area;
    (b) The number of members resident in the area of each Approved Society which has members so resident; and
    (c) The total number of insured persons resident in the area, i.e. (a) plus the total of (b).
(Nos. 5, 7, and 9 of 1913 Regulations.)

Electoral Unit.

(12) Having ascertained the number of insured persons within the area of the Committee, the Clerk proceeds to determine an electoral unit figure. This is arrived at by dividing the total number of insured persons resident in the Committee's area by the total number (three-fifths of the Committee's total membership) of representatives of insured persons on the Committee. Any fraction is disregarded (No. 6 of 1913 Regulations).

Deposit Contributors' Representatives.

(13) The number of representatives to be allocated to Deposit Contributors is the figure ascertained by dividing the total number of Deposit Contributors resident in the area of the Committee by the unit figure. A fraction of one-half or more than one-half of the unit figure is regarded as equivalent to the unit figure. A fraction of less than one-half is disregarded. Where the total number of Deposit Contributors is less than the unit figure one representative is allowed (No. 7 of 1913 Regulations).

Approved Societies' Representatives.

(14) The number of representatives allocated to Approved Societies is the total number of representatives of insured persons less the number allocated to Deposit Contributors. The representatives of members of Societies are divided into two classes, viz. :—

> (a) Representatives to be appointed direct by individual Societies whose membership within the area equals or exceeds the unit figure—called for convenience " A " Societies ; and
>
> (b) Representatives to be elected jointly by Societies whose membership in the area is less than the unit figure—called " B " Societies.

(Nos. 8 and 9 of 1913 Regulations.)

(15) The number of representatives allocated to "B" Societies is the figure ascertained by dividing the total number of members, resident in the Committee's area, of all " B " Societies having members resident in such area, by the unit figure. A fraction of less than one-half of the unit figure is disregarded, and a fraction of one-half or more than one-half is regarded as equivalent to the unit figure. If in any case the total number of members of " B " Societies resident in the Committee's area is less than the unit figure, one representative is allowed (No. 10 of 1913 Regulations).

(16) The number of representatives of " A " Societies is the difference between the total number of representatives allotted to Approved Societies and the number allotted to " B " Societies.

(17) The number of representatives allocated to each " A " Society is the figure ascertained by dividing the number of members of the Society resident in the Committee's area by the unit figure, *any fraction being disregarded.*

(18) The allocation is commenced with the " A " Society which has the largest number of members resident in the Committee's area. The Clerk then proceeds to allocate the appropriate number of representatives to the Society having the next largest number of members resident in the Committee's area, and so on.

(19) If, as may happen owing to the ignoring of fractions,

any representatives remain unallocated, one of these is assigned to the Society in the case of which the largest fraction was disregarded, the next to the Society in the case of which the next largest fraction was disregarded, and so on until the allocation is completed.

(20) It may happen, as a consequence of Deposit Contributors and " B " Societies being each entitled as a minimum to one representative, that the quota of representatives allotted to " A " Societies is not sufficient to complete the allocation among the Societies in the manner above described. In such circumstances, if the preliminary allocation has resulted in an " A " Society having more than one representative, a readjustment will require to be made, and one of its representatives will be given to the " A " Society which the preliminary allocation may have left unprovided for. If there are more " A " Societies than one having two or more representatives, the necessary readjustment is made by taking one representative from that Society in the case of which the smallest fraction was disregarded (paragraph (17)). If there is no " A " Society having more than one representative, the matter requires to be reported to the Commissioners, who have power to direct that a representative shall be taken from the " B " Societies, or that the allocation shall be completed in such other manner as they may think right (Nos. 11 and 12 of 1913 Regulations).

Return of Allocation of Representatives of Insured Persons.

(21) The Clerk must, before a date in April specified in the Regulations, complete the allocation of the representatives of insured persons in the manner described above, and furnish the Commissioners with a copy of a return in a form prescribed in the First Schedule to the Regulations, showing how the representatives have been allocated.

(22) The Commissioners have power to direct the Clerk to make alterations on the return. This power enables the Commissioners to verify the return in matters as to which a Society may not have the necessary information.

(23) On receiving the copy of the return back from the Commissioners, the Clerk must forthwith publish an intimation of it in a newspaper or newspapers circulating in the Committee's area, and must send a copy of the return to each Society whose name appears therein, and to the Association of Deposit Contributors, or where there is no such Association, to each representative of Deposit Contributors on the existing Committee. He must also display a copy of the return at his office for seven days for inspection by all persons concerned.

(24) If within seven days from the date or last date of the newspaper advertisement, the accuracy of the return is not challenged in writing by any authorised person or body, the return is to be treated as final and conclusive. Provision is made for the

determination of objections by the Committee within seven days, subject to appeal to the Commissioners, and for the return becoming final and conclusive ten days after the Committee's decision, or, if any appeal has been lodged with the Commissioners, when the objection is finally disposed of and the decision intimated (Nos. 14–17 of 1913 Regulations).

Notices.

(25) Within three days from the date on which the return becomes final and conclusive, the Clerk must—
- (1) Send by registered letter a notice (*a*) to the Association of Deposit Contributors (if any), and (*b*) to each "A" Society, stating, *inter alia*, the number of representatives to be appointed by them, and calling upon them to make the appointments and intimate the names of the persons appointed within twenty-eight days from the date on which the return became final and conclusive;
- (2) Send by registered letter in a prescribed form a notice to each "B" Society stating, *inter alia*, the number of representatives to be appointed by the group of "B" Societies, and calling upon the Committee of Management of each Society to appoint a delegate to attend a joint meeting at which the election of the representatives of the "B" Societies is to be carried through (Nos. 18, 20, and 22 of 1913 Regulations).

Appointment of Deposit Contributors' Representatives.

(26) If a recognised Association of Deposit Contributors exists, the representatives of Deposit Contributors are to be elected by vote of the members taken in accordance with the Association's Rules, and the names must be intimated to the Clerk by registered post within the 28 days referred to in the preceding paragraph. Regulations under which Associations of Deposit Contributors may be established were made on 11th April 1913 (Associations of Deposit Contributors Regulations (Scotland), 1913), but no Association has been formed thereunder.

Where no such Association exists, the representatives of Deposit Contributors are to be appointed by vote of the Insurance Committee within the time mentioned (No. 19 of 1913 Regulations).

Appointment of " A " Societies' Representatives.

(27) The representatives of "A" Societies are appointed by the Committees of Management of the Societies concerned, and it is contemplated that those Committees in making the appointments will wherever possible be guided with regard to the persons to be appointed by the advice of the branches operating in

the area. The names of the representatives so appointed must be intimated to the Clerk by registered post within the 28 days already referred to in paragraph (25) (No. 23 of 1913 Regulations).

Appointment of " B " Societies' Representatives.

(28) Within 14 days from the date on which the return becomes final and conclusive, the Committee of Management of each " B " Society is required to appoint a delegate, and intimate his name and address to the Clerk by registered post. The names and addresses of two other persons should also be intimated in order that one or other of them may take the place of the appointed delegate at the joint meeting in the event of the latter's being unable to attend. Notice of the date and place of the meeting is sent by the Clerk to the appointed delegate only. If unable to attend, he should hand the notice to one of the persons nominated as substitutes.

(29) Within 17 days from the date on which the return becomes final and conclusive, the Clerk must fix a date and place for the joint meeting, and intimate the same to the appointed delegates by registered post, giving them not less than 7 days' notice of the meeting. Unless with the consent of the Commissioners the place of meeting must not be outside the area of the Committee.

(30) The Clerk acts as Returning Officer at the meeting. He must call to the chair the delegate in attendance from that " B " Society which has the largest number of members resident in the Committee's area, and in the event of such delegate refusing to act or leaving the meeting prior to the business being completed, the delegate of the next largest Society, and so on in succession. If two or more Societies have an equal number of members so resident, the order in which the delegates shall have the right to be called to the chair is determined by lot by the Clerk. The Chairman so appointed must thereupon ask the delegates to nominate and elect the required number of representatives on the Committee. Power is given him to decide finally all points of order.

(31) The election is made by vote of the delegates in attendance. Each delegate has a number of votes equal to the required number of representatives of the " B " Societies on the Committee.

(32) If more persons are proposed and seconded for membership than the required number of representatives, the Clerk must call the roll of delegates. Each delegate in attendance as shown by the roll-call (including the Chairman), must then write down the names of the persons so proposed and seconded for whom he votes. He must use all his votes, and give not more than one vote to each person, otherwise his voting paper will be regarded as spoiled.

(33) The Clerk counts the votes so recorded, and declares to

be elected the required number of representatives having the largest number of votes.

(34) If the voting is inconclusive, owing to equality of votes, the meeting decides by show of hands which of the persons having an equality of votes are to be regarded as elected. The Chairman determines the order in which the persons having an equality of votes are to be set against each other. He has both a casting and a deliberative vote. In accordance with the result of the voting so taken, the Clerk declares the required number of representatives to have been elected.

(35) In the event of any delegate being dissatisfied with the elections made as above provided, he may move that they be set aside, and that a "card" vote be taken. If at least one-third of the delegates in attendance support the motion, the elections are set aside, and the votes of each delegate as previously recorded are, subject to the provision set forth in the next paragraph, thereupon multiplied in each case by the number of members, resident in the Committee's area, of the Society he represents. The Clerk counts the votes resulting from the multiplication, and declares to be elected the required number of representatives having majorities. If the voting is inconclusive, as a result of equality of votes, the procedure detailed in the preceding paragraph is carried out, and the Clerk declares the required number of representatives elected accordingly.

(36) If the number of delegates present and voting exceeds twenty, and the multiplication of the votes would involve an unduly long sitting, the Clerk need not proceed with it at the meeting. He must, however, complete it as soon as possible. If an equality of votes rendering the election inconclusive is disclosed, he must call upon the Chairman of the meeting (or, if there were successive Chairmen, the Chairman who presided last) to exercise a casting vote or votes. As soon as the result of the voting is ascertained, the Clerk must intimate it by post to each delegate, stating the names of all persons proposed and seconded, the number of votes recorded for each, and the names of the persons declared by him to have been duly elected (No. 21 of 1913 Regulations).

Intimation to Commission of Names, etc., of Representatives.

(37) Within seven days after the expiry of the time within which the representatives of insured persons are required to be appointed or elected, the Clerk must send to the Commissioners a list containing the names and addresses of all such representatives, and he is also required to display a copy of the list at his office for a period of seven days for inspection by all concerned (No. 24 of 1913 Regulations).

Double Membership.

(38) Membership of more than one Insurance Committee at the same time is prohibited, except in special circumstances

and with the consent of the Commissioners. Any representative of insured persons appointed to more than one Committee concurrently, who does not obtain the consent of the Commissioners, is to continue a member only of the Committee to which he was first appointed. Provision is made for filling vacancies so created (No. 25 of 1913 Regulations).

Default.

(39) In the event of any default taking place in the election or appointment of representatives of insured persons, the Commissioners may at any time thereafter order that the default be made good by election or appointment in such manner as they may direct. In giving directions for making good any default, the Commissioners will follow as nearly as seems expedient the lines of procedure laid down for ordinary appointments. If the default is not made good by a date in the month of June specified in the Regulations, the appointment of representatives to supply the default is to be forthwith made by the Commissioners in such manner as they may think proper (No. 26 of 1913 Regulations).

Term of Office.

(40) Representatives of insured persons on Insurance Committees hold office for three years. Retiring members are eligible for re-appointment or re-election. A member appointed to fill a casual vacancy holds office only for the unexpired portion of the three years' period (No. 27 of 1913 Regulations and No. 2 of Amending Regulations).

Disqualification.

(41) The choice of representatives of insured persons is not restricted to persons possessing any particular qualification, and persons are accordingly eligible who are not themselves insured under the Act or who are not members of the Society appointing them. Where, however, a representative of insured persons who, at the date of becoming such, was a member or an official of the "A" Society appointing him or of one of the "B" Societies participating in his election, ceases to be a member or official, as the case may be, of such Society, his tenure of office as a member of the Committee is, if the Society so decides, terminable ten days thereafter, or at such later time as may be fixed by the Society. The Secretary of the Society is to intimate any decision to this effect to the Clerk by registered post. The Clerk must thereupon send notice of the Society's intimation to the member in question, and must also notify the Commissioners that a vacancy will arise ten days after the date of his receipt of the Society's intimation, or at any later

date that the Society may have specified. Forms for giving the intimation and notices are prescribed.

The member in question may appeal to the Commissioners against the termination of his tenure of office, and the decision of the Commissioners on his appeal is final.

If the member was elected to represent a group of " B " Societies and has transferred from one Society to another in the group, the Commissioners are required to take this fact into consideration in dealing with the appeal.

Pending the decision of the appeal, the member is to continue to hold office if the Commissioners so determine (No. 28 of 1913 Regulations).

(42) Six consecutive months' absence from meetings without leave of the Committee involves unconditional disqualification of a representative of insured persons unless the cause of absence is the member's employment in the naval or military forces during the present war. The six months are counted from the date of the first meeting which the representative failed to attend, and at the end of the period he ceases to be a member of the Committee. " Meeting " is to include meetings of any Sub-Committee of the Insurance Committee as well as meetings of that Committee or any of its Sub-Committees in conference with persons not members of the Committee (No. 2 of Amending Regulations and No. 3 of National Health Insurance (Appointment of Representatives of Insured Persons on Insurance Committees) Amendment Regulations (Scotland), 1914 (No. 2)).

Vacancies.

(43) If a representative of insured persons loses his seat on the Committee (paragraphs 41 and 42), dies, or demits office, the Clerk is to call upon the appropriate body to appoint another representative in his room.

Where the vacancy is among the representatives of " B " Societies, the remaining representatives of " B " Societies on the Insurance Committee elect a member of the Committee in place of the former member. The election takes place at a meeting to be convened by the Clerk to the Committee as soon as possible after the occurrence of the vacancy. Such meeting must be held within 28 days of the date of the notice summoning it. The place of meeting is determined by the Clerk. The Chairman of the Insurance Committee, or failing him, another member of the Committee (not being a representative of insured persons) to be nominated by him presides at the meeting, and has a casting but not a deliberative vote. Two representatives of the " B " Societies, in addition to the Chairman or other member of the Committee presiding, form a quorum. The nominations are made and the voting conducted in such manner as the meeting may determine.

In the event of there being less than two remaining representatives of " B " Societies on the Committee, the procedure outlined above does not apply. In such circumstances the Commissioners themselves, after such consultation with the " B " Societies as seems proper to them in the circumstances, appoint a member in place of the former member.

If any default in filling a vacancy takes place, the Commissioners forthwith fill the vacancy in such manner as they think proper.

A member appointed to fill a vacancy retires with the other representatives of insured persons at the end of their three years' term of office (No. 2 of Amending Regulations, 1914).

(44) The fact that vacancies may exist among the representatives of insured persons does not invalidate the proceedings of the Committee. The remaining representatives are treated as duly representing insured persons until the vacancies are filled (No. 30 of 1913 Regulations).

Technical Errors.

(45) Unless the Commissioners so determine, no election held or appointment made under the Regulations is to be invalidated in consequence of any neglect to give proper notice or to make proper advertisement, or of any other technical defect in the proceedings which has not been prejudicial, in the opinion of the Commissioners, to the interests of any party concerned (No. 34 of 1913 Regulations).

Representation of Women.

(46) In order to secure an adequate number of women representatives of insured persons, the Commissioners have strongly recommended that where a Society contains both men and women members, or where there is comparatively a considerable number of women Deposit Contributors, the question of the appointment of women representatives or, as the case may be, of instructing delegates to vote for women representatives, should be considered by the body electing or appointing the representatives or delegates (Memo. No. 313 I.C.).

(vi.) REPRESENTATIVES OF COUNTY AND TOWN COUNCILS.

(47) The number of duly qualified medical practitioners to be appointed by the Council of the county or burgh (see paragraph 7) is 1, 2, or 3, according as the total membership of the Insurance Committee is under 60, 60 and upwards, or 80. These members are in addition to the Council's representation extending to one-fifth of the total membership of the Committee (Sec 59 (2) (d) of 1911 Act).

(48) Of the members appointed by the County Council or a Town Council at least two must be women (Sec. 59 (2) (ii.) of 1911 Act). Moreover no person except a medical practitioner may represent the Council unless he or she is, in the case of a County Council, a member of a Local Authority within the county under

the Public Health (Scotland) Act, 1897, or, in the case of a Town Council, a member of that Council. This requirement is, however, waived so far as women are concerned, if women thus qualified are not available (Sec. 80 (7) of 1911 Act). It has been suggested to the Councils that it should be made a condition of the appointment of their representatives that they should cease to be members of the Insurance Committee on ceasing to be members of the Local Authority.

(49) The Commissioners are empowered to increase the one-fifth representation of any County or Town Council which may have assumed liability to make good one-half of any deficiency in the income available for the administration of medical or sanatorium benefit. The increase is to be met by a corresponding diminution in the representation of insured persons, to be made in the manner and for the period which the Commissioners may determine (Secs. 15, 17, and 59 (3) of 1911 Act, and No. 33 of Appointment of Representatives of Insured Persons (Scotland) Regulations, 1913).

(vii.) REPRESENTATIVES APPOINTED BY MEDICAL PRACTITIONERS.

(50) The first appointments of their two representatives by the medical practitioners were made in the manner prescribed by the Election of Medical Representatives on Insurance Committees Regulations (Scotland), 1912 (Regulations No. 7). The two members of the Insurance Committee fell to be elected by an association of duly qualified medical practitioners, resident in the area of the Committee, formed for that purpose, or, if no such association were formed, by such practitioners at a meeting convened in accordance with the Regulations (Sec. 59 (2) (c) of 1911 Act).

(51) The meeting might be summoned by an existing medical association or committee acting within the area of the Committee including in its membership at least one half of the registered medical practitioners resident in the area, or by any accredited official of the association or committee or by any duly qualified medical practitioner resident therein. Written notice of the meeting was required to be posted not less than seven days prior to the meeting to every duly qualified medical practitioner resident in the area whose name appeared in the then current edition of the Medical Register. The notice was required to specify the time and place of meeting, and that the association, if formed, or the meeting itself, might proceed forthwith to the election of two members to serve on the Insurance Committee. Similar notice had to be given by advertisement in a newspaper circulating in the area, at least seven days before the meeting (No. 6 of Regulations).

(52) If the meeting were summoned by, or on behalf of, an existing association or committee, the notice had to be sent to all practitioners whether members of the association or

committee or not. Non-members could attend the meeting and take part in the proceedings on payment of a sum (not exceeding 1s.) fixed by the association or committee to cover expenses and specified in the notice (No. 6 of Regulations).

(53) The quorum in a burgh was one-fourth of the duly qualified medical practitioners resident in it, but in no case less than five, and in a county, one-sixth of the duly qualified medical practitioners resident in it, but in no case less than five, except in the counties of Argyll, Bute, Inverness, Orkney, Ross and Cromarty, Sutherland and Zetland, where it was three (No. 6 of Regulations).

(54) The meeting was required to appoint a Chairman and Clerk, and the latter was to transmit to the Commissioners a report of the proceedings of the meeting, duly authenticated by the Chairman, and specifying the names of the practitioners present at the meeting, the business transacted, any motions and amendments duly proposed and seconded, and the numbers voting therefor, and the names and addresses of the members, if any, elected to serve on the Insurance Committee (No. 6 of Regulations).

(55) Where no election was made the Commissioners might convene by advertisement a meeting of the practitioners (Regulations Nos. 7, 8, and 9).

(56) The term of office of these members has not yet been fixed by Regulation, and is meantime determined by the electors. Any medical practitioner whose name is removed from the Register by the General Medical Council ceases *ipso facto* to be a member of the Committee (No. 10 of Regulations).

(57) Any vacancy occurring in the representation of the local medical practitioners is to be filled by the appointment of another member at a meeting summoned in accordance with the Regulations (No. 10 of Regulations). The procedure to be followed is on the lines of that detailed in the foregoing paragraphs (No. 6 of Regulations).

(viii.) REPRESENTATIVES OF THE COMMISSIONERS.

(58) Of the members appointed by the Commissioners to an Insurance Committee, at least two must be women, and at least one must be a duly qualified medical practitioner (Sec. 59 (2) (ii.) of 1911 Act). The Commissioners have endeavoured to secure that large employers of labour, nursing and other associations, etc., who have an interest in but no direct right of representation under the scheme of National Insurance, should be represented, and, where practicable, that one of their representatives should be a chemist resident in the area. In cases where the total medical representation on the Committee under the Act would amount to less than 10 per cent. of members, the Commissioners have agreed to include among the members to be appointed by them such further number of medical representatives as will suffice to raise the total number of medical representatives to the proportion mentioned. The term of office of the Commissioners'

representatives has been fixed for the present at a period expiring three years after 15th July 1913. Persons appointed subsequently to 15th July 1913 hold office for the unexpired portion of the three years' period.

(ix.) COMBINATION OF COMMITTEES.

General.

(59) Any two or more Insurance Committees may, and, if required to do so by the Commissioners, must, combine for the exercise of any powers or duties under the Acts (Sec. 59 (5) of 1911 Act). The Committees entering into a combination are required to appoint from their respective members a Joint Committee for any purpose in respect of which the combination is effected. The costs incurred by the Joint Committee will form a charge upon the funds of the separate Committees in such proportion as may be agreed to by them. Failing agreement the apportionment will be determined by the Commissioners who will have regard, *inter alia*, to the number of insured persons residing within the area of each of the Committees interested (No. 12, Insurance Committees Procedure Regulations (Scotland), 1912).

(60) The number of members to be appointed by each of the Committees concerned will be fixed by arrangement between them, or failing agreement, by the Commissioners. The time and method of appointment and the tenure of office of members will be fixed by the Committees respectively appointing them. The proceedings of the Joint Committee are regulated by the Standing Orders of the Committee (No. 12, Procedure Regulations).

Drug Accounts Committee.

(61) All Insurance Committees in Scotland were required by resolution of the Commissioners, dated 12th December 1914, to combine as from 1st January 1915 for certain purposes connected with the scrutinising of expenditure on drugs and appliances. Regulations have been issued adapting the provisions of the Act to the combination (National Health Insurance (Drug Accounts Committee) Regulations (Scotland), 1914). Provision is made for the election of a Joint Committee to manage the affairs of the combination, under the title of "The Drug Accounts Committee."

(62) The purposes of the Drug Accounts Committee are—

(*a*) to scrutinise the accounts furnished to each Insurance Committee for drugs and appliances supplied to insured persons, and make such reports thereon as may be necessary for the purposes of the Insurance Committee;

(*b*) to make and furnish such statistical and other returns and such reports with reference to the accounts as the Commissioners may require; and

(c) to do such other things as are incidental or conducive to the attainment of the above purposes (No. 5 (1), Regulations).

(63) Insurance Committees are required to forward to the Committee at such times as may be agreed upon all the accounts in respect of drugs and appliances supplied to insured persons. Failing agreement, the Commissioners fix the times at which the accounts are to be sent to the Drug Accounts Committee. After the accounts have been scrutinised the Drug Accounts Committee are required to return them with reports thereon to the Committees which sent them (No. 5 (2), Regulations).

(64) The Drug Accounts Committee consists of fourteen members, of whom ten are members of Insurance Committees, two are medical practitioners, and two are chemists (No. 6, Regulations).

Eight of the Insurance Committee members are respectively elected by eight electoral divisions into which the Committees are grouped (No. 8, Regulations). These must be members of an Insurance Committee in the electoral division they represent (No. 6, Regulations). The Insurance Committee for the Burgh of Glasgow is entitled to appoint two of its members to the Drugs Accounts Committee (No. 7, Regulations).

(65) A list showing the composition of the electoral divisions and the value of the vote of each Insurance Committee is given in Appendix II. (B). Each Committee may nominate one candidate (No. 8 (3) of Regulations). The election is conducted by a Returning Officer appointed by the Commissioners (No. 8 (1), Regulations). Only one vote may be cast by each Committee, but different values are assigned to the votes of the various Committees (No. 9 (1), Regulations).

If the election is inconclusive owing to the candidates at the top of the poll having an equality in value of votes, a second poll is taken as between those candidates. If this is similarly inconclusive, the Returning Officer decides by lot which candidate is to be considered elected (No. 9 (4), Regulations).

(66) The medical representatives must be panel practitioners. They are elected by the Panel Committee, but need not be members of a Panel Committee. The chemists' representatives must be persons registered under the Pharmacy Act, 1868, as amended by the Poisons and Pharmacy Act, 1908. They are elected by the Pharmaceutical Committee, but need not be members of a Pharmaceutical Committee (Nos. 6 and 11 (3) (d), Regulations).

For the purpose of the election of the medical and chemists' representatives, the Panel and Pharmaceutical Committees are each divided into two groups, viz. Burghs and Counties, and the vote of each Committee is of the same value as the vote of the Insurance Committee for the same area. Glasgow in this case forms part of the Burgh group, and the value of its vote is seven. Each group elects one member of the Drug Accounts Committee. The election is carried out exactly as if the groups were Insurance Committee electoral divisions, except that in the event of an equality in value of votes there is no second poll, the Returning Officer deciding by lot (No. 11, Regulations).

(67) Provision is made in the Regulations that casual vacancies caused by loss of qualification, absence without leave for six consecutive months from meetings, resignation or death, are to be filled by a new election (No. 18 of Regulations). The remaining members may act notwithstanding a vacancy. The term of office of members of the Drug Accounts Committee is three years. The members retire in a body in favour of a new Committee, which must be elected triennially within three months from the expiration of the term of office of representatives of insured persons on Insurance Committees (No. 15 of Regulations).

(68) The quorum of the Committee is five (No. 17 of Regulations). The Committee's proceedings are regulated by the Standing Orders prescribed in the Insurance Committees Procedure Regulations (Scotland), 1912 (see paragraph (70) below), except where these are inconsistent with the purposes of the Drug Accounts Committee or with the Drug Accounts Committee Regulations (No. 4 of Regulations).

(69) The expenses of the Drug Accounts Committee are met by Insurance Committees in proportion to the number of prescriptions respectively furnished to each Committee during the year.

Where a Panel or Pharmaceutical Committee agrees to make a contribution towards the share payable by the Insurance Committee of the area of the annual expenses of the Drug Accounts Committee, the Insurance Committee will supply the contributing Committee with such reports by the Drug Accounts Committee as may be agreed upon. The reports will enable the contributing Committee to consider and deal with cases of alleged excessive ordering of drugs under No. 40 of the Medical Benefit Regulations without the necessity of making an exhaustive analytical examination of the drug accounts for themselves. The Commissioners have strongly recommended Panel and Pharmaceutical Committees to take advantage of this provision (No. 20 of Regulations).

SECTION (II.)—PROCEDURE, OFFICES, Etc.

(i.) STANDING ORDERS.

(70) The National Health Insurance (Insurance Committees Procedure) Regulations (Scotland), 1912, embody a set of Standing Orders in accordance with which the proceedings of every Committee must be regulated, subject to the power of the Committee to suspend any one or more of the Orders in a case of urgency or upon a motion for the purpose provided that two-thirds of the members present and voting so decide (No. 5 of Regulations).

The Standing Orders are as follows :—

Meetings.

(1) The Committee shall, in addition to the first meeting at which the Committee is constituted and any adjournment or postponement thereof, hold such ordinary or special general meetings as shall be necessary for the transaction of business. The date, time, and place of meeting shall be fixed by the Committee.

(2) The Committee shall, at the first meeting, appoint a Chairman and Vice-Chairman of the Committee. In the event of difficulty arising from an equal division of votes the matter shall be settled by lot.

(3) The Clerk may at any time, on the instructions or with the concurrence of the Chairman, or, in cases of urgency, without such concurrence, call a special meeting of the Committee. He shall call a special meeting on receiving a requisition signed by one-fifth of the members of the Committee, which requisition shall state the business to be brought up at such meeting. Should the Clerk fail to call a meeting within seven days after receiving such requisition, the requisitionists shall be entitled themselves to call a meeting.

(4) All meetings shall be called by circular delivered or posted at least seven days before the meeting, except in case of urgency, of which the Chairman or the Clerk shall be the judge. The circular shall specify the items of business so far as known.

Order of Business.

(5) The order of business at all meetings of the Committee shall be as follows :—
   (a) The Chairman, or in his absence, the Vice-Chairman, shall take the chair ; if both are absent, the members present shall appoint a Chairman of the meeting. In the event of difficulty arising from an equal division of votes the matter shall be settled by lot.
   (b) The Clerk shall read the circular and the statutory authority, if any, for the meeting.
   (c) The sederunt shall be taken.
   (d) The minutes of last meeting shall be read, and, when confirmed, signed by the Chairman.
   (e) Business required by statute to be done at the meeting.
   (f) Business continued from previous meeting.
   (g) Reports of committees or officials.

(h). Business of which notice has been given.
(i) Special business brought forward by direction of the Chairman.
(j) Any other competent business.

The Committee may at any meeting vary the above order, so as to give precedence to urgent business, but not so as to postpone consideration of statutory business.

Motions, etc.

(6) No motion to rescind any resolution which has been passed within the preceding six months, nor any motion to the same effect as any motion which has been negatived within the preceding six months, shall be in order, unless notice of the same be given in the circular calling the meeting.

(7) Every amendment must be relevant to the motion on which it is moved. The Chairman shall be the sole judge of relevancy.

(8) A relevant motion or amendment once made and seconded shall not be withdrawn without the consent of the mover and seconder thereof, and of the meeting.

(9) Every motion or amendment shall be reduced to writing, and shall be moved and seconded before it is put to the meeting.

(10) A member shall not speak more than once on any motion or amendment (save in explanation), but the mover of a resolution may reply. After the mover has been called on by the Chairman to reply, no other member shall speak to the question. The decision of the Chairman on all questions of order, relevancy, and regularity shall be final; and it shall be the duty of the Chairman to stop any discussion which, in his judgment, is irrelevant or outside the work of the Committee.

Voting.

(11) Every question shall be determined by a show of hands, unless three members demand a division, in which case the names, for and against the motion or amendment, shall be taken down and entered on the minutes.

(12) The Chairman or Vice-Chairman or other member presiding in the absence of the Chairman in case of equality shall have a casting as well as a deliberative vote.

Employment of Officers.

(13) The Committee may appoint officers and servants for the conduct of its business, and shall appoint such officers and servants as are necessary for the carrying out of the powers and duties conferred and imposed

on it by the Act, including the keeping of proper records of its proceedings, books, and accounts, and the preparation of reports and returns. The number and remuneration of such officers and servants shall be fixed by the Committee, due regard being had to the provisions of the Act prescribing the sums available for administrative expenses of the Committee, and shall be subject to the approval of the Commissioners.

Vacancies.

(14) In the event of the death, resignation, or disability of the Clerk or other official, the Chairman shall make such temporary arrangements as may be necessary for the performance of the duties of the office, and shall, as soon as may be, call, or cause to be called, a meeting of the Committee to decide what action is to be taken.

(15) When there are more than two candidates for any office, and the first voting does not show an absolute majority of the members present and voting in favour of any candidate, the candidate having the least number of votes shall be struck off the list, and a fresh voting shall take place; and so on, till an absolute majority shall be obtained in favour of one candidate.

(16) Personal canvassing of members shall be prohibited by the Committee, who may declare any candidate infringing this rule to be disqualified for election.

Signing of Deeds.

(17) All deeds, contracts, and writs of importance, granted or entered into by the Committee, shall be in name of the Committee, and may be signed by two members and the Clerk.

In addition the Act of 1913 has made it necessary that a Standing Order should be made to provide for the proper custody of the Seal of the Committee, for securing that it shall only be affixed in pursuance of a resolution of the Committee, and for its proper authentication, which should be by two members and the Clerk as above.

Suspension and Alteration of Standing Orders.

(18) Any one or more of the standing orders in any case of urgency or upon motion made may be suspended at any meeting, so far as regards any business at such meeting, provided that two-thirds of the members of the Committee present and voting shall so decide.

Quorum.

(19) The quorum of the Committee in each county and burgh shall consist of the number of persons mentioned in the Regulations (*see* Appendix II. (A)).

(20) If within twenty minutes or such longer time as the Committee may appoint after the time appointed for a meeting a quorum of members be not present, the Chairman, or in his absence, the Vice-Chairman, shall adjourn the meeting. In the event of the failure of a quorum and the absence of both Chairman and Vice-Chairman, the Clerk shall minute that owing to the want of the necessary quorum no business was done.

(ii.) OFFICES.

(71) Any Committee may, subject to the approval of the Commissioners, provide suitable office accommodation, including accommodation for its meetings. For this purpose it may use any offices belonging to a Local Authority, *i.e.* an Authority which has power to levy a rate directly or by precept or requisition, including therefore a County Council, Town Council, School Board, District Committee, Landward Committee, and Secondary Education Committee, with the consent and during the pleasure of the Authority with or without payment as may be agreed. No Committee may take steps to acquire premises or accommodation for meetings or offices until it has satisfied itself that accommodation cannot be obtained in the offices of a Local Authority (No. 6 of Insurance Committee Procedure Regulations (Scotland), 1912).

If a majority of the Committee so agree, meetings may be held in premises which are situate outwith the area of the Committee (No. 7 of Regulations).

SECTION (III.)—POWERS AND DUTIES.

(i.) ADMINISTRATION OF BENEFITS.

(72) The main duties entrusted to an Insurance Committee are the administration of —
- (*a*) Medical Benefit, and any additional benefit in the nature of Medical Benefit, of all insured persons in their area except members of the Seamen's National Insurance Society (Secs. 14 and 48 (12), 1911 Act).
- (*b*) Sanatorium Benefit of all insured persons in their area except members of the Seamen's National Insurance Society (Secs. 14 and 48 (12), 1911 Act).
- (*c*) All the benefits of Deposit Contributors in their area (Sec. 14, 1911 Act).

In view of the great importance of these duties, they are dealt with separately in detail in Chapters IV., V., and VI. respectively of the Handbook. It is here proper to mention, however, that where an Insurance Committee in Scotland thinks it desirable, owing to sparseness of population, difficulties of communication, or other special circumstances, to modify or suspend any benefits for the administration of which it is responsible, it has power to do so if the consent of the Scottish Insurance Commissioners is obtained. Where this power is exercised, the Committee must (with the consent of the Commissioners) make provision for the increase of other benefits or the grant of one or more additional benefits to an amount equivalent to the value of the modification or suspension (Sec. 80 (9), 1911 Act). As regards Medical Benefit alternative or supplementary arrangements may be made in cases of difficulty (Sec. 11 of 1913 Act).

(ii.) MISCELLANEOUS.

Reports and Returns.

(73) Insurance Committees are required to make such reports as to the health of insured persons within their areas as the Commissioners, after consultation with the Local Government Board for Scotland, may prescribe. Insurance Committees must also furnish such statistical and other returns to the Commissioners as they may require. On their own initiative Committees may make such reports regarding the health of insured persons and the conditions affecting the same, with such suggestions in reference thereto, as they may see fit, the reports when made being forwarded by the Commissioners to the Local Authorities affected by or interested in them. The Committees are also to collect information which will enable an analysis and classification of Deposit Contributors to be made (Sec. 60 (1) (*a*), 1911 Act).

Health Lectures, etc.

(74) Another duty placed upon Insurance Committees is the dissemination of knowledge on health subjects by provision for the giving of lectures and the publication of information on questions relating to health. In this connection arrangements may, if the Committee thinks fit, be made with local education authorities, universities, and other institutions (Sec. 60 (1) (*b*), 1911 Act).

Contributions to Hospitals and for Nursing.

(75) An Insurance Committee may grant such subscriptions or donations as it may think fit to hospitals, dispensaries, and other charitable institutions, or for the support of district nurses, and may appoint nurses for the purpose of visiting and nursing insured persons. Any expenditure thereby incurred is to be

treated as expenditure on such benefits under the Act as may be prescribed by regulations. No regulations on the subject have yet been issued (Sec. 21, 1911 Act).

Excessive Sickness.

(76) Where it is alleged by the Insurance Commissioners or any Approved Society or Insurance Committee interested that there is excessive sickness amongst the persons for the administration of whose sickness or disablement benefit the Society or Committee is responsible, and that the excess is due to—
 (1) The conditions or nature of employment of such persons;
 (2) Bad housing or insanitary conditions in the locality;
 (3) An insufficient or contaminated water supply;
 (4) Neglect on the part of any person or authority
  (*a*) to observe or enforce the provisions of any Act relating to the health of workers in factories, workshops, mines, quarries, or other industries, or relating to public health, or the housing of the working classes, or any regulations made under any such Act, or
  (*b*) to observe or enforce any public health precautions;
the Commissioners, Society, or Committee may claim from the person or authority alleged to be in default payment of the excess expenditure incurred (Sec. 63 of 1911 Act).

Failing agreement on the subject, the Home Secretary or the Local Government Board, as the case may be, may, on the application of the Commissioners, Society, or Committee, appoint a " competent person " to hold an inquiry. The person holding the inquiry is to report to the authority by whom he was appointed (*i.e.* the Home Secretary, or the Local Government Board), who will consider the report and decide whether any, and, if so, what action is to be taken (Secs. 63 and 80 (11) of 1911 Act). Should it be proved that the amount of sickness
 (1) During a period of not less than three years before the date of the inquiry; or
 (2) If there has been an outbreak of any epidemic, endemic, or infectious disease during any less period;
has been in excess of the average expectation of sickness by more than ten per cent., and that such excess was in whole or in part due to any of the causes before-mentioned, the amount of any extra expenditure found to have been incurred is to be made good by the following persons or authorities to the respective extents to which they are found responsible, viz. :—
 (*a*) *the employer* where the excess or part thereof is due to
  (i.) The conditions or nature of the employment;
  (ii.) Any neglect on his part to observe or enforce any of the Acts or Regulations above mentioned :

(b) *the local authority* where the excess or part thereof is due to—
  (i.) Bad housing;
  (ii.) Insanitary conditions in the locality;
  (iii.) Neglect on the part of the local authority to observe or enforce any of the Acts or Regulations or precautions above mentioned;
  (iv.) The insanitary condition of any particular premises, and it is found that the local authority is responsible therefor:

(c) *the owner, lessee, or occupier of premises* where the excess or part thereof is due to—
  The insanitary condition of any particular premises, and it is found that such person is responsible therefor:

(d) *a local authority, company, or person by whom water is supplied, or who, having imposed on them the duty of affording a water supply, have refused or neglected to do so* :—
  Where the excess or part thereof is due to an insufficient or contaminated water supply, unless it is proved that the insufficiency or contamination was not due to any default on their part, but arose from circumstances over which they had no control (Sec. 63 (2) of 1911 Act).

The local authority have recourse against the owner, lessee, or occupier of any premises, by whose act or default the extra expenditure may have been caused, provided a notice has been served on such owner, lessee, or occupier by the local authority. It is presumed that the notice would require to be served prior to the time of the inquiry in order that the person served might have an opportunity of being heard if he so wished (Sec. 63 (3) of 1911 Act).

The "average expectation of sickness" is to be calculated in accordance with Tables to be prepared by the Commissioners, who will also make Regulations for the procedure at inquiries. (Sec. 63 (4) and (5) of 1911 Act).

An order by the Home Secretary or the Local Government Board dealing with the subject of costs and expenses in connection with excessive sickness may, with leave of the Court of Session, be enforced in the same manner as a judgment or order of the Court (Sec. 63 (5) of 1911 Act).

Any sum ordered to be paid by a local authority may, in accordance with the regulations of the Secretary for Scotland, with the approval of the Treasury, be deducted from sums payable to the local authority out of the Local Taxation (Scotland) Account (Sec. 63 (6) of 1911 Act).

Grouping of Approved Societies for Valuation.

(77) At triennial valuation periods Societies having less than 5000 members, unless they form a voluntary association large enough to bring the total membership up to not less than 5000 (exclusive of married women suspended from receiving ordinary benefits who are not special voluntary contributors and of members who are not insured persons (Sec. 18 of Act of 1913)), are to be grouped together for the purpose of valuation, and of pooling surpluses and deficiencies. The Insurance Committee for these purposes only is to act as a central financial committee of the grouped Societies within its jurisdiction. Except, however, so far as relates to the power of refusing to make good any part of a deficiency due to maladministration, no power of control over the administration of the grouped Societies is conferred on the Committee (Sec. 39, 1911 Act).

Protection of Insured Persons against Diligence.

(78) Other matters committed to the charge of Insurance Committees include the keeping of a special Register of medical certificates granted for the purpose of the protection of sick insured persons against the sale of their goods under warrant for debt or ejectment from their homes for non-payment of rent (Sec. 68 of Act of 1911).

Note.—The powers and duties of Insurance Committees in connection with finance, including such matters as the payment of the travelling and subsistence expenses of members and the payment of subscriptions to an Approved Association of Insurance Committees (Sec. 31, 1913 Act), are dealt with in the chapter on Finance.

CHAPTER II.

CONSTITUTION, PROCEDURE, POWERS, AND DUTIES OF SUB-COMMITTEES OF INSURANCE COMMITTEES.

SECTION (I.)—SUB-COMMITTEES.

(i.) MEDICAL SERVICE SUB-COMMITTEE.

Appointment.

(79) EVERY Insurance Committee must appoint one, and may with the consent of the Commissioners appoint two or more, Medical Service Sub-Committees (Nos. 45 (1) and (5), Medical Benefit Regulations (Scotland), 1913).

The Medical Service Sub-Committee must consist of equal numbers of representatives of insured persons and of representatives of medical practitioners with a neutral Chairman. The minimum membership is seven—three persons to be appointed from and by the members of the Insurance Committee who represent insured persons, one by the Local Medical Committee, and two by the Panel Committee with the Chairman. If there is no Local Medical Committee, or if that Committee does not exercise its right of appointment, the Panel Committee appoints three members. With the consent of the Commissioners the number of representatives of insured persons may be increased by one or two (*i.e.* to make a total of four or five), but in such a case the number of members appointed by the Panel Committee must be increased to the same extent.

Unless one of the members appointed by the Local Medical Committee or the Panel Committee is a woman, the representatives of insured persons must include a woman in their selection. Where this is necessary the woman so appointed need not herself be a member of the Insurance Committee (No. 45 (2) (i.) of Regulations).

Chairman.

(80) The Chairman must be selected by the members of the Sub-Committee from among those members of the Insurance Committee who were appointed by the Council of the County or Burgh and by the Commissioners respectively, and who are neither insured persons, practitioners, nor registered pharmacists. In default of a selection by the members of the Sub-Committee the Chairman must be appointed by the

persons who are eligible themselves to become Chairman. The Insurance Committee may provide for the appointment of a Vice-Chairman in the same manner as that in which the Chairman is appointed. The Vice-Chairman will act as Chairman when the latter is not present, and may attend meetings at which the Chairman is present, but has then no vote and must take no part in the proceedings (No. 45 (2) (ii.) and (4) of Regulations).

Member Interested.

(81) If in the opinion of the Chairman any member of the Medical Service Sub-Committee is interested, or is partner or assistant to a practitioner interested, in a question referred to them, that member is debarred from taking any part in the hearing. Another person having the same qualification, if any, as the member who has withdrawn, must be appointed for the purpose by the remaining members who represent practitioners or insured persons respectively, as the case may be, and the Chairman (No. 45 (3) of Regulations).

Committee's Jurisdiction.

(82) Any question arising between a practitioner on the panel and a person entitled to treatment from him, as to the treatment given (including the granting of certificates) or as to the conduct of the person while receiving treatment, stands referred automatically to the Medical Service Sub-Committee (No. 45 (1) of Regulations).

Any question raised by an Approved Society as to the action of a practitioner on the panel with regard to any certificate which he is required under his agreement with the Committee to furnish to a member of the Society, is to stand similarly referred to the Sub-Committee. In addition the Insurance Committee may refer to the Sub-Committee any other question arising in connection with the administration of medical benefit or to the discharge by the practitioner of his duties under his agreement (No. 45 (1) and (15) of Regulations).

Procedure.

(83) Any person desiring to have a question raised for the hearing of the Sub-Committee, must state in writing to the Clerk of the Committee the substance of the question (No. 45 (6) of Regulations).

The Clerk must, within 3 days,* send copies of the statement to the person in respect of whom the question is raised and to the Chairman of the Sub-Committee, and must, upon receipt of any reply or further statement made by either party, send copies thereof to the other party and the Chairman. Not less than 7 days'* notice of the meeting at which the question

* The details of procedure depend on the rules actually adopted by the Committee and approved by the Commissioners.

is to be considered must be given to both parties, and each member of the Sub-Committee must be supplied at the meeting with copies of the statement and the reply, if any, thereto, and of any further statement made by either party (Model Rules for Administration of Medical Benefit No. 5, see Appendix III.).

The Sub-Committee must meet at regular intervals and special meetings may be called (Rules No. 4).

Either party is entitled at the hearing to make such statement and produce such evidence, whether written or otherwise, as he may think fit (Rules No. 5).

Admission to Hearing.

(84) The proceedings at a hearing before the Medical Service Sub-Committee are private, and no person shall be admitted except—

- (a) the person raising the question and the person with respect to whom the question arises;
- (b) the secretary or other officer of the Society, if any, to which the insured person belongs;
- (c) the secretary or other officer of the Panel Committee;
- (d) such other person, not being counsel or a solicitor or other paid advocate, as the Sub-Committee may upon the application of either party admit by reason of the fact that his attendance is required for the purposes of the proceedings or to assist either party in the presentation of his case; and
- (e) such officers and servants of the Insurance Committee as they may appoint for the purpose.

(No. 45 (7) of Regulations.)

Quorum, etc.

(85) Subject to the above provisions, the quorum of the Sub-Committee, their term of office, the procedure with regard to the hearing of any question, the nature of the evidence admitted, and so on, are matters for the determination of the Committee, with the approval of the Commissioners (No. 45 (8) of Regulations).

Report.

(86) The duty of the Sub-Committee is to draw up a report stating such relevant facts as appear to them to be established by the evidence placed before them, together with a recommendation as to the action, if any, which should be taken, and to present the report to the Insurance Committee. Any finding of fact contained in the report is to be accepted by the Committee as conclusive (No. 45 (9) of Regulations).

Range of Medical Service.

(87) Where in the course of any investigation it appears to the Sub-Committee that a question arises as to whether an

operation or other service is of a kind which can consistently with the best interests of the patients be properly undertaken by a general practitioner of ordinary competence and skill, they must refer the question to the Local Medical Committee for decision. The decision of that Committee, if acquiesced in, or of Medical Referees, is binding on the Sub-Committee (No. 45 (14) of Regulations). The question is more fully treated in paragraphs (177) and (178).

(88) The powers of the Committee and the action which may be taken following on the report, are dealt with in Chapter IV. Section (V.), paragraphs (259) to (276).

(ii.) PHARMACEUTICAL SERVICE SUB-COMMITTEE.

(89) The provisions relating to this Sub-Committee are similar to those applying to the Medical Service Sub-Committee. Every Insurance Committee must appoint one, and may with the consent of the Commissioners appoint two or more, Pharmaceutical Sub-Committees (No. 46 (1) and (4), Medical Benefit Regulations (Scotland), 1913).

Constitution.

(90) The Pharmaceutical Committee must consist of six persons (exclusive of the Chairman and Vice-Chairman), and there is no discretion allowed to increase this number. Its constitution is as follows :—

(i.) Three persons appointed by and from the members of the Insurance Committee who represent insured persons;

(ii.) Three registered pharmacists appointed by the Pharmaceutical Committee;

(iii.) A Chairman selected from the neutral members of the Insurance Committee (*i.e.* members appointed by the Council of the County or Burgh and the Commissioners respectively, who are neither insured persons, practitioners, nor registered pharmacists). The selection must be made by the persons appointed to be members of the Sub-Committee, or in default of selection being made by those persons, by the members of the Insurance Committee who are qualified themselves to become Chairman.

Unless one of the persons appointed by the Pharmaceutical Committee is a woman, at least one of the persons appointed by the representatives of insured persons must be a woman, and in the latter case the person appointed need not be a member of the Insurance Committee (No. 46 (2) of Regulations).

(91) Paragraph (80) above, applying to the Chairman and Vice-Chairman of the Medical Service Sub-Committee, and paragraphs (81), (83), (84), and (85), relating respectively to the disqualification of members interested in questions referred to the

Medical Service Sub-Committee, admission to the hearing, the conduct of proceedings of the Sub-Committee, and the quorum, etc., also apply, with the necessary alterations, to the Pharmaceutical Service Sub-Committee (No. 46 (3) and (5) of Regulations).

Duties.

(92) The function of this Sub-Committee is to deal with any complaint made by a person entitled to treatment from a panel practitioner against a person supplying drugs or appliances. Such a complaint may relate to the quality of the drugs or appliances supplied or to the failure to supply them within a reasonable time. Any question of this nature is to stand referred from the Insurance Committee to the Sub-Committee (No. 46 (1) of Regulations).

The Sub-Committee's powers are restricted to reporting on such complaints and submitting recommendations in regard to them. As in the case of the Medical Service Sub-Committee any finding of fact contained in the report must be accepted as conclusive by the full Committee (No. 46 (5) of Regulations).

(iii.) JOINT SERVICES SUB-COMMITTEE.

Constitution.

(93) A Joint Services Sub-Committee must be constituted by every Insurance Committee, to consist of 6 persons, exclusive of the Chairman and Vice-Chairman. Two practitioners, 2 registered pharmacists, and 2 representatives of insured persons are to be appointed by and from among the members of the Medical Service Sub-Committee, the Pharmaceutical Service Sub-Committee, and the representatives of insured persons on the Insurance Committee respectively. There must be at least one woman upon the Joint Services Sub-Committee, and, unless either of the two appointing Sub-Committees select a woman for one of their members, the representatives of insured persons must do so. In the latter case the woman need not herself be a member of the Insurance Committeee (No. 47 (1) of Regulations).

Chairman.

(94) The Chairman and Vice-Chairman (the latter appointment is optional) are to be selected in the same manner, and to have the same powers, as the corresponding officers of the Medical Service Sub-Committee (*see* par. (80), and No. 47 (4) of Regulations).

Disqualification of Member Interested.

(95) Any member of the Sub-Committee who is, in the opinion of the Chairman, interested in a question referred to it, or is a partner or assistant to a person so interested, is not allowed

to take part in the hearing of the question. His place must be filled temporarily by a person with the same qualifications as himself, to be appointed by the remaining members of the class to which he belongs and the Chairman (No. 47 (2) of Regulations).

Quorum, etc.

(96) The **quorum,** term of office, procedure, etc., of the Sub-Committee must be determined by the Insurance Committee, subject to the approval of the Commissioners. The provisions detailed in pars. (83) to (86) as to the hearing and reporting of proceedings, and the persons entitled to be present at the proceedings, of the Medical Service Sub-Committee are applicable to the Joint Services Sub-Committee, except that the secretaries or other officers of *both* the Panel and the Pharmaceutical Committees are entitled to be present (No. 47 (4) of Regulations).

Duties.

(97) To the Joint Services Sub-Committee must be referred all matters which lie at the same time within the provinces of the two constituent Sub-Committees. That is to say, where in the opinion of the Medical Service Sub-Committee any matter before it involves also a question relating to a person supplying drugs or appliances, or where in the opinion of the Pharmaceutical Service Sub-Committee any matter before it involves also a question relating to a practitioner on the panel, that Sub-Committee cannot deal with the matter itself, but must refer it to the Joint Services Sub-Committee (No. 47 (3) of Regulations).

Report.

(98) As in the cases of the other statutory Sub-Committees, the final decision is reserved for the full Committee, and the Sub-Committee's duty is to submit a report and recommendation, but the finding of the Sub-Committee on questions of fact is to be held conclusive (No. 47 (4) of Regulations).

(iv.) GENERAL.

Other Sub-Committees.

(99) In addition to the statutory Sub-Committees which are directed to be established, an Insurance Committee may appoint such other Sub-Committees as it may think expedient (No. 8, Insurance Committee Procedure Regulations (Scotland), 1912). In general the Committees have found it convenient to set up a Sanatorium Benefit Sub-Committee, a Medical Benefit Sub-Committee, a Deposit Contributors Sub-Committee, and a Finance and General Sub-Committee.

Co-option of Members.

(100) Sub-Committees may consist wholly or partly of members of the Committee as the Committee in its discretion may decide,

but a majority of the members of every Sub-Committee must consist of members of the Committee. This requirement does not, however, apply to any Sub-Committee appointed with advisory powers only, or appointed to supervise or report upon the administration of benefits, or for any purpose where no power of incurring expenditure is conferred upon it (No. 9, Procedure Regulations).

Representation of Interests.

(101) In the appointment of Sub-Committees and the selection of persons to serve on them, a fair apportionment of duties and work between all members of the Committee should be arranged, and the balance of representation of interests provided by the Act in the case of the Committee itself must be secured where reasonably practicable (No. 10, Procedure Regulations).

(102) Every Sub-Committee formed for the purpose of dealing with the administration of any benefit must contain at least one woman member (Sec. 30 (2), National Insurance Act, 1913).

Proceedings.

(103) The proceedings of Sub-Committees are regulated *mutatis mutandis* by the Standing Orders of the Committee as set forth in paragraph (70) above (No. 11, Procedure Regulations).

General Powers of Remit.

(104) No expenditure may be incurred by a Sub-Committee without the previous consent of the Committtee, and powers and duties in regard to the following matters may not be delegated with full powers to any Sub-Committee, and may not be delegated at all to a Sub-Committee appointed to act within a portion only of the area of the Insurance Committee :—
  (a) The arrangements for the treatment of tuberculosis.
  (b) All negotiations with practitioners or Local Medical Committees or pharmacists or chemists in regard to the terms on which, and the general conditions under which, medical treatment, medicines, and appliances will be supplied.
(No. 8 (1) and (2), Procedure Regulations.)

Powers of Remit in Sanatorium Benefit.

(105) Special attention should be directed to (b) in the last paragraph, in so far as it relates to Sanatorium Benefit. The general effect of the Regulations is that a Committee may remit to a Sub-Committee to make all necessary enquiries as to—
  (a) action being taken by the Public Health Local Authorities and negotiations with such Authorities for the provision of treatment ;
  (b) accommodation available for sanatorium treatment ;

(c) the terms on which insured persons may be admitted to sanatoria or other institutions if recommended for treatment;
(d) the provision which it is possible to make for the treatment of insured persons otherwise than in sanatoria or other institutions;
(e) the terms on which such treatment can be obtained;
(f) the procedure to be followed generally in dealing with applications for either sanatorium or domiciliary treatment.

(106) These powers cannot in any case be remitted without reservation to a Sub-Committee. The Committee itself must have ultimate control, and rules should therefore be made by the Committee prescribing the exact preliminary procedure to be followed in such matters as, for example, the following :—

(a) evidence that the applicant is an insured person;
(b) certificate from the regular medical attendant;
(c) report by the Medical Officer of Health or other medical adviser as to the case and the treatment required;
(d) report by an expert adviser appointed by the Committee to report on all cases reported by the Medical Officer of Health or other medical adviser as suitable for sanatorium treatment. This may be unnecessary where the Medical Officer of Health or other medical adviser is himself an expert.

(107) The Sub-Committee should report whether the case complies with the requirements and is one to be recommended for treatment; the method of treatment to be recommended; and if sanatorium treatment is to be recommended, any special grounds for selection of the case—such as prospect of cure or need for isolation.

(108) Although arrangements may be tentatively made by the Sub-Committee in order to secure immediate admission to a sanatorium on the Insurance Committee recommending the case, the Sub-Committee should have no power on its own initiative to recommend cases for immediate treatment, to arrange for actual admission to a sanatorium unless the expert medical adviser has certified the case as one in which immediate treatment is necessary; or to bind the Insurance Committee to continue treatment in the sanatorium, granted under such a certificate of urgency, beyond the date of the next meeting of the Committee. A Sub-Committee taking action on ground of urgency as above described should be required immediately thereafter to submit a special report of such action to the full Committee.

(109) It should be explicitly provided that a Sub-Committee must not in any case arrange for admission to a sanatorium on higher terms than may have been agreed on by the Insurance Committee.

CHAPTER III

LOCAL MEDICAL COMMITTEES, PANEL COMMITTEES, AND PHARMACEUTICAL COMMITTEES.

SECTION (I.)—LOCAL MEDICAL COMMITTEE.

Statutory Sanction.

(119) STATUTORY provision was made by the Act of 1911 for the recognition, if duly formed, of Local Medical Committees representative of all duly qualified medical practitioners resident in the area of an Insurance Committee or District Committee. The initiative in forming such a Committee rests with the practitioners themselves. The Committee's function is, broadly speaking, to represent the views of such practitioners on all *general* questions affecting the administration of medical benefit in the area (Sec. 62 of 1911 Act).

Recognition.

(120) Before a Local Medical Committee is entitled to be consulted by the Insurance Committee or District Committee on these matters, it has to secure the recognition of the Commissioners and the Joint Committee (Sec. 62, 1911 Act, and Joint Committee Regulations, 1911, No. 16 (*d*)). Committees were recognised originally for a period terminating not later than 1st March 1914, when recognition was extended, on application by the Committees, to 1st March 1915. For the period of the war, special consideration is given by the Commissioners, with a view to avoiding work and difficulties in the application of the ordinary requirements.

(121) The number of Local Medical Committees in Scotland which have been recognised is fifty-two. A list of the Committees is given in Appendix (IV.)

(122) The Commissioners require to be satisfied that the Committee is in fact representative of all duly qualified medical practitioners resident in the area. To some extent the personnel of the Local Medical Committee and of the Panel Committee may be identical, and it was provided by the Amending Act of 1913 that in any area in which, within six months of the date of passing the Act (15th August 1913), no Local Medical Committee

had been recognised, the Panel Committee might itself be recognised as the Local Medical Committee for that area (Sec. 32, 1913 Act).

Constitution.

(123) The Commissioners before awarding recognition required that a regular form of constitution providing for the election of the Committee and governing its proceedings should be adopted by the practitioners at a meeting called on due notice. Two Model Forms of constitution were, at the request of the practitioners, proposed by the Commissioners for their guidance. The constitutions finally adopted follow one or other of these models very closely.

(124) The Local Medical Committee was composed under Model A. of the whole body of the duly qualified medical practitioners resident in the area, and under Model B. of selected individuals appointed by and representative of such practitioners.

Functions.

(125) The Local Medical Committee is entitled to be consulted by the Insurance Committee (or the District Insurance Committee) on all general questions affecting the administration of medical benefit, including the arrangements made with medical practitioners giving attendance and treatment to insured persons (Sec. 62, National Insurance Act, 1911). The Committee is, moreover, at liberty to make any representations on such matters to the Insurance Committee or to the Commissioners. The nature of the questions which will arise is described fully in the following paragraphs relating to Panel Committees, and the powers and duties therein set out are common to the Local Medical Committee and the Panel Committee. The exceptions are the making of arrangements for the supply of drugs and appliances by a practitioner, the examination of the accounts of persons supplying drugs and appliances, the rate at which advances are to be made to practitioners, and remuneration is to be calculated, arrangements for enabling insured persons to be assigned to a practitioner on the panel (Reg. 21 (4)), and the defraying of the expenses of the Panel Committee. Those are points which affect more particularly the payment of panel practitioners. With them the Local Medical Committee is not concerned.

(126) The Local Medical Committee has in addition certain specific duties of a very responsible kind. In the first place, it has the duty of considering any complaint made by one practitioner on the panel against another, involving any question of the efficiency of the medical service of insured persons. It may make application to the Commissioners to remove the name of the practitioner against whom the complaint is made from the panel (No. 48, Medical Benefit Regulations (Scotland), 1913).

(127) In the second place, if an Insurance Committee is of

opinion that a question has arisen or may arise as to whether an operation or other service is of a kind which can, in the words of the practitioner's agreement, " consistently with the best interests of the patient be properly undertaken by a general practitioner of ordinary professional competence and skill," it must refer the question to the Local Medical Committee. Such a question may also arise in the course of the proceedings of the Medical Service Sub-Committee, and, if so, it is similarly to be referred to the Local Medical Committee (No. 50, Medical Benefit Regulations).

(128) If the Insurance Committee and the Local Medical Committee are unable to agree upon a decision in the case, or if the Commissioners in any event so determine, the provisions of the Regulations as to the appointment of referees come into force. These provisions are dealt with at length in Chapter IV. If an agreement is reached by the two Committees, the Insurance Committee is bound to report the matter to the Commissioners, who may, if they think fit, themselves refer it to referees for consideration (No. 50 of Medical Benefit Regulations).

SECTION (II.)—PANEL COMMITTEE.

Sanction.

(129) Section 32 of the National Insurance Act, 1913, provides for the appointment of a Panel Committee for every Insurance Committee area by the medical practitioners who are under agreement with the Insurance Committee.

Election.

(130) The method of election for the first Panel Committees and the number of members thereof for the various areas were prescribed by Regulations (Panel and Pharmaceutical Committees Regulations (Scotland), 1913).

Membership.

(131) The number of members for each area is set out in Appendix V. Not less than two-thirds of the members were required to be practitioners on the panel for the area, while the remainder might be duly qualified medical practitioners whether on the panel or not and whether or not resident in the area. The electors were the practitioners under agreement with the Insurance Committee for the area as at 13th October 1913. A Returning Officer was appointed by the Commissioners in each case (Nos. 3 and 4, Panel and Pharmaceutical Committees Regulations (Scotland), 1913).

Vacancies.

(132) The first members of the Committee hold office until 31st March 1916, when a new Committee will be constituted in accordance with Regulations which will be made for that purpose.

Should the war not have terminated by March 1916 Regulations will be made postponing the election till the termination of hostilities. Casual vacancies arising before that date must be filled by the remaining members of the Committee, who are within three months to appoint a duly qualified person. In default of an appointment by the Committee within that period, the Commissioners will fill the vacancy. Where the member whose place has been vacated was at the time of his appointment a panel practitioner for the area, the person appointed in his place must also possess the qualification. In any case a new member will hold office only until 31st March 1916. The existence of a vacancy is not to invalidate the proceedings at any meeting of the Committee (Nos. 8, 16 (4), and 17 of Regulations).

(133) A vacancy will arise if a member dies, or submits his resignation in writing to the Secretary of the Committee (who is to communicate it to the Clerk to the Insurance Committee), or if the member—

    (a) was at the time of his appointment a practitioner on the panel for the area, and subsequently ceases to be such ;

    (b) is absent without leave of the Committee from its meetings for a period of six consecutive months commencing from the date of the first meeting from which he was absent, unless the absence is due to employment in the naval or military forces during the present war.

(No. 16 of Regulations and Panel and Pharmaceutical Committees Amendment Regulations, 1915).

Quorum.

(134) The quorum fixed for each Committee is given in Appendix V. (No. 15 of Regulations).

Secretary.

(135) Every Panel Committee was required to appoint a Secretary at its first meeting, who was under the obligation to notify his appointment to the Commissioners. If it is necessary to appoint a new Secretary on account of death or resignation, the appointment must be similarly intimated to the Commissioners. The names and addresses of the Secretaries of Panel Committees in Scotland are given in Appendix V. (No. 14 (2) of Regulations).

Powers and Duties.

(136) The position of the Panel Committee is in the main that of an advisory body which is to be consulted by the Insurance Committee, where it is the duty of the latter to ascertain, in respect of any matter affecting the administration of medical benefit in its area, the opinions and wishes of the panel practitioners. The Panel Committee has in addition any powers and duties which may be conferred upon it by the Commissioners.

It will be recalled (*see* par. (122)) that where, within six months of the passing of the Amending Act (*i.e.* before 15th February 1914), no Local Medical Committee has been recognised, the Panel Committee may be recognised as the Local Medical Committee for the area (Sec. 32, 1913 Act). The Panel Committee for the County of Orkney was so recognised on 1st April 1914.

Consultation by Committee.

(137) The Medical Benefit Regulations impose upon all Insurance Committees the duty of consulting the Panel Committees for their areas before exercising any of the following powers :—

(a) Embodying in a draft agreement the terms upon which it is proposed to invite practitioners to undertake the treatment of insured persons (No. 5 (1), Medical Benefit Regulations (Scotland), 1913).

(b) Submitting to the Commissioners any alteration in the terms of service of practitioners (No. 16 (1)).

(c) Fixing, varying, or abolishing an income limit for the receipt of medical benefit under arrangements made by the Committee (No. 14 (2)).

(d) Making Rules under Section 14 of the Act of 1911 with regard to the administration of medical benefit (No. 81, Medical Benefit Regulations (Scotland), 1913).

(e) Preparing the list of drugs and appliances, known as the Drug Tariff; or making any alteration of the Drug Tariff, or of the terms upon which the supply of drugs and appliances is to be undertaken (Nos. 8 and 18 (1)).

(f) Making arrangements, with the consent of the Commissioners, where an insured person is resident in a rural area at a distance of more than one mile from the place of business of the nearest chemist, for the supply to that person by the practitioner attending him of such drugs and appliances as would otherwise ordinarily be supplied by a chemist (No. 12 (1)).

Arrangements for Medical Benefit.

(138) The Commissioners will, before approving the arrangements proposed by the Insurance Committee for the administration of medical benefit, consider any representations on the subject from the Panel Committee (No. 82, Medical Benefit Regulations).

Consideration of Chemists' Accounts.

(139) With regard to the accounts of persons supplying drugs and appliances, the Panel Committee is entitled to require that such accounts shall be submitted to them, together with any report made by the Pharmaceutical Committee, and if the Panel Committee take objection to any items in the accounts or

to any recommendation contained in the report, the Insurance Committee must decide as to the validity of the objection. The Panel Committee may, either with or without an examination of the accounts, indicate their willingness to accept all or any of them, and in so far as they are accepted they will be binding on all the practitioners on the panel. These powers also apply to the provision of medicine to temporary residents (Nos. 39 (3) and (4) and 42 (8), Medical Benefit Regulations).

Excessive Prescribing.

(140) Moreover, where it appears to the Panel Committee that, owing to the character or amount of the drugs ordered for insured persons by any practitioner or practitioners on the panel, the cost of the supply of those drugs and appliances is in excess of what may reasonably be necessary for the adequate treatment of those persons, the Panel Committee may, and, if any representation to the effect indicated is made to them by the Pharmaceutical Committee, must, make an investigation into the circumstances, and, after hearing the Pharmaceutical Committee and any practitioner concerned, report to the Insurance Committee (No. 40, Medical Benefit Regulations). The reports should deal with the question of whether there has been excessive prescribing, and if so, whether in character or amount and to what extent, and may include a recommendation as to surcharge. The decision as to surcharge and the amount thereof rests with the Insurance Committee.

Income Limit.

(141) In the event of an income limit being fixed, the Panel Committee is entitled, by giving notice in writing, to dispute the right of any insured person to receive medical benefit under the arrangements made by the Insurance Committee on the ground that his income exceeds the limit so fixed (No. 14 (3), Medical Benefit Regulations).

Advances to Practitioners.

(142) The rate at which advances are to be made to each practitioner after the end of each quarter is to be a matter of arrangement between the Insurance Committee and the Panel Committee (No. 37, Medical Benefit Regulations).

Scheme for Treatment.

(143) One of the most important duties of the Panel Committee is to make arrangements with the Insurance Committee to enable an insured person, who is not on the list of a practitioner, to obtain on application treatment without delay and to be assigned to a practitioner (No. 21 (4) of Regs.). The adoption of such a scheme is a preliminary to a scheme for the apportionment

amongst and payment to the practitioners of the balance of the Practitioners Fund (Reg. 35 (1)).

Complaints.

(144) The Panel Committee have certain rights in regard to the appointment and proceedings of the Medical Service Sub-Committee and the Joint Services Sub-Committee, and the conduct of any inquiry as to a complaint against a practitioner. The Commissioners are bound to hold such an inquiry on a sufficient representation from the Panel Committee (Parts V. and VI. Medical Benefit Regulations).

Expenses.

(145) As regards administrative expenses the Insurance Committee may, if requested to do so by the Panel Committee and the Pharmaceutical Committee or either Committee, allot for this purpose a sum or sums not exceeding in all one penny for each insured person entitled to obtain treatment from insurance service practitioners. The amount is to be determined by the Insurance Committee with the consent of the Commissioners (Sec. 33 (2), National Insurance Act, 1913).

(146) If the two Committees decide to put forward such a request it is desirable that they should come to an agreement as to how the amount to be allotted to them is to be divided. If one Committee only makes application the Commissioners require that the application should be submitted to the other Committee for its observations.

SECTION (III.)—PHARMACEUTICAL COMMITTEE.

Sanction.

(147) The appointment and recognition of Pharmaceutical Committees was provided for by Section 33 of the National Insurance Act, 1913.

General.

(148) The provisions relating to Pharmaceutical Committees are similar to those in the case of Panel Committees. (Parts III. and IV., Panel and Pharmaceutical Committees Regulations (Scotland), 1913.) Special Regulations have been made to meet the case of Zetland County.

Membership.

(149) The number of members of the Pharmaceutical Committee for each area is given in Appendix VI. Not less than two-thirds must be registered pharmacists, and all must be electors. The electors for the first Committee consisted of the pharmacists and others, and one representative of each firm and body corporate, under agreement with the Insurance Committee as at 13th October 1913, to supply drugs, medicines,

or appliances to insured persons, whether or not their place of business or residence was within the area of the Committee (Nos. 9 & 10 of Regulations).

Term of Office.

(150) The first members hold office until 31st March 1916. Casual vacancies must be filled by the remaining members of the Committee within three months, or in default by the Commissioners. The term of office of all members expires on 31st March 1916. Where a person whose seat is vacated was at the time of his appointment a person supplying drugs or appliances in the area, the person appointed in his place must have the same qualification (Nos. 12 and 17 of Regulations).

Vacancies.

(151) A casual vacancy will occur if a member dies, or resigns in writing addressed to the Secretary of the Committee (who is to notify the Clerk to the Insurance Committee of the resignation), or where a member—

(a) was at the time of his appointment a person supplying drugs or appliances in the area, and has subsequently ceased to be such ; or

(b) has been absent without leave of the Committee from its meetings for a period of six consecutive months, commencing from the date of the first meeting from which he was absent, unless the absence is due to employment in the naval or military forces during the present war.

(No. 16 of Regulations and Panel and Pharmaceutical Committees Amendment Regulations, 1915.)

Quorum.

(152) The quorum fixed for each Committee is given in Appendix VI. (No. 15 of Regulations).

Secretary.

(153) A Secretary to the Committee was appointed at the first meeting, and was required by the Regulations to notify his appointment to the Commissioners. Similar intimation must be given by any new Secretary appointed (No. 14 (2) of Regulations). The names and addresses of the Secretary of each Committee are given in Appendix VI.

Consultation by Committee.

(154) The Insurance Committee is bound to consult the Pharmaceutical Committee for its area in regard to the following matters :—

(a) The preparation of the Drug Tariff for ordinary drugs and prescribed appliances, and the method by which payment for drugs not included in the Tariff is to be calculated (No. 8, Medical Benefit Regulations).

(b) Any alterations which it is desired to make in the Drug Tariff or in the terms upon which the supply of drugs and appliances is undertaken (No. 18 (1), Medical Benefit Regulations).

(c) Arrangements proposed to be made, with the consent of the Commissioners, where an insured person is resident in a rural area at a distance of more than one mile from the place of business of the nearest chemist for the supply by a practitioner of drugs and appliances which would ordinarily be supplied by a chemist (No. 12 (1), Medical Benefit Regulations).

(d) Fixing, varying, or abolishing an income limit (No. 14 (2), Medical Benefit Regulations).

Drug Accounts.

(155) If the Pharmaceutical Committee so require, the accounts incurred for drugs and appliances must be submitted to them for examination, and they will make a report stating which items in the accounts ought, in their opinion, to be accepted, and which, if any, ought to be reduced or disallowed. The recommendations of the Committee are binding on the persons furnishing the accounts. If, however, the accounts are considered by the Panel Committee objections may be made by them to any item of an account or recommendation of the Pharmaceutical Committee. The Insurance Committee must decide as to the validity of any such objection. The Pharmaceutical Committee may at any time make representations to the Panel Committee that the character or amount of the drugs ordered for insured persons is in excess of what may reasonably be necessary for adequate treatment (Nos. 39 (2) and 40, Medical Benefit Regulations).

Complaints.

(156) It is the duty of the Pharmaceutical Committee to consider any complaint made by a person supplying drugs and appliances against any other such person, involving any question as to the efficiency of the service, and they may apply to the Commissioners to remove from the parel list the name of the person against whom the complaint has been made (No. 49, Medical Benefit Regulations).

Panel List.

(157) The Insurance Committee is required to submit its list of persons who have agreed to supply drugs and appliances to the Pharmaceutical Committee before it is issued in any year. The arrangements proposed for the administration of medical benefit must be submitted to the Commissioners, who will

before approving them consider any representations of the Pharmaceutical Committee (Nos. 11 (1) and 82, Medical Benefit Regulations).

Income Limit.

(158) The Committee has the right at any time to dispute the title of an insured person to receive medical benefit under the arrangements made by the Insurance Committee on the ground that the person's income exceeds any limit which may have been fixed (No. 14 (3), Medical Benefit Regulations).

Advances to Chemists.

(159) The sums to be paid in advance to persons supplying drugs and appliances, on rendering their accounts, are to be agreed upon between the Pharmaceutical Committee and the Insurance Committee (No. 39 (8), Medical Benefit Regulations).

CHAPTER IV.

MEDICAL BENEFIT.

General.

(160) THE most important duty of an Insurance Committee is that of making proper arrangements for the administration of Medical Benefit within its area.

By Section 8 of the Act of 1911 Medical Benefit is defined as Medical Treatment and Attendance, including the provision of proper and sufficient medicines and such medical appliances as may be prescribed by Regulations to be made by the Commissioners. Medical Benefit is declared by Section 8 (6) of the Act not to include any right to medical treatment or attendance in respect of a confinement.

(161) In terms of Section 15 (1) of the 1911 Act every Insurance Committee is bound, for the purpose of administering Medical Benefit, to make arrangements with duly qualified medical practitioners in accordance with Regulations made by the Commissioners. Under Section 15 (5) every Committee is further required to make provision for the supply of proper and sufficient drugs and medicines and prescribed appliances also in accordance with Regulations made by the Commissioners.

Regulations.

(162) The Medical Benefit Regulations at present in force are the National Health Insurance (Medical Benefit) Regulations (Scotland), 1913, dated 14th November 1913, and the Medical Benefit Regulations (Scotland), 1914, dated 22nd October 1914. Copies of the Regulations may be obtained from H.M. Stationery Office (Publications Branch), 23 Forth Street, Edinburgh, at the price respectively of 4d. and 1d. per copy, including postage. (S.O. references to be quoted, H.C. 28 and H.C. 42 respectively.)

(163) Generally, in pursuance of the requirements of Section 15, the provisions of the regulations secure that insured persons, including exempt persons entitled to medical benefit under Section 9 of the Act of 1913, shall be enabled to receive adequate medical attendance and treatment. The regulations require the adoption by the Insurance Committee of such system as will secure—

    (*a*) the preparation and publication of lists of (i.) medical practitioners who have agreed with the Insurance Committee to treat insured persons, and (ii.) persons, firms, and bodies corporate who have agreed to supply drugs, medicines, and appliances to insured persons;

(b) a right on the part of any duly qualified medical practitioner or of a person, firm, or body corporate who is desirous of being included in such list of being so included;

(c) a right on the part of any insured person of selecting, at such periods as may be prescribed, from the appropriate list, the practitioner by whom he wishes to be attended and treated, subject to that practitioner's consent;

(d) the distribution amongst, and so far as practicable under arrangements made by, the several practitioners whose names are on the lists, of the insured persons who after due notice have failed to make any selection, or who have been refused by the practitioner whom they have selected;

(e) the provision of medical attendance and treatment on the same terms as to remuneration as those arranged in regard to insured persons to members of societies who were at the date of the passing of the principal Act entitled as such members to medical attendance and treatment, and who were either over sixty-five years of age at the commencement of the Act, or were at that date, on account of permanent disablement, not qualified to become insured persons.

The main features of the Regulations are referred to in the Sections which follow.

(164) The Medical Year has been fixed by the Commissioners as the calendar year, *i.e.* 1st January to 31st December, and the Quarters as the periods commencing on 1st January, 1st April, 1st July, and 1st October (Reg. 2).

SECTION (I.)—ARRANGEMENTS WITH PRACTITIONERS AND INSTITUTIONS.

(i.) PRACTITIONERS.

(A) *Panel List.*

(165) If a duly qualified medical practitioner, other than one whose name has been removed by the Commissioners from the panel of an Insurance Committee in the United Kingdom, at any time makes application to a Committee for that purpose, the Committee must include his name in their panel list (Reg. 17). For the purpose of providing treatment for insured persons a Committee is required to enter into written agreements with such practitioners as are willing to undertake the treatment of insured persons on the terms of the agreement (Reg. 4). Each Committee must cause to be prepared and issue at least fourteen days before the end of the medical year a medical list of the

practitioners who have entered into agreements with it (Regs. 6 and 17).

(166) The list is to contain the name of each practitioner, his private address, the address of any surgery, dispensary, or other place at which he undertakes to attend for the purpose of treating insured persons, and particulars of the days and hours at which he undertakes to be in attendance at each place. If the Committee so decides the exact area in which each practitioner undertakes treatment may be shown. Where practitioners are in partnership a reference to the partnership may appear in the list (Regs. 6 and 5). Steps must be taken to enable insured persons to inspect an up-to-date copy of the list at the Committee's offices, at any Post Office, and at any other suitable places, and a copy must also be sent to the Commissioners and to every person, firm, or body corporate supplying drugs or appliances or both. The Commissioners must also be informed as soon as possible of any alteration on the list (Regs. 6 (4) and 17 (5)).

(B) Conditions of Service.

(167) The Medical Benefit Regulations prescribe certain conditions which must form part of every agreement, and the Regulations themselves are also deemed to be incorporated in the agreement. Insurance Committees are bound to consult with Local Medical Committees and Panel Committees, and to prepare for the approval of the Commissioners a draft agreement upon the terms of which practitioners are to be invited to take service (Reg. 5 and First Schedule). A copy of the Model Form of Agreement between the Committee and the practitioner forms Appendix VII.

Places and Times of Attendance.

(168) The practitioner's agreement must state the places and hours at which patients may attend and receive treatment, but in addition any patient on the doctor's list whose condition is such that a visit is required is entitled to be so visited. Ordinarily the patient will be at the address given when he was accepted by the doctor, but the agreement provides that a visit shall be paid if necessary even when he is elsewhere, provided that the distance by road from the doctor's residence does not exceed the number of miles which may be specified in the agreement.

The places, days, and hours of attendance may be altered by the practitioner with the consent of the Committee (which cannot be unreasonably withheld), but in such an event he must take steps to the satisfaction of the Committee to bring the changes to the notice of the persons entitled to obtain treatment from him (First Schedule, 4 and 5).

Practitioner's List.

(169) Every practitioner on the panel must be supplied by the Committee with a list of the persons for whose treatment he is

responsible, *i.e.* of the persons accepted by him or assigned to him by the Committee. An approved institution has a right to receive corresponding information (Reg. 25).

Deputy.

(170) In normal circumstances the practitioner is bound to give treatment personally. If, however, this is impossible, owing to urgency of other professional duties, temporary absence from home, or other reasonable cause, he must to the best of his ability provide for some other practitioner to act as his deputy. Although the places at which treatment may be given by a deputy may be altered, due regard must be had to the convenience of the patient (First Sch. 7).

Breach of Agreement.

(171) The practitioner is liable to make good any expense or loss which the Committee or a patient may suffer owing to a breach on his part of the agreement. The amount involved may be recovered by deduction from any sums due to the practitioner under the agreement, or in any other competent manner, but unless the Medical Service Sub-Committee or the Joint Services Sub-Committee have already had the matter before them, the Committee must refer it to the Medical Service Sub-Committee before taking action. In any case the practitioner or his legal personal representative has a right of appeal to the Commissioners within fourteen days after he has received notice of the Committee's decision (First Sch. 9). A dispute or question between a Committee and a practitioner as to the construction of the agreement or their respective rights and liabilities is referred to the Commissioners unless other machinery for its settlement is specially provided by the Regulations, *e.g.* Medical Service Sub-Committee (Reg. 45) Referees (Reg. 50), etc. (First Sch. 10).

Alteration of Conditions.

(172) An Insurance Committee may, after consultation with the Local Medical Committee and the Panel Committee, and subject to the approval of the Commissioners, make alterations in the conditions of service. The proposals will, after being submitted to the Commissioners and approved by them, take effect at the beginning of the following year, or from such later date as the Commissioners may determine. Six weeks' notice prior to the commencement of the year must be given by the Committee to the practitioner (Reg. 16).

Withdrawal from Panel.

(173) Unless a practitioner gives written notice to the Committee at least four weeks before the beginning of the year that he desires to withdraw, his agreement will stand for the following year, subject to any alterations of which notice may have been given to him. If intimation of withdrawal is received four

weeks or more before the end of the year the practitioner's name must be removed from the list at the end of the year (Reg. 17).

(174) Withdrawal may take place during the course of the year only under the following circumstances :—

    (*a*) If both panel and other practice is to be discontinued in the area to which the practitioner's agreement applies, he may have his name removed from the list on giving due notice to the Committee. The Committee may, if it thinks fit, refuse to remove the name before two months have elapsed from the date of the notice.

    (*b*) The Committee may, if it wishes, consent to the removal of the name even where the practitioner proposes to continue his other practice and desires to discontinue his panel practice only.

    (*c*) The name of any practitioner who dies or whose name is directed to be removed from the list by the Commissioners should be removed at once. In the case of death, the legal personal representative may appoint a practitioner (who need not be on the panel) to undertake the treatment of such persons as do not apply to be transferred to the list of another practitioner, as if he were a deputy of the deceased practitioner. Notice of the desire to adopt this course must be given by the representative within seven days of the death, and treatment under such arrangement may be given for such period as the Committee thinks fit. (*See* also par. 241.)

(Reg. 17.)

    (*C*) *Supply of Drugs by Practitioners.*

(175) If an Insurance Committee is satisfied that a person entitled to medical benefit will have difficulty in obtaining drugs or appliances from a chemist on the panel, it must, if the practitioner concerned so desires, make arrangements for the supply of the drugs and appliances by the practitioner attending him.

The Committee has, moreover, a discretionary power to make similar arrangements after consultation with the Panel Committee and Pharmaceutical Committee and subject to the consent of the Commissioners, where a person is resident in a rural area at a distance of more than one mile from the place of business of the nearest panel chemist. The Commissioners' decision on any question arising under the regulation is final (Reg. 12). The distance of one mile is to be measured by road or path.

The arrangements made by the Committee with a practitioner as above will stand until the end of the medical year even if a chemist should start business within such a distance of the person's residence that the necessity for the special arrangement no longer exists (Reg. 12). If, however, the insured person changes his place of residence during a year to a place within a mile of a chemist under agreement with the Committee the doctor is not entitled to continue to dispense.

(176) The Committee must also arrange with panel practitioners to supply in all cases drugs which are necessarily or ordinarily administered by a practitioner in person, and drugs and appliances required for immediate administration or application, or required for use before a supply can conveniently be obtained in the ordinary way through a panel chemist (Reg. 12 (3)).

(D) Range of Service.

(177) The treatment which the practitioner is required to give is " of a kind which can consistently with the best interests of the patient be properly undertaken by a general practitioner of ordinary professional competence and skill," but he is bound to advise the patient as to what steps should be taken to obtain any treatment beyond this which the condition of the patient may demand. The practitioner is not required by his agreement to give, or entitled thereby to charge for, treatment to any person in respect of a confinement.

The conditions of the Parliamentary Grant to the Committee require that the domiciliary treatment of persons on panel-lists recommended for sanatorium benefit shall be undertaken by the practitioners by whom they are attended. (First Schedule to Agreement.)

(178) The question of whether a particular operation or other service can consistently with the best interests of the patient be properly undertaken by a general practitioner of ordinary professional competence and skill is one for determination, having regard to the conditions and practice of the locality and the degree of urgency of the patient's need. No rules for rigid application can be stated, but for the guidance of Committees certain general principles on which the practice appears to proceed may be indicated :—

    (a) Special experience and skill of a particular practitioner on the panel is not to be exploited.

    (b) The standard of competence and skill is, however, that of the average general practitioner, and the incompetence of a particular practitioner is not a ground for excluding a particular operation or service, or for reducing the general standard of the service.

    (c) The exigencies of service in districts removed from hospital practice demand a degree of competence and skill in a general practitioner as regards operations and other services which, in the interests of the patient, may in more favoured districts be better left to hospital or specialist treatment.

    (d) In any district urgent need for immediate treatment will extend the range of service.

The matter is, in each instance, one for consideration in the first place by the Local Medical Committee, and as has been mentioned in paragraph (87) may arise out of a complaint dealt with by the Medical Service Sub-Committee. The Insurance Committee and the Local Medical Committee may agree upon the decision, but, in the event of failure to come to an agreement, or where the Commissioners do not agree with a decision of both the Local Medical and Insurance Committees, the Commissioners will appoint three referees to hear evidence and decide the question at issue. The referees comprise two practitioners in actual practice in Great Britain and a member of the Faculty of Advocates or enrolled law-agent, in actual practice. The procedure in connection with an inquiry has been prescribed by Rules, dated 3rd September 1914, which are printed in Appendix VIII. The referees may decide any question by a majority, and subject to the Regulations and Rules may determine their own procedure. The decision must be reported to the Insurance Committee, and by them to the Commissioners, and the referees must state whether in arriving at their decision they have had regard to any custom or practice of the medical profession which is peculiar to the area (Reg. 50).

(E) Standard of Treatment.

(179) The conditions of the Special Parliamentary Grant to the Committee of 2s. 6d. per person entitled to medical benefit require that the general arrangements made by the Committee shall be such as to secure to insured persons a standard of treatment satisfactory to the Commissioners.

(F) Remuneration.

(180) The basis of payment for services is explained in Chapter VI. It is to be noted that a practitioner is precluded from accepting any fee or other remuneration in respect of treatment which he is required to give under his agreement except as the agreement provides.

(G) Medical Records.

(181) It is a condition of the payment to the Insurance Committee of the special Parliamentary Grant that the practitioner shall keep such records of the diseases of his patients as is required by the Commissioners. In view of the importance of the statistics of diseases which it is hoped to obtain from this source the necessity for making the records both complete and accurate cannot be too strongly emphasised. There are two alternative forms of record— the Medical Day-Book and the Medical Record Card. Only one system may be in use in any Committee area, and the choice is a matter for decision by the Panel Committee, subject to the approval of the Commissioners. The records of a practitioner who is on the panel for two or more adjacent Insurance Committee areas, whether in book or in card form, *must be kept separate.*

(182) *Medical Day Books* are issued by the Insurance Committee. Each page of the book is current for a calendar month, and

contains spaces for details regarding 30 patients. All attendances and visits (including special visits, etc.) upon persons entitled to medical benefits must be entered. The page is divided into three portions, the left hand portion for notes to be retained by the practitioner, the middle portion to be sent to the Insurance Committee *within* 14 *days* of the end of the month to which it refers, and the right hand portion to be sent to the Commissioners within the same period. Two points of detail may be mentioned, attention to which will obviate much correspondence. In the first place, if two or more pages are used in any month, each portion of the first page should be lettered " A," each portion of the second page " B," and so on. In the second place, if the treatment of a particular patient did not terminate during the month, the nature of the illness, even if diagnosed, should not be entered for that month, but the patient's name should be carried forward at once to the next month, and in the space for " nature of illness " in the first month there should be inserted the serial letter of the page and the number against which the name of the patient is entered in the second month. It is possible that a patient whose name is carried forward may not require any attendances or visits during the second month. If this is the case, a zero should be entered in the appropriate column, and if the practitioner is still of opinion that treatment is not concluded, the name should again be carried forward and a reference to re-entry made.

In dealing with the month of December a modification of this procedure is necessary for statistical purposes. For that month both the nature of illness and a reference to the re-entry in January should be given in cases which are not concluded.

It is important that a return should be made although no patients may have been seen during any month.

Where a panel practitioner is acting as deputy say for an absent colleague, treatment given to persons on the absent colleague's panel list should appear on the records of the absent colleague.

(183) Each *Medical Record Card* is applicable to a single patient and is current for a complete calendar year. There are two portions—one to be sent to the Insurance Committee, and one to the Commissioners, between 1st and 14th January of the year following that to which the card refers. A practitioner will not require to write a Record Card for any person unless and until that person receives treatment, and *not more than one Record Card should be initiated in respect of any person in the same year.* The cards are self-explanatory, and no " reference to re-entry " is necessary. Before they are despatched to the Commissioners the name of the Insurance Committee, and of the practitioner, should be entered in the spaces provided.

The Card system has many advantages in practice over the Day Book one, and its use is steadily extending. There is no doubt that it presents advantages to the practitioner, and is adaptable to other uses than simply keeping records, but like all card systems regular and timeous use is essential to its success. The form of card in use is shown in Appendix IX.

(H) *Certification of Incapacity.*

(184) It is a further condition of the Special Parliamentary Grant to Insurance Committees that certificates shall be furnished to every insured person, where he so desires and requests, in such form, on such occasions, and generally in such manner as the Commissioners may determine, for the purposes of any claim made by him for sickness or disablement benefit or for the purpose of determining or calculating the period during which sickness benefit is or would, but for any Section of the Act disentitling him, have been payable, or of calculating arrears. The Commissioners have made Rules for the giving of such certificates and have issued model forms of first, intermediate, and final certificates. The new uniform system of certification came into force on 1st January 1915. It was fully explained in Memo. 211 I.C., issued by the Commissioners for the information of doctors and Approved Societies, and a copy of that Memorandum with the Rules and Model forms of Certificates appended is printed in Appendix X.

(ii.) SYSTEMS OR INSTITUTIONS.

(185) Under Section 15 (4) of the Act of 1911 any system or institution which provides medical attendance and treatment and which was in existence at the date when the Act passed (16th December 1911) can apply through its Board of Management or other authority for approval by the Insurance Committee or Committees affected and the Commissioners. Where such approval is given medical attendance and treatment (including the provision of drugs and applicances) given through it to persons entitled to medical benefit is treated as medical benefit, and a contribution towards the cost is made from the funds of the Committee.

The application must be made in the first instance to the Committee, who are required to inform the Commissioners whether they approve the system or institution, and to supply certain particulars of its management, rules, finances, staff, the scope of treatment, etc. The essential conditions for the approval or the continued approval of the Commissioners are—

    (*a*) that the system or institution shall make such alterations in and additions to its rules as the Commissioners may require, and shall not make any alterations or additions affecting the rights of insured persons except with the consent of the Commissioners;

    (*b*) that it shall be conducted in such a manner as to comply with any conditions for the receipt of the Parliamentary Grant applicable to the giving of treatment by panel practitioners (*e.g.* the keeping of records of diseases and treatment given);

(c) that any person under the system or institution shall be entitled, if he so elects at the prescribed date, to obtain medical benefit in the ordinary way from a practitioner on the panel in place of from the institution.

No institution has been approved in Scotland.

Post Office System.

(186) The Post Office Medical System is the only system approved in Scotland. A list of the Insurance Committee areas for which it has been approved is given in Appendix XI. Under it members of the Post Office staff entitled to free medical attendance are generally placed on the " capitation list " of the medical officer attached to the office at which they are employed. In respect of each officer on his list the medical officer receives from the Department a fee of 8s. 6d. per annum, in return for which the staff under his care are entitled to receive at his surgery (or at the Post Office when the medical officer attends there) advice and treatment such as a general medical practitioner is accustomed to render to his patients in the course of ordinary practice, including the domiciliary treatment of tuberculosis in the case of persons recommended for such treatment under Sanatorium Benefit, and also such medicine as they may require. Officers who are too unwell to leave home are entitled to be visited at their home if they live within the medical officer's visiting area, which is measured by a circle of three miles radius described round the office to which the medical officer is attached, or in the case of a medical officer attached to a group of rural offices by circles of three miles radius round each office. Officers living outside the visiting area of the medical officer of the office at which they are employed are treated exceptionally, and are placed on the " capitation list " of the medical officer nearest to their homes if they live within his visiting area.

Officers normally entitled to free medical attendance, but not attached to any definite headquarters, as, for example, labourers in the Engineering Department, are not placed on capitation lists, but are allowed to avail themselves of the services of the medical officers of the districts they are employed in when they fall ill, and the privilege of consulting the neighbouring medical officer is also conceded to officers who fall ill while absent from their headquarters on official business. The payments made to medical officers for attendance on such "itinerants" are at the rate of 2s. 6d. per visit to or by the patient, subject to a maximum payment of 8s. 6d. per half-year for each officer attended.

SECTION (II.)—ARRANGEMENTS WITH CHEMISTS AND PHARMACISTS.

General.

(187) The general provisions of the Acts and Regulations as to the steps to be taken by the Insurance Committee to arrange for the supply of drugs, medicines, and appliances follow very closely those relating to medical treatment. Thus in virtue of Section 15 (5) (*b*) of the Act of 1911 any person, including a firm, or body corporate has the right to have his name placed on the panel list of the Committee, and to enter into an agreement with the Committee for the purpose of supplying such drugs and appliances or any of them as he is legally entitled to supply unless the Commissioners and the Joint Committee after inquiry are satisfied that the inclusion of the name on the panel, either initially or after removal by the Commissioners from any panel in the United Kingdom, would be prejudicial to the efficiency of the service. No person is, however, entitled to dispense medicines under the agreement except a chemist who undertakes that all medicines supplied shall be dispensed either by a registered pharmacist, or under the direct supervision of a registered pharmacist, or by a person who, for three years immediately prior to 16th December 1911, acted as a dispenser to a duly qualified medical practitioner or a public institution. "Chemist" is the term used in the Medical Benefit Regulations to mean any person, firm, or body corporate entitled to carry on the business of a chemist or druggist under the provisions of the Pharmacy Act, 1868, as amended by the Poisons and Pharmacy Act, 1908, and by "registered pharmacist" is meant a person who is registered as a chemist or druggist under the Pharmacy Act, 1868 (Regs. 9 and 19 (1)).

Panel List.

(188) A person may enter into an agreement to supply drugs only, including or excluding scheduled poisons or appliances only, or both, and may or may not be entitled to dispense medicines. A list of names and addresses of persons who have entered into agreements must be prepared by the Insurance Committee, and must distinguish between the persons entitled to supply drugs only, appliances only, and to dispense medicines (Reg. 10).

(189) The list must be submitted to the Pharmaceutical Committee before it is issued, and must be issued at least 14 days before the beginning of each medical year. A copy must be sent to the Commissioners and to every practitioner on the panel, and a copy kept up to date must also be available for the inspection of insured persons at the office of the Committee, and such other places (*e.g.* Post Offices) as the Committee think fit. Any alteration which takes place must be communicated to the Commissioners as soon as possible (Reg. 19).

Notice.

(190) Every person on the list must exhibit at his place of business a notice in the following form so far as applicable :—

National Insurance Acts, 1911 *to* 1913.

(*Name of Person or Firm contracting*).

Under contract with the Insurance Committee for the County (or Burgh) of........................

To dispense medicines.
To supply drugs.
To supply drugs (except scheduled poisons).
To supply appliances.
(Reg. 11 (3) and Fourth Schedule.)

Form of Agreement.

(191) A draft agreement embodying the conditions upon which persons are invited to undertake the supply of drugs and appliances must be prepared by each Insurance Committee after consultation with the Pharmaceutical Committee, and submitted to the Commissioners for approval. The agreement must include the conditions set forth in the Third Schedule of the Regulations and the Drug Tariff (Reg. 10). A Model Form of Agreement has been issued for the guidance of Committees, and is printed in Appendix XII.

Conditions of Agreement.

(192) The conditions of the agreements for the supply of drugs and appliances are *mutatis mutandis* similar to those applicable to agreements between the Committee and panel practitioners. (See Appendix VII.) Disputes and questions regarding the agreements are to be settled in the same manner. The provisions worthy of special notice are those requiring the chemists (1) to supply drugs and appliances of good quality ; (2) to supply with reasonable promptness ; (3) to supply the drugs and appliances free of charge to the person entitled to medical benefit ; (4) to provide, free of charge to the insured person, proper bottles or other vessels for any substances to which Section 5 of the Poisons and Pharmacy Act, 1908, or the Regulations made under Section 1 of the Pharmacy Act, 1868, relate ; (5) to provide proper bottles or vessels in other cases on the price being deposited by the insured person, which will be refunded upon the return of the bottles or vessels in a clean condition.

Drug Tariff.

(193) The " Drug Tariff " is the list of the prices prepared by the Committee after consultation with the Local Medical Committee, the Panel Committee, and the Pharmaceutical Committee, on the basis of which the sums to be paid for the drugs ordinarily supplied and for the prescribed

appliances are calculated. The method of ascertaining the amount of the payment by the Committee to the chemist for drugs not included in the Tariff is also incorporated in the agreement and is determined by the Insurance Committee after consultation with the Committees mentioned (Reg. 8). Both the Tariff and the method of pricing non-tariff drugs and medicines are subject to the approval of the Commissioners. In order to avoid the difficulties and anomalies which it was feared might be attendant on different tariffs in different areas in Scotland the Pharmaceutical Standing Committee for Scotland prepared and submitted to the Commissioners a Model Form of Tariff which was adjusted and issued to Committees for their guidance. The Model Form has been adopted in all areas in Scotland.

Emergency Provisions.

(194) Owing to the outbreak of war certain drugs were subject to a considerable rise in price. To meet the hardship to chemists attendant on extreme fluctuation of prices, a special grant was made available by the Government in 1914 which permitted an increase on the contract price to be allowed in the case of certain drugs. In the 1915 Tariff drugs which it was anticipated would be subject to substantial fluctuation in prices were " starred," and arrangements were made for a monthly revision of the price.

Proper and Sufficient Medicines.

(195) Questions with reference to what are to be regarded as proper and sufficient drugs and medicines were dealt with in Circular No. 389 and Memo. 587, issued by the Commissioners for the assistance of Committees.

Certain drugs and medicinal substances are relatively cheap, while others are comparatively costly. Even of drugs which are in common and necessary use a number are somewhat expensive. In normal circumstances expense, however, by itself should never be a bar to the supply of a drug under National Insurance. The insured person, subject to the provisions of the Acts, is entitled to receive proper and sufficient medicines, but in order that he may do so restrictions must be imposed on improper or excessive prescribing. During the period of the war, when the supplies of certain drugs are restricted, care is especially necessary in order that the available supply may be made use of to the best advantage. Preparations which are the same in substance may figure under different titles, varying in cost according to the proprietary or other names by which they are designated in prescriptions. In this connection Circular 389 was issued by the Commissioners for the general guidance of Insurance Committees and others in endeavouring to arrive at a decision with regard to particular questions which might emerge, and in cases of reasonable doubt the Commissioners have been prepared to advise Committees, if requested to do so, without prejudice to their own position in determining matters formally submitted to them as a dispute.

If the Panel Committee in any Insurance area, acting as expert advisers on methods of prescribing, desire to inform the Insurance practitioners of the method which they as a Committee propose to adopt in the scrutiny of prescriptions, and if it be their considered opinion that certain preparations should not be supplied, or that certain others should only be prescribed in a particular form or under a particular name, they would in the view of the Commissioners be entitled to declare their method and express their opinion by means of a circular issued by them to practitioners on the panel. The specific compounds or preparations which the Panel Committee regard with disfavour will necessarily vary to some extent with local medical custom, and the views of the Panel Committee could not be held as binding on a particular doctor in the administration of a particular form of a remedy to a particular patient; but if the doctor, knowing the opinion of the Panel Committee to be opposed to the use of the particular form, and being advised of the method which they propose to adopt in scrutinising prescriptions, elects to prescribe the remedy in the particular form, it would devolve upon him to justify his procedure and to show cause why he should not be surcharged.

Panel Committees in a number of Scottish areas have already taken useful action by circularising their practitioners on these matters. In any area where the Panel Committee desire to take this course, the Insurance Committee should offer them every facility, by conference and otherwise, towards carrying out their design.

Emergency Drugs and Appliances.

(196) In approving schemes of Committees for the issue to their practitioners of a supply of emergency drugs and appliances the Commissioners have required that the quantities ordered at one time should be restricted within definite limits. Their object in so determining has been to enable Committees to control the frequency and amount of such orders by reference to the number of insured persons on the panel lists of practitioners and other relevant circumstances.

Appliances.

(197) The medical and surgical appliances which may be supplied as part of medical benefit are in terms of Section 8 (1) of the Act, such as may be prescribed in regulations made by the Commissioners. The following have been prescribed (Reg. 7 and Second Sch.):—

BANDAGES—
    Calico, bleached.
    Calico, unbleached.
    Crepe.
    Domette.
    Elastic-web.

BANDAGES—continued—
    Flannel.
    Indiarubber.
    Muslin.
    Plaster of Paris.
    Open-wove.

GAUZES—
    Unmedicated.
    Boric.
    Carbolic.
    Cyanide.
    Iodoform.
    Picric.
    Sal-alembroth.
    Sublimate.

LINTS—
    Unmedicated.
    Boric.
    Sal-alembroth.

COTTON WOOL
    Unmedicated.
    Boric.
    Sal-alembroth.

Wood wool.
Tow, plain.
Oiled silk.
Oiled paper.
Oiled cambric.
Gutta-percha tissue.
Adhesive plaster.
Ice-bags—
    Indiarubber.
    Check sheeting.
Splints.
Catheters.
    Gum elastic.
    Soft rubber.

Where loan would be practicable, the Committee may make provision for lending any of these appliances, and if this has been done and the practitioners and chemists have been informed of the fact, an insured person is not entitled to the appliance otherwise than under the lending arrangement (Reg. 22).

(198) The Drug Tariff under the Medical Benefit Regulations is the list of prices for drugs ordinarily supplied, and for prescribed appliances. There are ex-list drugs, not on the Tariff, which may be ordered also, and the manner of calculating payment for these is provided for in the Regulations (see paragraph (193) above); but the only appliances which may be supplied are those named above.

It has come under notice that in certain areas such appliances as douches, syringes, trusses, nebulisers, throat brushes, and jaconette have been ordered. Articles of this kind are not prescribed appliances; and if supplied should not be paid for by an Insurance Committee.

Tuberculosis and the Drug Fund.

(199) Consideration of the prescriptions investigated in course of inquiries has indicated a certain amount of overlapping between Medical and Sanatorium Benefits. When substances commonly regarded as remedies for consumption figured in large quantities under the Drug Fund, the question emerged whether owing to the failure of practitioners to write the appropriate index marks on prescription forms, the medicines of patients recommended for domiciliary treatment under Sanatorium Benefit were being improperly charged to the Drug Fund, or whether patients who were qualified for domiciliary treatment under Sanatorium Benefit were being retained for any reason under Medical Benefit.

On either alternative the Drug Fund would be called upon to bear a burden from which it should be immune and the general tendency to shortage would be accentuated.

The Commissioners have expressed the opinion that procedure under this head is worthy of careful consideration by Committees.

Temporary Residents.

(200) Similar precautions should be observed in the case of temporary residents receiving medical treatment within the area of a Committee. Care should be taken by practitioners to mark prescriptions for such persons in the manner directed by the Committee, in order that the cost may be duly charged against the Central Medical Benefit Fund.

The Commissioners have recommended Committees to take steps with a view to protecting their Drug Funds against improper claims from this source.

Shortage of Drugs owing to State of War.

(201) Serious questions regarding the supply of drugs and medicines have arisen in consequence of the state of war now existing in Europe, the effect of which has been to produce in this country a shortage in the supply of certain drugs and prescribed appliances. In the case of some preparations it is probable that no further consignments can be obtained until the termination of hostilities; in the case of others it may be possible to procure quantities from sources not hitherto drawn upon. The duration of shortage will vary with different substances, to an extent which it is not possible at this juncture to foresee.

The question at issue with regard to the use of such articles is not wholly or mainly one of price. Nor is it one which solely affects the Insurance Medical Service. Apart from these considerations, it is essential at present that all existing stocks of remedies for disease should, as far as possible, be husbanded, by reserving drugs in which there is a shortage for cases to whose treatment they are indispensable, and endeavouring to provide for the needs of others by other remedies of similar action.

The position has been brought under the notice of practitioners and Insurance Committees for their part should, as far as possible, co-operate with Panel Committees in the adoption of any recommendations or other measures which may seem likely to prove of service.

Facilities.

(202) Arrangements must be made by the Insurance Committee with the Pharmaceutical Committee to secure that in its area so far as practicable one or more places of business of persons supplying drugs and appliances shall at all reasonable times be open to persons entitled to obtain drugs or appliances (Reg. 10 (3)).

Alterations in Agreements.

(203) The Committee must, after consultation with the Local Medical Committee, Panel Committee, and Pharmaceutical Committee, submit for the approval of the Commissioners a statement of any alterations which they may desire to make in the Drug Tariff, or other conditions in the agreements for the supply of drugs or appliances. No alterations can, however, take place before the beginning of the following medical year, and if any such alterations are approved by the Commissioners due notice must be given by the Committee to each person, etc., concerned not later than six weeks before the beginning of the year (Reg. 18).

In the year 1915, however, this is subject to the special emergency arrangements due to the war of a monthly revision of the prices of "starred" drugs, and to a right to revise the contracts once during the course of the year if the Commissioners so approve (Medical Benefit Regulations, 1914).

Termination of Agreement.

(204) If a person, including a firm or body corporate desires to cancel his agreement he may do so by giving notice to the Committee in writing at least four weeks before the beginning of any medical year, and the agreement will then terminate at the end of the current year. Unless such notice is given the person, firm, or body corporate will be deemed to have continued the agreement, subject to any alterations in the conditions which may have been notified to him or them under the last paragraph. The agreement cannot be determined at any time *during* the year except with the consent of the Committee. In the event of death the person's name is removed from the list at once, provided that where the business of the person is carried on in accordance with the provisions of the Pharmacy Act, 1868, as amended by the Poisons and Pharmacy Act, 1908, by a person who is his executor or administrator or the trustee of his estate within the meaning of Section 16 of the former Act, that person is deemed to be on the list so long as these conditions continue (Reg. 19).

SECTION (III.)—THE REGISTER.

(i.) GENERAL.

(205) Each Insurance Committee must prepare and keep to the satisfaction of the Commissioners a Register of Persons resident in its area entitled to Medical or Sanatorium Benefits and all Deposit Contributors so resident. The Register consists of three lists :—

(a) Approved Society members, including members of the Navy and Army Insurance Fund ;
(b) Deposit Contributors ;
(c) Exempt persons.

The lists must show the addresses of the persons whose names are included therein, and must distinguish between those entitled to (i.) Medical and Sanatorium Benefit; (ii.) Medical Benefit only; (iii.) Sanatorium Benefit only; (iv.) neither Medical nor Sanatorium Benefit. Approved Society members must be distinguished as (i.) members of the Navy and Army Fund; (ii.) members of other Societies.

Deposit contributors must be distinguished as having or not having attained the age of 70 years at the commencement of the current medical year (No. 3 of Payments to Insurance Committees Regs., 1914). The Register is necessary in order that the Committee may know who are the persons for whom arrangements in regard to medical treatment must be made. To prepare and maintain the Register it is necessary that the Committee should be supplied with information as to the members of Approved Societies, Deposit Contributors, and Exempt Persons entitled to benefit who are resident in its area. This information is supplied by Approved Societies for their members and by the Commissioners for Deposit Contributors and Exempt Persons. A card system of Register has been adopted by every Committee. The Register, in addition to constituting a record of insured persons entitled to medical and to sanatorium benefits, or either of them, is also utilised in connection with the administration of sickness, disablement and maternity benefits of Deposit Contributors and with the finance of the Committee, as explained in the Section dealing with that subject.

(ii.) Preparation of Register.

(206) The Register includes (a) the Index Register; (b) the Suspense Register; and (c) Deposit Contributors not entitled to Medical or Sanatorium Benefit.

The Index Register.

(207) The Register is comprised of notifications on thin cards of uniform size called "Index Slips." In order that they may be readily distinguished index slips of Society members entitled to medical and sanatorium benefits are in colour—white for men and blue for women. Deposit Contributors' Index Slips are yellow for men and green for women. The index slip of the exempt person is red. Further, members of Societies entitled to medical benefit only, viz. the special married women voluntary contributors (classes of contribution card H^1 and H^2) are distinguished by pink slips. Members of Societies who having entered insurance at 65 or over, on attaining the age of 70, have less than 27 contributions properly paid in respect of them lose their right to medical benefit, and are shown in the Register by means of mauve slips. Deposit Contributors who attain the age of 70 retain their title to medical and sanatorium benefit provided they comply with the conditions of the Deposit Contributors Benefits Order, 1914 (No. 2)

(*see* paragraph (371))). Voluntary Contributors, it may be noted, under Section 10 of the Act of 1913, are not allowed to receive medical benefit if their total income from all sources exceeds £160 a year, the contribution which would otherwise be payable being in that case reduced by one penny.

Suspense Register.

(208) Where the index slip of an insured person who has established his title to benefit cannot readily be traced a " Suspense Slip " is prepared by the Committee. Slips so written are kept apart from the slips comprising the Index Register.

Arrangement of Register.

(209) For ease in access and handling index slips are usually arranged in a filing cabinet under—
1. Societies,
2. Deposit Contributors, and
3. Exempt Persons,

in alphabetical order according to the surname of the insured persons, and are further subdivided into men and women. Some Committees arrange slips for Societies with Branches under branch subdivisions.

(iii.) KEEPING OF REGISTER.

The Index Register is kept up to date in the following manner:—

Approved Society Members.

(210) *New Members.*— An index slip should be sent by the Society to the Committee of residence not later than seven days after a person is admitted as an insured member (Reg. 29 (4)). In the case of a person in Class B (Soldiers, Sailors, and Marines in the service of the Crown, who are not entitled to medical or sanatorium benefit), the index slip is not sent until the member transfers from Class B to some other Class and becomes eligible for these benefits.

(211) Failure on the part of the Society to send the index slip on admission of the member to insurance will result in delay in the issue of the medical card to the member, who may thus be prejudiced in obtaining medical benefit. Effective membership begins on the date subsequent to entry into insurance from which the Society undertakes to admit the insured person. The index slip should be forwarded without delay, and on no account must its despatch be deferred until the Contribution Card has been received. In the case of a voluntary contributor, however, the Society should satisfy itself that the contributor has entered insurance by the payment of at least one contribution.

(212) *Transfers.*—The fact that a person has transferred from

another Society or Branch, or from the Deposit Contributor or Exempt Person Classes, should be noted in the appropriate space on the back of the index slip sent by the Society.

(213) *Deaths and changes of status* affecting the position of members of Societies in regard to medical or sanatorium benefit are notified to Insurance Committees by means of orange slips and pink slips. The former slips are used for intimating cessation of membership owing to death or resignation, and suspension from benefit owing to joining army or navy, removal abroad, or ceasing insurance on marriage, the latter for notifying that the persons in respect of whom they are issued are no longer employed owing to marriage, have elected to become Special Voluntary Contributors, and have ceased to be eligible for sanatorium benefit.

(214) On receipt of an *orange slip* from the Society, the corresponding index slip should be traced and destroyed in cases where the member has died, is suspended from benefit, or has ceased to be insured. Where the person has been expelled or has resigned (otherwise than on transfer) the fact of expulsion or resignation should be noted on the index slip, which should be retained pending certification from the new Society or the Commissioners. Where the Committee does not hold an index slip, but has prepared a suspense slip the Society should be requested to state to what Committee the index slip was sent, and steps should be taken to recover the index slip and destroy it. The doctor or institution and the insured person should be notified and the medical index amended. On receipt of a *pink slip* the corresponding blue index slip must be destroyed. The doctor or institution should be notified of the new name and address and the Medical Index amended. Where removal from the area has taken place the pink slip will be transmitted on receipt of the half medical card. Where it is noted on the index slip that the person was formerly a member of another Society, the index slip of the former Society must be *destroyed*. If the person was formerly a Deposit Contributor or an Exempt Person the index slip must be *returned* to the Commissioners.

(215) Under the medical card system the index slip of an Approved Society member who removes temporarily (*i.e.* for a period up to 3 months) to another Committee area is retained by the Committee in whose area the member ordinarily resides, and the slip will not be transferred to the Committee of new address, in the case of permanent removal to another area, until the individual applies for medical benefit therein. Removal slips received from Societies notifying changes which occurred after 11th January 1914, do not therefore require to be acted on unless the change is to an address in the Committee's own area or the insured person has removed to Ireland. In the latter case the slip should be forwarded to the Irish Insurance Committee concerned. Societies must notify changes of address of members which occurred prior to 11th January 1914, to another

area, intimation thereof being made by means of removal slips and effect should be given thereto.

Deposit Contributors.

(216) On a Deposit Contributor's account being opened in the books of the Commissioners an index slip is sent to the Committee. When the amount standing to the contributor's credit is insufficient to meet the charge for medical benefit, notice of suspension from benefits is conveyed to the Committee by means of an orange slip. If after the receipt of further contribution cards it is found that some Deposit Contributors are again qualified for medical benefit the Committee is again informed by means of a Reinstatement List. Suspensions and reinstatements take place as from the end or beginning of the medical quarters —which correspond to the quarter dates of the calendar year.

When a Deposit Contributor joins an Approved Society, dies, or passes out of insurance in any way, notice is sent by the Commissioners to the Committee by means of an orange slip. The index slip in these cases must be immediately destroyed by the Committee. The procedure in regard to change of address and suspension from benefit is explained in paragraphs (430) and (431). All reallotment of Deposit Contributors' index slips must be done through the Commissioners. If an Insurance Committee is in doubt as to whether a particular Deposit Contributor who has applied to them is entitled to medical benefit the necessary information can be obtained from the Commissioners. The procedure is dealt with in detail in Chapter VI., Section (VI).

Exempt Persons.

(217) *Suspension from Benefits* owing to inadequacy of contributions or the exempt person having joined the Military or Naval Forces of the Crown for the duration of the war.—The Commissioners advise the exempt person of his suspension from benefit and forward an orange slip to the Committee. The method of dealing with orange slips is as follows :—

(A) Where an index slip is in the Committee's possession :—
- (a) The orange slip should be substituted for the index slip in the Index Register, and the medical slip should be removed from the Medical Index. Both slips withdrawn should be retained in a drawer reserved for such slips, so that they may be reinstated should occasion arise. The Committee will keep what note is necessary to enable them to adjust the figures when the count is made. Reinstatement should be made only in cases where the exempt person again becomes entitled to benefit as an exempt person, and in such cases a reinstatement slip is issued to the Committee;
- (b) If the exempt person is on the list of any doctor on the panel or obtaining benefit through an approved

system in the area of the Committee, the doctor or system should be notified at once.

(B) Where an index slip is not in the Committee's possession :—
The orange slip should be listed on Form No. 591 and returned to the Commissioners.

Cancellation of Exemption Certificates.—Where owing to death or change in status (*e.g.* becoming an insured person, ceasing employment, or removing abroad) a Certificate of Exemption is cancelled, intimation of the fact is made to the Committee on Form 507A, and in such cases the Committee are required to recall the Medical Card and to return the relative index slip to the Commissioners.

Removals.—Where the change of address does not involve a change of area, the form of intimation is issued by the Commissioners to the Insurance Committee holding the index slip, and should be dealt with in accordance with the instruction in paragraph (*a*) below.

Where the change of address involves a change of area, it is issued to the new Committee, who should proceed as indicated in paragraph (*b*) below.

(*a*) If the new address is in the area of the Committee, the Clerk should alter the index slip for the exempt person.

(*b*) When the change of address involves a change of area, the Insurance Committee of the new area should take steps to recover the medical card in the exempt person's possession, or, if he has not received or has lost his medical card, to get the exempt person to choose a doctor in the new area. The front part of the medical card (or a declaration from the exempt person that he has not received or has lost his Medical Card) should then be forwarded to the Committee of the old area, who will surrender the index slip to the Commissioners, the slip subsequently being forwarded by the Commissioners to the Committee of the new area.

Under no circumstances should a Committee re-allocate the index slip of an exempt person direct to another Committee. Where an exempt person advises the Committee direct of his loss of right to benefit, the Commissioners should be informed thereof by the Committee.

(iv.) ROUTINE PROCEDURE.

(218) On receipt of an index slip the address should first be examined to ascertain if it is proper to the area. If the slip belongs to another area it should be transmitted at once and the Society informed. The slip, if applicable to the area, should be compared with the index slips already in the Register to see if it is a duplicate, and with the Suspense Register to see if there is a suspense slip in existence. Duplicate index slips should be destroyed. Where a suspense slip is found it should be destroyed and the choice of doctor noted on the index slip, a

medical card issued if necessary, and the person placed on a doctor's list, if this has not already been done. The association of all duplicates is a matter of great importance in keeping the Register accurately. Questions of considerable difficulty are involved in many cases where there are differences in particulars of name, address, or number in the Society. No general rules can be laid down, but it may be pointed out that in the case of men where the name and address is the same, there is no presumption that either one or two persons are represented. Only by inquiry can it be determined whether there is duplication of slips or there are different individuals, e.g. a father and son or even two persons unrelated. In the case of women and especially women employed in such occupations as domestic service there is a strong presumption that two persons of the same or essentially the same name are not employed at the same address. The practice of certain Committees has shown that much can be done by care, ingenuity, and common sense to eliminate duplicates without involving many individual enquiries.

Where a new index slip is found to be in order, a blank medical card should be issued, and Committees are recommended to enclose a circular letter instructing the person to choose a doctor without delay. The date of the issue of the medical card should be noted on the index slip. It is advisable to keep these new index slips separate until the medical card is returned, as when the medical card comes back with Part A filled in the doctor's name must be noted on the back of the index slip. The person's name should then be entered in the medical index under the proper doctor, and if any note as to mileage or dispensing is contained on the medical card the particulars should in turn be noted on the doctor's list.

The index slips should then be placed in strict alphabetical order in the proper drawer of the Index Register, and the medical card should be returned to the insured person with the doctor's name, the Committee's cipher, and the date stamped on page 1.

On receipt of an index slip from another Committee, in response to an application by means of Med. 50, the Med. 50 record should be noted and a medical card issued as above.

If the index slip is received on application by means of the first half of a medical card, the name of the doctor already chosen should be entered on the slip and the person placed on that doctor's list. The new medical card to be issued to the insured person should be stamped with the date and cipher, the name of doctor should be entered thereon, and Part A cancelled.

(v.) CENTRALISATION PROCEDURE.

(219) Committees and Societies experienced much difficulty in tracing index slips issued to the wrong area in the first issues or issued in duplicate or in error, and very considerable correspondence was involved. Questions also arose as to whether an

index slip had been issued by the Society or received by the Committee. As special emergency and temporary measures the Commissioners undertook (*a*) the centralisation of suspense slips and the issue of a list thereof, (*b*) the centralisation society by society of all index and suspense slips issued to Committees in Scotland, and their association, and where deemed necessary comparison with contribution cards. Duplicates have been destroyed and slips written by the Society where necessary; (*c*) periodical issue to all Committees of lists of orange slips not associated by the Committee to which they were sent by the Society. Full explanations and instructions for Committees' guidance are contained in the relative circulars.

SECTION (IV.)—ARRANGEMENTS IN REFERENCE TO INSURED PERSONS.

(i.) INTIMATION.

(220) Particulars of the arrangements made by an Insurance Committee for the medical benefit of insured persons, including a statement of the places where the various lists of doctors, chemists, etc., may be seen and copies of the necessary forms obtained, are required to be published by the Committee in such a manner that the persons interested may, as far as possible, be duly informed (Reg. 15).

(ii.) MEDICAL CARD.

Form of Voucher.

(221) An insured person who desires and is entitled to select a practitioner on the panel may make application for that purpose in such manner as the Insurance Committee, with the approval of the Commissioners, may require, and, subject to the consent of the practitioner, shall be entitled to obtain treatment from him (Reg. 21 (1)). Where under any arrangement approved by the Commissioners the Committee, or the Society of which the insured person is a member, provides him with a voucher for the purpose, the practitioner is entitled to require him to produce such voucher as a condition of receiving treatment (Reg. 21 (2)). A voucher, known as a "medical card," has been adopted by all Scottish Insurance Committees; the form of it is shown in Appendix XIII.

Other Uses.

(222) The medical card contains instructions to insured persons as to their rights and obligations in connection with medical benefit, and also brings to their notice the rules for the administration of medical benefit in force within the area of the Committee issuing the card. Apart from serving as a method of choosing a doctor which, alike on the ground of accuracy and convenience, possesses many advantages, the card may be used by persons already on panel lists when removing to a new

address and ceasing thereby to be able to get treatment from the doctor who had accepted them. Provision is made on the card for the insertion of the Committee cipher and the number allotted on its list to the doctor or institution responsible for the treatment of the insured person. It will generally be found convenient to assign a number to each doctor and mark the number on the lists or other records, as the Committee cipher and list number combined form a reference key which, when quoted, will enable the Committee to refer readily to the insured person's slip in the Medical Index, and thence to the slip in the Index Register. The Card is also employed by insured persons desiring to receive medical treatment when on holiday or otherwise temporarily away from home.

Application for Card.

(223) Insured persons who have not chosen a doctor are required to apply for a card to the Insurance Committee by means of a form (Med. 50) to be obtained at a Post Office. To new entrants into insurance and Exempt Persons, cards are issued by the Insurance Committee on receipt of an index slip from the Approved Society or in the case of a Deposit Contributor or Exempt Person, the Commissioners.

Presentation to Doctor.

(224) On receiving his card the insured person presents it to the doctor by whom he desires to be attended. The doctor, if he accepts the insured person, signifies his acceptance by signing and forwarding the card to the Insurance Committee. It will probably be found convenient to arrange that cards bearing acceptances should be periodically transmitted to the Committee, for example, in weekly batches.

Return to Insured Person.

(225) The Committee, after making the necessary entries and impressing the card with their stamp, return it to the insured person. Corresponding provisions apply in the case of Deposit Contributors and Exempt Persons.

Change of Doctor.

(226) Under Article 21 of the Medical Benefit Regulations, where an application has been received by a practitioner by means of a medical card, or by the special forms provided for transfer from one doctor to another, he must within one week inform the Committee of his acceptance or rejection of the application. The medical card or form should not be retained by the practitioner if he does not desire to accept the applicant or if the latter has not properly completed the card or form. The Committee on receipt of the acceptance issue to the insured person a new medical card bearing their stamp and with the name of the doctor, etc., endorsed. The insured person is regarded as on the list of the doctor as from the date of issue of the card.

Lost Card.

(227) The medical card is the property of the Commissioners, and the person to whom it is issued is required to give immediate notice to the Insurance Committee if it is lost.

Change of Area of Residence.

(228) In a case of change of address from another area, the new Committee must apply direct to the old Committee for the index slip, forwarding the first half (*i.e.* pages 1 and 2) of the old card if it is available for the satisfaction of the Committee of origin, and retaining the other half for its own protection pending the receipt of the index slip. The latter Committee must at once forward the index slip and strike the insured person off the list of the doctor or institution on whose list he had been placed.

Temporary Change of Residence.

(229) If the removal is temporary only (*i.e.* is likely to last for less than three months), the card must be presented by the person to the doctor or institution by whom he desires to be treated during his temporary residence, page 4 having been completed. In all cases such applications should be dealt with by the doctor at once; the transmission of the card to the Committee should not be delayed until the next periodical dispatch. The Committee should make arrangements to deal specially with all such cases with a view to the card being stamped and returned to the insured person by return of post. Before the card is returned to the person surrendering it the signature on page 4 might usefully be compared with the signature or signatures of the person to whom the card was issued as appearing on page 3.

(230) The medical card will enable the insured person to obtain treatment during temporary residence in one area only and from one doctor. When the spaces provided for the purpose have been used, it will be necessary for the person to surrender the card to the Committee by whom it was issued in order that a new card may be issued. The old card will thus come under the notice of the Committee by whom it was issued before a further occasion can arise which might result in a case value debit to its funds; and it will therefore be in a position to investigate any circumstances which call for inquiry.

Intimation to Committee of Origin.

(231) In all cases in which a medical card is stamped for the purpose of treatment during temporary residence, the new Committee, immediately upon receipt of the card, should communicate with the Committee of origin to the effect that arrangements are being made for the treatment of the temporary resident, in order that the Committee of origin may, if the insured person has already been suspended from medical benefit, or if, for any

other reason, it desires to dispute his title to receive the treatment, *at once* communicate the facts to the new Committee. In practice it is suggested that the new Committee should assume that no question will be raised unless it receives the objections of the Committee of origin within the shortest period within which it would be reasonably possible for that Committee to reply by post. In the cases which should be rare in which the notification by the new Committee elicits the fact that the insured person is suspended, it must at once give notice to the doctor, who will refuse any further treatment to the insured person except as a private patient. The insured person is thus debarred from obtaining any further treatment in that area, or in any other area, as a temporary resident, or otherwise, without the knowledge of the Committee.

Record of Temporary Treatment.

(232) Committees require to keep a record of all cards received and stamped by them for the purpose of treatment during temporary residence in their area, and of the date in each case on which the stamp was impressed for the purpose of dealing with accounts rendered by doctors in respect of such treatment; and a record should also be kept by each Committee for the purpose of entering the notifications received from other Committees by whom treatment during temporary residence is given upon production of medical cards issued by the Committee.

Own Arrangers.

(233) As stated elsewhere, insured persons who have been allowed to make their own arrangements for medical treatment are not entitled to participate in the special arrangements made for the treatment of insured persons during temporary residence. Upon removal, however, other than temporary to the area of another Committee, the permission given to them by the old Committee to make their own arrangements lapses, and they will be again entitled to select a method of treatment. Although, therefore, such persons may not require a medical card for production to their doctors when applying for treatment, it is necessary to issue cards to the persons for other purposes, *e.g.* to enable them to obtain treatment upon removal (other than temporary) and to assist the new Committee to trace the index slip. It will probably also be found convenient to require the production of a medical card when a contribution is claimed.

(234) A special procedure must be observed in issuing cards to these persons. The front page must be endorsed "Receiving medical benefit under own arrangements," and Part C on page 4 and the relevant paragraph on page 2 must be cancelled. A covering letter should be sent with the card, and should state that the card must be carefully preserved for use in the event of removal (otherwise than for a period of less than three months) into another area, or, if no such removal takes place, for pro-

duction when a contribution is claimed at the end of the year, that if on removing for three months or more into another area the insured person desires to continue to make his own arrangements he must apply to the new Insurance Committee (whose address will be found in the list in the Post Office in the new area) for permission to do so, and that if on such removal he wishes to sèlect a doctor on the panel or approved institution he should fill up Part B and present the card to the doctor or institution selected.

Exempt Persons, etc.

(235) Medical cards specially endorsed should be issued also to exempt persons entitled to medical benefit and to persons receiving their benefit through the Post Office as an approved institution.

(iii.) TRANSFER DURING THE YEAR.

(236) A person entitled to medical benefit cannot ordinarily change from the list of one practitioner to that of another in the same area during the course of any medical year. Any transfer must take place as from the beginning of a year, except in certain special circumstances referred to below. Notice of the desire to transfer must be sent to the Committee by the person before 1st December in the year preceding that for which he desires to transfer (Reg. 30).

(237) These remarks also apply to any change in the method of obtaining treatment, for example, the change from the list of an Approved System or Institution to that of a Panel Practitioner.

(238) The special circumstances under which transfer may take place during a year are detailed in Reg. 26 as follows :—

(a) where the name of a practitioner is removed from the medical list during the year;

(b) where a practitioner dies;

(c) where an insured person and a practitioner both agree to a transfer; and

(d) where an insured person is transferred as a result of a complaint against the practitioner attending him.

(239) With regard to (a), the practitioner's name may be removed from the medical list at his own request, or because he has ceased to practice within the area in which he undertook treatment. In such a case the practitioner must notify to the Committee and to the insured persons concerned that he has made arrangements for their transfer to the list of another practitioner or other practitioners on the panel. Unless the insured person gives notice to the Committee within fourteen days of the receipt of the doctor's intimation, it is assumed that he has consented to be transferred as arranged. If such notice of objection is sent, however, the person has a right to select another practitioner on the panel as if he had not previously made a selection.

(240) The practitioner's name may be removed from the list by

the Commissioners, and if so, notice of the removal must be given to the insured persons concerned by the Committee. The insured persons are then entitled at once to select another practitioner.

(241) As regards (b) paragraph (174) deals with the temporary arrangements which may be made on the death of a practitioner on the panel, and the action which may be taken in this matter by the legal personal representative of the practitioner. The period for which temporary arrangements may remain in force is fixed at the discretion of the Committee, and at any time before the expiration of the period the legal personal representative may notify to the insured persons concerned that they are to be transferred to the list of another practitioner, or other practitioners, on the panel, and the rules as to the lodging of objection by the patient and his right to select another practitioner if he so desires are the same as those which apply in the case of a practitioner's name being removed from the list in accordance with the last paragraph.

If the practice of a doctor who has died is not carried on by a representative, notice of the death must be given by the Committee to all insured persons concerned, who are at once entitled to make another selection.

(242) Persons who are entitled to obtain treatment through an Approved Institution, have the right to select another method of treatment immediately upon the Institution ceasing to be approved. Notice of the withdrawal of approval must be given by the Committee to the persons on the list of the Institution.

(243) It will be seen that under exception (c) there is provision made for the case where a practitioner and a person on his list arrange by consent for a transfer during the course of a year to a practitioner to whom the person wishes to transfer and who is willing to accept him. If such a transfer is arranged, notice must be given to the Committee within 7 days by the new doctor. A form for this purpose can be obtained from the Committee, and it must be signed by the insured person and by both doctors concerned.

(244) With regard to exception (d), reference should be made to the paragraphs (259) to (276) on the subject of inquiries as to complaints.

(iv.) RULES FOR ADMINISTRATION OF MEDICAL BENEFIT.

(245) In terms of Section 14 (3) of the 1911 Act and Article 81 of the Medical Benefit Regulations, rules for the conduct of persons in receipt of medical benefit must be framed by every Committee after consultation with the Local Medical Committee and the Panel Committee. When approved by the Commissioners they are binding on all persons receiving or entitled to treatment under arrangements by the Committee, who may in its discretion inflict a fine (not exceeding 10s., or in the case of repeated

breach 20s.) for any breach of any of these rules, or of any of the provisions of the Act relating to medical benefit, or of the Regulations, or for any imposition or attempted imposition in respect of medical benefit, and may in the case of repeated breaches suspend the right to medical benefit for a period not exceeding one year. No insured person is, however, subject to any penalty on account of refusal to submit to vaccination or inoculation of any kind, or to a surgical operation, unless such refusal, in the case of a surgical operation of a minor character, is considered by the Committee, or, on appeal, by the Commissioners, unreasonable.

(246) If any act or omission alleged to constitute a breach of these rules is of such a nature as to amount to a breach of any rule of a Society of which the insured person is a member, the Committee must refer the matter to the Society, and, unless the Society has unreasonably refused to take action, or the action taken by the Society appears to the Committee to be inadequate, the latter cannot deal with the matter itself except by way of transferring the insured person, in cases where after inquiry it thinks fit, to another practitioner on the panel. Any question arising between the Committee and a Society must be referred to the Commissioners.

The rules of Committees also provide that any complaint by an insured person which is adjudged by them to be frivolous or vexatious, shall be regarded as a breach of their Rules.

(247) A model set on which Insurance Committees have framed their rules will be found in Appendix III. already referred to (*see* paragraph (83)).

(v.) TRAVELLERS.

(248) Special arrangements have been made for the provision of medical benefit to insured persons who frequently move from place to place in the course of their employment, *e.g.* actors, commercial travellers, etc. Persons desirous of being admitted to the special arrangement apply to their Insurance Committee, or to their Society, for the appropriate form of application. The form when filled in by the insured person and countersigned by his employer is sent to his Approved Society to certify as to his title to medical and sanatorium benefits. The Society, after completing the necessary certificate, send the form to the Insurance Committee, who then considers whether it will recommend the applicant for admission to the special arrangement. Deposit Contributors send the form to the Committee through the Commissioners. If the Committee recommends the application it transmits the form to the Commissioners with the insured person's index slip, care being taken that the insured person's name is removed from any panel list on which it has been placed, and that the medical index is corrected in this respect (Reg. 78).

(249) Insured persons who by means of the form have shown

themselves qualified for special arrangements, are provided with a traveller's voucher which they may present to a doctor on the panel in any area in Great Britain where they happen to require medical benefit. The voucher provides for medical records being kept. Payment is on an attendance basis according to a scale, and is made out of the Central Medical Benefit Fund (Regs. 42 and 78 (3)). Drugs are ordered on the usual order forms, prescriptions being specially distinguished. The special traveller's voucher is current for six months only from the date of issue, and holders of vouchers are instructed to make application for renewal not later than a month prior to expiry (Reg. 78).

(vi.) OWN ARRANGEMENTS.

(250) Arrangements for medical treatment and for obtaining drugs and appliances may be made by an insured person himself if—

(a) he is required to do so (1) under any decision of the Committee fixing an income limit (he might also in very exceptional cases be required to do so owing to the fact that the Committee is unable to make arrangements for his treatment); or (2) because as an exempt person his total income from all sources exceeds £160 a year (Section 9 of the Act of 1913); or

(b) he makes application to the Committee for permission to make his own arrangements, and is allowed to do so.

Income Limit.

(251) An income limit under (a) may be fixed by an Insurance Committee as provided by Section 15 (3) of the Act of 1911 and Article 14 of the Regulations, made thereunder after consultation with the Local Medical Committee, the Panel Committee, and the Pharmaceutical Committee, on giving due public notice of its intention. Before fixing such a limit the Committee is required by the statute to take into consideration representations made to it by any Society having members resident in its area, or by the Association of Deposit Contributors where such has been formed for the County. There is, however, no such association in existence in Scotland. Any variation or abolition of the income limit can be effected only after the same formalities and notice of the fixing, varying, or abolishing of an income limit must be given to the Commissioners. Exemption from the requirements to make their own arrangements may be given to any persons who, in the opinion of the Committee, should be exempted owing to the circumstances of their occupation or method of remuneration, and so on. It should be noted that an income limit can be fixed, varied, or abolished only as from the beginning of a medical year.

(252) Where a limit has been fixed, any Approved Society having members in the area or the Association of Deposit

Contributors for the area, if such there be, or the Panel Committee, or Pharmaceutical Committee, may dispute the right of any person to receive medical benefit under the arrangements made by the Committee, on the ground that his income exceeds the limit. Objection must be made in writing to the Committee who may give notice to the persons that unless within the specified period he shows that his income does not exceed the limit, or that if it does exceed the limit, he is entitled to be exempted from the requirement, he will be required to make his own arrangements.

Exempt Persons.

(253) It is the duty of any Exempt Person who comes within the requirement to make his own arrangements, to notify the fact to the Insurance Committee.

Persons Allowed to make Arrangements.

(254) As regards persons who may be *allowed* to make their own arrangements, the following provisions apply :—

Application for permission to adopt this course is usually made to the Committee by the person on a form supplied by the Committee. The form of application, under Reg. 80, must be approved by the Commissioners. The application may be made by an individual person, or by a number of persons collectively, but in either case intimation of consent or refusal to the application must be given by the Committee within a reasonable time (Reg. 14).

(255) The Committee can demand such evidence as it thinks sufficient to show that the arrangements proposed to be made by the person are satisfactory, *i.e.* that they are such as to secure treatment (including medicines and appliances) not inferior in nature, quality, or extent, to that provided under the arrangements made by the Committee. If the persons make their own arrangements, and these conditions are not satisfied, the Committee may withhold any contribution towards the cost of the treatment, or make such a deduction from the contribution as it may determine (Reg. 44 (1)).

The general conditions which must be secured, and evidence of which must be obtained by the Committee, include in addition to those referred to above an undertaking (by contract or otherwise) by the medical man with whom the person makes his arrangements that he will keep and forward in due course to the Committee and the Commissioners proper records of diseases and treatment in the form prescribed ; that he will furnish such certificates as may be required in claims for sickness and disablement benefit, and that in the event of the person being recommended for sanatorium benefit, he will, if called upon, provide him with domiciliary treatment. In the case of keeping of records and the provision of domiciliary treatment, the Committee should obtain an enforceable contract.

(256) In all cases it is entirely within the discretion of the Committee whether applications to make own arrangements are granted or refused, but in no case is the Parliamentary Grant payable unless an obligation has been given by the practitioner that he will observe the conditions attaching to the payment of the Grant. As stated elsewhere (*see* paragraphs (233) and (234)), medical cards should be issued to persons who are allowed or entitled to make their own arrangements.

Removal from Area.

(257) If a person who is required or allowed to make his own arrangements removes from the area of the Committee and intends to be absent for a period of three months or more he comes under the arrangements for transfer described in paragraph (234). If the removal is for less than three months, he is not entitled to obtain medical benefit under the arrangements made by the Committee into whose area he moves (Reg. 44).

Finance.

(258) The financial matters in connection with Own Arrangements are dealt with in paragraphs (516) to (519).

SECTION (V.)—COMPLAINTS.

(i.) BY OR AGAINST DOCTOR.

(259) Any question arising between a person entitled to obtain treatment from a practitioner on the panel and the practitioner attending him in respect of the treatment (including the granting of certificates) rendered by the practitioner, or the conduct of the insured person while receiving that treatment stands referred, in terms of Article 45 of the Medical Benefit Regulations, to a special Sub-Committee constituted by the Insurance Committee for the purpose and known as the Medical Service Sub-Committee. The Insurance Committee may also, if it thinks fit, refer to the Sub-Committee any other question arising with reference to the administration of Medical Benefit, or to the discharge by the practitioner of his duties under his agreement with the Committee.

The procedure of the Sub-Committee in matters of this nature is detailed in Section (I.) of Chapter II., paragraphs (79) to (88). It is the duty of the Sub-Committee to prepare a report upon any question referred to it, which must state such relevant facts as appear to the Sub-Committee to be established by the evidence placed before it, and to make any recommendation which it considers necessary. The Committee must accept as conclusive any finding of fact contained in the report (Reg. 45 (9)).

If the question at issue relates to the conduct of the patient, and in the opinion of the Sub-Committee the allegation is substantiated, the Committee may, at the request of the practitioner, arrange for the transfer of the person to the list of another practitioner. In addition the Committee may impose a fine or inflict a suspension of benefit in accordance with its rules (Reg. 45 (10)).

Where, however, the inquiry relates to the treatment given by the practitioner, and the Committee is satisfied that the complaint is substantiated, it may at its discretion accede to any request from the person that arrangements may be made for his transfer to the list of another practitioner The agreement between the Committee and the practitioner may also contain special provisions for transfer, but in any case the Committee may decide that it will, on the application of any person on the practitioner's list, make arrangements without further inquiry for the person's transfer to another list, provided it is satisfied that—

    (a) owing to the excessive number of persons on his list the doctor is unable to give adequate treatment to all of them ; or

    (b) the conduct of the doctor has been such as to afford grounds for desiring to be transferred.

(Reg. 45 (11).)

(260) The practitioner must be informed of any decision of the Committee regarding him, and he is entitled to appeal from that decision to the Commissioners within 14 days after he has received the intimation (Reg. 45 (16)).

(261) In serious cases, the Committee may make representations to the Commissioners that the efficiency of the service under medical benefit would be prejudiced by the continuance of the practitioner on the panel (Reg. 45 (12)).

(262) A practitioner may, under his agreement, be liable to refund to the Committee any expenses reasonably and necessarily incurred owing to his breach of the agreement, and if the insured person has been put to such expense, the Committee must pay over the amount of the expenses incurred. If, owing to a breach of the agreement, a portion of the Special Parliamentary Grant of 2s. 6d. per insured person payable to the Committee is withheld by the Commissioners, the practitioner is liable to pav or refund the amount to the Committee (Conditions of Service, 9 (i.)).

(ii.) BY OR AGAINST CHEMIST.

(263) The provisions in the Regulations for the decision of questions arising between persons entitled to medical benefit and persons supplying drugs or appliances are drawn up on lines similar to those which govern the relations between the insured person and the practitioner. The Sub-Committee to which such qu s i ns stand referred is the Pharmaceutical Service Sub-Committee, the procedure of which is prescribed in paragraphs (80) and (81) and (83) to (86) (Reg. 46).

(264) The proceedings at the investigation into the complaint must be reported to the Insurance Committee, and if the allega-

tions against a person supplying drugs or appliances are proved action may be taken in accordance with the terms of the agreement. If part of the Special Parliamentary Grant is withheld by the Commissioners liability is incurred for its payment to the Committee. Extreme cases may be submitted to the Commissioners with a view to the removal of the name of the person from the list. A person entitled to obtain drugs or appliances, who has been put to any expense by the chemist's breach of his agreement, is entitled to have repaid to him the amount of such expenses out of any sums recovered by the Committee. Notification of the Committee's decision must be sent to the person concerned, and appeal may be made by him to the Commissioners within 14 days after the receipt of such notice (Reg 46 (7) and (8)).

(iii.) BY OR AGAINST DOCTOR AND CHEMIST.

(265) The Joint Services Sub-Committee may be concerned in complaints of the nature referred to, if they involve both a practitioner on the panel and a chemist under agreement with the Committee. The remarks as to the treatment of complaints and the presentation of a report apply in the same way to these cases (Reg. 47).

(iv.) INQUIRY AS TO CONTINUANCE ON THE PANEL OF DOCTOR.

Representation.

(266) Special Regulations have been made to meet cases in which representations may be made to the Commissioners that the continuance of a practitioner upon the panel of any Committee is prejudicial to the efficiency of the medical service of persons entitled to receive medical benefit (Medical Benefit Regs. Part VI.). Such representations may be made by any Insurance Committee, Local Medical Committee, or Panel Committee, and the Commissioners will then hold an inquiry in accordance with the special provisions. The questions dealt with by the Local Medical Committee and the Insurance Committee on reports from the Medical Service or Joint Services Sub-Committee may involve an application of this nature to the Commissioners. Representations may also be made by any other person or body, but in such a case the Commissioners may refuse to hold an inquiry if they consider that no good cause has been shown why it should be held (Regs. 53 and 56).

Any representation must contain a concise statement of the alleged facts and grounds on which it is based, and a list of all the documents which the complainer proposes to put in evidence, and must be signed. The Commissioners may also require the complainer to verify by a statutory declaration the allegations, or where an alleged fact is not within the personal knowledge of the complainer, to state the source of his information, the grounds for his belief in its truth, and any other particulars. The complaint may be treated as withdrawn if any of the above conditions are not satisfied or documents founded on are not produced (Regs. 54, 55, and 59).

Notices.

(267) Where the Commissioners propose to hold an inquiry, the complainer and the practitioner will be informed. The latter will be supplied with a copy of the representation, and a notice that he may, if he so desires, admit or dispute the truth of any or all of the allegations by statement in writing addressed to the Commissioners within a specified time. The practitioner may, moreover, on giving due notice in writing to the complainer, inspect (either personally or by an authorised agent) the documents referred to in the representation. The complainer is bound to give reasonable facilities for this purpose. Alternatively, the practitioner may make application to the Commissioners to inspect the documents, who will arrange with the complainer for the documents to be deposited with them or with an Officer appointed by them (Regs. 57 and 58).

Not less than 14 days before the date appointed by the Commissioners for the holding of the inquiry the Commissioners will send notice to the complainer and the practitioner concerned informing them of the date, time, and place proposed. A similar notice will be sent to each Committee on whose list the practitioner's name appears. The inquiry may be postponed by the Commissioners on the application of either party (Regs. 61 and 62).

Withdrawal or Amendment of Representation.

(268) The representation may be withdrawn or amended at any time before the date of the inquiry if the Commissioners give their consent, subject to any conditions which may be imposed (Regs. 64 and 65).

Committee of Inquiry.

(269) The Committee of Inquiry for each case is to be constituted by the Commissioners, and to consist of two practitioners and one other person who must be a member of the Faculty of Advocates, or an enrolled Law Agent in actual practice. The Joint Committee have power to establish a body of practitioners from whom the practitioners are to be selected for this purpose. The Chairman (one of the three members) and the Clerk will be appointed by the Commissioners (Reg. 60).

Appearance.

(270) The Commissioners must give notice of the inquiry to any Insurance Commtttee on whose panel the practitioner's name appears, and such Committee are entitled to be present. Such Committee, and any other Committee, Local Medical Committee,

Panel Committee, or other body entitled to appear may be represented by the Clerk or other Officer duly appointed for the purpose, or, if the Chairman of the Inquiry Committee consents, they may be represented by Counsel or a Solicitor (Regs. 61 (2) and 63 (1)).

The complainer, unless one of the bodies just mentioned above, may, with the consent of the Chairman appear—
- (a) by Counsel or Law Agent; or
- (b) by any member of his family; or
- (c) by any officer or member of any Society or other body of persons of which he is a member, or with which he is connected.

Application for the Chairman's consent to appear, in cases where this is required, must be made at least 10 days before the date of the enquiry by notice addressed to the Clerk of the Inquiry Committee (Reg. 63 (2) and (3)).

Forms.

(271) The various forms for representation, notice, etc., which must be followed substantially in the procedure relating to inquiries, are printed in the sixth Schedule to the Medical Benefit Regulations (Reg. 52 (2)).

Rules for Procedure.

(272) The procedure of the Inquiry Committee is governed by the following rules, unless the Inquiry Committee, with the approval of the Commissioners, otherwise determine—
- (a) The Inquiry Committee shall be at liberty to proceed with the inquiry on the appointed day in the absence of either party (whether represented or not), if they are of opinion that it is just and proper to do so.
- (b) The Inquiry Committee may adjourn the inquiry from time to time as they think fit, and hold adjourned sittings at such time and place as may appear to them suitable.
- (c) Witnesses may be heard at the inquiry on behalf of either party, and all witnesses (including the parties) shall be subject to examination and cross-examination as nearly as may be as if they were witnesses in an ordinary action.
- (d) The Chairman of the Committee shall preside at the inquiry, but, subject to the decision of the Chairman as to the admissibility of any question, any member of the Committee may put questions to any witness, and the Committee may, if they think fit, call for such documents and examine such witnesses as appear to them likely to afford evidence relevant and material to the issue, although not tendered by either party.
- (e) Subject to the provisions of Part VI. of the Medical

Benefit Regulations and of these Rules, the proceedings at the inquiry shall be conducted in such manner as the Inquiry Committee may direct.
(Reg. 66 and Seventh Schedule.)

Inquiry without Representation.

(273) The Commissioners may institute an inquiry on their own initiative, and notwithstanding that no representation has been made or has been withdrawn after having been made (Reg. 67). The Commissioners must send to the practitioner a statement of the facts and grounds which appear to them to justify the holding of an inquiry (Reg. 68). Every Insurance Committee on whose panel the doctor's name appears must receive notice of the time and place of the inquiry, and any such Committee may appear and take such part in the proceedings as the Inquiry Committee think proper (Reg. 69). Generally speaking, the ordinary provisions as to the constitution and procedure of the Inquiry Committee still apply. The Commissioners will in this instance appoint some person to appear in support of the allegations (Reg. 70).

Report of Inquiry Committee.

(274) The report of the Inquiry Committee must be presented to the Commissioners as soon as possible after the conclusion of the inquiry. It must contain a statement of the facts established by the evidence, and the inferences of fact which the Committee consider may be drawn therefrom. The Commissioners' decision will be published in due course and in the manner which they think best (Reg. 71).

General.

(275) An inquiry may be stopped temporarily by the Commissioners if they are of opinion that the alleged facts which form the basis of the complaint are, or may be, the subject of investigation by another tribunal, *e.g.* a Court of Law or the General Medical Council (Reg. 72).

(276) Provision is made for the procedure in serving and sending notices (Reg. 73).

(v.) INQUIRY AS TO ADMISSION TO OR CONTINUANCE ON PANEL OF CHEMIST.

(277) With the substitution of "Pharmaceutical Committee" for "Local Medical Committee," and any other necessary modifications, the preceding paragraphs may be taken as applicable to an inquiry into any representation that the admission to or continuance of a person supplying drugs or appliances on the list of such persons would be prejudicial to the efficiency of the service. The Inquiry Committee is to consist of a member of the Faculty of Advocates or enrolled Law Agent in actual practice and two other persons (drawn from any body which may have been set up for the purpose by the Joint Committee) (Regs. Part VII.).

CHAPTER V.

SANATORIUM BENEFIT.

SECTION (I.)—ARRANGEMENT WITH PERSONS AND LOCAL AUTHORITIES, INCLUDING ARRANGEMENT WITH MEDICAL PRACTITIONERS.

(i.) GENERAL.

(278) *Definition.*—By Section 8 (1) of the principal Act Sanatorium Benefit is defined to be "Treatment in sanatoria or other institutions or otherwise when suffering from tuberculosis or such other diseases as the Local Government Board with the approval of the Treasury may appoint." This reference in the meantime is restricted to tuberculosis as no other diseases have yet been appointed.

(279) *Administration.*—By Section 14 (1) Sanatorium Benefit is to be administered in all cases by and through Insurance Committees.

(280) *Arrangements.*—By Section 16 (1) Insurance Committees are required to make arrangements to the satisfaction of the Scottish Insurance Commissioners for the purpose of providing treatment under Sanatorium Benefit. An Insurance Committee may not undertake or carry out treatment; its powers are restricted to arranging that treatment may be secured. It may thus contract for the treatment of insured persons in a sanatorium, but it cannot itself erect or manage such an institution.

(281) *Forms of Tuberculosis.*—The arrangements made by a Committee may cover both the pulmonary and the non-pulmonary forms of tuberculosis.

(282) *Forms of Treatment.*—The forms of Sanatorium Benefit for which a Committee may arrange are divided under Section 16 (1) into (*a*) treatment in sanatoria or other institutions, and (*b*) treatment otherwise than in sanatoria and other institutions. To class (*a*) belong residential treatment, hereinafter simply called *Institutional Treatment*, and *Dispensary Treatment*. Class (*b*) is equivalent to what has come to be known as *Domiciliary Treatment*. With regard to all these forms of treatment the approval of the Local Government Board is required, and it is expressly laid down that no arrangements may be made by Committees with any Poor Law Authority. The three forms of treatment named will be considered in order.

(ii.) INSTITUTIONAL TREATMENT.

(283) *Pulmonary Tuberculosis.*—Of the institutions now existing in Scotland for the treatment of pulmonary tuberculosis the majority belong to Public Health Local Authorities or combinations of such Authorities, or Boards representing such combinations. The number of sanatoria expressly erected by Local Authorities for the purpose of dealing with the disease is still somewhat limited, but new sanatoria are in course of planning or construction. In addition to institutions belonging to Local Authorities, there are several well-known sanatoria available for the insured, owned and managed by private persons or Trustees.

(284) *Non-pulmonary Tuberculosis.*—For the treatment of non-pulmonary tuberculosis, wards in a number of general hospitals are at the disposal of Committees, and certain Local Authorities also are prepared to receive non-pulmonary cases into their institutions.

(285) *Approval by Local Government Board.*—All institutions in which it is proposed to treat insured persons under arrangement with an Insurance Committee must be approved by the Local Government Board. This approval is granted for varying periods and subject to conditions as to maintenance of the standard of treatment and the due recording of cases.

(286) *Approved Institutions.*—Approval may lapse, by desire of the Local Authority or Committee of Management of an institution, or may be subject to withdrawal or renewal of approval as. the Board think fit. The list of approved institutions is thus liable to change from time to time. Timeous notice of such changes is sent by the Board to the Commissioners who will be prepared on request to inform Committees as to the currency of the approval of any institutions. A list of approved institutions is given in Appendix XIV.

(287) *Sanction by Commissioners.*—The approval of an institution by the Local Government Board for the purpose of Section 16 (1) of the principal Act is a guarantee of efficiency of treatment, and in so far as efficiency is concerned it carries the sanction of the Commissioners. The Commissioners, however, require to be satisfied also as to the payment to be made by the Committee in return for services rendered by the institution. It is open to a Committee either to retain beds in an institution for a fixed sum or to pay at a weekly rate. In the former case the sanction of the Commissioners is given for a stated period. In the latter case, once the weekly rate has been determined and approved, the Commissioners do not require Committees to report individual cases as they arise. Committees may continue to send cases to institutions without further notice so long as the charge and other details remain unaltered. Procedure with regard to institutions differs in this respect from that to be followed in domiciliary treatment, under which individual cases

are required to be brought to the notice of the Commissioners. (*See* paragraphs (295) and (301).)

(288) *Clothing.*—The Commissioners are not prepared to approve the purchase by Committees, for supply to insured persons on the point of admission to sanatoria or similar institutions, of an outfit of footgear, underclothing, or any wearing apparel. To meet the needs of insured persons for whom some equipment of this kind may be necessary in order to put them in a position to undergo treatment with advantage, it has been suggested that authorities controlling sanatoria should keep a stock of clothing, boots, and the like, to be lent to patients for their use while in residence. All arrangements made by Committees with Sanatorium Authorities should include the use of the foregoing items, where necessary, without extra charge.

(289) *Overhead Charge.*—The Commissioners require that any tariff proposed to be agreed to by Committees for institutional treatment should be at an overhead rate to include all charges. They are not prepared to sanction payment for extras, such as washing, medicines, or special courses of treatment. They intend that in any institution to which an insured person may be admitted all the resources of that institution shall as a matter of course be available for his treatment. They also desire that Committees, in endeavouring to adjust their expenditure to their income, should not be subjected to the embarrassment of claims whose extent cannot be accurately foreseen.

(290) *Maintenance.*—Charges for lodging or maintenance at an institution will necessarily be included under the overhead rate.

(291) *Detention in Institution.*—The Commissioners are advised that Insurance Committees have no power to compel insured persons to remain in sanatoria or other institutions to which they have been admitted voluntarily under arrangements made by Committees. If, however, an insured person leaves an institution against the advice of the superintendent or other medical officer in charge before the expiry of the period of residence allowed, it would be open to his Committee to warn him that no further benefit would be given. Information of the facts should at the same time be sent to the Public Health Local Authority, or Authorities, concerned. Where difficulty is anticipated, it is suggested that insured persons before being sent to a sanatorium might be asked to sign an undertaking to remain therein until the medical superintendent or other responsible officer authorises their dismissal.

(292) *Burial.*—Charges for burial of the body of an insured patient who may have died in a sanatorium or other institution to which he had been sent by a Committee are not chargeable against the Committee. If the relatives of the insured person do not make arrangements to bury the body, it is the duty not of the Insurance Committee but of the Public Health Local Authority of the area in which the body lies—by direction of a Sheriff, Magistrate, or Justice—to undertake the burial. In

cases of doubt or dispute the Local Authority concerned should at once be approached with a view to its taking steps to bury the body, leaving the question of liability to be afterwards settled.

In any agreement which an Insurance Committee may enter into with a Local Authority or with the Board of Management of an institution the Committee should not undertake the burial of the body of any insured person sent to the institution by them for treatment, and dying there. (*See* also paragraph (333).)

(293) *Poor Law Institution.*—Certain Public Health Local Authorities have entered into agreement with Poor Law Authorities under which the Local Authorities undertake to defray the cost of treatment of persons suffering from tuberculosis admitted to Poor Law hospitals, either by meeting the charges for maintenance of staff, etc., or by payment at a tariff rate or otherwise. Such Poor Law hospitals have in some cases been approved by the Local Government Board for certain purposes in connection with the treatment of tuberculosis, though not for the purposes of the National Insurance Acts. They are to be regarded as institutions managed by Poor Law Authorities, and are therefore not eligible for insured persons or their dependants whose treatment is arranged for by an Insurance Committee. In any area in which a situation of the nature described exists it is essential that the Insurance Committee, if it arranges with the Local Authority for the institutional treatment of any persons, should stipulate that these persons shall receive treatment in an institution managed by the Authority itself, and not in any Poor Law institution regarding which the Authority has an agreement.

(iii.) Dispensary Treatment.

(294) *Tuberculosis Dispensaries.*—The work of Approved Tuberculosis Dispensaries is almost wholly restricted to the field of pulmonary tuberculosis. With scarcely an exception these dispensaries are under the management of Local Authorities. Their number is still comparatively small, and those which exist are situated principally in towns, but with the expansion of the tuberculosis schemes of Local Authorities it may be anticipated that others will come into being.

(295) *Approval by Local Government Board.*—As in the case of residential institutions, dispensaries for the treatment of insured persons require the approval of the Local Government Board. Such approval satisfies the Commissioners as regards efficiency of the dispensary treatment. When, however, it is proposed to supplement the dispensary treatment by the provision of medical comforts, the Commissioners require that the housing and other conditions shall be such as to comply with (*a*) the requirements of the Board as to manner of treatment of domiciliary cases (*see* paragraph (312)) and of the Commissioners' requirements for domiciliary treatment (*see* Section (I.) (iv.) *infra*).

(296) *Sanction by Commissioners.*—The terms of payment proposed to be arranged between an Insurance Committee and the authority controlling a dispensary must be to the satisfaction of the Commissioners, and must be duly submitted to them for approval. The form and basis of the arrangements made have varied considerably in different Scottish areas, and the Commissioners in proceeding to consider the question of approval have taken all the circumstances into account.

(297) *Insured Persons outwith area.*—Whether furnishing treatment by means of residential institutions or dispensaries, Local Authorities are not restricted to making provision for insured persons resident within their own area. They may also provide for the insured who reside outside their area. This liberty of action, conferred upon Authorities by Section 16 (1) (*a*) of the principal Act, has been exercised in the interest of Insurance Committees in whose areas sanatoria are either not yet in operation or if in operation are not of sufficient extent to meet all local demands.

(iv.) DOMICILIARY TREATMENT.

(298) *Meaning of Term.*—The expression Domiciliary Treatment, which does not occur in the National Insurance Acts, has come by usage to be held as covering treatment otherwise than in sanatoria or other institutions as referred to in Section 16 (1) (*b*) of the principal Act.

(299) *Summary of Conditions.*—The conditions relating to arrangements made by Insurance Committees with a view to domiciliary treatment, detailed under Section 16 (1) (*b*), may be thus summarized :—

(*a*) Arrangements must be to the satisfaction of the Commissioners ;
(*b*) Arrangements must be with a view to providing treatment ;
(*c*) Arrangements must be with persons and local authorities undertaking treatment ;
(*d*) Treatment must be otherwise than in sanatoria or other institutions ;
(*e*) Treatment must be in a manner approved by the Local Government Board ;
(*f*) Arrangements may not be made with Poor Law Authorities.

(300) *Model Scheme.*—The model scheme of management for the domiciliary treatment of tuberculosis issued by the Commissioners has been drawn up in such a manner as to give practical effect to these conditions. The model scheme (Form No. 603) and covering circular (Memo. No. 602) appear in Appendix XV.

The following comments will serve to explain the general principles involved.

(a) *Arrangements must be to the satisfaction of the Commissioners.*

(301) *Reporting and Approval of cases.*—In the case of residential treatment the Commissioners have been content to sanction certain general arrangements, and to exempt Committees from the submission of individual cases so long as the general conditions were fulfilled. Under domiciliary treatment the Commissioners will require each case to be separately reported. Sanction, however, need not to be asked if the arrangements for the case are in accordance with a general scheme for the domiciliary treatment of tuberculosis of which the Commissioners have already expressed approval. (*See* Memo. 602.)

(b) *Arrangements must be with a view to providing Treatment.*

(302) *Medicines and Medical Comforts.*—It will be patent that the domiciliary treatment of tuberculosis will include a number of medicines and appliances which in the case of a non-tuberculous patient would fall within the scope of medical benefit. In addition, however, to medicines in the stricter sense, medical comforts also may be allowed. The expression medical comforts, as here employed, refers to substances other than medicines which may be regarded as essential to treatment. Many of these belong either wholly or in part to the class of foods, but since the object of sanatorium benefit is expressly laid down as treatment, the provision of foods by way of maintenance is necessarily excluded. When, therefore, it is proposed to allow to an insured person in respect of his domiciliary treatment a substance which is often or habitually used for the purpose of subsistence, or for a purpose other than the treatment of disease, the quantity of the substance allowed ought to be only the excess beyond the amount needed for ordinary use. This excess quantity should be expressly ordered by the medical practitioner in attendance, as required for the treatment of the tuberculosis from which the patient is suffering (App. XV., Form 603 (5)). It is impracticable, owing to individual differences, to define by rule the amount required for ordinary use; but, so as to give effect to the principle, the total amount allowed as part of treatment, including medicines, appliances, and medical comforts, should be so limited that the inclusive cost shall not exceed 5s. weekly. If, in exceptional cases, this sum is regarded as insufficient, the special approval of the Commissioners must be obtained before treatment in excess of that amount is given. It should, however, be borne in mind that none of the articles in question should be ordered as a matter of routine; they should be given only if and so far as required for the individual needs of separate cases.

(303) *Clothing.*—Under domiciliary treatment the provision of clothing like the provision of ordinary sustenance falls outwith the sphere of an Insurance Committee (App. XV., Form 603 (11)). An insured patient who does not possess the requisite clothing will

require to be supplied with it either by private parties or by a Poor Law Authority.

(304) *Bedding.*—The same limitation excludes the provision of bedding and bed clothes for use in the patient's own house (App. XV., Form 603 (10)). The employment of a shelter in this connection presents special features to which reference is made in paragraph (310).

(c) *Arrangements must be with persons and Local Authorities undertaking treatment.*

(305) *Medical Practitioners.*—As regards insured persons, conformity to this requirement is secured by the inclusion in the agreements between medical practitioners and Insurance Committees of the condition that the domiciliary treatment of persons on panel lists recommended for sanatorium benefit shall be undertaken by the practitioners by whom they are attended. Arrangements for the supply to the patient of medicines and medical comforts should be made by the Committee through the practitioner in attendance, and orders presented to purveyors should be signed by him as applying to articles which he had ordered (App. XV., Form 603 (15 and 16)).

(306) *Dependants.*—As insurance practitioners are under agreement with Committees to give domiciliary treatment to the insured, no occasion should arise for Committees to seek to make arrangements with Local Authorities in respect of the treatment of insured persons. Committees, however, who have extended sanatorium benefit to dependants will require to arrange for the domiciliary treatment of any dependants whom they may recommend for this form of treatment, either with Local Authorities or with private medical practitioners.

(307) *Money payment to patients.*—The patient himself, whether an insured person or a dependant, not being a person undertaking treatment, cannot be permitted to supervise or negotiate the conduct of his own case. The same restriction applies to the patient's friends. A patient therefore, either himself or through his representative, can not be supplied by a Committee with any money to be disbursed on his behalf, but the Committee should make arrangements with a view to the supply by purveyors to the patient of medicines, appliances, and medical comforts (App. XV., Form 603 (14)).

(308) *Extra Rent.*—The Commissioners have been invited on sundry occasions to sanction the payment by Committees of extra rent for an insured person, or of the expense of an additional room, with a view to domiciliary treatment under more spacious conditions, or with a view to the more effective isolation of the patient from the other members of his household. They have, however, been advised that the landlord or factor of a property, with whom arrangements by a Committee for such a purpose would fall to be made, cannot be regarded as a person undertaking treatment in terms of Section 16 (1) (*b*) of the 1911 Act.

They are for this and other reasons unable to approve proposals of this class (App. XV., Form 603 (12)).

In the event of an instance of inadequate housing coming under the notice of a Committee it would appear to be open to the Committee to bring the facts under the notice of the Public Health Local Authority of the area.

(d) Treatment must be otherwise than in Sanatoria or other Institutions.

(309) *Shelters.*—Under this heading it will be appropriate to deal with shelters—portable structures convenient for erection on ground adjoining the houses of patients. They may be obtained as part of arrangements made with persons or Local Authorities undertaking treatment. Boards of Management of Sanatoria or Public Health Local Authorities in town or county districts would be in a position to furnish shelters for the use of the insured (App. XV., Form 603 (8)).

(310) *Beds and Bedding in Shelters.*—Shelters being freely open to the air do not require to be of large size. For this reason among others it will occur from time to time that no bed in the patient's house can conveniently be fitted into the shelter provided. Under such circumstances it would be proper that there should be made available, in addition, such equipment of bed, bedding, and bedclothes for the shelter as may be thought desirable.

(311) *Cost of Shelter.*—The charge, if any, made for the use of the shelter by the person or Local Authority providing it, with whom arrangements are made, should include all costs of transport and erection. Such charge will not be reckoned by the Commissioners in any calculation as to the weekly limit of expenditure on patients undergoing domiciliary treatment.

(e) Treatment must be in a manner approved by the Local Government Board.

(312) *Approval by Local Government Board.*—The formal approval of treatment by the Local Government Board for the purpose of Section 16 (1) (b) of the 1911 Act is contained in their Circular of 1st December 1913. In ascertaining whether the terms of the Board's Circular are duly complied with, Committees will look for guidance to their medical advisers, who are in Scotland, almost without exception, Medical Officers of Health or Officers on the Staff of the Public Health Departments of Local Authorities.

(313) It will be observed from the Board's Circular that by arrangement with the Commissioners they are to obtain the names and addresses of all persons to whom domiciliary treatment is granted.

(f) Arrangements may not be made with Poor Law Authorities.

(314) *Treatment by Officers of Poor Law Authority.*—Domiciliary treatment under Poor Law auspices is expressly ruled out by

Section 16 (1) (*b*) of the 1911 Act. Alike in the case of institutional and domiciliary treatment this disqualification applies both to arrangements proposed to be made directly between an Insurance Committee and a Poor Law Authority, and to arrangements proposed to be made indirectly between these bodies through the agency or participation of a Public Health Local Authority. With regard to the insured whose domiciliary treatment is already matter of agreement between insurance practitioners and Committees and with regard to dependants whose treatment may be arranged for directly with insurance or other practitioners, questions affecting a Parish Council will not arise. But in no area would an arrangement be proper between the Public Health Local Authority and the Parish Council by which the Parish Council would undertake to carry out the treatment of patients in their homes on behalf of the Local Authority, nor in such an event would it be proper for the Insurance Committee to recommend any dependant for domiciliary treatment under the care of the Local Authority unless on the understanding that such treatment would be given by other hands than those of the Parish Council.

SECTION (II.)—EXPENSES OF SANATORIUM BENEFIT AND MISCELLANEOUS ADMINISTRATIVE QUESTIONS.

(i.) FINANCIAL BASIS.

(315) *Sums Available.*—The sums available for defraying the expenses of sanatorium benefit in each year by Section 16 (2) of the 1911 Act are—

(*a*) one shilling and three pence in respect of each insured person resident in the Insurance county or burgh, payable out of the funds out of which benefits of insured persons are payable, and

(*b*) one penny in respect of each such person, payable out of moneys provided by Parliament, the whole or any part of which may be applied by the Commissioners for the purpose of research.

(316) *Treatment.*—With regard to each sum of 1s. 3d. payable to the Committee, it will be recalled that there is set aside 6d. to provide for the remuneration of the practitioner in respect of his obligation to afford domiciliary treatment to recommended insured persons on his list eligible for sanatorium benefit. The remaining 9d. is available to meet the other charges against sanatorium benefit, including the cost of administration.

(317) *Research.*—For the year 1914 and until further notice the sum of 1d., payable out of moneys provided by Parliament, will be retained and paid into a fund called the Medical Research Fund, under the control and management of the Joint Committee by whom Regulations for the application of the sum to the purposes of research have been made.

(318) *Migrants*.—The incidence of cost of sanatorium benefit as between Insurance Committees in the case of persons changing their residence during the year is provided for in Regulations made under paragraph (*f*) of the First Schedule to the Act of 1913 (Payments to Insurance Committees Regulations (Scotland), 1914).

Where an insured person entitled to sanatorium benefit has removed from one area to another, and makes application for sanatorium benefit within three months from the date of his removal, the benefit is to be administered for him by the Committee of the area to which he has removed subject to the following conditions :—

   (*a*) On applying for benefit the insured person must inform the Committee whether he intends to remain in the area for a period of three months or more from the date of his removal into it.
   (*b*) If he does not intend to remain for three months, or if when he removed his case was under recommendation by the Committee area from which he came, the cost of any treatment afforded falls on the Committee's ordinary sanatorium funds.
   (*c*) In any other case if the person is recommended for sanatorium benefit a "case value" in respect of him is to be transferred from the funds of the Committee in whose Register the person's name was included immediately before the date of removal to a Central Sanatorium Benefit Fund, and from that fund a payment of a sum bearing the same proportion to the fund as the number of recommendations made by the Committee bears to the number of recommendations made by all Committees is made to the Committee affording treatment.

(319) *Travellers*.—Insured persons who from the nature of their employment move frequently from place to place, and who hold a voucher indicating that they have been admitted to a special arrangement by which they may receive benefits, apply for sanatorium benefit to the Insurance Committee of the area where they happen to be. The Committee is recouped for the cost of any treatment given by a contribution from the Central Sanatorium Benefit Fund.

(320) *Soldiers, Sailors, etc*.—The case of soldiers, sailors, etc., who are members of an Approved Society and discharged from the service of the Crown, is met by provision being made for a payment to the Insurance Committee affording treatment from the Central Sanatorium Benefit Fund on a "case value" basis (Payments Regs. 24).

Difficulties arising out of the special position created by the war have been met by an emergency arrangement concurred in by the War Office, the Admiralty, the Treasury, and the Local

Government Board for Scotland whereby all insured soldiers, seamen and marines discharged from military or naval hospitals and certified to be suffering from tuberculosis for which a period of institutional treatment is required are immediately placed in a sanatorium. The necessary accommodation has been made available by the patriotism and organising ability of Public Health Local Authorities and certain of the privately owned institutions in Scotland. The Commissioners, acting as a central clearing house on behalf of the Insurance Committees, arrange for the admission of the case to the institution having a bed available nearest to the proposed place of residence of the soldier, seaman or marine, and advise the Committee concerned, which is invited to assume liability therefor. Where the patient is a member of an Approved Society a special grant from public funds of £10 is made available together with the payment from the Central Sanatorium Benefit Fund referred to above. Where he is a member of the Navy and Army Fund the actual cost incurred in the treatment will be defrayed from that Fund. The emergency arrangement is more fully explained in Memo I.C. 53 and 53A.

(321) *Sickness Benefit.*—Where an insured person, being a member of an Approved Society, is an inmate of a sanatorium or similar institution in which he is receiving treatment under arrangements duly made by an Insurance Committee, the sum which would otherwise have been payable to him on account of sickness or disablement benefit is required by Section 12 (2) (*b*) of the 1911 Act, if he has no dependants, to be paid to the Insurance Committee towards the general purposes thereof.

(ii.) Recommendation for Sanatorium Benefit.

(322) *Discretion of Committees.*—By Section 16 (3) of the Act of 1911 an insured person is not entitled to sanatorium benefit unless the Insurance Committee recommends the case for such benefit. This provision recognises the discretionary power of Committees in the selection of cases for treatment. A Committee should exercise this power after consultation with its medical adviser, and should proceed with due regard to the amount of its income.* Many administrative difficulties are avoided if the Committee makes such arrangements as will keep its expenditure within the amount which its income estimated on a quarterly basis permits, and thus is enabled to continue its administrative functions throughout the year. *Where, however, the Committee has during any year incurred liabilities which necessitate its discontinuing arrangements for treatment, it is desirable that early notice should be given to the Local Authority in order that the latter body may make arrangements for taking over the treatment of current cases.*

(323) *A Specified Period.*—Every recommendation for sana-

* Safeguards against incurring expenditure in cases where right to benefit has been lost were suggested in the Circular Letter (80835) of 8th April 1915.

torium benefit should be reviewed at stated intervals, which should not in any case exceed three months, provided that a Committee may at the close of any period of recommendation, if it thinks fit, extend such recommendation (App. XV., Form 603 (18)).

(324) *Erroneous Procedure in Prescribing.*—It should be kept in mind that an insured person suffering from tuberculosis, until he has been recommended for sanatorium benefit, is entitled to medical benefit only, and may, therefore, be supplied only with such drugs and prescribed appliances as the conditions of that benefit authorise. In any area in which the medical benefit drug order forms of the Insurance Committee are permitted to be adapted for the purposes of domiciliary treatment under sanatorium benefit by writing the index mark D in the appropriate space, Insurance practitioners should always be satisfied, before entering the index mark, that the insured person undergoing treatment has been duly *recommended* for sanatorium benefit. The chemist to whom the order is presented has no means of checking the correctness of the entry or of ascertaining the facts with regard to recommendation. When the order form marked D has merely prescribed drugs regarded as proper and sufficient under medical benefit, any error arising on the index mark can be subsequently rectified without great difficulty; where, however, the misleading order is for substances of the nature of medical comforts which could not have been prescribed under medical benefit, no adjustment is possible, and the practitioner must be held responsible for any charges payable to the chemist in respect of the erroneous entry.

(325) *Concurrent Disease.*—It should at the same time be noted that where a patient who is receiving domiciliary treatment for tuberculosis under the scheme suffers concurrently from a disease or injury not arising out of his tuberculosis, any medicines or appliances ordered by his panel doctor for the treatment of the concurrent disease or injury should be charged to the Medical Benefit Drug Fund, since the patient, in respect of the concurrent disease or injury, would be under medical benefit.

(326) *Index Mark.*—Every precaution should also be taken by practitioners to ensure that, where they are ordering drugs for insured persons known to be recommended for domiciliary treatment, they do not omit to write the symbol D in the space provided on the form. This omission has the effect of inflating the Drug Account of the Committee. In any area in which a Committee is aware of the existence of lax procedure under this head appropriate instructions should be issued to Insurance practitioners and chemists.

(327) *Intimation to Practitioners.*—In order to obviate misunderstanding on these and other matters, and generally in the interests of effective administration, the recommendation of any insured person for sanatorium benefit should as soon as possible be followed by an intimation to that effect from the

Committee Clerk to the practitioner responsible for treatment (Form 603 (19)).

(328) *Retrospective Sanction.*—In certain cases the Commissioners have been invited to give a retrospective sanction to recommendations of Committees for sanatorium benefit. The patient may have been under treatment by a practitioner prior to his application for benefit, or he may have been admitted on his own initiative into an approved institution, and have submitted his application for benefit while in residence there, or an interval may have elapsed between the date of recommendation by the Committee and the coming into effect of the arrangements made under the recommendation. Under these or similar conditions the Commissioners are not prepared to give retrospective sanction. Arrangements made by the insured person himself, or by his friends or by other private persons on his behalf, whatsoever the reason for such arrangements may be, do not comply with the terms of Section 16 (1) of the 1911 Act. The date from which the sanction of the Commissioners runs, provided that the arrangements conform in other respects to requirements, is the date on which arrangements made by the Committee, subsequent to recommendation, take effect.

(iii.) EXPENSES OF CONVEYANCE.

(329) *Travelling Expenses.*—By Section 16 (4) of the 1911 Act, an Insurance Committee may defray in whole or in part the expenses of the conveyance of an insured person to or from any institution to which he may be sent for treatment therein, or may make advances for the purpose.

(330) *Advances and Routine.*—The permission given to Committees by the foregoing provision should be exercised with a careful regard to the needs of the insured person and to his ability himself to defray in whole or in part the cost of his conveyance. Any advances made should be accurately adjusted to the actual or proposed outlays. Nothing of the nature of a routine advance to insured persons on the point of admission to a sanatorium by way of a contribution towards their possible travelling expenses should ever be contemplated by a Committee.

(331) The Commissioners have had occasion to consider the position of insured persons recommended by Insurance Committees for Sanatorium Benefit who, in order to receive institutional treatment, are removed from the parish in which they are resident to a sanatorium in another parish, and who, on the expiration of their period of treatment, having no home to which to return, may be in a position which may possibly necessitate the intervention of the Poor Law. With a view to avoiding difficulties which might arise in local administration owing to the discharge of such persons in an area with which they have no connection, the Commissioners recommended that Insurance Committees in Scotland should consider the advisability of securing that patients

are in a position to return to the area from which they were originally removed. As pointed out in the preceding paragraph, Section 16 (4) of the Act of 1911 gives to Committees a permissive power to pay the cost of conveyance of an insured person both to and *from* an institution, and the Commissioners accordingly suggested that in such cases as have been referred to arrangements should be made by Committees to return the patients to the parishes from which they were taken, if that course is, in the particular circumstances, reasonable and satisfactory for the patient (Circular No. 370).

(332) *Recurrent Expenses.*—The Commissioners have been invited to approve the payment by a Committee of the daily travelling expenses of an insured person, proposed to be submitted to tuberculin treatment, to and from a dispensary in a town at a distance of some miles from his place of residence. The Commissioners are of opinion that the terms of Section 16 (4) do not cover payment under the circumstances in question, and they have therefore been unable to sanction the proposal.

(333) *Conveyance of Dead Body.*—The question has also been put to the Commissioners whether an Insurance Committee would be in order in defraying the cost of conveyance home for burial of the body of an insured person who had died in a sanatorium to which he had been sent under the Committee's arrangements. In the view of the Commissioners a Committee has not the power to defray such cost. The obligations of a Committee with regard to burial itself have been dealt with in paragraph (292).

It is inevitable that the question of the burial or conveyance of the dead body of an insured person may from time to time arise through the unexpected death of a patient sent to a sanatorium with a reasonable prospect of recovery or improvement. In many cases of advanced disease a fatal termination may have to be anticipated within a comparatively limited time. It is for the Committee to consider in any such case which they may propose to recommend whether it is expedient that it should be sent to a sanatorium or hospital at any great distance from home.

SECTION (III.)—EXTENSION OF SANATORIUM BENEFIT TO DEPENDANTS.

(i.) General Conditions of Extension.

(334) *General Consideration.*—Section 17 (1) of the 1911 Act empowers an Insurance Committee, if it thinks fit, to extend sanatorium benefit to the dependants of insured persons resident in its area or any class of such dependants, and in such case the arrangements of the Committee are required to include arrangements for the treatment of such dependants and the sums available for sanatorium benefit are applicable to such treatment.

(335) By Section 17 (2) if in any year the amount available for defraying the expenses of sanatorium benefit is insufficient to meet the estimated expenditure on sanatorium benefit for insured persons and such dependants, the Insurance Committee may, through the Commissioners, transmit to the Treasury and the Council of the county or burgh an account showing the estimated expenditure for the purpose and the amount of the sums available for defraying the expenses of sanatorium benefit, and the Treasury and Council may, if they think fit, sanction such expenditure.

(336) By Section 17 (3) the Treasury and the Council of the county or burgh sanctioning such expenditure as aforesaid shall thereupon each be liable to make good in the case of the Treasury out of moneys provided by Parliament, and, in the case of the Council of the county or burgh out of the general purposes rate or the Public Health general assessment, as the case may be, one-half of any sums so sanctioned by them and expended by the Insurance Committee on sanatorium benefit for insured persons and their dependants in the course of the year in excess of the amount available for defraying the expenses of the Committee on sanatorium benefit.

(337) *Position of Dependants.*—The extension of sanatorium benefit by an Insurance Committee in terms of Section 17 (1) of the 1911 Act places dependants in the same position as the insured so far as the general administration of the benefit is concerned. What has been said above with regard to recommendation of benefit, conditions of approval of arrangements and the like in the case of the insured is to be taken as generally applicable to dependants also, when benefit has been extended.

(338) *Domiciliary Treatment of Dependants.*—It should, however, be noted that the remuneration of practitioners at a capitation rate of 6d. per insured person in respect of their obligation to afford treatment under sanatorium benefit does not cover the case of dependants, and it will accordingly be necessary for an arrangement to be made by the Committee for the payment of practitioners in charge of dependants treated at home, preferably by an inclusive weekly or other periodic charge.

(339) *Class of Dependants.*—In lieu of extending benefit to all dependants, it is open to a Committee to limit the extension to a particular class of dependants. A class of dependants for this purpose is to be defined with respect to the individuals composing the class, not with respect to their diseases. Manner of dependence, for example, or degree of relationship or residence within an area, would be appropriate considerations, but the type of tuberculosis or its severity, or the organ or organs principally affected, could not be employed as bases of classification. While, therefore, a Committee might properly extend sanatorium benefit to the wives or alternatively to the wives and children of the insured, or to dependants resident within the area of the Committee, extension to, say, dependants

suffering from non-pulmonary tuberculosis, or to dependants in early stages of pulmonary tuberculosis, would not be competent.

(340) *Discretion of Committee.*—Apart from these limitations, it lies within the discretion of a Committee to determine whether it will or will not extend sanatorium benefit to dependants or specified classes of dependants. Having decided to extend, the Committee may, if it anticipates a deficit, submit an estimate thereof in terms of Section 17 (2) of the 1911 Act to the Town or County Council who may or may not agree to sanction expenditure in terms of Section 17 (3). But the right of the Committee to extend is not governed or conditioned by these contingencies. With or without an estimate, and with or without the sanction of the Local Authority, the Committee may, if after consideration of the circumstances it so elects, extend sanatorium benefit to the dependants of insured persons.

(ii.) EXTENSION AS AFFECTING LOCAL AUTHORITIES.

(341) *Estimate of Expenditure.*—The Committee's estimate of expenditure on the sanatorium benefit of insured persons and dependants, for transmission under Section 17 of the 1911 Act to the Treasury and the Local Authority concerned, is required to be forwarded in the first place to the Commissioners. Care should be taken in preparing estimates for transmission to ensure that any arrangement included in the estimate as a basis for the expenditure anticipated has already received the approval of the Commissioners. If this precaution is omitted, it may be necessary for the Commissioners either to delay transmission of the estimate pending inquiry as to the arrangement proposed, or to refer the estimate back to the Committee for readjustment.

(342) *Constituent Authorities.*—Section 22 of the 1911 Act enables provision to be made by agreement between a County Council and a Local Authority for the contribution towards the Committee's deficit in respect of the area of the authority to be measured by the cost based on the actual incidence of the disease, in place of a rateable proportion of the total expenditure, where it is deemed desirable so to localise liability, instead of spreading it over a wider area.

(343) *Allocation of Liability.*—Under the Public Health Acts, cases of infectious disease, including tuberculosis, fall to be dealt with by the Local Authority of the area in which they emerge, and at the charge of that Local Authority who have no power to reclaim against the Authority to whose area the patient belongs. An Insurance Committee, on the other hand, by means of the Central Sanatorium Benefit Fund, may be in a position to recover the cost of treatment of insured persons who, though coming under notice within its own area, are nevertheless resident in the area of another Committee. A Town or County Council, therefore, which has sanctioned expenditure

under Section 17 (2) of the 1911 Act may be enabled through its own Insurance Committee to obtain a refund of the cost of treatment of cases not belonging to its own area from the area to which they belong. The Commissioners have expressed the view that, apart from financial considerations, the extension of sanatorium benefit to dependants by an Insurance Committee, together with the sanction of the necessary expenditure on behalf of the Local Authority, serves to effect a useful administrative alliance in which the realm of treatment is reserved to the Local Authority, while the duty of making arrangements with a view to treatment is entrusted to the Insurance Committee.

(344) *Co-ordination.*—If the County Council in an Insurance county, as noted in the Annual Report of the Commissioners for 1913-14, acting under Section 64 of the 1911 Act and Section 41 (3) of the 1913 Act, elect to be the executive authority for the treatment of tuberculosis, combined action between the Insurance Committee and the County Council links up and unifies into a single system all agencies within the insurance area which otherwise might be disunited and ineffective. Such co-ordination may be strengthened by an agreement between the County Council and the Committee either under the alternative after-mentioned or under Section 17 of the 1911 Act. If, on the other hand, the County Council do not proceed as authorised in Sections 64 of the 1911 Act and 41 (3) of the 1913 Act, the co-ordinating influence of the Insurance Committee is still of great value. In counties which contain burghs of few inhabitants and low valuation, administrative action tends to be unequal or dispersed in local effort, and the charges for the treatment of tuberculosis, which would fall lightly if spread over an extensive field, may press heavily on some of the separate authorities whose resources are more restricted. In such areas the County Insurance Committee, which possesses jurisdiction, for its purposes, in landward districts and burghs having a population under 20,000 alike, exerts through the National Insurance Acts a powerful co-ordinating influence. It can recommend cases for treatment, irrespective of the question whether they come under notice in a landward or a burghal area. It can deal not only with insured persons, but also, by extending sanatorium benefit, with the dependants of the insured. It can defray from its funds the expenses of treatment, in so far as its funds are available, and, if the County Council has sanctioned expenditure under Section 17 (3) of the principal Act, the expenditure, so far as it forms a local charge for cases not covered by the Committee, is distributed over the combined area by the General Purposes Rate, and it can secure uniformity of treatment by declining to enter into any general or special arrangement with Local Authorities in its area who do not maintain a high standard of efficiency in treatment.

(345) *Letter to Mr. Henry Hobhouse.*—There has been provided an alternative to Section 17 of the 1911 Act in the offer made by the Treasury, in a letter dated 31st July 1912 from the Chancellor

of the Exchequer to Mr. Henry Hobhouse (Appendix XVI.), to meet one-half of any deficit on a tuberculosis scheme by a Local Authority for the treatment of its whole community. The offer holds good whether or not the Local Authority has been a party to sanctioning expenditure under Section 17 (2). A Local Authority which does not elect to defray one-half of the deficit of the Insurance Committee, nor decide to proceed itself without regard to funds available to the Committee, may desire to enter into an agreement with the Insurance Committee under which in respect of the Committee's undertaking to pay over to the Local Authority the balance of its Sanatorium Benefit Fund after deduction of the amount required to meet domiciliary treatment of insured persons, administration, and any payments to the Central Sanatorium Benefit Fund, the Local Authority will undertake to afford treatment to all insured persons recommended by the Committee in the form recommended by them. Such an agreement may be so framed as to grant to the Local Authority and the Committee the advantages of the alternative under Section 17.

(346) *General Agreements.*—It is provided by Section 64 (4) of the 1911 Act that an Insurance Committee may, with the consent of the Commissioners, enter into agreements with any person or Authority, other than a Poor Law Authority, that in consideration of such person or Authority providing treatment in a sanatorium or other institution or otherwise for persons recommended by the Committee for sanatorium benefit, the Committee will contribute out of the funds available for sanatorium benefit towards the maintenance of the institution or provision of such treatment, such annual or other payment and subject to such conditions and for such period as may be agreed, and any such agreement shall be binding on the Committee and their successors, and any sums payable by the Committee thereunder may be paid by the Commissioners and deducted from the sums payable to the Committee for the purposes of sanatorium benefit.

(347) In connection with the foregoing provisions, and particularly the Hobhouse Letter, the Commissioners would be prepared to consider the terms of any agreements proposed to be made between Insurance Committees and persons or Local Authorities. It will be noted that, as in the case of arrangements under Section 16 of the Act, it would not be competent for a Committee to enter into an agreement with a Poor Law Authority. Agreements with Local Authorities proposed for consideration would necessarily proceed on the lines of reserving to Insurance Committees their duty of recommending cases for treatment together with the relevant arrangements, and committing to the hands of Local Authorities, under their Scheme for dealing with tuberculosis, the actual treatment of cases. The Commissioners think it essential that any agreements should be such as to enable advantage to be taken of the right secured by Insurance Committees under their

arrangements with medical practitioners of having treatment afforded without extra charge to all insured persons recommended for domiciliary treatment, and desirable that provision should be made for securing the advantages dealt with above which follow from co-ordination of the various authorities and the distribution of liability. The Commissioners, apart from special circumstances, would not be prepared to approve a general agreement between the Committee and the Local Authority unless and until the latter body has received the approval of the Local Government Board and the Commissioners to a general scheme for the treatment of tuberculosis within its area, and has built the sanatoria, hospitals and dispensaries, and completed the arrangements necessary to enable treatment to be given by the Authority itself.

(348) Where the Local Authority has, under an approved general scheme, completed the erection of sanatoria, hospitals and dispensaries, and made adequate arrangements for the treatment of all tuberculosis cases within its area, the Commissioners ordinarily would not approve of arrangements for the institutional treatment by the Insurance Committee of insured persons otherwise than with the Local Authority of the area under either a general arrangement or arrangements for individual cases. In a county where the County Council has not itself formulated and carried out a scheme under Section 41 (3) of the 1913 Act the Commissioners as a rule would not be prepared to approve a general arrangement with a Local Authority which would deal only with part of the Committee's area, unless there were simultaneously submitted similar agreements with the other Local Authorities in the area.

CHAPTER VI.

DEPOSIT CONTRIBUTORS.

SECTION (I.)—CONTRIBUTIONS.

(349) SECTION 42 of the 1911 Act makes special provision for Deposit Contributors, *i.e.* insured persons who have not joined an Approved Society within the prescribed time, or who, having been members of an Approved Society, have been expelled or have resigned and have not joined another Society. The position of a Deposit Contributor differs from that of a member of an Approved Society in respect that the former draws on his own credits in the Deposit Contributors Fund, and not on a general fund in which other persons have also an interest. Insurance Committees are specially concerned with Deposit Contributors as they have important duties in administering the money benefits of this class of insured persons.

(350) The contributions in respect of Deposit Contributors are paid in the same way as those for members of Approved Societies. A Deposit Contributor obtains his contribution card from the Commission, and returns it to them at the end of the period of currency, except where a claim for benefit is made. In that case the current contribution card is forwarded with the claim to the Insurance Committee, which issues a fresh card for the remainder of the half year.

(351) The Insurance Committee holds in its Register a record of the names and addresses of all the Deposit Contributors resident in its area. Any changes of address notified by Deposit Contributors should at once be intimated to the Commissioners.

(352) The weekly rates of contributions payable in respect of Deposit Contributors vary according to the classes of contributors. The following tables give the rates relating to the different classes and the portions payable respectively by the employer and the insured person :—

[TABLE.

RATES OF CONTRIBUTIONS.

(a) *Employed Contributors.*

TABLE showing the Amount of the Joint Weekly Contribution and its Division between Employer and Worker.

Rate of remuneration means the rate *for a full working day*, and not the earnings for less than a day's work.	Wages, &c.	Value of Stamp to be affixed by Employer. Men.	Value of Stamp to be affixed by Employer. Women.	Amount recoverable from Worker. Men.	Amount recoverable from Worker. Women.
		d.	d.	d.	d.
Where the worker receives wages or other money payments either from his employer or from some other person; and (a) is between 16 and 21—whatever the rate of remuneration		7	6	4	3
(b) (1) **is 21 or upwards**, and the rate of remuneration exceeds 2s. 6d. a working day, OR WHERE BOARD AND LODGING ARE PROVIDED, WHATEVER THE RATE OF REMUNERATION		7	6	4	3
(2) **is 21 or upwards**, and board and lodging are not provided, and the (i.) Rate of remuneration exceeds 2s. but does not exceed 2s. 6d. a working day		7	6	3	3
(ii.) Rate of remuneration exceeds 1s. 6d. but does not exceed 2s. a working day		6	5	1	1
(iii.) Rate of remuneration does not exceed 1s. 6d. a working day		6	5	0	0

(b) *Sections 47 and 53.*

The employed rate of contributions, for persons under these Sections, is reduced by 2d. a week for men and by 1½d. a week for women. The employer accepts responsibility for payment of full remuneration to the employee during six weeks of sickness, and his share of the contribution is reduced by a penny for a man and a ½d. for a woman. The share of the employee, whether man or woman, is reduced by a penny.

Employers can adopt the Section only by giving notice to the Commissioners on a form obtainable from them, and only in respect of certain classes of employment.

(c) *Outworkers.*

Contributions in respect of outworkers may be paid by reference to the work actually done by them instead of to the weeks in which they are employed. Where an employer has received the Commission's permission to adopt this method of paying contributions, he affixes a stamp to the worker's card for each "unit" of work (the "unit" being an amount of work fixed by the Commission) irrespective of the time taken to complete the "unit." The contributions and their incidence on employer and employee respectively are as shown in the table on p. 103, the "unit" being normally taken as a guide to the rate of remuneration.

(d) *Voluntary Contributors.*

RATES of contribution payable by persons entering into Insurance before the 13th day of October 1913.

England, Scotland, and Wales.

Age at entry into Insurance. (1)	Weekly Contribution for Men. (2) s. d.	Weekly Contribution for Women. (3) s. d.
Under 45	0 7	0 6
45 and under 46	0 9	0 8
46 ,, 47	0 9	0 8½
47 ,, 48	0 9½	0 8½
48 ,, 49	0 10	0 9
49 ,, 50	0 10	0 9
50 ,, 51	0 10½	0 9½
51 ,, 52	0 10½	0 9½
52 ,, 53	0 11	0 10
53 ,, 54	0 11½	0 10½
54 ,, 55	1 0	0 11
55 ,, 56	1 0½	0 11
56 ,, 57	1 1	0 11½
57 ,, 58	1 1½	1 0
58 ,, 59	1 2	1 0½
59 ,, 60	1 2½	1 1
60 ,, 61	1 2½	1 1
61 ,, 62	1 3	1 1½
62 ,, 63	1 3½	1 1½
63 ,, 64	1 3½	1 1½
64 ,, 65	1 3½	1 1½
65 ,, 66	1 3	1 0½
66 ,, 67	1 3	1 0½
67 ,, 68	1 3	1 0½
68 ,, 69	1 3	1 0½
69 ,, 70	1 3	1 0½

(d) *Voluntary Contributors*—continued.

Rates of contribution payable by persons entering into Insurance on or after the 13th day of October 1913.

England, Scotland, and Wales.

Age at entry into Insurance. (1)	Weekly Contribution for Men. (2) s. d.	Weekly Contribution for Women. (3) s. d.
16 and under 17	0 7	0 6
17 ,, 18	0 7	0 6½
18 ,, 19	0 7½	0 6½
19 ,, 20	0 7½	0 6½
20 ,, 21	0 7½	0 6½
21 ,, 22	0 7½	0 6½
22 ,, 23	0 7½	0 6½
23 ,, 24	0 7½	0 6½
24 ,, 25	0 7½	0 6½
25 ,, 26	0 8	0 7
26 ,, 27	0 8	0 7
27 ,, 28	0 8	0 7
28 ,, 29	0 8	0 7
29 ,, 30	0 8	0 7
30 ,, 31	0 8	0 7
31 ,, 32	0 8½	0 7½
32 ,, 33	0 8½	0 7½
33 ,, 34	0 8½	0 7½
34 ,, 35	0 8½	0 7½
35 ,, 36	0 9	0 8
36 ,, 37	0 9	0 8
37 ,, 38	0 9	0 8
38 ,, 39	0 9½	0 8
39 ,, 40	0 9½	0 8½
40 ,, 41	0 9½	0 8½
41 ,, 42	0 9½	0 8½
42 ,, 43	0 10	0 9
43 ,, 44	0 10	0 9
44 ,, 45	0 10½	0 9½
45 ,, 46	0 10½	0 9½
46 ,, 47	0 11	0 10
47 ,, 48	0 11	0 10

8

(d) *Voluntary Contributors*—continued.

			s. d.	s. d.
48 and under 49		.. ..	0 11½	0 0½
49 ,, 50		.. ..	0 11½	0 10½
50 ,, 51		.. ..	1 0	0 11
51 ,, 52		.. ..	1 0½	0 11
52 ,, 53		.. ..	1 0½	0 11½
53 ,, 54		.. ..	1 1	1 0
54 ,, 55		.. ..	1 1½	1 0½
55 ,, 56		.. ..	1 2	1 0½
56 ,, 57		.. ..	1 2½	1 1
57 ,, 58		.. ..	1 3	1 1½
58 ,, 59		.. ..	1 3½	1 2
59 ,, 60		.. ..	1 4	1 2½
60 ,, 61		.. ..	1 4½	1 2½
61 ,, 62		.. ..	1 4½	1 3
62 ,, 63		.. ..	1 5	1 3
63 ,, 64		.. ..	1 5	1 3
64 ,, 65		.. ..	1 5	1 3
65 ,, 66		.. ..	1 4½	1 2
66 ,, 67		.. ..	1 4½	1 2
67 ,, 68		.. ..	1 4½	1 2
68 ,, 69		.. ..	1 4½	1 2
69 ,, 70		.. ..	1 4½	1 2

(e) *Late Entrants.*

Employed Deposit Contributors aged 17 or upwards entering Insurance after 13th October 1913, whose time has not been spent in a school or college or in indentured apprenticeship or otherwise in instruction without wages or otherwise in the completion of their education, and who wish to qualify for full benefit must pay an additional weekly contribution according to the following tables:—

MEN.				WOMEN.			
			d.				d.
17 and under 18		..	—	17 and under 18		..	0½*
18 ,, 19		..	0½*	18 ,, 19		..	0½*
19 ,, 20		..	0½*	19 ,, 20		..	0½*
20 ,, 21		..	0½*	20 ,, 21		..	0½*
21 ,, 22		..	0½*	21 ,, 22		..	0½*
22 ,, 23		..	0½*	22 ,, 23		..	0½*
23 ,, 24		..	0½*	23 ,, 24		..	0½*
24 ,, 25		..	0½*	24 ,, 25		..	0½*

* In these cases there being no ½d. insurance stamp, a 1d. insurance stamp should be affixed every other week.

(e) *Late Entrants*—continued.

MEN.			d.	WOMEN.			d.
25 and under 26			1	25 and under 26			1
26	,,	27	1	26	,,	27	1
27	,,	28	1	27	,,	28	1
28	,,	29	1	28	,,	29	1
29	,,	30	1	29	,,	30	1
30	,,	31	1	30	,,	31	1
31	,,	32	$1\frac{1}{2}$	31	,,	32	$1\frac{1}{2}$
32	,,	33	$1\frac{1}{2}$	32	,,	33	$1\frac{1}{2}$
33	,,	34	$1\frac{1}{2}$	33	,,	34	$1\frac{1}{2}$
34	,,	35	$1\frac{1}{2}$	34	,,	35	$1\frac{1}{2}$
35	,,	36	2	35	,,	36	2
36	,,	37	2	36	,,	37	2
37	,,	38	2	37	,,	38	2
38	,,	39	$2\frac{1}{2}$	38	,,	39	2
39	,,	40	$2\frac{1}{2}$	39	,,	40	$2\frac{1}{2}$
40	,,	41	$2\frac{1}{2}$	40	,,	41	$2\frac{1}{2}$
41	,,	42	$2\frac{1}{2}$	41	,,	42	$2\frac{1}{2}$
42	,,	43	3	42	,,	43	3
43	,,	44	3	43	,,	44	3
44	,,	45	$3\frac{1}{2}$	44	,,	45	$3\frac{1}{2}$
45	,,	46	$3\frac{1}{2}$	45	,,	46	$3\frac{1}{2}$
46	,,	47	4	46	,,	47	4
47	,,	48	4	47	,,	48	4
48	,,	49	$4\frac{1}{2}$	48	,,	49	$4\frac{1}{2}$
49	,,	50	$4\frac{1}{2}$	49	,,	50	$4\frac{1}{2}$
50	,,	51	5	50	,,	51	5
51	,,	52	$5\frac{1}{2}$	51	,,	52	5
52	,,	53	$5\frac{1}{2}$	52	,,	53	$5\frac{1}{2}$
53	,,	54	6	53	,,	54	6
54	,,	55	$6\frac{1}{2}$	54	,,	55	$6\frac{1}{2}$
55	,,	56	7	55	,,	56	$6\frac{1}{2}$
56	,,	57	$7\frac{1}{2}$	56	,,	57	7
57	,,	58	8	57	,,	58	$7\frac{1}{2}$
58	,,	59	$8\frac{1}{2}$	58	,,	59	8
59	,,	60	9	59	,,	60	$8\frac{1}{2}$
60	,,	61	$9\frac{1}{2}$	60	,,	61	$8\frac{1}{2}$
61	,,	62	$9\frac{1}{2}$	61	,,	62	9
62	,,	63	10	62	,,	63	9
63	,,	64	10	63	,,	64	9
64	,,	65	10	64	,,	65	9

(e) *Late Entrants*—continued.

MEN.		WOMEN.	
	d.		d.
65 and under 66	9½	65 and under 66	8
66 ,, 67	9½	66 ,, 67	8
67 ,, 68	9½	67 ,, 68	8
68 ,, 69	9½	68 ,, 69	8
69 ,, 70	9½	69 ,, 70	8

(f) *Mercantile Marine.*

The ordinary rate of contribution applies in the case of seamen when serving on home trade ships. In the case of men serving on foreign-going ships and ships engaged in regular trade between foreign ports the employed rate and the employer's contribution are each reduced by a penny. The employer's share of the contribution is payable in respect of every week in which the seaman is employed, but every four contributions paid by the seaman in any calendar year are treated as five. There is credited to the contributor's account a sum equal to two-fifths of the amount of the contributions actually paid in respect of him, and an equal sum is treated as having been expended on sickness benefit, the Parliamentary Grant being paid thereon (Sec. 48 (2), proviso (b)).

SECTION (II.)—REFUNDS.

(i.) On Permanently ceasing to reside in the United Kingdom.

(353) Where a Deposit Contributor shows that he has permanently ceased to reside in the United Kingdom, he is entitled to a refund of 4/7ths (or ½ in the case of a woman) of the amount standing to his credit in the Deposit Contributors Fund (1911 Act, Sec. 42 (g)). The refund cannot be made, however, until the contributor has permanently ceased to reside in the United Kingdom. It can be paid either to the contributor or to some person in the United Kingdom nominated by him. Where the remittance is sent abroad the cost is in all cases deducted from the amount to be refunded.*

(354) A Deposit Contributor who intends to leave the United Kingdom and desires to claim a refund should apply to the Insurance Committee in whose area he is resident for the forms necessary for making the claim after he has left the United Kingdom. (These Forms are 174, 175, and 198.)

(355) When the Committee has satisfied itself that the contributor has permanently ceased to reside in the United Kingdom, a certificate to that effect (Form 332) is prepared and forwarded to the Commissioners, together with the Index Slip. The refund

* No refund will be made to an alien enemy.

is then made and the Committee notified on Form 394B/A.G.D. (Scotland).

(356) As refund is made in some cases to the contributor himself after he has gone abroad it is necessary that the Clerk should furnish on Form 332 the full postal address of the contributor so that the letter containing the Money Order or Postal Order may not be returned on account of insufficient address.

(ii.) ON THE DEATH OF A DEPOSIT CONTRIBUTOR.

(357) Section 42 (f) of the 1911 Act provides that on the death of a Deposit Contributor 4/7ths (or $\frac{1}{2}$ in the case of a woman) of the amount standing to his credit in the Deposit Contributors Fund shall be paid to his nominee, or in default of a nomination to the person who would be entitled to receive the sum, as if it were money payable on the death of a member of a registered Friendly Society.

(358) When, therefore, an Insurance Committee receives intimation of the death of a Deposit Contributor, the Clerk should immediately notify the Commissioners.

(359) Where a Deposit Contributor has nominated a person to whom the 4/7ths (or $\frac{1}{2}$ in the case of a woman) of the amount standing to his credit is to be paid at his death, the nomination will be in the custody of the Commissioners, who will pay the money over to the nominee on receiving a certificate of death in proper form. An outstanding claim for benefit whether made by the contributor or, after his death, by his legal representative would be met in priority to the claim of the nominee.

(360) Where the contributor has made no nomination but has left a will, the Commissioners cannot in general pay the portion of the sum standing to his credit in the Deposit Contributors Fund (which he might have disposed of by nomination) to his executor without production of confirmation. The Commissioners have no power to dispense with proof of title however small the estate.

(361) Where the Deposit Contributor has died intestate and without making any nomination, the Commissioners will pay the appropriate sum to any person who has been appointed Executor-Dative and has duly confirmed to the estate; but where no Executor-Dative or other legal representative has been appointed, the Commissioners are empowered to distribute the money among those persons who appear to them to be entitled by law to receive it (*i.e.* to the husband or wife, or children, or other next of kin).

(362) In a case where no nomination has been made, the Commissioners may have to obtain the assistance of the Insurance Committee in ascertaining whether the deceased contributor—

    (*a*) has left a will upon which executors have obtained confirmation; or

(b) has died intestate and an Executor Dative has been appointed and taken out confirmation; or

(c) has died intestate and no Executor Dative has been appointed;

in which last case the Insurance Committee will be asked to ascertain who are legally entitled to the money.

(363) It should be borne in mind that unless the amount standing to the credit of the contributor, together with the value of the stamps on the last contribution card, exceeds 5s. 4d. in the case of a man and 6s. 2d. in the case of a woman, the representatives of the deceased will probably consider that it is not worth while incurring the cost of a certificate of death (viz. 3s. 1d.), and if in any such case a claim is intimated to the Committee it should be pointed out to the applicants that the amount payable will not exceed the cost of the certificate.

(364) If in connection with the death of a Deposit Contributor the Insurance Book and Contribution Card of the deceased should come into the hands of the Committee, they should at once be sent to the Commissioners.

SECTION (III.)—RULES.

(365) Insurance Committees are required to make rules, subject to the approval of the Commissioners, with regard to the administration by the Committee of the benefits of Deposit Contributors. A model form of Rules was issued by the Commissioners for the assistance of Committees (Appendix XVII.), and has been generally adopted (Section 14 (3) of 1911 Act).

SECTION (IV.)—MEDICAL AND SANATORIUM BENEFITS.

(366) The medical and sanatorium benefits of Deposit Contributors are administered by Insurance Committees under the same general conditions as those of members of Approved Societies. Reference should therefore be made to Chapters IV. and V.

(367) The cost of these benefits is, however, defrayed in a different way. The cost of all the benefits of a Deposit Contributor (sickness, disablement, and maternity, as well as medical and sanatorium) is met from the amount standing to his credit in the Deposit Contributors Fund. In the case of British subjects seven-ninths of the cost (three-quarters in the case of a woman) is defrayed by the contributions paid on behalf of the contributor and the remainder is met from the State grants.

(368) The right to benefits is suspended when the sum standing to the credit of a Deposit Contributor is exhausted. An Insurance Committee may, however, allow a Deposit Contributor to continue to receive medical benefit or sanatorium benefit after the expiration of the period for which his account has been debited.

(369) Under the Deposit Contributors Scheme, unless the contributor accumulates in one period a sufficient credit to ensure medical and sanatorium benefits in the next, he will lose those benefits, and Committees in administering benefits should see that this is explained to contributors, *e.g.* it would not be desirable to grant sickness or maternity benefit as so to exhaust the credit of the contributor, and thus disentitle him to benefits during the ensuing year without previously warning him of the effect on his right to medical and sanatorium benefits. While the contributor has anything at his credit, the Committee, however, has not the right to withhold payment of sickness or maternity benefit to which he may be entitled, if, after having been duly warned, he insists on his claim. It is, however, provided by the Deposit Contributors Benefits Order, to which reference is made in paragraph (371), that towards the end of the year no payment on account of sickness or maternity benefit is, unless the Commissioners otherwise determine, to be made to any contributor of an amount greater than the excess (if any) of the amount standing at his credit over the sums payable for medical and sanatorium benefits and administration expenses for the succeeding year—any unpaid balance of benefits being paid as soon after the beginning of the year as possible.

(370) Section 42 (*e*) of the 1911 Act provides for the deduction at the beginning of each year of the sums payable in respect of a Deposit Contributor for medical and sanatorium benefit and administration expenses from the amount standing to his credit in the Deposit Contributors Fund. If at the commencement of any year he has not sufficient to provide these charges he will not be entitled to any benefits during that year unless the Insurance Committee consents, except so far as may be authorised by the Deposit Contributors' Benefits Order. The Insurance Committee may attach conditions to the payment of benefits provided with its consent.

(371) To meet the case of a considerable number of deposit contributors who, while not having sufficient at the beginning of the year at their credit to pay for a full year's medical and sanatorium benefits, had either then or later on in the year sufficient to provide themselves with these benefits for a part of the year, the terms of Section 42 have from time to time been modified by Orders of the Commissioners made under Section 78 of the 1911 Act. According to the Order applicable to 1915, the year was divided into quarters, and each deposit contributor who had not sufficient at the commencement of the year to pay for the full year's benefits was provided with medical and sanatorium benefits for such quarters as could be paid for out of the sum at his credit. To meet the case of new entrants into insurance during the first half of 1914, it was provided that each person returning a stamped card for that half year was to be entitled to medical and sanatorium benefits for the first quarter of 1915 irrespective of the amount at his credit. After the first quarter,

however, he only got those benefits for such of the remaining quarters as after taking account of the charge for the first quarter could be paid for out of the sum at his credit. The Order is No. 94 (Scotland), and its full title is the National Health Insurance (Deposit Contributors' Benefits) Order (Scotland), 1914, No. 2.

(372) Section 3 of the Act of 1913 provides that contributors do not cease to be entitled to medical benefit at the age of 70, provided that, in the case of persons 65 years of age or upwards on entry into insurance, at least 27 contributions have been paid. If less than 27 contributions have been paid, the contributor ceases to be entitled to medical benefit although still eligible for sanatorium benefit except, under the said Order, where he attained 70 after 5th July 1914, in which case he need only have been in insurance for over 26 weeks.

If a contributor, 65 years of age or upwards on entry into insurance, has paid less than 27 contributions on attaining the age of 70, but has been at least 27 weeks in insurance, it will be open to him, by the payment of arrears, to bring the number of his contributions up to 27, and thus qualify for medical benefit after attaining the age of 70. A contributor aged 65 or upwards on becoming insured, who has not been in insurance at least 27 weeks, cannot, however, in any circumstances qualify to receive medical benefit after attaining the age of 70.

SECTION (V.)—SICKNESS BENEFIT.

(A) *QUALIFICATIONS.*

(373) Sickness benefit is payable under certain conditions in respect of total incapacity for work resulting from a specific disease or a bodily or mental disablement. A contributor in order to be entitled to benefit must possess the following qualifications :—

    (i.) He must have been in insurance for 26 weeks.
    (ii.) He must have paid 26 weekly contributions.
    (iii.) He must be resident in the United Kingdom.
(i.) and (ii.) call for no comment.

(iii.) RESIDENCE.

(374) Where a Deposit Contributor becomes temporarily resident in some place outside the area of the Committee, but in the United Kingdom, or in the Isle of Man, or in the Channel Islands, the Committee, if satisfied that his residence outside the area of the Committee is temporary only, may take into consideration any application by him for the payment of any sickness or maternity benefit. If a Deposit Contributor is resident outside the United Kingdom elsewhere than in the Isle of Man or the Channel Islands, and at the date of his leaving the United Kingdom was in receipt of sickness benefit, the Committee may allow him whilst so resident to continue to receive sickness benefit.

(B) SUSPENSION OR MODIFICATION.

(375) Moreover, there are certain circumstances in which payment is suspended or modified. These include the following, which are further described in the paragraphs below :—

    (iv.) When the contributor is in receipt of or entitled to compensation or damages in respect of the injury or disease causing incapacity.

    (v.) When the contributor is in a poorhouse, or in a charity or rate-supported hospital, asylum, convalescent home, infirmary, or sanatorium.

    (vi.) When the contributor enters insurance on or after 13th October 1913, and is on the date of entry of the age of 17 or upwards and not entitled to the benefit of Section 9 (4) of the 1911 Act (*see* paragraph (390)).

    (vii.) When the contributor is unmarried and under the age of 21.

    (viii.) When the contributor is an alien.

    (ix.) When the contributor is insured under Section 47 of the 1911 Act.

    (x.) When the contributor is in the Mercantile Marine.

    (xi.) In the case of a woman contributor suspended from ordinary benefits on marriage or who returns to employment after suspension.

    (xii.) In the case of a woman contributor incapacitated as a result of a confinement.

    (xiii.) When the contributor has become a seaman, marine, or soldier.

(iv.) PAYMENT OF COMPENSATION OR DAMAGES IN RESPECT OF THE INCAPACITY.

(376) The Act of 1911 (Sec. 11) provides that sickness or disablement benefit shall not be paid to an insured person in respect of any injury or disease where the insured person has received or recovered, or is entitled to receive or recover, compensation or damages under the Workman's Compensation Act, 1906, or any scheme certified thereunder, or under the Employers' Liability Act, 1880, or at Common Law, if—

    (1) the weekly sum ; or

    (2) the weekly value of any lump sum paid or payable is equal to or greater than the benefit which would otherwise be payable to such persons.

(377) The Act further provides that where any such weekly sum or the weekly value of any such lump sum is less than the benefit in question, such part only of the benefit will be paid as, together with the weekly sum, or the weekly value of the lump sum will be equal to the benefit. Thus, if a Deposit Contributor otherwise entitled to sickness benefit at the rate of 10s. per week, were receiving or were entitled to receive compensation amount-

ing to 10s. or more per week, no sickness benefit would be payable in respect of the incapacity. If, however, the contributor were entitled to receive as compensation, say, 8s. per week, and his rate of sickness benefit were 10s. per week, he would be entitled to receive as sickness benefit 2s. per week, that being the difference between the amount of the compensation and his rate of sickness benefit.

(378) Sickness benefit may be advanced to a contributor pending the settlement of the question of compensation on the understanding that any sums so advanced shall be refunded by the contributor if and when compensation is received. The amount advanced may be recovered by deduction from or suspension of future benefits.

(379) As regards the duration of benefit, it should be noted that where partial sickness benefit is paid as described in paragraph (377), the maximum duration of such benefit is still 26 weeks. Thus, if a contributor is continuously sick and is receiving 2s. per week benefit and 8s. per week compensation, not more than 26 weekly payments of 2s. can be made to him.

(380) Where, however, the contributor has been in receipt of such partial benefit, then recovers from his illness, and subsequently again becomes ill, special provision is made in the 1913 Act as to the calculation of continuing illness. In the ordinary case where full benefit is paid, two unconnected periods of illness are reckoned as continuous for the purpose of calculating when the 26 weeks' duration of benefit expires, unless the periods are separated by at least 12 months.

(381) If partial benefit only was paid, however, the contributor is treated as having been in receipt of benefit not for the whole period during which partial benefit was paid but for a period which bears to the whole period the same proportion as the amount of partial benefit paid bears to the full benefit to which the contributor would otherwise have been entitled.

The period so calculated is to be treated as continuous, and as having expired on the last day of incapacity for which the partial benefit was paid.

Thus, suppose the contributor has received 8s. per week compensation and 2s. per week sickness benefit for 10 weeks, and then recovers. For the purpose of "linked-up" sickness he would be held to have received sickness benefit for two weeks, the two weeks expiring on the last day of his incapacity.

If the compensation is greater than the sickness benefit would have been, and consequently no benefit at all is paid, the period is not to be counted towards the 26 weeks.

Territorials and Special Reservists.

(382) Section 11 of the Act of 1911 will normally not apply to members of the Territorial or Special Reserve Forces injured while in training at drills, at the annual camp, etc. During such

training the contributor is employed in the Military Service of the Crown, which employment is specifically excepted from the provisions of the Workmen's Compensation Act and the Employers' Liability Acts. No compensation is, therefore, payable, and although the Army Regulations allow the payment of certain sums in cases of injury, such payments are entirely *ex gratia*, and sickness benefit should not be withheld.

(v.) CONTRIBUTOR IN A POORHOUSE, ETC.

(383) The following statement shows the effect of the special provisions of the Acts where a Deposit Contributor is in a poorhouse, hospital, asylum, convalescent home, or infirmary supported by any public authority, or out of any public funds, or by charity, or by voluntary subscriptions, or in a sanatorium or similar institution approved under the Acts.*

If the contributor is an inmate of an institution which does not fall within the above definition, *e.g.* a private nursing home, the ordinary provisions as to payment of benefit apply.

(384) No sickness benefit must be paid to any person during any period when he is an inmate of any institution as above defined. It should be noted in this connection that the word "inmate" will not ordinarily extend to a nurse in the hospital in which she is employed or to persons regularly employed in or about a hospital, who are accustomed to receive there such treatment and attendance as they may require.

(385) Where the contributor has dependants, the sickness benefit which he would otherwise receive must be applied for the relief or maintenance of the dependants after consultation, wherever possible, with the contributor.

(386) If the contributor is an inmate of a poorhouse, hospital, asylum, convalescent home or infirmary, and he has no dependants, the benefit may be used to provide any surgical appliances required on his behalf, or otherwise for his benefit when he ceases to be an inmate. The amount still outstanding must be paid in cash to the contributor after he leaves the institution, either in a lump sum or in instalments, as the Committee thinks fit.

(387) All sums paid or expended in any of the ways above referred to are to be treated as payments in respect of sickness benefit for the purpose of determining the rate and duration of that benefit.

(vi.) LATE ENTRANTS.

(388) A Deposit Contributor who being 17 or over at the time becomes an Employed Contributor after 12th October 1913, will be entitled to sickness benefit at the rates shown in the Table below.

* A list of sanatoria and other similar institutions approved by the Local Government Board for Scotland, under Part I. of the National Insurance Act, 1911, will be found in Appendix XIV.

TABLE showing the reduced rate of sickness benefit for employed contributors entering into Insurance after 12th October 1913:—

Age next birthday after entry into insurance.	Rate of Sickness Benefit.	
	MEN.	WOMEN.
	s. d.	s. d.
17	No reduction.	No reduction.
18	No reduction.	7 0
19	9 0	6 6
20	8 6	6 0
21	8 0	5 6
22	8 0	5 0
23	7 6	5 0
24	7 0	5 0
25	7 0	5 0
26	6 6	5 0
27	6 6	5 0
28	6 0	5 0
29	6 0	5 0
30	5 6	5 0
Over 30	5 0	5 0

(389) An Employed Contributor may qualify for the payment of sickness benefit at the full rate (10s. a week for men and 7s. 6d. a week for women) by paying an additional weekly contribution from the date of his entry into insurance. The increased contributions applicable to various ages are given in the Table in paragraph (352). Since, however, a Deposit Contributor is entitled to benefit only so far as the amount standing to his credit will allow, the payment of the additional contribution will not be of full benefit to him until he joins a Society.

(390) A Deposit Contributor who being 17 or over becomes an Employed Contributor after 12th October 1913, is entitled to sickness benefit at the full rate (so far as the amount standing to his credit allows), if he can prove that his time since he became 17 has been spent in a school or college, in indentured apprenticeship or otherwise under instruction *without wages*, or otherwise in the completion of his education.

(vii.) UNMARRIED MINORS.

(391) A Deposit Contributor under the age of 21, who is unmarried and has no dependants, is entitled to sickness benefit

at the rate of 6s. a week (women 5s. a week) with a reduction to 5s. a week (women 4s.) after the first 13 weeks. A contributor under 21 who is married or has any member of his family wholly or mainly depending on him is entitled to sickness benefit as though he were over 21.

(viii.) ALIENS.

(392) The rates of sickness benefit applicable to aliens are seven-ninths of the ordinary rates in the case of men and three-quarters in the case of women. It should be observed, however, that British women contributors who marry aliens are treated as British subjects and receive full benefits according to date of entry in respect of their own insurance.

(ix.) SECTIONS 47 AND 53.

(393) Where a person is insured under Section 47 of the 1911 Act his employer undertakes to pay full wages during the first 6 weeks of sickness, and sickness benefit is not payable during this period. It is deemed to have been paid, however, and accordingly commences in ordinary circumstances at the beginning of the seventh week of sickness (not on the fourth day of the seventh week) (see paragraph (399) below), and continues for twenty weeks from the first day for which sickness benefit is paid, *i.e.* it ordinarily terminates at the end of the twenty-sixth week of actual incapacity.

As regards the precise period for which the employer is liable, it may generally be stated that contributors under Section 47 if engaged by their employer for a term of less than six months certain cannot claim sickness benefit until they have been ill *for six weeks in all in any period of* 12 *months*. They then receive their ordinary sickness benefit, and may continue to receive it for 20 weeks (provided they have sufficient standing at their credit), at the end of which the benefit stops even though they are still ill. If engaged for a term of not less than six months certain they are not entitled to sickness benefit until they have been ill for *six weeks in succession*, unless their employment terminates during an illness which has been going on for less than six weeks, in which case benefit become payable on the termination of the employment. They then receive ordinary sickness benefit and may continue to receive it (provided that the amount standing at their credit is sufficient) up to the expiration of 20 weeks from the commencement of sickness benefit.

(394) Section 53 applies these provisions to certain persons employed under the Crown, not excepted under Part II. (*b*) of the First Schedule to the 1911 Act, and provides that where $\frac{2}{3}$ only of the remuneration is payable for a period of not less than 3 months in any year, $\frac{2}{3}$ shall be substituted for full wages, and 3 months for 6 weeks. The contributor is, however, deemed to have re-

ceived Sickness Benefit for 6, not 13 weeks, for the purpose of calculating the duration of benefit.

(x.) MERCANTILE MARINE.

(395) Under Section 48 of the 1911 Act a master, seaman or apprentice is not entitled to receive sickness benefit while the owner of the ship is liable for the cost of his medical attendance and maintenance. The Act of 1913 (Section 23 (1)), however, provides that if a Deposit Contributor *serving on a home trade ship* has dependants and the owner, though liable for his maintenance and medical attendance, is not liable to pay wages to him, the Committee may pay the sickness benefit in whole or in part to the dependants or apply it for their relief or maintenance in such manner as the Committee (after consultation wherever possible with the contributor) thinks fit.

(396) Whether the contributor has or has not dependants the whole period of incapacity during which the owner has maintained him is to be treated as if he had been in receipt of sickness benefit for the purpose of calculating the rate and duration of sickness benefit (Section 48 (1)).

(xi.) SUSPENSION FROM ORDINARY BENEFITS ON MARRIAGE.

(397) A woman Deposit Contributor is suspended from ordinary benefits on ceasing to be employed on or after marriage. Two-thirds of the sum standing to her credit in the Deposit Contributors Fund may be applied in providing a sum of 5s. a week on confinement during a period not exceeding four weeks on any one occasion; or under certain conditions and in the discretion of the Committee, in providing payments during any period of sickness or distress (1911 Act, Section 44 (4), and Married Women's Consolidated Regulations, 1915). If at any time after suspension she again becomes employed she will be entitled to ordinary sickness and maternity benefits only after the usual waiting period of 26 weeks, and after payment of 26 contributions.

(xii.) INCAPACITY DUE TO CONFINEMENT.

(398) An unmarried woman is not entitled to sickness benefit for a period of four weeks after her confinement unless she is suffering from an illness not connected directly or indirectly with her confinement (1911 Act, Section 8 (6)). Subject to the above condition, no distinction should be drawn as regards the payment of sickness benefit between incapacity due to pregnancy and incapacity due to other causes. The additional maternity benefit for insured married women (*see* paragraph (409)) is given in lieu of sickness benefit in respect of the four weeks after confinement.

(xiii.) SEAMEN, MARINES, AND SOLDIERS.

(399) Seamen, marines, and soldiers are not entitled to sickness benefit during service. On discharge, they are treated, subject

to the provisions of Sec. 79 of the Act of 1911, as employed contributors (unless, being qualified, they become voluntary contributors), and they therefore become entitled to the ordinary benefits subject to the usual conditions. A discharged man whose state of health would prevent him from gaining admission to an Approved Society will normally not return to Deposit Insurance, but will become entitled to the ordinary benefits out of the Navy and Army Fund.

(C) PAYMENT.

(400) Sickness benefit is ordinarily payable as from the fourth day of the incapacity. It should be noted in this connection that a Sunday is not treated as a day of incapacity for the purposes of the waiting period unless the insured person would, but for the illness, have worked on that day (1913 Act, Section 13).

Where, however, a Deposit Contributor has received sickness benefit for one illness and falls ill again within 12 months of his recovery, his second illness is to be treated as a continuation of the first, *i.e.* sickness benefit begins from the first day and can only continue until 26 weeks' benefit (*including the first illness*) has been paid (but *see* paragraph (381)) above for procedure in compensation cases where only partial sickness benefit is paid in respect of the first incapacity) (1911 Act, Section 8 (5)), as amended by 1913 Act, Section 12).

(D) PROCEDURE IN DEALING WITH CLAIMS.

(401) The procedure to enable a Deposit Contributor to claim sickness benefit is as follows:—

The contributor (like a member of a Society) will be furnished by his doctor with a certificate on Form Med. 40 in lieu of the certificate at the back of the ordinary claim form (Form 27/I.C.) which was used prior to 1st January 1915.

When the contributor receives a first certificate of incapacity on Form Med. 40 he should complete it and send it to the Insurance Committee, who will thereupon send him Form 27/I.C. with instructions for its completion and return with the next certificate received.

When the contributor receives a second (Intermediate or Final) certificate, he should complete the front page of Form 27/I.C., attach the certificate to it, and forward both to the Insurance Committee together with his insurance book and current contribution card. The Committee should furnish its certificate to the Commissioners (39 Buckingham Terrace, Edinburgh) on Form 335/A.G.D. If the illness continues after the date of the second medical certificate the contributor should fill up the right hand side of the further certificates received from the doctor and send them to the Committee. Further claims on Form 27/I.C. are not necessary.

(402) A copy of Form 625/A.G.D., notifying certain changes

in procedure, should be attached by the Committee to each Form 27/I.C. issued, the doctor's certificate forms and the first four instructions on the back of that form being cancelled before issue. When returned by the contributor, the Form 27/I.C. should be retained by the Committee.

(403) In examining claims prior to certification the Insurance Committee should satisfy itself—

    (*a*) that the medical certificates are duly signed and in order;

    (*b*) that the incapacity for work is not due to an accident or disease in respect of which compensation would seem to be payable.

    (*c*) that the contributor if employed under Section 47 or 53 (which is generally shown by the rate of contribution on his card) has received payment of wages according to that Section.

Where it is ascertained that a contributor is in receipt of compensation at a lower weekly rate than that of the sickness benefit to which he would otherwise be entitled the claim should be certified in the usual way, and the rate of compensation stated on the certificate.

(404) Since it has been the experience of the Commissioners that confusion has arisen at various times between two persons of the same name and resident at the same address (more especially in the case of Model Lodging Houses), the Committee should in every case insist on the contributor forwarding his insurance book with his claim. Where the insurance book is not available the Deposit Contributor's number should be stated, failing which Form 301D/A.G.D. should be completed by the contributor in order that his identity as a Deposit Contributor may be established. It is also essential that the current contribution card should be obtained and forwarded to the Commissioners.

(405) Should the Committee receive an application for sickness benefit from a person in respect of whom it does not hold an index slip, Form 335/A.G.D. should be noted " No index slip received," and forwarded to the Commissioners together with the contributors insurance book or Form 301D/A.G.D.

SECTION (VI.)—DISABLEMENT BENEFIT.

(406) When a contributor's right to sickness benefit has been exhausted, *i.e.* after 26 weeks' sickness benefit has been paid, he becomes entitled to Disablement Benefit if properly qualified. The qualifications necessary are that the contributor must have been in insurance for 104 weeks and have paid 104 contributions. The benefit commences immediately sickness benefit ceases.

Owing to the basis of the deposit scheme, however, these conditions can be fulfilled at present only by a Deposit Contributor who has been transferred from an Approved Society from which he has received Disablement Benefit or Sickness Benefit for a period approaching the maximum.

SECTION (VII.)—MATERNITY BENEFIT.

GENERAL.

(407) Maternity Benefit is a payment in respect of a confinement, the word "confinement" meaning labour resulting in the issue of a living child or labour after 28 weeks of pregnancy resulting in the issue of a child whether alive or dead.

(408) The amount of the payment is 30s. in ordinary circumstances, and where the sum standing to the credit of the contributor permits of the full benefit being paid. In the case of aliens, the amount is reduced by $\frac{2}{5}$ths if the benefit is in respect of a man's insurance, and by $\frac{1}{4}$th if in respect of a woman's insurance (1911 Act, Section 45). It should be noted, however, that this reduction does not apply in respect of the insurance of an alien whose wife before marriage was a British subject, and of such a woman's own insurance (1913 Act, Section 20).

(409) Where a woman is married (or in the case of a posthumous child a widow) and uninsured, one Maternity Benefit is payable in respect of her husband's insurance. An insured woman is entitled to receive two Maternity Benefits, one in respect of her own insurance and one in respect of her husband's. If her husband is not insured or not qualified for Maternity Benefit on account of insufficiency in number of contributions paid or in the sum standing to his credit she may receive two Maternity Benefits from her own insurance (1913 Act, Section 14).

Thus if the husband is or was a member of a Society, but Maternity Benefit is not payable owing to the qualifying contributions not having been paid, or to arrears, the woman, if she is a Deposit Contributor is entitled to two Maternity Benefits if, and so far as, the balance in her account in the Deposit Contributors Fund admits (1913 Act, Section 14 (2) (*a*)).

If the husband is a Deposit Contributor but the amount standing to his credit is insufficient to provide the full Maternity Benefit in respect of his insurance, the woman, if she is a Deposit Contributor is entitled (if, and so far as, the balance in her account admits) to both Maternity Benefits less the amount paid from her husband's insurance (1913 Act, Section 14 (2) (*b*)). (In connection with the payment of these claims see paragraph (412) below).

(410) In this connection it should be observed that a woman receiving a second Maternity Benefit must abstain from remunerative employment during the four weeks following her confinement under the Rules made by the Committee in pursuance of Section 14 (3) of the 1913 Act. Any penalties imposed for breaches of this rule should not exceed in the aggregate the sum payable in respect of the Maternity Benefit.

(411) Maternity Benefit is in all cases the mother's benefit, whether payable in respect of her husband's or her own insur-

ance, and the Committee must administer it in the interest of the mother and child in cash or otherwise as they think fit. If the benefit is to be paid to the husband, the wife's authority for making the payment to him must be obtained before the certificate of payment is sent to the Commissioners.

QUALIFICATIONS.

(412) The necessary qualifications for any payment of Maternity Benefit are as follows :—
- (a) The contributor must have been in insurance for 26 weeks (in the case of a voluntary contributor for 52 weeks).
- (b) He must have paid 26 contributions (in the case of a voluntary contributor 52 contributions).
- (c) In the case of a male contributor, either he or his wife must be resident in the United Kingdom, or in the case of a female contributor, she must reside in the United Kingdom (but see paragraph following).

(413) Where Maternity Benefit is payable in respect of the husband's insurance it will be paid if either he or his wife is in the United Kingdom at the time of the confinement. It will be payable from the husband's insurance if he is at the time of the confinement temporarily living in the Isle of Man, or the Channel Islands, even although the wife is resident abroad. Where the benefit is payable in respect of the wife's insurance, it will be paid if, at the time of the confinement she is in the United Kingdom, or temporarily living in the Isle of Man or the Channel Islands, but not if she is abroad.

(414) With regard to contributors who have emigrated, but whose wives have remained in this country, it must be remembered that no benefit is payable in respect of any contributor who has ceased to be an insured person. The first question to be determined, therefore, is whether he is, or is not, still an insured person. If it is known that he is only abroad temporarily, he remains an insured person; and the fact of his wife's continuance in the United Kingdom may ordinarily be taken as sufficient evidence that he has not yet permanently taken up his residence abroad. If, however, he has definitely removed his residence no benefit is payable in respect of his insurance unless he does in fact return to the United Kingdom under circumstances that indicate that his absence was temporary and did not involve cessation of insurance. In the meantime he is treated as being out of insurance, and in consequence his wife, if she is herself an employed contributor, is entitled both to ordinary and to second maternity benefit from her own Society.

MODIFYING CIRCUMSTANCES.

(415) There are certain circumstances under which, although the qualifications mentioned in paragraph (412) above may be

satisfied, Maternity Benefit is not payable, or at least is payable only subject to modifications as described in the paragraphs following. These circumstances are :—
    (d) when the woman to whom benefit is payable is in a poorhouse, or charity or rate-supported hospital, asylum, convalescent home, infirmary, or sanatorium (*see* paragraph (383) above).
    (e) When arrangements are made for providing the services of a midwife or doctor as part of the benefit.

Benefit when the Mother is in Hospital, etc.

(416) No payment can be made on account of Maternity Benefit while the mother is in any charity or rate-supported institution as defined in paragraph (383) above.

(417) If the mother has dependants, it must be applied in whole or in part for the relief of such dependants in such a manner as the Committee thinks fit after consultation with the mother wherever possible.

Where, however, an additional Maternity Benefit is payable as well as the primary benefit (*e.g.* in the case of the insured married woman) provision for the wife's dependants is made out of the additional Maternity Benefit. The primary benefit is not available for dependants.

(418) If the woman to whom benefit is payable is an inmate of a hospital, asylum, convalescent home, or infirmary, any of the benefit which is not paid to dependants may be applied in the provision of surgical appliances. If not so expended it must be paid in cash to the contributor when she leaves the institution, either in a lump sum or in instalments, as the Committee thinks fit.

Provision of Midwife or Doctor.

(419) Under Section 18 of the Act of 1911 Insurance Committees have power to administer Maternity Benefit " in cash or otherwise." A Committee may, therefore, if it thinks fit, instead of paying the whole of the benefit in cash, administer part of it by arranging that the mother will have the services of a midwife possessing the qualifications prescribed in the Qualifications of Midwives (Scotland) Regulations, 1912, or a doctor. The value of the services rendered will then be part of the Maternity Benefit, and the balance will be available for payment in cash or otherwise.

(420) In any such arrangements, however, due effect must be given to the proviso to Section 18 of the 1911 Act that the mother shall have free choice in the selection of the doctor or midwife by whom she is to be attended, and for this purpose it will be necessary for the Committee to supply to Deposit Contributors on application lists of the doctors or midwives whose services are available.

PROCEDURE.

(421) Claims for Maternity Benefit may be made according to the circumstances as follows :—
- (a) by a husband from his own account ;
- (b) by a wife from her husband's account ;
- (c) by a wife or unmarried woman from her own account ;
- (d) a wife may claim further benefit from her own account because—
    - (1) her husband is a member of a Society, but nothing has been paid by his Society as he is not qualified ;
    - (2) her husband is a Deposit Contributor, but full Maternity Benefit has not been paid in respect of his insurance ;
    - (3) her husband is not insured.
- (e) by the wife of a sailor or soldier on service in respect of her husband's insurance.

(422) In every case notice of the confinement should be given to the Insurance Committee within seven days, and where the claim for Maternity Benefit is in respect of the husband, it should be accompanied by a copy of his marriage certificate or such other evidence of the marriage as the Committee may think fit.

(a) *Claim by Husband.*

(423) When a Committee receives intimation of a claim for benefit, a Form 27B/I.C., should be issued to the husband.

If the husband is an alien, information should be obtained as to the wife's nationality before marriage (*see* paragraph (408) above). On receipt of the completed form the Committee should certify the claim on Form 341/A.G.D. and forward it to the Commissioners with the current Contribution Card and Insurance Book, or Form 301D as in the case of claims for Sickness Benefit (*see* paragraph (404) above). (*See* also paragraph (411) above in regard to authority for making payment of Maternity Benefit to the husband.)

(b) *Claim by Wife from Husband's Account.*

(424) Where the wife claims Maternity Benefit from the husband's account a Form, 27B/I.C., should be sent to the wife, and the husband's signature to the claim obtained. If for any reason this cannot be procured, the Committee should ascertain his present address and request an extract certificate of marriage (*see* paragraph (422) above). On receipt of the claim it should be certified on Form 341/A.G.D. as described in the preceding paragraph.

If there is no evidence to show that the husband is aware of the claim, he should be informed that Maternity Benefit is being claimed, so that if he should have a prior claim for Sickness

Benefit he may be able to inform the Committee. In this case the certificate on Form 341/A.G.D. should not be sent to the Commissioners until a week has elapsed after the date of the notification sent to the husband.

(c) *Claim by Mother from own Account.*

(425) A Form 27C/I.C. should be issued to and completed by the claimant and certified by the Committee on Form 341A/A.G.D.

(d) *Further claim by Wife from own Account.*

(1) *Husband Society Member.*

(426) A signed statement from the husband's Society should be obtained from the wife showing that he is not entitled to Maternity Benefit and giving the reason. A supplementary certificate on Form 341A/A.G.D. should then be forwarded to the Commissioners.

(2) *Husband Deposit Contributor.*

If the husband is a Deposit Contributor, but full Maternity Benefit has not been paid in respect of his insurance as in case (d) (2) above the husband's number as a Deposit Contributor should be obtained and a supplementary certificate submitted in the ordinary way. (The Committee will ordinarily be able to satisfy itself that less than the full amount has been paid in respect of the husband's insurance by reference to the notifications of payments received from the Commissioners.)

(3) *Husband not Insured.*

Where the wife claims further payment from her own account because her husband is not insured, a certificate should be obtained from the husband to the following effect,

" I declare that I am the husband of.................... Deposit Contributor No............ that I am not liable to compulsory insurance under the National Insurance Acts, and that I am not insured thereunder as a voluntary contributor."

A supplementary certificate on Form 341A/A.G.D. should then be forwarded to the Commissioners.

(427) The Committee should in no circumstances delay forwarding the certificate for payment of the wife's claim for payment of benefit from her own account because a supplementary claim in respect of the first Maternity Benefit is pending, or is under investigation.

(e) *Claim by Wife of Soldier or Sailor in respect of Husband's Insurance.*

(428) (a) *If the husband is a Seaman or Marine,* Active Service rating, application for a claim form should be made by the wife to the Accountant General of the Navy, Admiralty, London, S.W. The form contains full instructions as to how to make the claim.

(b) *If he is a regular Soldier* (including those now enlisted for the period of the war), application for a claim form should be made by the wife to the Paymaster by whom the wife's Separation Allowance is paid. The form contains full instructions as to how to make the claim.

(c) *If he is a Naval Reservist or Naval Volunteer, or entered in the Navy for the period of the war, or an Army Reservist or Territorial,* application should be made by the wife to the Secretary, National Health Insurance Commission, 29 Queen Anne's Gate, London, S.W.

To avoid delay in the payment of benefit it will be well to apply about a month before the expected date of confinement.

It is desirable that information should be given when the application for the claim form is made, as to whether any cards were stamped for him before service, and if so, how each card was disposed of. If he has a Deposit Contributor's Insurance Book it should be enclosed with the application where possible, or his number as a Deposit Contributor should be quoted in the letter.

To avoid delay it is important that all applications and letters should show the husband's full name, his ship or regiment, his rating or rank, and his official or regimental number.

SECTION (VIII.)—ADMINISTRATIVE PROCEDURE IN CONNECTION WITH DEPOSIT CONTRIBUTORS.

(429) With the view of relieving Insurance Committees of a large amount of administrative detail, the *accounts* of Deposit Contributors are kept on a centralised system at the offices of the Commissioners.

On an account being established in respect of a Deposit Contributor an *index slip* is issued by the Commissioners to the Insurance Committee of the area in which such Deposit Contributor is resident.

The slips are sent out in batches under cover of Form 311 A.G.D. Should any of the index slips sent to an area be found to be in respect of Deposit Contributors resident in other areas, the index slips should be sent to the proper area and the Commissioners notified by attaching to the receipt for the index slips (Form 311 A.G.D.) a Form. 312 A.G.D., giving the numbers of the index slips reallotted. A separate Form, 312 A.G.D., should be used for each new area. Should any index slips be forwarded to an area which are not applicable to that area, and for the reallotment of which there is insufficient knowledge the index slips should be returned to the Commissioners with a list on Form 313 A.G.D.

(430) On a Deposit Contributor intimating a *change of address* which involves a change of area, a removal slip giving the old and new addresses is sent to the Insurance Committee of the

new area. It falls to this Committee to see that the contributor surrenders his medical card, the appropriate part of which should be forwarded to the former Insurance Committee, who will then send the index slip to the Commissioners. They will have the change recorded and the slip sent to the new Committee who will issue a new medical card.

(431) When a Deposit Contributor is *suspended from benefits* an orange slip is sent to the relative Insurance Committee, who should inform the contributor and the doctor. After having had further contributions credited to his account a Deposit Contributor may be reinstated in benefits. A list of all such cases is sent to the Insurance Committee, who advises the doctor and the contributor. If, on receiving notification of suspension or reinstatement an Insurance Committee has a removal slip showing that the Deposit Contributor has recently removed to the area, the steps indicated above in respect of change of address should be expedited. Should, however, an Insurance Committee find that it has neither index slip nor removal slip, the suspension slip or reinstatement notice should be returned to the Commissioners with a statement to that effect.

(432) When a Deposit Contributor *joins an Approved Society*, the Insurance Committee is notified by means of the removal slip. In this instance search should be made as to whether an index slip has been received from the Society to which the Deposit Contributor has transferred. If the Society Index Slip is traced the Deposit Contributor's Index Slip should be returned to the Commissioners at once, but, should the Society Index Slip be missing, the Deposit Contributor's Index Slip should be retained, the Society communicated with, and the Deposit Contributor's Index Slip returned to the Commissioners on receipt of the Society Index slip.

(433) In cases where an Insurance Committee receives intimation that a Deposit Contributor is *deceased or has passed out of Insurance*, or where by receipt of a Society Index Slip duly noted as being in respect of a former Deposit Contributor it comes to their knowledge that a Deposit Contributor has joined an Approved Society, the Deposit Contributor's Index Slip should be returned to the Commissioners with a reference to the name of the Society and the membership number therein.

There should never be any necessity for an Insurance Committee to retain in its Index Register a suspense slip in respect of a Deposit Contributor. On application to the Commissioners the Committee will be advised whether an account for the contributor has been opened, and if so where the index slip is.

CHAPTER VII.

FINANCE AND ACCOUNTING OF INSURANCE COMMITTEES.

(434) REFERENCE is made in dealing with this division of the subject to the following Regulations :—
  (1) National Health Insurance (Payments to Insurance Committees) Regulations (Scotland), 1914 ;
  (2) National Health Insurance (Medical Benefit) Regulations (Scotland), 1913 ;
  (3) National Health Insurance (Accounts of Insurance Committees) Regulations, 1915 (issued in Draft, and dated 3rd August 1915).

Throughout the Chapter the first of these is referred to as the "Paragraph (F) Regulations" from their being framed under the provisions of Section 28 and Paragraph (F) of the First Schedule to the National Insurance Act, 1913 ; the second "the Medical Benefit Regulations," and the last "the Accounts Regulations."

SECTION (L)—INCOME.

(435) The income of Insurance Committees is dealt with under the following heads :—
  (1) Medical Benefit, including Ordinary and Special Income ;
  (2) Sanatorium Benefit ;
  (3) Administration ;
  (4) General Purposes ;
  (5) Transfer between Funds.

1. MEDICAL BENEFIT INCOME.

(a) GENERAL MEDICAL BENEFIT FUND.

(436) This fund is established by the Commissioners in accordance with the provisions of Part IV. of the Medical Benefit Regulations. Into the fund are carried all the sums at the disposal of Insurance Committees for the purposes of medical benefit. They include the sums available under Sections 15 (6) and (8) and 42 (d) and (e) of the Principal Act and Sections 1 and 9 of the Act of 1913.

(436) The annual cost of a full year's medical attendance and treatment of each insured person entitled to benefit is at present as follows :—

	s.	d.
Charge to Societies and Deposit Contributors and for exempt persons, (less State Grant in case of British subjects)	6	0
Special Parliamentary Grant (including Aliens) ..	2	6
Transfer from sanatorium income for domiciliary treatment	0	6

(437) The major part of the income raised by these debits is the sum derived from the charge made against Societies and Deposit Contributors and for exempt persons in respect of the cost of medical benefit. Of the actual amount, which, in terms of Article 32 of the Medical Benefit Regulations, is reached by agreement between Societies and Insurance Committees, or in the other two cases is fixed by the Commissioners, there is charged to the Society 7/9ths in respect of male and 3/4ths in respect of female members who are British subjects. These amounts are supplemented by the State's proportion of 2/9ths and 1/4th as the case may be, as provided by Section 3 of the 1911 Act. The full amount is charged to the Society in respect of Aliens (Section 45 (1) (*d*) of 1911 Act).

(438) In the case of Societies the method of ascertaining the sum payable is, under the provisions of Article 5 of the Paragraph (F) Regulations, as follows :—

(*a*) The Commissioners ascertain the number of insured persons (other than persons who are masters, seamen, or apprentices on foreign-going ships in the Mercantile Marine) whose contribution cards for the first half-year of the year in respect of which the calculation is made have before a date to be determined by the Commissioners been forwarded by each Society to the Commissioners, and who were for the whole or any part of that half-year entitled to medical benefit.

(*b*) Each Society ascertains, as on a date to be determined by the Commissioners, and furnishes to the Commissioners a return of (i.) the number of members of the Society who were at the commencement of the said year of the age of seventy and upwards, and were during the first half-year of that year entitled to medical benefit, and (ii.) the number of members, being masters, seamen, or apprentices in foreign-going ships in the Mercantile Marine in respect of whom contributions were paid for that half-year, and who were during the whole or any part of that half-year entitled to medical benefit.

(*c*) The sum of the three numbers so obtained is the number upon which the amount to be debited to each Society is based.

Cards which are surrendered after the date fixed by the Commissioners are included when surrendered in the numbers for the year then under calculation.

(439) *Alternatively*, a Society may, if the Commissioners so allow or require, be charged on the ascertained number of its members entitled to medical benefit at the end of the first half-year of any year and the sum payable by the Society in respect of Medical benefit for that year will then be calculated on the basis of the number so ascertained.

(440) Power is reserved to the Commissioners to make (*a*) such adjustments as may be necessary to secure that the sum debited to each Society is equal to the amount which is determined to be payable, and (*b*) such further adjustments, if any, as are in their opinion required to meet the case of insured persons who have in the course of the year been transferred from one Society to another, or being Deposit Contributors have become members of Societies or *vice versa*, or who during the year become or cease to be insured under the provisions of Section 46 of the Principal Act as amended by the National Insurance (Navy and Army) Acts of 1914 and 1914 (Session 2). (*See* List of Acts, Appendix I.)

(*b*) DISTRIBUTION OF CENTRAL POOL TO COMMITTEES.

Apportionment of Fund.

(441) The General Medical Benefit Fund or Pool having thus been formed, its apportionment among the various Insurance Committees takes place as follows :—

(1) In the case of each Committee the number of insured and exempt persons included in the Register of the Committee at the commencement of each quarter of the year and entitled at that date to medical benefit, as ascertained by the quarterly Counts made by the Committee but subject to any adjustments in terms of Article 29 of the Medical Benefit Regulations, is calculated and the sum of the four numbers divided by four.

(2) Subject to any adjustments between the General Medical Benefit Fund and any similar funds under the control and management of the English or Welsh Insurance Commissioners, made by the Joint Committee under the powers conferred on them by Sub-Section (2) of Section 83 of the 1911 Act, and to any deductions made in respect of persons the cost of whose medical benefit is defrayed out of the Central Medical Benefit Fund, in accordance with any Regulations for the administration of medical benefit made by the Commissioners and for the time being in force, the sums in the General Medical Benefit Fund are to be apportioned amongst the several Committees in proportion to the number obtained in the case of each Committee

under the provisions of the preceding part of this paragraph, and the sum so apportioned to each Committee is the sum available to that Committee for the purposes of medical benefit in that year. (Par. (F), Regs. 12.)

(442) As it is thus in practice not possible to constitute the Fund and to pay or credit at the commencement of each year to each Committee the income available to it, provision is made by Article 5 (2) of the Paragraph (F) Regulations for a provisional debit to Societies in any year of an amount calculated by reference to the amounts payable by the Society for the previous year, or in the case of a new Society calculated in such manner as the Commissioners may determine.

Advances to Committees.

(443) In order that Insurance Committees may not be without funds, advances are made to them out of the General Medical Benefit Fund of such sums as may be required for the purpose of medical benefit to an extent such that the advances do not exceed the proper proportion of the sums estimated to be due to the Committee. In the event of any Committee requiring money before any sums have been credited to the General Medical Benefit Fund the Commissioners may, if they think fit, make such advances from the General Balances in the Scottish National Health Insurance Fund as appear to them to be reasonable, pending the ascertainments of the accounts due to be credited to its several accounts (Par (F), Regs. 11).

(*c*) MEDICAL BENEFIT FUND ACCOUNT.

(444) All moneys payable to an Insurance Committee out of the General Medical Benefit Fund, including the State Grant and the Special Parliamentary Grant of 2s. 6d. per insured person, but excluding the Special Drug Fund and Mileage Fund are carried to the credit of the Committee's Medical Benefit Fund Account (Medical Benefit Regs. 33 (1)). In practice it is also found convenient to carry to the credit of this fund before distribution the sum payable from the Sanatorium Benefit Account in respect of the obligation to treat cases recommended for domiciliary treatment of tuberculosis. The allocation of the Fund by Committees is dealt with under Section II. of this chapter.

(*d*) CENTRAL MEDICAL BENEFIT FUND.

Constitution.

(445) The fund is established for the purpose of defraying the cost of the medical benefit of temporary residents (Medical Benefit Regs. 41). A temporary resident is a person who has moved into

the area with the intention of residing there for a period of less than three months.

(446) The following is an outline of the system under which this fund is worked. Medical treatment given to persons temporarily resident outwith the area of their home Insurance Committee (except persons making own arrangements) and to all persons in possession of " travellers' vouchers " is paid for upon the basis of the scale of fees set out in the Fifth Schedule to the Medical Benefit Regulations. It should be kept in mind that the capitation fees (including the domiciliary 6d.) in respect of persons holding travellers' vouchers are not credited to Committees, but are carried direct to the Central Medical Benefit Fund.

(447) To facilitate financial adjustments between the funds of individual Committees, a special system has been devised.

A "case value" obtained by dividing the amount of the Panel Service Fund by the number of cases of disease or disablement of persons upon panel lists who receive treatment throughout the year is annually ascertained by the Commissioners in respect of each Committee. The basis of the calculation is the information derived from the Medical Records kept by the practitioners. Similar " case values " are also ascertained for persons entitled to receive treatment through approved institutions.

(448) The Committee will then be debited with the relative " case value " in respect of each person for whose treatment it is responsible, who has obtained any treatment as a temporary resident during the year. Careful note is kept of the methods of receiving treatment in his home area selected by each such "temporary resident," in order that the debits against the Committee may be placed against the appropriate funds, Practitioners and Drug Funds, or Institutions Fund, as the case may be (Medical Benefit Regs. 41).

(449) The debits referred to, other than those for international temporary residents, together with any sums similarly receivable from the other Commissions in respect of English, Welsh, or Irish insured persons who have received treatment in Scotland, are carried to the Central Medical Benefit Fund, and the total, including capitation fees in respect of travellers, is subdivided into Central Panel and Central Drug Funds, in the proportions of 13/17ths and 4/17ths respectively (Medical Benefit Regs. 41 and 42).

Distribution to Committees.

(450) The accounts presented by the Insurance Committees whose panel practitioners and chemists have given treatment, drugs, and appliances to " temporary residents " or " travellers " are then considered and the amounts thereof ascertained.

(451) The accounts of doctors and approved institutions for treatment should be calculated in accordance with the scale in the Fifth Schedule to the Medical Benefit Regulations and those

of chemists, doctors, and institutions for drugs according to the Drug Tariff. The sums so ascertained should be credited to the practitioners, chemists, and institutions by the Committee, and an account thereof be sent to the Commissioners within one month after the end of the year (Medical Benefit Regs. 42 (1)).

(452) The Central Drug Fund is first applied as far as it will go in crediting Committees with the amounts of the drug bills presented, and so much of the resulting balance, if any, as does not exceed one-fourth of the amount originally carried to the Fund is transferred to the Central Panel Fund, but any further balance remains to the credit of the Central Drug Fund in the ensuing year (Medical Benefit Regs. 42 (3) and (4)). The principle of the "floating sixpence" is thus applied to the Central Medical Benefit Fund.

(453) The Central Panel Fund augmented as above is then divided amongst Committees in proportion to the amounts of doctors' bills submitted by each, and the amounts so ascertained are advised to Committees as special credits. It is to be noted that the sums paid to Insurance Committees from the Central Medical Benefit Fund do not pass into the Panel Service Fund for the general purposes of that fund, but are to be carried to the Temporary Residents Fund Account, and paid direct to the individual doctors who have given treatment to temporary residents.

Distribution to Doctors and Chemists.

(454) The procedure to be adopted by Insurance Committees in allocating to individual doctors and chemists the amounts credited out of the Central Panel and Central Drug Funds is as follows :—

(455) In the first place the chemists' accounts are met either in full or to such lesser extent as the sum transferred from the Central Drug Fund will permit (Medical Benefit Regs. 42 (3)).

(456) The sums obtained from the Central Panel Fund are to be distributed to practitioners or institutions giving treatment to temporary residents in proportion to the amounts of accounts submitted. The amounts so paid may involve a discounting of the accounts or a dividend thereon, but the whole sum available is distributed annually, and the rate of discount or bonus is a flat one for the whole country, whether the temporary residents are of Scottish, English, Welsh, or Irish origin (Medical Benefit Regs. 42 (7)).

(e) DIAGRAM.

(457) The diagram which is printed in Appendix XVIII. displays graphically but not exhaustively the passage of medical benefit moneys through the various accounts. It illustrates the passage of the money from its various sources to its ultimate destinations, but no attempt has been made to illustrate the respective funds by comparison. It has to be kept in view that some of the funds are central ones others local.

(f) Special Income for Medical Benefit.

(458) The ordinary income of the Committee for medical benefit, including the Special Parliamentary Grant of 2s. 6d. per insured person and the sum of 6d. per insured person, specially transferred from sanatorium benefit has been dealt with above. In addition there is available for Committees the following additional sources of special income : —

(1) Parliamentary Special Mileage Grants.
(2) Parliamentary Special Drug Grant.

Special Mileage Grants.

(459) Special Mileage Grants have been provided for Highland and Lowland County Committees. The Grant for the Highlands and Islands, including the Highlands of Perthshire, was in the past made to the Commissioners and distributed by them to the Committees under a scheme approved by the Treasury. (*See* Appendix XIX.) In future this Grant will form part of the monies placed at the disposal of the Highlands and Islands Board for the improvement of the Medical Service in the Highlands and Islands, and falling to be distributed under a scheme to be approved by the Secretary for Scotland and the Treasury.

The Grant for the Lowland Counties amounted to £16,000, being the share allocated to Scotland of a Grant of £50,000 to the National Health Insurance Joint Committee. The Scheme under which the sum of £16,000 was distributed ·to the Committees was approved by the Treasury and is printed in Appendix XIX. The circumstances of each Committee were fully considered by the Commissioners following on inquiry into the circumstances of each area, and grants made accordingly. These amounts are disbursed by the Committees to the doctors in the area for mileage and special charges under the scheme. A distinct record of the expenditure out of these grants must be kept by Committees.

For 1915 the Grant to the Joint Committee is £54,000, and the share apportioned to Scotland £20,000, the additional £4000 or such part thereof as is necessary being applied for the improvement of the medical service of sparsely populated and necessitous districts in the lowlands.

Special Drug Grant.

(460) The Special Drug Grant of £30,000 per annum for the whole United Kingdom was voted by Parliament to meet deficits on drug funds of Committees due to special charges consequent on the outbreak of an epidemic of disease in the area or other abnormal conditions. It is to be administered under a scheme prepared by the Joint Committee and approved by the Treasury.

2. SANATORIUM BENEFIT INCOME.

(a) GENERAL SANATORIUM BENEFIT FUND.

Constitution of Fund.

(461) The income under this head is derived from the charges made to Societies and Deposit Contributors, being the amount of 1s. 3d. per insured person resident in the area of each Insurance Committee which is made available by Section 16 (2) of the Act of 1911, together with the premium of the same amount in respect of each exempt person in terms of Section 9 of the Act of 1913. In terms of Sections 3 and 45 (1) (*d*) of the 1911 Act there is contributed except in respect of aliens from monies provided by Parliament 2/9ths in the case of men and 1/4th in the case of women of the amount due for the cost of sanatorium benefit. Societies and Deposit Contributors with certain exceptions and the Exempt Persons Fund are accordingly charged with the remaining 7/9ths or 3/4ths, and the amounts arrived at, together with the State proportion, are carried to an Account in the Commissioners books known as the General Sanatorium Benefit Fund. The method of forming this General Fund or Pool is set out in Part III. of the Paragraph (F) Regulations.

(462) Under Section 61 of the 1911 Act it is provided that " all sums available for sanatorium benefit . . . in any year shall be paid or credited to the Insurance Committee at the commencement of that year." In view of this provision and of the fact that the amount of a Committee's Sanatorium Benefit Income is not like its Medical Benefit Income determined by agreement but fixed by the Statute itself, it follows that, under the 1911 Act, the Sanatorium Benefit Income of the Committee required to be fixed for any year by reference to the number of insured persons resident in the area at the beginning of the year without adjustment either in respect of any fluctuations in the insured population of the area occurring subsequently during the year or in repect of any increase during the year of the insured population throughout the whole country.

(463) Part III. of the Paragraph (F) Regulations, however, in virtue of the terms of Section 28 of the 1913 Act, embodies an important modification in the basis of crediting Insurance Committees with their Sanatorium Benefit Income. Under the Regulations. the credits to Committees for sanatorium benefit are based, like those for medical benefit, upon a mean calculation of the insured population of each area and of the country as a whole during the year.

Distribution of Fund amongst Committees.

(464) The General Sanatorium Benefit Fund as made up is thus allocated to Insurance Committees by the same method as that employed in the case of the General Medical Benefit Fund already described, save that the basis of calculation is the number

of insured persons entitled to sanatorium benefit instead of the number entitled to medical benefit. The sums so apportioned to Committees are subject to deductions to meet "case values" which fall to be credited to the Central Sanatorium Benefit Fund in respect of "Strays" as explained in the immediately following paragraphs, and also to the transfer to medical benefit of 6d. per insured person in respect of the obligation of practitioners on the panel to afford domiciliary treatment of tuberculous persons on their lists if recommended by the Committee, and to the transfer by the Committee to its Administration Account of a reasonable sum to cover cost of administration.

(b) CENTRAL SANATORIUM BENEFIT FUND.

Provision for " Strays."

(465) While provision is made as above described for the income of Committees being adjusted to the fluctuations in their insured population due, *inter alia*, to removals in and out of the area, financial machinery is established under Part IV. of the Paragraph (F) Regulations whereby further adjustments are effected in respect of a particular class of removals which deserve special consideration.

(466) It has been found that difficult questions are apt to arise as to the liability of Committees to entertain applications for sanatorium benefit from insured persons temporarily resident in, or having recently removed into, a given area, and as to the principles determining, in any given set of circumstances in which an insured person desired to exercise his undoubted right under the National Insurance Acts of applying for the benefit, the Committee upon whom devolves under those Acts the corresponding duty of considering and dealing with his application. A procedure has accordingly been devised whereby a "case value" adjustment is effected, subject to certain conditions, in respect of a class of insured persons termed for the purpose of the regulations "removal cases."

(467) Experience suggests that in the case of persons who become tuberculous there is a distinct tendency to migrate soon after infection, and this in many cases not with any intention to return, but with the object of escaping from the surroundings in which the disease was contracted, securing more favourable climatic conditions, taking advantage of more efficient treatment, or for other reasons which differentiate their case from that of the "temporary resident" under medical benefit. In such cases it would appear that the area to which the tuberculous person removes is at a distinct disadvantage as against the area which has hitherto derived benefit from his contributions during health, and the system of case value adjustment is accordingly applied not, as in the case of medical benefit, to those insured persons who enter the area with the intention of not remaining for more than three months, but (subject to the exceptions in-

dicated below) to those persons who apply to the Committee for sanatorium benefit within three months of their removal into the area. In a " removal case," therefore, recommended by a Committee for sanatorium benefit, a case value will (subject to the exceptions specified later) be debited against the Committee from whose area the removal took place.

(468) The adjustments as between Scottish Insurance Committees in this connection fall to be made on the basis of a national case value arrived at by dividing the total expenditure on sanatorium benefit (exclusive of payments to doctors for treatment of domiciliary cases and sums transferred to the administration account) by the total number of cases recommended for all kinds of treatment. International adjustments will be made between the Scottish Central pool and the Central pools in England, Wales, and Ireland, the respective debits being adjusted between the Commissions.

(469) The case value debits, when ascertained, along with the monies available in respect of travellers, as after mentioned, are pooled in a Central Sanatorium Benefit Fund. This Fund as finally constituted in respect of the year will be distributed amongst Insurance Committees in the proportions which the number of each Committee's recommendations of cases of removal into the area for which a case value debit is made against another Committee, and of travellers, soldiers, and sailors after mentioned bears to the total number of recommendations of such cases.

(470) For the proper protection of the funds of Insurance Committees some exceptions require to be made from the general rule that a case value debit is payable in respect of every insured person who is recommended for sanatorium benefit on an application made within three months of his removal into the area. It would obviously be unreasonable that an insured person whose case had already been under consideration by one Committee, and who was entitled under their recommendation to the form of treatment nominated by them, should be at liberty to create a charge upon the funds of that Committee by voluntarily withdrawing himself from the treatment afforded and by making application elsewhere with the hope of getting some other or more desired form of treatment. Again, even if the insured person's removal was unavoidable and was not dictated by any such motives, it would be unfair that the Committee of origin, who had already given, perhaps, a considerable amount of treatment, and who would have continued the treatment had the patient been able to remain, should be burdened in addition with a case value charge upon their funds.

(471) For these reasons, under Article 21 (2) of the Paragraph (F) Regulations no case value adjustment is made in respect of any removal case " if at the date of his removal he was entitled to treatment under any recommendation for sanatorium benefit."

(472) An insured person, again, not already entitled to sanatorium benefit by virtue of any Committee's recommendation,

might conceivably apply for the benefit to a Committee in whose area he did not propose to stay for more than a few days or weeks. If a case value adjustment were to be made in such a case some inequity would result. The Committee would by their recommendation be responsible for causing a full case value to be debited against the Committee of origin, although the liability they would incur by considering the case would be strictly limited in time; and, further, on the insured person's return to the area of the Committee of origin, that Committee would become responsible for the cost of his treatment (although they had already been debited) without themselves becoming entitled to any share of the Central Fund. Article 21 (2) also provides, therefore, that no case value adjustment should be made unless the applicant expresses his intention of remaining in the area for a period of at least three months from the date of his removal thither.

(473) In effect every "removal case" who gives rise to a case value adjustment automatically becomes, for the purposes of registration and medical benefit, a permanent resident in the new area. On application, therefore, being made by a "removal case" who expresses his intention of remaining in the area beyond the period of three months from removal, the index slip falls to be recovered from the Committee of origin, and a new medical card issued in substitution for the old.

Sanatorium Benefit of Travellers.

(474) The sums available in respect of the sanatorium benefit (excluding domiciliary treatment) of travellers are also pooled in the common Central Sanatorium Benefit Fund, together with the case values debited in respect of "removal cases," payment being made in both classes of case on the lines indicated in paragraph (469) above. Further, provision is made for a payment from the Central Sanatorium Benefit Fund in respect of the recommendation for benefit of an insured person who has ceased to be a "traveller," but whose application was made within three months of the cancellation of his yellow voucher.

Soldiers, Sailors, etc., applying for Sanatorium Benefit shortly after Discharge.

(475) In the case of soldiers and sailors who are members of Approved Societies or Deposit Contributors, and whose benefit is paid for on the insurance premium basis (*i.e.* at 1s. 3d. per head per annum), some hardship has been occasioned in the past by the fact that, on discharge from the military or naval hospital in which they were treated prior to discharge, they usually make application to the Insurance Committee for an area with which they have only an accidental association. In these circumstances Committees affected, who have not, of course, previously received any contributions paid in respect of the applicants, may be placed at a serious financial disadvantage by

the proper discharge of their obligations. The case of such insured persons is not, however, different in nature from that of the "removal cases"; and provision is made for a payment to the Committee affording treatment from the Central Sanatorium Benefit Fund in respect of each soldier or sailor recommended on an application within three months of his discharge. There is, however, in this case no Committee of origin against whom a case value can be debited; but as the General Sanatorium Benefit Fund contains, on normal insurance assumptions, the sum representing the average amount contributed in respect of healthy insured persons towards defraying the liability of Committees in respect of tuberculous insured persons, the Regulations provide for a sum being transferred from the General Sanatorium Benefit Fund to the Central Sanatorium Benefit to meet the cost of such additional payments. Owing to special difficulties arising out of the war an emergency arrangement in supplement of that of Part IV. of the Paragraph (F) Regulations has been made. This is described in paragraph (320) above.

3. ADMINISTRATION INCOME.

(476) The income under this head may be subdivided into—
(1) General Administration chargeable as follows :—
(a) members of Societies in terms of Section 61 (2) of the Act of 1911 at the rate of 1d. per insured person resident in the area of an Insurance Committee. Supplemented by the Government Grant, this sum becomes 1¾d. in the case of men and 1⅛d. in the case of women;
(b) Deposit Contributors who had not before the commencement of the year attained the age of 70, and members of the Navy and Army Fund. The cost of administration in both these cases has been fixed at 1s. 9d. per annum per insured person—in the former by Order of the Commissioners and in the latter by arrangement with the Authorities controlling the Navy and Army Fund;
(2) Medical Benefit Administration derived from
(a) charges made against Societies in terms of Section 15 (6) of the 1911 Act, together with the due proportion payable by the State in the case of British subjects. By the existing agreements between the Societies and the Committees the sum payable to the Committee per annum was fixed at 1½d. per member entitled to benefit, subject to an increase up to 2⅖d. if necessary.
(b) Deposit Contributors who had before the commencement of the year attained the age of 70, and exempt persons. In these cases the rate has been fixed by the Commissioners at 3d. and 4½d. respectively per head per annum.

(3) the amount carried from the Sanatorium Benefit Fund as representing the cost of administration of sanatorium benefit.

(477) The General Administration Fund which receives the aggregate of the amount under the foregoing heads is distributed among Insurance Committees by the same method of apportionment as that followed in the case of the General Medical Benefit Fund and the General Sanatorium Benefit Fund already referred to.

(478) An additional source of administrative income also requires to be noted. In relief of the liability imposed on Approved Societies and others for the cost of administration of medical benefit in respect of insured persons under the provisions of Section 15 (6) of the principal Act, a Special Parliamentary Grant is given under conditions framed by the Treasury. This special Parliamentary Grant is distributed among Committees according to the following sliding scale :—

No. of members of Approved Societies entitled to Medical Benefit residing in the area of the Committee.	Annual Grant at the rate of
Not exceeding 10,000	£22, 10s. per 1,000
Exceeding 10,000	£22, 10s. per 1,000 for the first 10,000, and then £3 per 1,000.

(479) The number of members of Approved Societies resident in the area of the Committee is, for the purpose of the special grant, the same number as that determined for the purpose of the credit to the Committee for the cost of medical benefit; and the grant represents $\frac{9}{170}$ths of the amount credited for medical benefit exclusive of the transfer of the domiciliary 6d. from Sanatorium Benefit in respect of members of Societies up to £4,250 and $\frac{3}{125}$ths of such amount in excess of £4,250.

(480) The scheme, under which the grant is distributed, empowers the Commissioners to make additional grants in the following circumstances if satisfied that a Committee's administrative expenditure is reasonable :—

(a) Where the total income of a Committee for administrative purposes from all sources (excluding sums paid by Approved Societies in respect of travelling under Section 61 (2) proviso of the National Insurance Act, 1911) is less than £300, a further grant may be made sufficient to raise the income of the Committee to a sum not exceeding £300, strictly subject to the qualifications mentioned above. In the case of certain Highland and Island Committees, where it is shown to the satisfaction of the Commissioners that special circumstances exist, they may, to such extent and subject to such conditions as they think necessary, authorise the payment of an additional grant notwithstanding that the income of the Committee exceeds £300.

(b) Where the travelling expenses of members of the Committee at the approved rates exceed the maximum amount available for the Committee under the proviso to Section 61 (2) of the National Insurance Act, 1911, a further grant equal to the difference may be given.

(481) To permit of the repayment of the travelling expenses of members, County Insurance Committees, in terms of Section 61 (2) of the 1911 Act, receive, in addition to their apportionment of the foregoing funds, the proceeds of a special levy on Societies not exceeding 1d. per member resident in the area of the Committee, as authorised by the Commissioners.

(482) The power of the Commissioners to authorise the repayment of travelling expenses of members of County Insurance Committees in special circumstances has by Section 31 (2) of the Act of 1913 been extended to Burgh Committees. The circumstances of burghs will, however, seldom necessitate payment of travelling expenses to members, and no expenditure under this head will thus ordinarily arise.

(483) In terms of Section 31 (1) of the Act of 1913 an Insurance Committee may also pay to its members subsistence allowance and compensation for loss of remunerative time, in accordance with a scheme to be prepared by the Committee and approved by the Commissioners.

Only members of Insurance Committees are entitled to payment under such schemes, and attendance at meetings of Insurance Committees and of Sub-Committees only may be taken into consideration for this purpose. No charge can therefore be made under the terms of the scheme for expenses incurred by delegates in attending general conferences with representatives of other bodies. Subsistence allowance should be separated from compensation for loss of time, and a member may be allowed to claim under each head in respect of the same attendance if qualified to do so. Members of Committee who reside beyond the County or Burgh area are entitled to claim only on the basis of the amount which would have been charged had their residence been at the boundary of the County or Burgh area. In those cases in which Committee meetings are held outside the area of the Committee, the Commissioners are prepared to take the special circumstances of the Committee into consideration when the details of the schemes are submitted for approval. In the case of Burghs it is seldom necessary to pay subsistence allowances or compensation for loss of remunerative time, especially the latter, if the meetings are held in the evening.

(484) As regards subsistence allowances a member of an Insurance Committee is not required to prove actual expenditure on subsistence, the scale adopted by Committees providing only

for repayment of such expenses as would reasonably be incurred by the members generally. The charges embodied in the scheme under this head in no case exceed the following scale :—

Where absence from home is not less than 4 hours but less than 8 hours . . . 2s. 6d.

Where absence from home is not less than 8 hours but does not include a night . . . 3s. 6d.

Where absence from home includes a night, for each night . . . . 10s. 0d.

The allowance for a night covers any period up to 24 hours, commencing from the time of leaving home.

Where a member claims compensation for loss of time in addition to subsistence allowance, the allowance for a night does not exceed 8s.

(485) Compensation for loss of remunerative time is paid only in those cases in which a member has actually lost wages through attendance at meetings of Committees or Sub-Committees. This includes the case of a person who had to incur expense in providing a substitute, but excludes persons on fixed weekly or yearly salaries who incur no pecuniary loss, and persons working on their own account or not in employment. Actual loss of wages incurred by members who make claims under this head need not be investigated, provided the member has certified his loss and a fixed scale of payment has been laid down by the Committee. The maximum allowance which may be embodied in a Committee's scheme cannot exceed 3s. 6d. for each half-day on account of which the member suffers loss of wages. A scale of payment for periods of less than a half-day may, however, be allowed.

(486) Allowances out of the grant are made from time to time to Committees to enable them to repay members the cost of these expenses.

4. GENERAL PURPOSES INCOME.

(487) The income to be credited to the General Purposes Fund Account is obtained from the following sources :—

(a) Sickness benefit payable in respect of insured persons who have no dependants and who are in receipt of sanatorium benefit.

(b) Subscriptions and donations received from Local Authorities in terms of Sec. 61 (3) of the 1911 Act.

(c) Fines payable by virtue of any rules made under Sub-section (3) of Section 14 of the 1911 Act.

(d) Excess of any interest credited to the Committee in respect of sums in the hands of its bankers over bank charges debited to or paid by or on behalf of the Committee.

(e) Incidental receipts.

5. TRANSFER BETWEEN FUNDS.

(488) The whole available income of Committees, ordinary or special, for all purposes of benefit or administration, has been contributed and voted for specific purposes, and the Regulations and Schemes framed by the Commissioners with the approval where required of the Treasury have proceeded on the basis of allowing to Committees wide discretion within the ambit of their purposes. The contracts and commitments which Committees required to enter into have in general had the effect of earmarking all available monies. Under the Accounts of Insurance Committees Regulations, 1915, a Committee has, however, the power to transfer, subject to the express approval of the Commissioners in each case, any monies available in the General Purposes Fund to the Administration Fund, the Sanatorium Benefit Fund, or the Medical Benefit Fund as the case may be; provision is also made in these Regulations for a transfer from the Sanatorium Benefit Fund Account to the Administration Fund Account of a sum not exceeding the expenditure charged against the latter account in respect of the administration of Sanatorium Benefit. The purpose for which the money transferred is to be applied must be one within the powers of the Committee, the terms of the Acts, and the conditions of the Grants (Accounts Regs. 4 (1) (iii.), 5 (2) (c), 6 (1) (ii.), and (7) (1) (ii.)).

SECTION (II.)—EXPENDITURE AND ACCOUNTING.

(489) The income of Insurance Committees derived as indicated in the previous Section is expended in the following ways:—

(a) Payments to Doctors for treatment.
(b)   Do.   supply of drugs, etc.
(c) Payments to Chemists.
(d) Sanatorium Expenditure.
(e) Administration Expenses.
(f) General Purposes Expenditure.

The further classification of expenditure is referred to in connection with the separate accounts into which the income and expenditure are carried, which are dealt with in the following paragraphs.

1. GENERAL.

(490) In order that a proper record of all income and expenditure may be kept, Insurance Committees, in addition to the register of persons entitled to benefits administered by the Committee provided for in the Paragraph (F) and Medical Benefit Regulations, are required to keep certain registers, records, and accounts prescribed by the National Health Insurance (Accounts of Insurance Committees) Regulations, 1915, as follows:—

1. Sanatorium Benefit Register in a form approved by the Commissioners.
2. General Cash Book in a form approved by the Commissioners.
3. Minute Book showing, *inter alia*, the payments authorised by the Committee.
4. Inventory of the property of the Committee not being moneys or securities.
5. Register of instruments, agreements, and contracts entered into by or on behalf of the Committee.
6. Ledger, containing the following accounts, together with, as respects each particular account, such subsidiary accounts as the Commissioners may from time to time require :—
    (a) Current Account with the Commissioners.
    (b) Administration Fund.
    (c) General Purposes Fund.
    (d) Sanatorium Benefit Fund.
    (e) Medical Benefit Fund.
    (f) Panel Service Fund.
    (g) Institutions Fund.
    (h) Special Arrangements Fund.
    (i) Temporary Residents Fund.
    (j) Deposit Contributors Benefits Account.
    (k) Such other accounts as may be found necessary or desirable.
7. Register of sums due and paid to medical practitioners in a form approved by the Commissioners.
8. Register of sums due and contributed towards the expenses of systems or institutions approved under Subsection (4) of Section 15 of the Act in a form approved by the Commissioners.
9. Register of sums due, and paid in respect of the supply of drugs, medicines, and appliances in a form approved by the Commissioners.
10. Register of claims received from and payments made to insured persons required or allowed to make their own arrangements in respect of medical benefit, in a form approved by the Commissioners.
11. Register of payments made in respect of benefits of Deposit Contributors in a form approved by the Commissioners.

(491) The explanations in the following paragraphs of this Section will be more easily understood if the following principles are kept in view :—

(a) Advances to the Committee on requisition prior to advice of the income for the year are to be entered in the Current Account with the Commissioners as a credit, but no entry thereof should be made in the ledger under any of the benefit fund or administration accounts.

(b) When the Committee receives the advices of its income for medical and sanatorium benefits and administration the amount of the advice should be entered in the appropriate Ledger Account as a credit, and a corresponding debit entered in the Current Account with the Commissioners.

(c) When payments are made by the Commissioners to the Committee's Bank Account in respect of income already advised, the Current Account with the Commissioners should be credited with the amount thereof, and the Bank Account debited. No entry should be made in the Ledger under any of the appropriate fund accounts.

(d) All actual payments for medical and sanatorium benefits and administration should be entered in the General Cash Book and posted to the appropriate Fund Account in the Ledger as a debit.

(e) The amount available to the Committee on each Fund for the remainder of the year is, subject to any further credits which may be receivable at any time, shown in the appropriate Ledger Fund Account as the difference between the advice credited and the actual payments debited plus expenditure incurred, but not yet paid.

2. GENERAL CASH BOOK.

(492) A form of General Cash Book has been circulated for use by Committees, and has been generally adopted. All cash transactions without exception must be entered in the Cash Book and subsequently posted to the appropriate account in the Ledger.

(493) The receipts side of the General Cash Book should be posted in the Ledger as follows :—(a) the advances received from the Commissioners should be credited to the "Insurance Commissioners Current Account"; (b) receipts from any other sources should be credited to the appropriate accounts in the Ledger.

(494) Any sums received direct by the Committee should be paid, without any deduction, into the account of the Committee at its bankers on the day of receipt, and a line should be drawn under the last item, in column 6 of Cash Book, so paid into bank, and the total of the amount paid into bank entered on the same line in column 7a.

(495) As regards payments, the entries in the "sundries" column of the General Cash Book should be posted separately to the debit of the proper Ledger Accounts, and the total of each of the other classification columns as a debit to the corresponding Ledger Account.

(496) In cases where postal orders are issued by the Commissioners payable to the Insurance Committee for benefits of Deposit Contributors, the value of the postal orders should be entered in column (6) of the General Cash Book, and any payments made in respect of the benefit should be recorded in column (14) of the General Cash Book. A subsidiary record of the receipts and payments in respect of each contributor's benefit so administered must be kept in the " Register of Payments made in respect of benefits of Deposit Contributors."

(497) The other payments falling to be recorded in the Cash Book are analysed under the headings given and should be posted to the respective accounts in the Ledger. These are referred to later under Ledger Accounts.

3. LEDGER ACCOUNTS.

(498) It is of the utmost importance that after the initial entries of transactions are made in the Cash Book, these should be posted forthwith to Ledger Accounts in order that the position of the different funds may be ascertained at any date.

The transactions of Insurance Committees are mainly in cash, and are entered in the Cash Book and posted to the Ledger. The income of Committees is advised to them by the Commissioners, and an advice note thereof is issued. On receipt of the advice the amounts may be posted direct to the appropriate Ledger Accounts, or if preferred may be recorded in a Journal before being posted. A Journal, however, has not been regarded as necessary and has not been prescribed.

(499) A trial balance should be made periodically to prove the Ledger. The entries in the Cash Book and the Journal, if kept, are posted to the debit and credit of Ledger Accounts, and if the cash and bank balances are taken into account, the debits in the Ledger should agree with the credits.

(500) The main transactions falling to be recorded in the principal Ledger Accounts are as follows :

Current Account with the Commissioners.

(501) The advice notes issued by the Commissioners show the income of the Committee under the following heads :—
   (*a*) Medical Benefit.
   (*b*) Sanatorium Benefit.
   (*c*) Administration.

On receipt of the advice, which shows what is due to the Committee, the Commissioners' Current Account should be debited and the appropriate Medical Benefit, Sanatorium Benefit, or Administration Fund credited.

(502) Committees from time to time apply to the Commissioners for advances, and the amount advanced is paid by them to the Committee's bank account. The Commissioners apportion

advances between the funds to enable Committees to decide as to what may be spent. Such apportioned amounts should not be credited to the particular funds, but the advance should be recorded in the Cash Book and from there posted to the credit of the Insurance Commissioners' Current Account. The actual income as distinct from an advance to account of that income should be posted to the appropriate Fund when the advice is received.

(503) The Insurance Commissioners' Current Account should show therefore what is due by the Commissioners to the Committee. As will be seen from the sample account given below, income advised is charged or debited to the account, whereas cash received to account is credited, any excess of the debit representing the indebtedness of the Commissioners to the Committee.

Example.
Current Account with the Commissioners.

Dr.	Cr.
To Medical Benefit Fund, per Advice Form 156.	By Cash, being advance from Commissioners.
,, Sanatorium Benefit Fund, per advice.	
,, Administration Fund, per advice.	

MEDICAL BENEFIT FUND.

(504) The amount of the Medical Benefit Fund as advised should be credited in the Ledger Account headed "Medical Benefit Fund," and transfers to the subsidiary medical funds be then made. Such transfers may be journalised.

Example.
Medical Benefit Fund.

Dr.	Cr.
To Panel Service Fund.	By General Medical Benefit Fund as advised by Commissioners.
,, Institutions Fund.	
,, Special Arrangements Fund.	
,, Practitioners Fund, amount of Domiciliary 6d.	,, Sanatorium Benefit Fund, amount of Domiciliary 6d.
,, Institutions Fund, do.	
,, Special Arrangements Fund, do.	

(Med. Benefit Regs. 33 (3) and 43.)

The income credited in this account being wholly apportioned to other funds, there will, in ordinary circumstances, be no balance to carry forward.

(505) The amount of income applicable to temporary residents obtained from the Central Medical Benefit Fund should be recorded separately from the ordinary medical benefit income (*see* paragraph (490) and Article 3 and First Sch. Accounts Regulations).

Panel Service Fund.

(506) Under Article 33 (3) of the Medical Benefit Regulations there is carried to the credit of the Panel Service Fund from the Medical Benefit Fund Account a sum calculated with reference to the number of persons on panel lists.

(507) Article 33 (3) further provides that the Panel Service Fund shall be apportioned as to thirteen-seventeenths to the Practitioners Fund, and as to four-seventeenths to the Drug Fund. The Regulations do not deal with the domiciliary sixpence, but this amount should appear to the credit of the Panel Service Fund and be apportioned to the Practitioners Fund.

(508) The Panel Service Fund will appear as follows in the Ledger :—

Example.
Panel Service Fund.

Dr.	Cr.
To Practitioners Fund 13/17ths (Arts. 33 (3)).	By Medical Benefit Fund, being amount apportioned as applicable to this Fund (Art. 33 (3)).
„ Drug Fund 4/17ths (33 (3)).	

The references are to the Medical Benefit Regulations.

This account should always be square, no balance appearing thereon.

Practitioners Fund.

(509) The 13/17ths referred to above as coming from the Panel Service Fund should be credited in this account, and to the debit be posted the cash paid to doctors as appearing in column in Cash Book headed "Practitioners Fund." There may also fall to be credited to this fund a transfer from the Drug Fund, viz., any balance on the Drug Fund remaining after meeting chemists' accounts which does not exceed one-fourth of the amount carried to the credit of the Drug Fund from the Panel Service Fund for the year. Any balance on the Drug Fund in excess of one-fourth of the amount credited for the year from the Panel Service Fund, *i.e.* excluding any balance brought forward from the preceding year, is carried forward to the credit of the Drug Fund for the next year. The account in the Ledger would be—

Example.
Practitioners Fund.

Dr.	Cr.
To Cash per monthly totals in Cash Book.	By Panel Service Fund, amount transferred (Art. 33 (3)).
	„ Drug Fund, amount transferred (Art. 39 (7)).
	„ Medical Benefit Fund, amount of Domiciliary 6d.

The references are to the Medical Benefit Regulations.

Drug Fund.

(510) The Drug Fund is to meet chemists' and doctors' accounts for drugs, medicines, and prescribed appliances, and amounts due to doctors for dispensing on a capitation basis. The payments to chemists and doctors should be posted from the Cash Book to the debit of the Drug Fund, and any credit balance on the Drug Fund after making these payments, not exceeding one-fourth of the initial credit to the fund for the year, *i.e.* excluding any balance from previous year, falls to be credited to the Practitioners' Fund Account, any further balance in excess of that amount being carried forward. The account summarised in ledger form is as follows :—

Example.

Drug Fund.

Dr.	Cr.
To Cash per Cash Book (c).	By balances brought forward (a).
,, Practitioners Fund, being one-fourth of amount credited at (b) (*see* Art. 39 (7)) (d).	,, Panel Service Fund, amount of 4/17ths transferred (b).
,, Balance carried forward (f).	
,, Bonus to Chemists (e).	

(f) must amount to $\frac{7}{24}$ of $((a)+(b))-(d)$ if the balance so permits.

The references to Articles are to those of the Medical Benefit Regulations.

The transfer (d) must not exceed one-fourth of (b), but it may in certain circumstances exhaust the Fund.

(e) is a special arrangement for the years 1913, 1914, and 1915. If, after the retransfer (d) there is a balance it is to be treated as follows :—

(1) The difference, if any, between (c) and $\frac{17}{24}$ of (a) plus (b), is paid to the Chemists as a bonus rateably, according to the total amount of their bills for the year.

(2) The balance, if any, is carried forward.

Institutions Fund.

(511) To this fund is carried the amount available for meeting the cost of medical attendance and drugs of insured persons who are receiving treatment through an approved system or institution. The only "institution" approved in Scotland is the Post Office Medical System.

(512) From the Medical Benefit Fund there is transferred the equivalent of what is transferred to the Panel Service Fund for ordinary cases of insured persons.

(513) Under the Medical Benefit Regulations, returns are to be

furnished by institutions at the commencement of each quarter, showing the number of insured persons who are members of the institution as also certificates as to the amount of expenditure. The Insurance Committees then disburse the income in this fund in repaying the institution

(a) the amount of its certified expenditure,

or

(b) a sum bearing the same proportion to the sum standing to the credit of the Institutions Fund as the number of insured persons of the institution bears to the total number of insured members of institutions, *whichever be the less.*

(Medical Benefit Regs. 43 (3).)

(514) The Committee therefore makes advances to institutions each quarter, but at the end of the year the certified expenditure on insured persons of all institutions will be aggregated. The amount of the Institutions Fund and the number of insured members in institutions being known, the cost per head can be ascertained, and according to Article 43 (3) of the Medical Benefit Regulations, the amount payable to institutions for the year may be either the actual expenditure or an amount calculated with reference to the cost per head, whichever is the less. In Scotland the Post Office have agreed to a rate of 8s. 6d. per person, and to give for that amount domiciliary treatment of tuberculosis to persons on their lists recommended for Sanatorium Benefit. Accordingly, subject to claims for case values, there will be a balance at the credit of the fund in respect of the domiciliary 6d., which should be retransferred to the credit of the Sanatorium Benefit Fund, to an amount not exceeding $\frac{1}{18}$ of the sum credited for the year.

(515) Any balance in the Institutions Fund after the retransfer to the Sanatorium Benefit Fund above referred to should be carried forward. The account in the Ledger will be as follows :—

Example.

Institutions Fund.

To Cash per Cash Book (b) . £	By balance brought forward . . £
,, Amount retransferred to Sanatorium Benefit Fund (c)	,, Medical Benefit Fund (including Domiciliary 6d) (a)
,, Balance carried forward (d) .	
£	£

(c) Should not exceed $\frac{1}{18}$ of (a).

Special Arrangements Fund.

(516) The amount available for this purpose is carried from the Medical Benefit Fund to the credit of this account (Med. Benefit Regs. 33 (3)). Thirteen-seventeenths of this amount is available to meet the cost of treatment and the remaining four seventeenths the cost of medicines, drugs, etc., and these proportions can be varied only with the express consent of the Commissioners (Medical Benefit Regs. 44 (2) (a)).

" Own arrangers " are divided into two classes :—

(a) Those who have contracted to obtain medical treatment in return for a fixed payment. In no case can a person making his own arrangements and contracting with a doctor for treatment at a fixed sum per annum receive more than the amount per head available to the Insurance Committee for medical benefit. The Special Arrangements Fund is charged with the cost of this class.

(b) Those who have not contracted and who require to produce doctors' and chemists' accounts as vouchers for the sums expended by them. The balance of the fund is divided into two parts, applicable respectively to the cost of treatment and to drugs as referred to above. The cost of treatment is kept quite distinct from the cost of medicines, etc., and any credit balance on the fund after liquidation of the accounts presented by the insured persons and admitted by the Insurance Committee on a scale of payment approved by them is carried forward, regard being had in the following year to the proportions of the balance available for treatment and for medicines respectively.

(517) Persons permitted to make " own arrangements " are during periods of absence from home of less than three months debarred from receiving medical attendance at the cost of the Insurance Committee in whose area they are thus temporarily resident. Those who have not contracted to pay a fixed sum may claim upon their home Committee for the amounts expended in obtaining treatment as private patients.

(518) In the case of permanent removal or periods of absence longer than 3 months, the following procedure obtains :—

Persons in both classes have the right, immediately upon entry into the new area, to select—subject always to the consent of the Committee concerned—a method of receiving treatment.

Persons in Class (b) present to their original Committee bills incurred during residence in its area, and to the new Committee those in respect of the period subsequent to removal.

In the case of persons in Class (a) removal is deemed to take place as at the end of the quarter current at exit and the original Committee makes payment of $\frac{1}{4}$, $\frac{1}{2}$, $\frac{3}{4}$ or the whole of the sum contracted for (not exceeding the amount available or 9s. per annum) as the case may be.

(519) Payments from the fund are recorded in the Cash Book in the columns provided for that purpose.

Example.

Special Arrangements Fund.

To Cash per Cash Book . . £	By balance brought forward (44 (3) of Med. Benefit Regs.). £
,, Treatment .	,, Medical Benefit Fund, being amount (including Domiciliary 6d.) transferred (33 (3) of Regs.).
,, Medicines, etc..	
,, Balance carried forward . £	
£	£

Temporary Residents Fund.

(520) All payments by the Committee for the purpose of providing persons temporarily resident in their area with Medical Benefit are to be charged to their account (Accounts Regs. 8 (2), and there are credited thereto all sums credited to the Committee from the Central Medical Benefit Fund (Accounts Regs. 8 (1)).

Special Transactions.

(521) The Ledger Accounts described above are those recording the transactions with the amounts available for Medical Benefit. Additional entries and accounts will have to be made on similar principles for special transactions, *e.g.* Mileage Grants and payments therefrom to doctors, deductions in respect of the failure of doctors to keep proper records as required by the conditions of the Special Parliamentary Grant, claims allowed on the Special Drug Grant, etc.

Sanatorium Benefit Fund.

(522) The amount available as detailed in paragraph (461) is ascertained from the advice issued by the Commissioners. The amount so advised should be debited to the Current Account with the Commissioners, and credited to this fund. Sums paid by the Commissioners to the credit of the Committee's Bank Account should be credited to the Current Account with the Commissioners. Payments from the fund are recorded and classified in the Cash

Book and thereafter posted to the Ledger. As returns of expenditure are called for, Committees should be careful to classify the expenditure in the form as given in the Classified Cash Book.

(523) There may be transferred from this fund to the Administration Fund a sum in respect of administration (Accounts Regs. 6 (2) (b)).

(524) If the Cash Book is squared off monthly, the Ledger will, unless kept in columnar form, require to be abstracted at the end of the year to show the final total under each heading of expenditure.

(525) The aggregate Ledger Account for the year would be as follows:—

Example.

Sanatorium Benefit Fund.

To Cash per Cash Book . . £	By Balance brought forward . . £	
,, Preliminary examination of patients .	,, Current Account with the Commissioners, amounts available .	
,, Domiciliary treatment .		
,, Drugs, medicines, and appliances .	(a) from the General Sanatorium Benefit Fund.	
,, Conveyance of patients to sanatoria .		
,, Hospitals and sanatoria .		
,, Dispensaries .	(b) from the Central Sanatorium Benefit Fund.	
,, Incidental expenses . .		
,, Medical Benefit Fund in respect of obligation to afford domiciliary treatment . .	(c) in respect of Special Parliamentary Grant.	
,, Balance carried forward	,, Cash received (if any) in terms of S. 17 (3) of 1911 Act .	
	,, Amount transferred from Institutions' Fund.	
£	£	

ADMINISTRATION FUND.

(526) Expenditure in respect of which a claim will be made on the Central Sanatorium Benefit Fund should be separately entered and earmarked.

The amounts available as detailed in paragraphs (476) and (478) including any sum transferred from the Sanatorium Benefit Fund should be credited in this account, the former being debited in the Current Account with the Commissioners, and the last to the Sanatorium Benefit Fund.

(527) Payments for administration are classified in the Cash Book, and if posted monthly to the Ledger should be aggregated at the end of the year to show the total under each heading.

Example.
Administration Fund.

	£		£
To Cash per Cash Book . .		By Balance brought forward .	
,, Remuneration of staff . .		,, Current Account with the Commissioners for	
,, Stationery, printing, and postage .		(a) Ordinary Income .	
,, Office accommodation .		(b) Special Grants (if any) .	
,, Incidental expenses, including travelling expenses on business of Committee .		,, Sanatorium Benefit Fund, amount for administration of that benefit (Accounts Regs. 4 (1) (iv)) .	
,, Travelling expenses of members attending meetings of Committee . .			
,, Allowance to members for subsistence and loss of remuneration when attending meetings of Committee			
,, Balance carried forward .			
	£		£

Deposit Contributors Benefits Account.

(528) This account in the Ledger is for recording the Committee's transactions in the administration of sickness, disablement, and maternity benefits of Deposit Contributors.

General Purposes Fund.

(529) Against this account are charged all payments made by the Committee in pursuance of the Act, otherwise than in respect of benefits or the administration of benefits, *e.g.*
  (1) Reports and returns as to the health of insured persons within the area ;
  (2) Provision for the giving of lectures and the publication of information on questions relating to health.
  (3) Subscription to Association of Insurance Committees and expenses of representatives thereon.

Expenditure chargeable against this account should not be incurred unless the Committee has a sufficient balance standing at the credit of the account of moneys derived from the above-mentioned source.

Alternative Forms of Books or Accounts.

(530) If any Committee satisfy the Commissioners that it is necessary or desirable that the Committee should keep any other books or accounts than those specified in the Schedule to the Accounts Regulations and explained above, the Commissioners may authorise their substitution therefor, provided—
  (a) the Committee submit the proposed books or accounts to the Commissioners ;
  (b) the books or accounts are of such a nature as to furnish substantially the same information as the prescribed ones.
  (c) the Commissioners approve thereof. (Accounts Regulations, 3 (2).)

Bank Account.

(531) The Commissioners have directed attention to the necessity for monies administered by the Committee being kept in a Bank Account in the name of the Committee itself, and for proper safeguards being imposed on operations on the account (Circulars 76 and 638 I.C.).

CHAPTER VIII.

GENERAL.

(i.) ADMINISTRATION.

(532) THE Offices of the Commissioners, the Inspectorate and the National Insurance Audit Department, with the areas of the Inspectoral Districts, and names of the Commissioners and principal officials are shown in Appendix XX.

(533) Information as to the names and addresses of Clerks of Insurance Committees in Scotland, with their telephone numbers, and the addresses of Clerks of the Committees in other parts of the United Kingdom, are contained in Appendix XXI., while the cipher references for Committees throughout the United Kingdom are shown in Appendix XXII.

(ii.) CONTRACTS, ETC.

(534) The Commissioners have expressed the view that in all contracts entered into by Insurance Committees a Fair Wages Clause should be inserted (*see* Appendix XXIII.).

(535) The Commissioners consider that it is highly inexpedient that a member of the Committee should enter into a contract with the Committee for the supply of any goods or services, and have recommended Committees to pass a formal resolution excluding such contracts (*see* Circular No. 427, Appendix XXIV.).

(536) Attendance at Committee and Sub-Committee meetings must be in person, and there is no provision by which a member of the Committee may be represented by a deputy.

(537) An official of the Insurance Committee, such as the Medical Officer to the Committee, is not eligible to serve as a member of the Committee while he holds office.

(538) Except in the case of the representatives of County and Town Councils, where such qualification is implied, there is no residential or franchise qualification for membership of an Insurance Committee.

(539) The Commissioners have expressed the opinion that it is undesirable that a Clerk to an Insurance Committee should hold a paid appointment under an Approved Society.

(540) The Commissioners have suggested to Insurance Committees that they should voluntarily apply by resolution the principles of Section 1 of the Local Authorities (Admission of the Press to Meetings) Act, 1908, to their meetings (Appendix XXV.).

APPENDIX I.

LIST OF ACTS AND PRINCIPAL REGULATIONS AND ORDERS.

(*See Introduction.*)

ACTS.

National Insurance Act, 1911. Price 6d. [By post, 8d.], or 1s. 3d. [By post, 1s. 6d.].
National Insurance Act, 1913. Price 1½d. [By post, 2d.], or 3d. [By post, 4d.].
National Insurance (Navy and Army) Act, 1914. Price ½d. [By post, 1d.].
National Insurance (Navy and Army) Act, 1914 (Session 2). Price ½d. [By post, 1d.].
National Insurance (Part I. Amendment) Act, 1915. Price ½d. [By post, 1d.].
Expiring Laws Continuance Act, 1915. Price ½d. [By post, 1d.].
Highlands and Islands (Medical Service) Grant Act, 1913. Price 1d. [By post, 1½d.].

ORDER.

Deposit Contributors Benefits Order, 1914 (No. 2), dated 26th November 1914 [Cd. 7705]. Price ½d. [By post, 1d.].

RULES.

Rules made under Article 50 *of the National Health Insurance (Medical Benefit) Regulations (Scotland),* 1913.

REGULATIONS.

Accounts of Insurance Committees Regulations, 1915 (Draft), dated 3rd August 1915 [H.C. 440]. Price 1d. [By post, 1½d.].
Administration of Benefits out of the Navy and Army Insurance Fund for discharged Seamen, Marines, and Soldiers Regulations, 1913, dated 22nd February 1913 (Provisional) [H.C. 529]. Price 1½d. [By post, 2d.]. Draft, 1½d. [By post, 2d.].
Appeals and Disputes Regulations, 1913 [H.C. 47], dated 19th March 1913. Price 1d. [By post, 1½d.].
Appointment of Representatives of Insured Persons on Insurance Committees Regulations, 1913 [H.C. 53], dated 2nd April 1913. Price 1d. [By post, 1½d.].
Appointment of Representatives of Insured Persons on Insurance Committees Amendment Regulations (Scotland), 1914, dated 7th May 1914 [H.C. 230]. Price ½d. [By post, 1d.].
Appointment of Representatives of Insured Persons on Insurance Committees Amendment Regulations (Scotland), 1914 (No. 2), dated 15th December 1914 [H.C. 78]. Price ½d. [By post, 1d.].
Associations of Deposit Contributors Regulations, 1913, dated 11th April 1913 [H.C. 68]. Price ½d. [By post, 1d.].

Constitution of District Insurance Committees Regulations, 1912, dated 8th July 1912 [H.C. 212]. Price ½d. [By post, 1d.].
County of Zetland Pharmaceutical Committee Regulations, 1914, dated 7th March 1914 [H.C. 146]. Price ½d. [By post, 1d.].
Deposit Contributors' Administration Expenses Regulations, 1914, dated 12th February 1914 [H.C. 102]. Price ½d. [By post, 1d.].
Deposit Contributors' Administration Expenses Regulations, 1914 (No. 2), dated 31st December 1914 [H.C. 77]. Price ½d. [By post, 1d.].
Deposit Contributors, Payment on Death Regulations, 1913 [H.C. 101], dated 18th April 1913. Price ½d. [By post, 1d.].
Drug Accounts Committee Regulations, 1914, dated 19th December 1914 [H.C. 141]. Price 1d. [By post, 1½d.].
Exempt Persons Benefits Regulations, 1914, dated 31st December 1914 [H.C. 68]. Price ½d. [By post, 1d.].
Election of Medical Representatives on Insurance Committees Regulations, 1912, dated 8th July 1912 [H.C. 210]. Price ½d. [By post, 1d.].
Insurance Committees Procedure Regulations, 1912, dated 8th July 1912 [H.C. 211]. Price 1d. [By post, 1½d.].
Medical Benefit Regulations (Scotland), 1913, dated 14th November 1913 [H.C. 28]. Price 3d. [By post, 4d.].
Medical Benefit Regulations (Scotland), 1914, dated 22nd October 1914 [H.C. 42]. Price ½d. [By post, 1d.].
Medical Research Fund Regulations, 1914, dated 21st March 1914 [H.C. 171]. Price ½d. [By post, 1d.].
Panel and Pharmaceutical Committees Regulations (Scotland), 1913, dated 3rd November 1913 [H.C. 27]. Price 1½d. [By post, 2d.].
Panel and Pharmaceutical Committees Amendment Regulations (Scotland), 1915, dated 17th March 1915 [H.C. 170]. Price ½d. [By post, 1d.].
Payments to Insurance Committees Regulations, 1914, dated 31st December 1914 [H.C. 69]. Price 1d. [By post, 1½d.].
Persons of Unsound Mind Regulations, 1915, dated 23rd July 1915.
Seamen's Medical and Sanatorium Benefit Regulations, 1914, dated 10th August 1914, modifying as regards members of the Seamen's National Insurance Society the provisions of the National Insurance Act, 1911, as to the Administration of Medical and Sanatorium Benefits [H.C. 446]. Price ½d. [By post, 1d.].
Seamen's Medical Benefit Regulations, 1914, dated 10th August 1914 [H.C. 453]. Price ½d. [By post, 1d.].

APPENDIX II.

(A) CONSTITUTION OF INSURANCE COMMITTEES.

(See Cap. I., Section (I.) (iii.) and (iv.), paragraphs (6) and (8), and Section (II.) (i.), paragraph 70).

COUNTIES.

Committee.	Total No. of Members.	Quorum.	Members Representing Insured Persons.	Members Appointed by County Council.	Members Representing Medical Practitioners.	Medical Practitioners Appointed by County Council.	Appointed by Commissioners.
Aberdeen	70	13	42	14	2	2	10
Argyll	50	7	30	10	2	1	7
Ayr	70	14	42	14	2	2	10
Banff	50	9	30	10	2	1	7
Berwick	30	6	18	6	2	1	3
Bute	30	6	18	6	2	1	3
Caithness	35	7	21	7	2	1	4
Clackmannan and Kinross	40	7	24	8	2	1	5
Dumfries	50	11	27	13	2	1	7
Dunbarton	60	11	36	12	2	2	8
Elgin and Nairn	50	10	30	10	2	1	7
Fife	70	14	42	14	2	2	10
Forfar	60	12	36	12	2	2	8
Haddington	40	8	24	8	2	1	5
Inverness	60	7	36	12	2	2	8
Kincardine	30	6	18	6	2	1	3
Kirkcudbright	35	7	21	7	2	1	4
Lanark	70	15	42	14	2	2	10
Linlithgow	60	11	36	12	2	2	8
Midlothian	60	12	36	12	2	2	8
Orkney	30	5	18	6	2	1	3
Peebles	30	6	18	6	2	1	3
Perth	60	12	36	12	2	2	8
Renfrew	70	13	42	14	2	2	10
Ross and Cromarty	60	7	36	12	2	2	8
Roxburgh	40	8	24	8	2	1	5
Selkirk	30	6	18	6	2	1	3
Stirling	60	12	36	12	2	2	8
Sutherland	30	5	18	6	2	1	3
Wigtown	30	6	18	6	2	1	3
Zetland	30	5	18	6	2	1	3

CONSTITUTION OF INSURANCE COMMITTEES—(*continued*).

BURGHS.

Committee.	Total No. of Members.	Quorum.	Members Representing Insured Persons.	Members Appointed by Town Council.	Members Representing Medical Practitioners.	Medical Practitioners Appointed by Town Council.	Appointed by Commissioners.
Aberdeen	60	14	36	12	2	2	8
Arbroath	30	8	18	6	2	1	3
Airdrie	30	8	18	6	2	1	3
Ayr	40	9	24	8	2	1	5
Clydebank	40	9	24	8	2	1	5
Coatbridge	40	10	24	8	2	1	5
Dumbarton	30	8	18	6	2	1	3
Dumfries and Maxwelltown	30	8	18	6	2	1	3
Dundee	60	14	36	12	2	2	8
Dunfermline	30	8	18	6	2	1	3
Edinburgh	70	16	42	14	2	2	10
Falkirk	40	9	24	8	2	1	5
Glasgow	80	19	48	16	2	3	11
Greenock	50	11	30	10	2	1	7
Hamilton	40	9	21	11	2	1	5
Inverness	30	8	18	6	2	1	3
Kilmarnock	40	9	24	8	2	1	5
Kirkcaldy	40	9	24	8	2	1	5
Leith	50	11	30	10	2	1	7
Motherwell	40	10	24	8	2	1	5
Paisley	50	11	30	10	2	1	7
Perth	40	9	24	8	2	1	5
Rutherglen	30	8	18	6	2	1	3
Stirling	30	8	18	6	2	1	3
Wishaw	30	8	18	6	2	1	3

(B.) ELECTORAL DIVISIONS AND VOTES FOR DRUG ACCOUNTS COMMITTEE.

(*See Cap. I., Section (I.) (ix.), paragraph (65).*)

Insurance Committees.	Value of Votes.	Insurance Committees.	Value of Votes.
ELECTORAL DIVISION I.		**ELECTORAL DIVISION II.**	
		Aberdeenshire	3
		Aberdeen Burgh	4
Zetland	1	Kincardine	1
Orkney	1	Forfar	3
Caithness	1	Arbroath	1
Sutherland	1	Perthshire	3
Ross and Cromarty	2	Perth Burgh	2
Inverness-shire	2	**ELECTORAL DIVISION III.**	
Inverness Burgh	1	Dundee	4
Argyll	2	Fife	4
Bute	1	Dunfermline	2
Elgin and Nairn	2	Kirkcaldy	2
Banff	2	Clackmannan and Kinross	2

ELECTORAL DIVISIONS AND VOTES FOR DRUG ACCOUNTS COMMITTEE—(continued).

Insurance Committees.	Value of Votes.
ELECTORAL DIVISION IV.	
Airdrie	1
Coatbridge	2
Hamilton	2
Motherwell	2
Rutherglen	1
Wishaw	1
Ayr Burgh	2
Kilmarnock	2
Dumbarton Burgh	1
Clydebank	2
Stirling Burgh	1
Falkirk	2
ELECTORAL DIVISION V.	
Ayrshire	4
Renfrew	3
Greenock	3
Paisley	3

Insurance Committees.	Value of Votes.
ELECTORAL DIVISION VI.	
Lanark	4
Linlithgow	3
Dunbartonshire	3
Stirlingshire	3
ELECTORAL DIVISION VII.	
Midlothian	3
Leith	3
Edinburgh	5
ELECTORAL DIVISION VIII.	
Peebles	1
Selkirk	1
Haddington	2
Berwick	1
Roxburgh	2
Dumfriesshire	2
Dumfries and Maxwelltown	1
Kirkcudbright	1
Wigtown	1

APPENDIX III.

MODEL RULES FOR ADMINISTRATION OF MEDICAL BENEFIT.

(See Cap. II., Section (I.), paragraph (83), and Cap. IV., Section (IV.), paragraph (247).)

(CONDUCT OF PERSONS IN RECEIPT OF BENEFIT, AND PROCEDURE OF THE MEDICAL SERVICE, PHARMACEUTICAL SERVICE, AND JOINT SERVICES SUB-COMMITTEES.)

1. CONDUCT OF PERSON IN RECEIPT OF MEDICAL BENEFIT.

An insured person in receipt of medical benefit shall comply with the following rules :—
(a) He shall obey the instructions of the practitioner attending him :
(b) He shall not conduct himself in a manner which is likely to retard his recovery :
(c) He shall not make unreasonable demands upon the professional services of the practitioner attending him :
(d) He shall, whenever his condition permits, attend at the surgery or place of residence of the practitioner attending him on such days and at such hours as may be appointed by the practitioner :
(e) He shall not summon the practitioner to visit him between the hours of   p.m. and   a.m., except in cases of serious emergency :
(f) He shall, when his condition requires a home visit, give notice to the practitioner, if the circumstances of the case permit, before   a.m. on the day on which the visit is required.

2. Offences.

(1) The Committee may in their discretion inflict a fine upon any insured person who is guilty of a breach of any of these rules, or of any of the provisions of the Act relating to medical benefit, or of the regulations, or of any imposition or attempted imposition in respect of medical benefit, of a sum not exceeding * shillings, or in the case of repeated breaches * shillings, and may, in the case of repeated breaches, suspend his medical benefit for a period not exceeding †: Provided that (i.) no insured person shall be subject to any penalty, or suspended from benefit on account of refusal to submit to vaccination or inoculation of any kind, or to a surgical operation, unless such refusal, in the case of a surgical operation of a minor character, is considered by the Committee, or, on appeal, by the Commissioners, unreasonable; and (ii.) if any act or omission alleged to constitute a breach of these rules is of such a nature as to amount to a breach of any rule of a Society of which the insured person is a member, the Committee shall refer the matter to the Society, and unless the Society has unreasonably refused to take action or the action taken by the Society appears to the Committee to be inadequate, shall not deal with the matter themselves except by way of transferring the insured person, in cases where after inquiry they think fit, to another practitioner on the panel.

(2) An insured person who has failed to pay a fine imposed on him under these rules within   weeks of the date on which it was so imposed may be suspended from medical benefit for a period not exceeding   .†

3. Infliction of Penalties.

Before inflicting any penalty upon an insured person or transferring him to another practitioner the Committee shall give notice to that person of their intention, and if within seven days from the receipt of the notice he gives notice to the Clerk that he desires to be heard in explanation of his conduct, the Committee shall, except in cases where the facts have already been investigated by any one of the Sub-Committees appointed under the Regulations for that purpose, fix a date for the hearing by the Committee, or shall refer the matter to the appropriate one of those Sub-Committees, and when the matter is heard by the Committee not less than seven days' notice shall be given to the insured person of the date fixed for the hearing.

4. Meetings of Sub-Committees.

(1) The Medical Service Sub-Committee shall meet at least once in every   weeks, and the Pharmaceutical Service Sub-Committee shall meet at least once in every   weeks.

---

* Section 14 (2) (a) of the National Insurance Act, 1911, provides that "*no fine imposed . . . shall exceed ten shillings, or. in the case of repeated breaches of rules, twenty shillings.*"

† Section 14 (2) (b) provides that "*no . . . rule shall provide for the suspension of any benefit for a period exceeding one year.*"

Section 69 (1) of the Act provides that, "*If, for the purpose of obtaining any benefit or payment . . . under this Part of this Act . . . any person knowingly makes any false statement or false representation, he shall be liable . . . . to imprisonment for a term not exceeding three months.*"

Section 71 of the Act provides, "*If it is found at any time that a person has been in receipt of any payment or benefit under this Part of this Act without being lawfully entitled thereto, he, or in the case of his death his personal representatives, shall be liable to repay to the Insurance Commissioners the amount of such payment or benefit, and any such amount may be recovered as a debt due to the Crown . . .*"

(2) In a case of urgency the Chairman of either Sub-Committee may summon a special meeting of the Sub-Committee by giving not less than seven days' notice to each member thereof.

(3) The Clerk shall summon a meeting of the Joint Services Sub-Committee as often as may be required by giving not less than seven days' notice to each member of the Sub-Committee.

5. Procedure of Medical Service and Pharmaceutical Service Sub-Committees.

Where under the provisions of the Regulations any question arising between a practitioner on the panel or a person supplying drugs or appliances and an insured person is referred to the Medical Service Sub-Committee or to the Pharmaceutical Service Sub-Committee the following procedure shall be adopted :—

(a) The Clerk shall, within three days, send copies of the statement made by the complainant to the respondent and to the Chairman of the appropriate Sub-Committee, and shall upon receipt of any reply or further statement made by either party send copies thereof to the other party and the Chairman.

(b) * Not less than seven days' notice of the meeting at which a question is to be considered shall be given to both parties.

(c) The Clerk shall at the meeting of the Sub-Committee supply to each member of the Sub-Committee copies of the statement and the reply, if any, thereto, and of any further statement made by either party.

(d) Either party shall be entitled to be present at the hearing and to give such evidence, either by himself or by witnesses, as the Sub-Committee may think relevant to the matters in issue, and may put such questions to the other party or to any witness called by him, either directly, or, if the Sub-Committee so direct, through the Chairman of the Sub-Committee, but, subject as aforesaid, the procedure at the hearing shall be such as the Sub-Committee may determine.

(e) The Sub-Committee may, before giving their decision, exclude from the proceedings the parties and other persons present at the hearing.

---

* The following paragraphs may be substituted for Paragraph (b) if it is desired that the Sub-Committee should have an opportunity of considering the statements made by the complainant, and dismissing the matter if it appears to them that no *prima facie* case has been shown. It should be observed, however, that the adoption of this procedure necessitates the case coming before the Sub-Committee at least twice, and consequently involves some delay :—

" (c) *The Sub-Committee shall consider the statement or statements made by the complainant, and if in their opinion the allegations contained therein disclose no case for inquiry the Clerk shall inform the complainant that unless, within seven days, the complainant submits a further statement, which in the opinion of the Sub-Committee discloses a case for enquiry, or gives notice to the Clerk that he desires to be heard in person by the Sub-Committee, the matter will be dismissed, and, if the complainant fails to submit such statement or give such notice as aforesaid within seven days, the matter shall stand dismissed.*

" (d) *If in the opinion of the Sub-Committee a case for inquiry is disclosed, or the complainant has given notice of his desire to be heard in person, the Sub-Committee shall, unless in the former case they decide, with the consent of both parties, to dispense with a hearing, appoint a day for the hearing and shall give not less than seven days' notice to both parties of the time and place at which the hearing will take place.*"

(f) If either party fails to appear at the hearing, and the Sub-Committee are satisfied that his absence is due to illness, incapacity, or other reasonable cause, they may postpone the hearing for such time as they think fit.

(g) In the case of the Medical Service Sub-Committee the Chairman, together with one representative of insured persons and one * of the persons appointed by the Local Medical Committee or Panel Committee, and in the case of the Pharmaceutical Service Sub-Committee the Chairman, together with one representative of insured persons and one registered pharmacist, shall form a quorum.

6. Procedure of Joint Services Sub-Committee.

Where under the provisions of the Regulations any question is referred to the Joint Services Sub-Committee the following procedure shall be adopted :—

(a) The Clerk shall, within three days, send copies of any statements or replies furnished to the Sub-Committee by which the matter is referred, to any third party to whom the question relates, and to the Chairman of the Sub-Committee, and shall, upon the receipt of any statement made by the third party, send a copy thereof to the other parties and the Chairman.

(b) The Chairman, together with one representative of insured persons, one practitioner, and one registered pharmacist shall form a quorum.

(c) Subject as aforesaid, the procedure of the Joint Services Sub-Committee shall be similar to that of the Medical Service Sub-Committee with such modifications as are rendered necessary by the inclusion of a third party.

7. Frivolous or Vexatious Questions.

Any insured person raising a question which, after investigation by the Committee or the Medical or Pharmaceutical Service Sub-Committee, appears to the Committee to be frivolous or vexatious, shall be deemed to have committed a breach of these rules.

8. Interpretation.

(1) Words and expressions used in these Rules have the same meaning as in the National Health Insurance (Medical Benefit) Regulations (Scotland), 1913, which are in these Rules referred to as " the Regulations."

(2) The expression " the Committee " means the Insurance Committee for the County [Burgh] of   , and the expression " the Clerk " means the Clerk or the Acting Clerk of the Committee.

(3) The expression " the complainant " means the person who raises any question within the meaning of Paragraph (1) of Article 45 of the Regulations, and the expression " the respondent " means the person in respect of whom the question is raised.

---

* In cases where the Medical Service Sub-Committee has been enlarged, with the consent of the Commissioners, under Article 45 (2) (1) of the Medical Benefit Regulations. it will be desirable to modify this rule. It is suggested that if the enlarged Sub-Committee consists of 9 members, the word " two " should be substituted for the word " one " where it appears in the rule, and that the word " three " should be similarly substituted if the enlarged Sub-Committee consists of 11 members.

APPENDIX IV.

LIST OF LOCAL MEDICAL COMMITTEES RECOGNISED BY THE COMMISSIONERS.

(Revised to 1st June 1915.)

(*See Cap. III., Section (I.), paragraph (121).*)

Counties.	Burghs.
Aberdeen.	Aberdeen.
Argyll.	Airdrie.
Ayr.	Ayr.
Berwick.	Arbroath.
Banff.	Clydebank.
Bute.	Coatbridge.
Clackmannan and Kinross.	Dumbarton.
Dumfries.	Dumfries and Maxwelltown.
Dunbarton.	Dundee.
Elgin and Nairn.	Dunfermline.
Fife.	Edinburgh.
Forfar.	Falkirk.
Haddington.	Glasgow.
Kincardine.	Greenock.
Kirkcudbright.	Hamilton.
Lanark.	Inverness.
Linlithgow.	Kilmarnock.
Orkney (Panel Committee).	Leith.
Peebles.	Motherwell.
Perth.	Paisley.
Renfrew.	Perth.
Ross and Cromarty.	Rutherglen.
Roxburgh.	Stirling.
Selkirk.	Wishaw.
Stirling.	
Sutherland.	
Wigtown.	
Zetland.	

APPENDIX V.

LIST OF PANEL COMMITTEES WITH MEMBERSHIP, QUORUM, AND SECRETARIES.

(*See Cap. III., Section (II.), paragraphs (131), (134), and (135).*)

COUNTIES.

Aberdeen—Members, 14; Quorum, 3—Dr. R. Bruce, Thoresby, Cults (Dr. J. E. Skinner, Westhill House, Skene, acting).

Argyll—Members, 12; Quorum, 3—Dr. J. A. Clarke, Milton House, Dunoon.

Ayr—Members, 15; Quorum, 5—Dr. W. A. Paterson, Elmbank House, Irvine. Communications to Mr. W. D. M'Michael, 84 John Finnie Street, Kilmarnock.

Banff—Members, 10; Quorum, 3—Dr. J. Taylor, Ugie House, Keith.

Berwick—Members, 8; Quorum, 3—Dr. A. J. Campbell, 47 Market Square, Duns.

Bute—Members, 7; Quorum, 3—Dr. J. S. Hall, 13 Battery Place, Rothesay.

Caithness—Members, 7; Quorum, 3—Dr. T. Wright, 13 Sinclair Terrace, Wick (Dr. Turnbull, 13 Sinclair Terrace, acting).

Clackmannan and Kinross—Members, 10; Quorum, 3—Dr. J. D. V. Wilson, Endrick, West Kellie Place, Alloa.

Dumfries—Members, 11; Quorum, 3—Dr. M. Bryson, Thornhill, Dumfriesshire.

Dunbarton—Members, 12; Quorum, 3—Dr. A. W. Sutherland, Barbain, Cardross.
Elgin and Nairn—Members, 10; Quorum, 3—Dr. J. A. Stephens, Murrayfield, Elgin.
Fife—Members, 15; Quorum, 5—Dr. G. C. Anderson, Denbeath House, Denbeath, Methil (Dr. Craig, Cowdenbeath, acting).
Forfar—Members, 12; Quorum, 3—Dr. G. C. Burgess, New Road, Forfar.
Haddington—Members, 10; Quorum, 3—Dr. T. P. Caverhill, The Hollies, Haddington.
Inverness—Members, 12; Quorum, 3—Dr. J. W. M'Kenzie, 5 Castle Street, Inverness.
Kincardine—Members, 8; Quorum, 3—Dr. H. Grey Brown, 47 Evan Street, Stonehaven.
Kirkcudbright—Members, 8; Quorum. 3—Dr. R. B. Lorraine, Castle Douglas.
Lanark—Members, 16; Quorum, 5—Dr. R. Thompson, Hawthornlaw, Uddingston. Communications to Mr. W. S. Mackenzie, Solicitor, Larkhall.
Linlithgow—Members, 12; Quorum, 3—Dr. J. Hunter, 16 Traquair Park, Corstorphine (Dr. Alexander Scott, Broxburn, acting).
Midlothian—Members, 13; Quorum, 3—Dr. Thomson, c/o J. B. Mackie, Esq., 25 George Street, Edinburgh.
Orkney—Members, 7; Quorum, 3—Dr. G. Sinclair, Queen Street, Kirkwall.
Peebles—Members, 7; Quorum, 3—Dr. T. D. Luke, St. Ronan's, Venlaw Brae, Peebles.
Perth—Members, 12; Quorum, 3—Dr. A. Trotter, Tayview House, Perth; Dr. J. H. Lyell, 15 Marshall Place, Perth. Correspondence to Dr. Lyell.
Renfrew—Members, 15; Quorum, 5—Dr. J. Barr Steven, Beechcroft, Renfrew.
Ross and Cromarty—Members, 10; Quorum, 3—Dr. J. Pender Smith, The Croft, Dingwall.
Roxburgh—Members, 11; Quorum, 3—Dr. W. T. Barrie, 18 Bridge Street, Hawick. Correspondence to Mr. E. Watson Simpson, Solicitor, Bank of Scotland Chambers, Hawick.
Selkirk—Members, 8; Quorum, 3—Dr. J. M. Menzies, Ettrick Lodge, Selkirk.
Stirling—Members, 13; Quorum, 3—Dr. J. Young, Mora, Bonnybridge.
Sutherland—Members, 7; Quorum, 3—Dr. J. B. Simpson, The Hollies, Golspie.
Wigtown—Members, 8; Quorum, 3—Dr. Jas. Dawson, Public Health Office, Newton-Stewart.
Zetland—Members, 7; Quorum, 3—Dr. J. F. Robertson, Viewforth, Lerwick.

BURGHS.

Aberdeen—Members, 15; Quorum, 5—Dr. C. Forbes, 54 King Street, Aberdeen. Communications to Mr. J. Johnstone, 80 Union Street.
Airdrie—Members, 6; Quorum, 3—Dr. Jas. Monie, Westfield, Airdrie.
Arbroath—Members, 5; Quorum, 3—Dr. J. E. G. Thomson, 13 Hill Terrace, Arbroath.
Ayr—Members, 7; Quorum, 3—Dr. J. Allan Thom, 19 Dalblair Road, Ayr.
Clydebank—Members, 7; Quorum, 3—Dr. T. M. Strang, 1 Drumry Road, Clydebank.
Coatbridge—Members, 8; Quorum, 3—Dr. Jas. Andrew, Arlington, Coatbridge.
Dumbarton—Members, 5; Quorum, 3—Dr. T. Miller, British Linen Bank Buildings, High Street, Dumbarton.
Dumfries and Maxwelltown—Members, 5; Quorum, 3—Dr. J. Dewar Robson, Dalston House, 1 Hope Place, Maxwelltown.
Dundee—Members, 15; Quorum, 5—Dr. G. F. Whyte, 12 Airlie Place, Dundee.
Dunfermline—Members, 7; Quorum, 3—Dr. J. Dalgleish, 12 Comely Park, Dunfermline.

Edinburgh—Members, 16 ; Quorum, 5—Dr. J. Craig, 216 Bruntsfield Place, Edinburgh.
Falkirk—Members, 7 ; Quorum, 3—Dr. G. Gardner, 2A George Street, Falkirk.
Glasgow—Members, 20 ; Quorum, 7—Dr. Jas. R. Drever, Lincluden, Clarkston Road, Cathcart, Glasgow.
Greenock—Members, 12 ; Quorum, 3—Dr. J. Miller, 35 Regent Street, Greenock.
Hamilton—Members. 8 ; Quorum, 3—Dr. H. Miller, Marie Lodge, Auchengramont Road, Hamilton.
Inverness—Members, 6 ; Quorum, 3—Dr. J. Munro Moir, 4 Ardross Terrace, Inverness.
Kilmarnock—Members, 7 ; Quorum, 3—Dr. J. Aitken, Allanhill, London Road, Kilmarnock.
Kirkcaldy—Members, 7 ; Quorum, 3—Dr. J. Isedale Greig, 23 Townsend Place, Kirkcaldy.
Leith—Members, 12 ; Quorum, 3—Dr. J. Mill, 188 Ferry Road, Leith.
Motherwell—Members, 8 ; Quorum, 3—Dr. R. Robertson, "Stronbuie," Motherwell.
Paisley—Members, 12 ; Quorum, 3—Dr. J. D. Holmes, 12 Neilston Road, Paisley.
Perth—Members, 7 ; Quorum, 3—Dr. A. Trotter, Tayview House, Perth ; Dr. J. H. Lyell, 15 Marshall Place, Perth. Correspondence to Dr. Lyell.
Rutherglen—Members, 7 ; Quorum, 3—Dr. A. D. Buchanan, Mossgiel. Rutherglen.
Stirling—Members, 6 ; Quorum. 3.—Dr. A. Vost, 11 Pitt Terrace, Stirling.
Wishaw—Members, 6 ; Quorum, 3—Dr. T. Scott Brodie, 21 Belhaven Terrace, Wishaw.

Note.—The membership and quorum of certain Highland and Island Committees where difficulty has been experienced in holding meetings is under consideration.

APPENDIX VI.

LIST OF PHARMACEUTICAL COMMITTEES WITH MEMBERSHIP, QUORUM, AND SECRETARIES.

(*See Cap. III., Section (III.), paragraphs* (149), (152), *and* (153).)

COUNTIES.

Aberdeen—Members, 9 ; Quorum, 3—J. R. Reith, St. Devenick's Pharmacy, Cults.
Argyll—Members, 7 ; Quorum, 3—J. R. Thomson, 9 Main Street, Campbeltown.
Ayr—Members, 9 ; Quorum, 3—W. G. Boyd, 68 Portland Street, Kilmarnock.
Banff—Members, 5 ; Quorum, 3—R. W. Garrow, Chemist, Mid Street, Keith.
Berwick—Members, 5 ; Quorum, 3—Wm. Elliot, Chemist, Coldstream.
Bute—Members, 5 ; Quorum, 3—G. C. Hill, 64 Montague Street, Rothesay.
Caithness—Members, 5 ; Quorum, 3—G. Banks, 26 Bridge Street, Wick.
Clackmannan and Kinross—Members, 5 ; Quorum, 3—T. Hetherington, Chemist, Tillicoultry.
Dumfries—Members, 5 ; Quorum, 3—A. G. Laidlaw, 84 High Street, Lockerbie.
Dunbarton—Members, 7 ; Quorum, 3—A. T. Campbell, 71 Bank Street, Alexandria.
Elgin and Nairn—Members, 5 ; Quorum, 3—A. Robertson, 94 High Street, Elgin.

Fife—Members, 7; Quorum, 3—C. Stewart, 231 High Street, Kirkcaldy.
Forfar—Members, 7; Quorum, 3—G. Forbes Johnston, 154 Brook Street, Broughty-Ferry.
Haddington—Members, 5; Quorum, 3—W. P. Wilson, 36 High Street, Haddington.
Inverness—Members, 7; Quorum, 3—R. Macdonald, 18 Church Street, Inverness.
Kincardine—Members, 5; Quorum, 3—A. Lyon Wood, 9 Market Square, Stonehaven.
Kirkcudbright—Members, 5; Quorum, 3—John Barr, 187 King Street, Castle-Douglas.
Lanark—Members, 11; Quorum, 5—J. A. Walls, The Pharmacy, 59 Main Street, Bothwell.
Linlithgow—Members, 5; Quorum, 3—F. Stuart, Chemist, Broxburn.
Midlothian—Members, 7; Quorum, 3—H. Dryerre, The Pharmacy, Bonnyrigg.
Orkney—Members, 5; Quorum, 3—B. Heddle, Albert Street, Kirkwall.
Peebles—Members, 5; Quorum, 3—W. J. Sanderson, 43 High Street, Peebles.
Perth—Members, 7; Quorum, 3—T. Harley, 29 High Street, Perth.
Renfrew—Members, 9; Quorum, 3—D. Penman, 28 High Street, Johnstone.
Ross and Cromarty—Members, 5; Quorum, 3—J. F. Hunter, 8 High Street, Dingwall.
Roxburgh—Members, 5; Quorum, 3—G. Cairns, 12 Sandbed, Hawick.
Selkirk—Members, 5; Quorum, 3—J. Henry, 24 Bank Street, Galashiels.
Stirling—Members, 7; Quorum, 3—R. Marshall, Chemist, South Bridge Street, Grangemouth.
Sutherland—Members, 5; Quorum, 3—J. Mennie, Chemist, Golspie.
Wigtown—Members, 5; Quorum, 3—J. Dunn, 64 Victoria Street, Newton-Stewart.
Zetland—Members, 2 to 5; Quorum, 2—A. A. Porteous, Union Bank Buildings, Lerwick.

BURGHS.

Aberdeen—Members, 7; Quorum, 3—W. F. Hay, 476 Union Street, Aberdeen.
Airdrie—Members, 5; Quorum, 3—W. S. Culbert, 39 Stirling Street, Airdrie.
Arbroath—Members, 5; Quorum, 3—F. W. M. Bennett, 238 High Street, Arbroath.
Ayr—Members, 5; Quorum, 3—Martin Meldrum, 7 Burns Statue Square, Ayr.
Clydebank—Members, 5; Quorum, 3—John Weir, 3 Glasgow Road, Clydebank.
Coatbridge—Members, 5; Quorum, 3—G. Clark Wilson, 110 Bank Street, Coatbridge.
Dumbarton—Members, 5; Quorum, 3—P. Mitchell, 8 Church Street, Dumbarton.
Dumfries and Maxwelltown—Members, 5; Quorum, 3—J. Fraser, The City Pharmacy, 84 High Street, Dumfries.
Dundee—Members, 7; Quorum, 3—G. J. Lindsay, 111 Nethergate, Dundee.
Dunfermline—Members, 5; Quorum, 3—R. Robertson, Abbey Pharmacy, 55 Moodie Street, Dunfermline.
Edinburgh—Members, 9; Quorum, 5—J. Muir, 7 Crichton Place, Leith Walk, Edinburgh.
Falkirk—Members, 5; Quorum, 3—D. Dunnet, 82 Main Street, Bainsford, Falkirk.
Glasgow—Members, 15; Quorum, 5—G. S. Kitchin, 116 Nithsdale Road, Pollokshields, Glasgow.
Greenock—Members, 5; Quorum, 3—T. L. Sinclair, 86 Roxburgh Street, Greenock.
Hamilton—Members, 5; Quorum, 3—B. Reekie, 18 Brandon Street, Hamilton.

Inverness—Members, 5; Quorum, 3—R. Macdonald, 18 Church Street, Inverness.
Kilmarnock—Members, 5; Quorum, 3—W. G. Boyd, 68 Portland Street, Kilmarnock.
Kirkcaldy—Members, 5; Quorum, 3—A. G. Adamson, High Street, West End, Kirkcaldy.
Leith—Members, 5; Quorum, 3—P. Nisbet, 3 Duke Street, Leith.
Motherwell—Members, 5; Quorum, 3—W. Morrison, 28 Brandon Street, Motherwell.
Paisley—Members, 5; Quorum, 3—H. Stewart, 81 High Street, Paisley.
Perth—Members, 5; Quorum, 3—T. Harley, 29 High Street, Perth.
Rutherglen—Members, 5; Quorum, 3—A. M'Haig, 198 Main Street, Rutherglen.
Stirling—Members, 5; Quorum, 3—J. Walker, 67 King Street, Stirling.
Wishaw—Members, 5; Quorum, 3—H. B. M'Minn, 17 Main Street, Wishaw.

APPENDIX VII.

AGREEMENT BETWEEN MEDICAL PRACTITIONER AND INSURANCE COMMITTEE.

Form Med. 18 (*Revised*).
(*Scotland.*)
(*January* 1915.)

(*See Cap. IV., Section (I.), paragraph* (167).)

PAYMENT BY CAPITATION.

AGREEMENT between the Insurance Committee for the
                    (hereinafter called the "Committee") of the one part and*
of   a duly qualified Medical Practitioner registered in the Medical Register in that name (hereinafter called the "Practitioner") of the other part, whereby it is agreed as follows:—

1. The National Insurance Acts, 1911 to 1913, and the National Health Insurance (Medical Benefit) Regulations (Scotland), 1913 (hereinafter called "the Regulations"), and the National Health Insurance (Medical Benefit) Regulations (Scotland), 1914, or other Regulations for the administration of Medical Benefit in force for the time being in the area of the Committee are incorporated in and form part of this Agreement.

2. (i.) The Practitioner shall as from the date of the commencement of this agreement give to all persons who are for the time being entitled to obtain treatment from him such treatment as is of a kind which can consistently with the best interests of the patient be properly undertaken by general practitioner of ordinary professional competence and skill: Provided that the Practitioner shall not by virtue of this agreement be required to give, nor entitled under this agreement to make, any charge for treatment to any person in respect of a confinement, that is to say, labour resulting in the issue of a living child, or labour after 28 weeks of pregnancy resulting in the issue of a child whether alive or dead.

(ii.) The Practitioner shall not accept any fee or other remuneration in respect of treatment which he is required to give under this agreement, except as provided in this agreement.

3. The persons entitled to obtain treatment from the Practitioner under this agreement (hereinafter called the "patients") are those persons who have been or may be accepted by him under the provisions of the

---

* The Practitioner should enter his name in the exact style in which he is registered in the Medical Register.

Regulations and such other persons as have been or may be assigned to him under any scheme or arrangements made in accordance with the Regulations by the Committee and the Panel Committee.

4. Where the condition of the patient is such as to require services beyond the competence of an ordinary practitioner, the Practitioner shall advise the patient as to the steps which should be taken in order to obtain such treatment as his condition may require.

5. (i.) The Practitioner shall attend and treat at the places, on the days and at the hours mentioned in the Third Schedule hereto, any patient who attends there for that purpose.

(ii.) The Practitioner may with the consent of the Committee, which shall not be unreasonably withheld, alter the places, days, and hours of his attendance, or any of them, and shall in that event take such steps as the Committee may consider necessary to bring the alteration to the notice of his patients.

6. (i.) The Practitioner shall visit at the place of residence of the patient any patient whose condition so requires.

(ii.) Where a patient is at any place other than his place of residence, the Practitioner shall visit him if his condition so requires, provided that he is within a distance of   miles by road from the place of residence of the Practitioner.

(iii.) For the purposes of this clause the place of residence of the patient means the place where he resided at the date on which he was accepted by or assigned to the Practitioner.

7. The Practitioner shall keep, and furnish to the Committee and Commissioners within 14 days of the expiration of the period to which such are applicable, records of the diseases of the patients attended by him, and of his treatment of them, in such one of the two forms set out in the Fourth Schedule hereto, as shall be agreed on between the Committee and the Panel Committee, and such further records as may at any time hereafter be agreed between the Committee and the Panel Committee, and shall, at the request of any patient, furnish such certificates as are referred to in the First Schedule hereto, and the services rendered by the Practitioner shall be of such a kind as to comply with the conditions set out in the First Schedule hereto (or any such modifications of those conditions as do not impose an additional burden on the Practitioner) being conditions respecting the nature and quality of treatment which must be complied with by reason of any scheme for the distribution of a Parliamentary Grant.

8. All treatment shall be given by the Practitioner personally, except where he is prevented by urgency of other professional duties, temporary absence from home, or other reasonable cause, and the Practitioner shall to the best of his ability provide that when he is so prevented some other practitioner will give attendance as his deputy on his behalf : Provided that where treatment is given by a deputy, the deputy shall be entitled to treat patients at places other than those mentioned in the Third Schedule hereto, due regard being had to the convenience of the patients.

9. The Practitioner shall, as soon as may be after the commencement of each quarter, furnish to the Committee on a form to be provided by the Committee a statement of the number of his patients, other than temporary residents, for that quarter, and shall as soon as may be after the expiration of each quarter furnish on a form to be provided by the Committee an account in respect of the treatment during that quarter of patients who are temporary residents.

10. The remuneration of the Practitioner in respect of patients other than temporary residents shall be calculated in accordance with the provisions of Part IV. of, and the First Schedule to, the Regulations on the basis of the rate contained in the Second Schedule hereto, and in respect of patients who are temporary residents shall be calculated in accordance with the provisions of Part IV. of the Regulations and on the basis of the scale contained in the Fifth Schedule to the Regulations.

11. The Practitioner shall order on a form provided by the Committee for the purpose such drugs and prescribed appliances as are requisite for

the treatment of any patient other than those which the Practitioner may under this agreement or any agreement hereafter to be made with the Committee himself supply, and if the Practitioner orders any drug not included in the list from time to time supplied to him by the Committee or orders any drug or appliance for a patient who is a temporary resident, he shall distinguish the order so given in such manner as the Committee may require.

12. (i.) The Practitioner shall himself supply to a patient where requisite drugs which are necessarily or ordinarily administered by a practitioner in person, and drugs and appliances required for immediate administration or application, or required for use before a supply can conveniently be obtained otherwise under the Regulations.

(ii.) The Practitioner shall furnish, together with the accounts for treatment of temporary residents, accounts for the drugs and appliances so supplied by him, and payment shall be made therefor at such rate or rates as may be agreed, or in default of agreement at the same rate or rates as agreed to be paid by the Committee to chemists and other persons supplying drugs or appliances.

13. (i.) If, owing to any breach on the part of the Practitioner of this agreement, any expenses have been reasonably and necessarily incurred by the Committee or by any patient, or the Committee are deprived of any sum which would otherwise have been payable towards the cost of providing medical benefit, the Committee shall be entitled to recover from the Practitioner or his legal personal representative, either by deduction from any moneys payable under this agreement or otherwise, the amount of the expenses so incurred and of the sum of which the Committee have been so deprived.

(ii.) Before taking action on any matter under the provisions of this clause, the Committee shall, unless the matter has previously been dealt with by the Medical Service Sub-Committee or Joint Services Sub-Committee, refer it to the Medical Service Sub-Committee, which shall deal with the matter in accordance with the Regulations relating to the powers and duties of that Sub-Committee.

(iii.) The Practitioner or his legal personal representative shall be entitled to appeal to the Commissioners against any decision of the Committee under this clause within fourteen days after receiving notice of the decision.

14. Any dispute or question (other than a question which under the provisions of the Regulations or of the last preceding clause hereof is referred to the Medical Service Sub-Committee, or is to be submitted for decision to referees appointed under the Regulations) arising between the Committee and the Practitioner or his legal personal representative relating to the construction of this agreement or the rights and liabilities of the Committee or the Practitioner or his legal personal representative hereunder shall be referred to the Commissioners.

15. In the event of the Commissioners exercising any of the powers conferred on them by the proviso to sub-section (2) of section 15 of the principal Act, or by the proviso (i.) to sub-section (5) of that section, or by section 11 of the amending Act, in respect of the area within which the Practitioner is under this agreement required to give treatment, this agreement shall be determined forthwith, but save as aforesaid, this agreement shall not be varied or determined otherwise than in accordance with the provisions of Part II. of the Regulations as amended by the said National Health Insurance (Medical Benefit) Regulations (Scotland), 1914, or in the special circumstances to which Regulation 83 (2) applies, in accordance with said Regulation.*

---

* Under Regulation 17 (2) a Practitioner who desires to withdraw from the panel may do so at the end of a year, as fixed by the Commissioners, by giving notice to the Committee not less than four weeks before the commencement of the succeeding year, and may with the consent of the Committee withdraw from the panel at any other time.

16. This agreement shall come into force on the 1st day of January 1915, or on the date of the agreement, whichever date is the later.

17. Except where the context otherwise requires, words and expressions used herein shall have the same meaning as in the Regulations.

In Witness whereof the parties hereto have executed this agreement, together with the said Schedules hereto, as follows :—

    Sealed with the Common Seal of the Committee,
       and subscribed on their behalf at
                     , the   day
      of   , One thousand
      nine hundred and
      in presence of

Name—————————————⎫
                                  ⎬ *Witness.*
Address ————————————⎭
                                   Signatures
Designation————————⎭ *on behalf*
                                      of
Name——— - ————————⎫ *Committee.*
Address ————————————⎬ *Witness.*
Designation————————⎭

    Signed and Delivered by the Practitioner at
                           , the
      day of
      One thousand nine hundred and
                   , in presence of

Name—————————————⎫
Address ————————————⎬ *Witness.*
Designation————————⎭

Name—————————————⎫
Address ————————————⎬ *Witness.*
Designation————————⎭

THE FIRST SCHEDULE.

    The conditions of a grant to the Committee will require that records shall be kept of the diseases of the insured persons in the area and of their treatment in such form as is required by the Commissioners,[*] and that certificates shall be furnished to every insured person, where he so desires, and requests, in such form, on such occasions, and generally in such manner as the Commissioners may determine, for the purposes of any claim made by him for sickness or disablement benefit or for the purpose of determining or calculating the period during which sickness benefit is or would, but for any section of the principal Act disentitling him, have been payable, or of calculating arrears, and that unless and until the Commissioners so deter-

---

   * *Note.*—The form is that set out in the Fourth Schedule to this Agreement.

mine such certificates shall be furnished for the purposes aforesaid as are required to be furnished in pursuance of the rules of the Society of which the insured person is a member or of the Committee, as the case may be, and that the general arrangements made by the Committee shall be such as to secure to insured persons a standard of treatment satisfactory to the Commissioners, and that the domiciliary treatment of persons on panel-lists recommended for sanatorium benefit shall be undertaken by the practitioners by whom they are attended and that a sum of 6d. per annum in respect of each such person eligible for sanatorium benefit shall be provided for the remuneration of those practitioners in respect of their obligation to afford such treatment.

THE SECOND SCHEDULE.

RATE FOR CALCULATING REMUNERATION.

The Practitioner shall be credited with a rate of
a quarter in respect of persons included in his list at the commencement of the quarter who are entitled to medical benefit and a further rate of
 a quarter in respect of persons so included who are eligible for sanatorium benefit.

THE THIRD SCHEDULE.

PLACES OF ATTENDANCE.   DAYS AND HOURS OF
                              ATTENDANCE AT EACH PLACE.

THE FOURTH SCHEDULE.

Form No. 1.

DAY BOOK RECORD.

Form No. 2.

MEDICAL RECORD CARD (*See* Appendix IX.).

APPENDIX VIII.

PROCEDURE IN INQUIRIES AS TO RANGE OF MEDICAL SERVICE.

(*See Cap. IV., Section* (*I.*), *paragraph* (178).)

RULES MADE BY THE SCOTTISH INSURANCE COMMISSIONERS UNDER ARTICLE 50 OF THE NATIONAL HEALTH INSURANCE (MEDICAL BENEFIT) REGULATIONS (SCOTLAND), 1913.

1. In these Rules unless the context otherwise requires—
"The Commissioners" means the Scottish Insurance Commissioners:
"Question" means a question as to whether an operation or other service is of a kind which can consistently with the best interests of the patient be properly undertaken by a general practitioner of ordinary professional competence and skill.

2. Where an Insurance Committee and a Local Medical Committee fail to agree as to the decision of any question, the Insurance Committee shall prepare and submit to the Local Medical Committee—
 (*a*) a written statement of the facts in connection with which the question has arisen; and
 (*b*) a written statement of the decision given by it and the grounds on which the decision is based.

3. The Local Medical Committee shall, as soon as may be after receipt

of the said statements, furnish to the Insurance Committee a written statement of the decision given by it and the grounds on which the decision is based, and shall inform the Insurance Committee whether it concurs in the statement of facts prepared by the Insurance Committee, and, if not, in what respects it does not concur in that statement.

4. The Insurance Committee shall send the statements prepared by both Committees to the Commissioners, and the Commissioners may, if they think fit, require both or either of the said Committees to furnish further particulars either with regard to the facts of the case or to the decision or the grounds of the decision.

5. The Commissioners shall furnish copies of all such statements or further statements to each of the Referees appointed by them for the purpose of deciding the question.

6. After consideration of the said statements the Referees shall inform the Commissioners whether in their opinion a hearing is desirable, and in the event of a hearing being required, the Commissioners shall fix the time and place of the hearing and shall give not less than seven days' notice thereof to the Insurance Committee and the Local Medical Committee.

7. Each Committee shall be entitled to appear at the hearing by the chairman, clerk, or secretary of the Committee, or by any other member thereof duly appointed for the purpose, or with the written approval of the Commissioners previously obtained by counsel or solicitor, and produce such evidence, whether orally or in writing, as in the opinion of the Referees may be relevant to the matters at issue.

8. The Referees shall as soon as may be after the hearing report to the Commissioners the decision at which they have arrived.

9. Where in the opinion of the Referees a hearing is not required, the Referees shall, as soon as may be after the matter has been referred to them, meet and consider the question and report to the Commissioners the decision at which they have arrived.

10.—(1) Where the Commissioners think fit to refer for decision to Referees any question on which the Insurance Committee and the Local Medical Committee are agreed, the Commissioners may require either or both of the said Committees to furnish written statements of the facts in connection with which the question has arisen and of their decision and the grounds on which the decision was based, and the Commissioners shall thereupon request the Referees appointed by them for the purpose to fix a day for the hearing.

(2) The statement or statements furnished in accordance with the provisions of the last preceding paragraph shall, for the purposes of the hearing, be evidence of the facts therein alleged.

(3) The Insurance Committee and the Local Medical Committee shall be given by the Commissioners not less than seven days' notice of a hearing held under this Rule, and shall be entitled to appear at the hearing by any of the persons mentioned in Rule 7.

11. At any hearing held under these Rules the Commissioners may produce such evidence, whether orally or in writing, as in the opinion of the Referees may be relevant to the matters at issue, and may appear by any one of themselves or of their officers or by counsel or solicitor.

12. The Commissioners may, if they think fit, dispense with any requirement of these Rules in any case where, regard being had to all the circumstances, it appears just or convenient to do so.

13. These Rules shall apply with the necessary modifications in the case of any question arising under Article 55 of the National Health Insurance (Administration of Medical Benefit) Regulations (No. 2) (Scotland), 1912.

Dated this third day of September in the year one thousand nine hundred and fourteen.

(Signed)   H. L. F. FRASER,
Assistant Secretary to the Scottish Insurance Commissioners, and a person authorised to sign on behalf of the Secretary.

175

Name _____
Address _____

Age _____ Sex _____
Occupation _____

a. = Surgery Attendance.   v. = Visit.

Mth.	1	2	3	4	5	6	7	8	9	10	11	12	13	14	15	16	17	18	19	20	21	22	23	24	25	26	27	28	29	30	31
Jan.																															
Feb.																															
Mar.																															
Apr.																															
May																															
June																															
July																															
Aug.																															
Sept.																															
Oct.																															
Nov.																															
Dec.																															

Machine perforation.

Mth.	1	2	3	4	5	6	7	8	9	10	11	12	13	14	15	16	17	18	19	20	21	22	23	24	25	26	27	28	29	30	31
Jan.																															
Feb.																															
Mar.																															
Apr.																															
May																															
June																															
July																															
Aug.																															
Sept.																															
Oct.																															
Nov.																															
Dec.																															

Mth.	Illnesses.	Total No. of	
		a.	v.
Jan.			
Feb.			
Mar.			
Apr.			
May			
June			
July			
Aug.			
Sept.			
Oct.			
Nov.			
Dec.			
	Total.		

Dr. _____ Insurance Committee.

Dr. _____ Insurance Committee.

Form Med. 15.
Scotland.

This portion to be forwarded to The National Health Insurance Commission (Scotland), EDINBURGH, between 1st and 14th January.

Doctor's Initials _____

Date _____ 191

Machine perforation.

NOTES.

This portion to be forwarded to The Clerk of Insurance Committee, at his Office, between 1st and 14th January.

APPENDIX X.

NEW SYSTEM OF MEDICAL CERTIFICATION OF INCAPACITY OF INSURED PERSONS FOR WORK.

(*See Cap. IV., Section (I.), paragraph* (184).)

Memo. 211 I.C.

MEMORANDUM FOR THE INFORMATION OF MEDICAL PRACTITIONERS AND APPROVED SOCIETIES.

1. The National Health Insurance Commissioners for England, Scotland. and Wales have given prolonged and careful consideration to difficulties brought under their notice as having been experienced by Approved Societies in dealing with claims for sickness benefit, especially as regards notice of illness and medical certificates, and by doctors in the giving of certificates and in their consequent relations with Approved Societies. As a result of this consideration, the Commissioners have decided to bring into operation a new system of medical certification, and of procedure in certain connected matters, which is explained in this memorandum.

2. In their investigation of the subject and in the development of the new scheme, the Commissioners have derived great assistance from conferences which they have held with the representatives of Approved Societies of all types on the Advisory Committees, and with representatives of the medical profession, including the medical members of the Advisory Committees and members of Panel Committees in many parts of the country. They have also been greatly assisted by the evidence bearing on the subject of medical certification which was collected in the course of the recent inquiry of the Departmental Committee appointed by Mr. Masterman to consider the question of sickness benefit claims (in England) under the National Insurance Act, and by the portions of the Report and Recommendations of that Committee which deal with the subject. [Cd. 7687].

3. It appears to the Commissioners that the difficulties which have been brought under their notice have been due partly to temporary causes which are gradually passing away; and partly to faults of individuals, inevitable in some degree under every system. In the main, however, they have been due to the fact that those concerned, including both doctors and those engaged in the administration of Societies, have not been able to arrive at such general understandings on matters of procedure as are necessary in order that each person concerned may carry out his own duties efficiently.

4. An official of an Approved Society normally has to deal with certificates given by a large number of doctors of most of whom he can have no personal knowledge, and who may differ widely in their standards of precision as regards both diagnosis and certification. Similarly, a doctor attending insured persons finds that his certificates of incapacity for work bring him into relation, directly or indirectly, with officials of a great number of Societies whose rules and methods of administration may be very varied. Moreover, the lack of the necessary mutual understanding exists not only between Societies on one side, and doctors on the other, but also between Societies among themselves, and between doctors among themselves. Doctors, for example, have frequently pointed out, in conference with the Commissioners, that the doctor who resists the importunity of his patient or of an official of a Society, to give improperly or to ante-date or post-date a certificate, causes offence and runs a risk of injuring his practice through the fact that, in the absence of any satisfactory check, some other doctor may be more complaisant. Societies similarly state that when making complaint of what they regard as undue laxity of procedure on the part of doctors, they may be met by the reply that other Societies do not so regard the practice criticised.

5. The Commissioners are satisfied that, while some improvement is attainable through local conferences between representatives of Societies

and doctors, such as have been held, and doubtless will continue to be held, with advantage, in various districts, the existing difficulties can only be substantially overcome by the establishment of a definite understanding between Societies and doctors generally, throughout the country. They are also satisfied that a general understanding of this kind can be brought about only through the intervention of the Commissioners.

6. Acceding, therefore, to representations made to them on behalf both of Approved Societies and of the medical profession, the Commissioners have framed the new scheme of procedure explained in this Memorandum, to apply to all cases in which insured persons need medical certificates of incapacity for work, in support of claims for sickness or disablement benefit,[*] or for other purposes under the Act. This new scheme will come into operation on 1st January 1915.

7. The scheme has two objects, first, to secure the necessary measure of uniformity of procedure on the part of Approved Societies, insured persons and doctors in respect of those matters which can satisfactorily be made the subject of definite rules, and, secondly, to bring about a general understanding amongst all concerned as to the procedure to be followed in dealing with various exceptional contingencies which cannot satisfactorily be dealt with by formal rules.

MAIN FEATURES OF THE SCHEME.

Forms of Certificates.

8. Under the scheme every medical certificate of incapacity of insured persons for work, required for the purposes of the Act, is to be in the appropriate form determined by the Commissioners.

9. Each medical certificate required will be given on a fresh form. The system, hitherto adopted by some Societies with the concurrence of the Commissioners, of issuing forms for the several successive certificates printed on one continuous sheet, will be entirely abandoned.

10. The forms will be contained in books kept by the doctor, so that they may always be available for his immediate use when occasion requires; they will be supplied to doctors through the Insurance Committees. Special care has been devoted to making the books so compact that they may be carried about with the least possible inconvenience.

11. The forms of Notice of Sickness, declaration of incapacity and claim for benefit, and of declaration off benefit, which insured persons are required to give to their Societies for the purposes of the Act, will be printed on the same slips as the medical certificates by which they have to be accompanied.

12. The forms of medical certificates provided include First, Intermediate, and Final Certificates. A First Certificate and a Final Certificate will be required in every case, and an Intermediate Certificate or certificates for all but very short periods of incapacity.

Dating of Certificates.

13. Every certificate will show plainly the date on which it was signed which will normally be also the date on which the doctor made the examination of the patient referred to in the certificate. In the exceptional cases in which the dates are not identical both dates will be stated.

14. The certificate is to be given, wherever practicable, at the time when the doctor sees the patient and makes the examination to which the certificate relates. When, for any exceptional reason, the certificate cannot be given at the time of examination, it is to be given as soon as possible thereafter.

15. The times of giving certificates will be governed mainly by the

---

[*] For brevity the term " sickness benefit " is used elsewhere in the document, but it must be understood as including disablement benefit, to which the same considerations apply.

arrangements which the doctor makes for seeing the patient in the ordinary course for the purpose of treatment, and will bear no necessary relation to any system adopted by the insured person's Society of paying benefit on some particular day of the week. Societies are advised to adopt an arrangement of paying benefit each week on and up to the day of the week most convenient for the purposes of their own administration, subject to a medical certificate having been given on some day since the last payment in each case, and to no Final Certificate having been received.

16. The ante-dating or post-dating of any certificate will be a breach of the doctor's agreement, and the arrangements under the new system, as above described, have been specially devised with a view to preventing those circumstances from arising which, in the past, have conduced to such practices. It is essential to efficiency of administration that doctors should resist any importunity from their insured patients or others and comply strictly with their obligation in this matter, and that Approved Societies should require their officials equally to abstain from any kind of direct or indirect pressure upon doctors to break the rule.

17. One of the main principles of the whole scheme is that certificates are to be retrospective, not prospective, in their effect. The certificates are so framed that (except as regards a very small group of cases mentioned in paragraph 31) the doctor certifies only as to the incapacity of the patient at and up to the time of making his examination, and not as to an anticipated incapacity on some future date.

Description of the Cause of Incapacity.

18. The doctor is required to certify, not only as to whether the insured person is incapable of work, but also as to the specific disease or bodily or mental disablement which is the cause of the incapacity. It is further definitely required that, except in certain special cases specifically provided for in the Rules, the cause of the incapacity shall be stated in such terms as will inform the Approved Society, as precisely as possible, of the condition of the patient so far as known at the time to the doctor. This matter is fully explained in paragraphs 42 to 52 below.

Uniformity.

19. The obligations of doctors respecting those matters in which uniformity of practice on their part is necessary have been made an integral part of the contract under which they treat insured persons. The agreements, for example, now entered into by panel practitioners with Insurance Committees provide that certificates shall be given (after 1st January 1915) in the form, and on the occasions, and generally in the manner determined by the Commissioners; and in pursuance of this provision the Commissioners have made the Rules appended to this Memorandum (*see* page 189).

20. As regards the procedure of Societies and of insured persons, the Commissioners are satisfied that the requisite measure of uniformity is secured in matters affecting the doctor's obligations under the scheme.

PROCEDURE UNDER THE SCHEME.

First Certificate and Notice of Sickness.

21. As soon as the doctor is satisfied that his patient is incapable of work, he will, if so desired by the patient, give him a First Certificate. The Rule does not lay upon the doctor the obligation of giving the certificate if the patient does not ask for it. It is important, however, in the interests of the insured person himself, that he should obtain his First Certificate, and send it with his Notice of Sickness to his Society, at the commencement of incapacity. Delay may cause him loss of benefit, or involve him in penalties, and must, in any event, occasion inconvenience and delay in obtaining benefit. Even if the insured person, for any reason, is not entitled to benefit, or does not wish to claim it, he may still be under the

necessity (under penalty of loss through delay or default) of furnishing to his Society a Notice of Sickness and a medical certificate as soon as he becomes aware that he is incapable of work.* It is in the power of a doctor, therefore, to assist his insured patients to avoid unfortunate results of oversight, ignorance, or misunderstanding on their part, by calling their attention to the matter on the first occasion in the course of an illness on which he finds them in such a state of health that a First Certificate can properly be given.

22. An insured person who has received a First Certificate is required to fill up the form of Notice of Sickness, on the right-hand side of the document containing the medical certificate, and to deliver the document at once to his Society.

23. The form of Notice of Sickness is a notice simply, and not an application for benefit, and no benefit will ordinarily be payable until a second medical certificate with the appropriate declaration has been delivered to the Society.

Second Certificates (Intermediate or Final).

24. The doctor is under obligation to give a second certificate, if so desired by the insured person, within eight days of the First Certificate. He is not required to give it on any particular day of the week. He is expected to give it on some occasion (within the eight days) on which he sees and examines his patient for purposes of treatment.

25. If, when giving the second certificate, the doctor is satisfied that the insured person, although incapable of work up to that date is fit to resume work immediately after that date, the second certificate will be in the form of a Final Certificate; but, if this be not so, he will give an Intermediate Certificate, and will give further certificates week by week during the period of incapacity, the last of the series being in the form of a Final Certificate, and the others in the form of Intermediate Certificates.

Further Intermediate Certificates.

26. The doctor is under obligation to give a certificate every week if one be desired by the insured person, and the insured person will, except in the cases referred to in paragraphs 36 and 37, and in some of the cases dealt with in paragraph 38, be required by the Society to produce a medical certificate as evidence of incapacity between each two weekly pay-days of the Society.

27. While it is not necessary that Intermediate Certificates should be given on any particular day of the week in order to enable a payment of benefit to be made on the next following ordinary pay-day of the Society, there are certain cases in which doctors will have it in their power, at the cost of little if any inconvenience to themselves, to facilitate the smooth working of the arrangements for payment of sickness benefit by having regard to the system of the Society, if informed of it by their patients. In the first place, if the doctor receives the necessary information through his patient, he may, by taking care to give his second certificate before the first ordinary pay-day, enable the member to receive any benefit to which he is entitled a week sooner than would otherwise be practicable. Secondly,

---

* It will be observed that as regards giving the First Certificate it makes no difference to the procedure whether the insured person is entitled to benefit and desirous of claiming it or not. As regards Intermediate Certificates there may be differences in the procedure as between the Society and the insured person, according to whether the insured person is or is not receiving sickness benefit. With a view to simplicity of explanation paragraphs 21 to 39 of the Memorandum are framed with reference to cases of persons who are receiving benefit: and the special requirements in the case of persons who, though incapable of work, are not receiving benefit, are explained separately in paragraph 40. It may be well to mention here, however, that (as will be seen from that paragraph), the points of difference between those two kinds of cases do not affect the doctor.

it is desirable that the interval between the date of examination of the patient and the date of payment should be as short as is reasonably possible, since the Society may often have no direct evidence of incapacity beyond the date on which the doctor found the patient to be incapable of work. It is believed that, except in very sparsely populated districts, doctors will find little difficulty in so arranging their work that any particular patient can always be seen on some one of any three consecutive days ; and that where this is so they will (as a matter, not of obligation, but of reasonable co-operation with the Societies) so arrange that, for example, a patient whose payment of benefit would ordinarily be made on a Friday, shall always be seen by the doctor either on Tuesday, Wednesday, or Thursday of that week, as may best suit the medical requirements of the case, and otherwise be most convenient.

Declaration by Insured Person.

28. The insured person, having received an Intermediate Certificate, will fill up the declaration on the right-hand side of the form, and deliver it at once to his Society. The Society, if satisfied that the insured person is eligible for benefit, and if a Final Cretificate has not been received in the meantime, will then be enabled to pay benefit up to whatever day after the date of the certificate its rules and ordinary practice determine.

Final Certificate and Declaration-Off.

29. A Final Certificate must be given by the doctor (whether asked for by the insured person or not) directly he comes to the conclusion, on any examination of the patient, that the latter is fit to resume work immediately after the date of the examination. The insured person having received the Final Certificate, will add, on the right-hand portion of the form, his declaration off the funds of the Society, and will deliver it to the Society.

30. The chief difficulties to which doctors have drawn attention as affecting the giving of Final Certificates' arise in respect of persons who, when seen by the doctor in the ordinary course, are found to be not quite fit for work, but likely to be fit within a few days. Such a person, in the absence of some precaution, may fail to see the doctor until some days after he has become fit for work. The doctor will then not be in a position to certify, from his personal knowledge, as to the day on which the patient in fact first became capable of work ; and in such circumstances the insured person will not be able to obtain from the doctor a Final Certificate, since the latter, in the form now required, is not only a certificate of fitness to resume work after the date of examination but also a certificate that the patient has, in the doctor's opinion, been incapable of work up to and including that date. In order to prevent this situation from arising, a space has been provided in the form of First and Intermediate Certificates, in which the doctor is required to insert the date on which the patient should come to see him again, if, at the time of giving one of these certificates, the doctor is satisfied that the patient, though not fit to resume work immediately, will be fit before a further certificate would next ordinarily be given (Rule 7).* It is believed that careful compliance with this Rule will enable doctors, in the great majority of cases, to avert the difficulties above-mentioned.

Special Final Certificates in certain Rural Areas.

31. It has been represented to the Commissioners that the procedure indicated in the preceding paragraph will not meet the difficulty completely in rural areas, in the case of patients living at a considerable distance

---

* While the doctor is required to make use of this space in the cases referred to in Rule 7, it is always open to him to fill it up in any other circumstances in which he may think it desirable, for the purpose of ensuring that the patient should see him again on some particular date.

from their doctors, to whom some hardship would be occasioned by requiring them to be seen a second time by the doctor within a very few days. A special arrangement has been made, therefore, to meet such cases by authorising the doctor, in these cases and these only, to give a prospective certificate. Under the provisions of Rule 8 it will be open to him, if on any occasion of seeing the patient he is satisfied that the patient is not fit to resume work at once but will be fit within three days, to give a certificate in the special form required by that Rule. This provision will operate in those districts only in which the Commissioners are satisfied that hardships of the kind above mentioned might frequently result from insistence on the ordinary requirements defined in Rules 6 and 7. A list of such districts will be determined by the Commissioners after consulting the Insurance Committees, and the doctors practising in those districts will be supplied with the requisite forms.

Necessity of care as to Final Certificates.

32. It is desired to draw the attention of doctors and officials of Societies specially to the point that a doctor is precluded by the Rules from giving a Final or other certificate of incapacity to an insured person who is found upon examination to have already become fit for work. Any question of injury or loss to the insured person arising in such a case will be one between him and the Society, with which the doctor is not concerned.

33. It is essential to the satisfactory working of the whole system that doctors should pay special attention to the giving of Final Certificates, since an insured person resuming work without producing a Final Certificate to his Society is at the risk of losing benefit or incurring penalties under the Society's rules. Furthermore, it will only be by a strict observance of the system of giving Final Certificates that the arrangement will continue to be possible under which Societies having fixed pay-days will not require that certificates should bear the date of any particular day of the week; and it is by this arrangement that doctors will be freed from the pressure from their insured patients and others, of which they have complained, to give certificates on some particular day. The Commissioners feel assured that, in recognition of the importance of these considerations, doctors will take special care not only to comply with the specific requirements of the Rules relating to Final Certificates, but also to act in accordance with the general principles of the whole system in this matter.

Remarks by Doctor.

34. A space has been provided in the certificate for remarks by the doctor, who is thus enabled to give any additional information which he may think it desirable to convey. This may include, for example, additional information as to the nature of the incapacitating disease or disablement, indications as to the probable duration of incapacity, or short particulars of directions which the doctor has given to the patient (*e.g.* as to his remaining in bed or indoors), of which he may think it well that the Society should be made aware.

PROCEDURE IN EXCEPTIONAL CASES.

Patients seen after the Commencement of Incapacity for Work.

35. In the first place, questions may arise as to the position of an insured person who for some reason was not seen by the doctor when he first became incapable of work, and who, therefore, cannot be certified by the doctor as having been incapable of work on the first day or days in respect of which he desires to claim benefit. The insured person in such a case should make special application to his Society stating the facts, and it is open to the Society, if satisfied by such evidence as he is able to furnish of his incapacity, to pay benefit accordingly. In such cases, doctors, although unable to certify as to the date when incapacity began, may be asked occasionally by their patients to make some statement, based on the condition of the

patient when first seen by them, which may be of assistance to the Society in considering a claim. Such a statement will be made, if at all, as an act of grace and not as a matter of obligation ; and it is desirable that it should be carefully worded so that the doctor may not be misunderstood as vouching for facts that are beyond his actual knowledge ; the value of his expression of opinion, as evidence in support of the claim, while varying widely in different cases, will consist only in his statement that the facts ascertained by him from his examination of the patient were such as to bear out, or were at all events not inconsistent with, the patient's own account of the case. It will be necessary for Societies to scrutinise such claims with special care, as it is obviously undesirable that insured persons should be encouraged to postpone placing themselves under proper care and supervision at times when they believe themselves to be incapacitated, by disease or disablement, for work.

Certificates in Cases of prolonged Incapacity for Work.

36. While it is contemplated that in the majority of cases it will be necessary for medical certificates to be furnished weekly during the continuance of incapacity, Societies may be satisfied with certificates at less frequent intervals in cases in which it appears certain that incapacity will be prolonged. Where the Society is satisfied from the information already in its possession that it is not necessary to require the insured person to obtain a medical certificate every week, the Society will inform the insured person accordingly, specifying the intervals at which certificates are to be obtained, and it will be for him to inform the doctor. It will, of course, always be within the power of the Society to terminate such an arrangement in view of any change of circumstances, and to require certificates again to be furnished weekly.

Certificates in respect of Patients away from Home.

37. The only other class of exceptions to the rule of weekly certification relates to certain cases of persons who, while still incapable of work, are sent away from home towards the end of an illness for rest and change. In a large proportion of such cases it will obviously be desirable that the patient should be under medical supervision during the period in question, and he will therefore be able to obtain such certificates as are necessary, so long as he remains incapable of work, from the doctor who is attending him in his place of temporary residence. There are, however, cases in which the doctor considers that the patient needs only a short period of change and rest to restore his working capacity, and that his condition does not make medical supervision necessary during this period. In these latter cases, provided that the insured person duly notifies the Society of his intention to leave home, and obtains the Society's permission required under its Rules, and provided also that the application is accompanied by a signed statement (*e.g.* inserted in the " other remarks " portion of an Intermediate Certificate given in the ordinary course) by the home doctor to the effect that the patient needs change for a specified period, but is not expected to need medical supervision while away, the Society, if otherwise satisfied, will be justified in paying benefit (as it becomes due) for a period not exceeding two weeks, on the strength of these statements, without the production of further medical certificates. A Final Certificate will, of course, be required in accordance with the ordinary rule, and, if this is not received by the Society before the third weekly pay-day after the date of the Intermediate Certificate last received, a further Intermediate Certificate will be required. If, through the patient's absence from home, his home doctor is not in a position to examine him, the certificate must be obtained from a doctor who, having examined him, is in a position to certify as to his incapacity for work. It will be understood that in all cases in which a patient goes away from home and the Society has not previously received from the doctor the intimations specified in this paragraph, it will be necessary for him to obtain certificates weekly from a doctor in the place

of his temporary residence, and he must therefore be transferred to the care of such a doctor under the special arrangements for the treatment of temporary residents.

Certificates in respect of In-Patients of Institutions.

38. A difficulty arises in the case of insured persons who are receiving treatment in Institutions from doctors who are under no obligation to furnish certificates required by the Society. Where the insured person is an in-patient of a Hospital or other Institution for the treatment of disease, and a certificate cannot be obtained from a Medical Officer of the Institution, the Society may be satisfied of the insured person's incapacity for work upon the evidence of a written statement, which may be furnished by any responsible officer (not necessarily medical) of the Institution, showing that the insured person is an in-patient of the Institution, and is receiving medical treatment there.

Out-Patients.

39. Where insured persons are out-patients of Hospitals and similar Institutions, and a certificate cannot be obtained from a Medical Officer of the Institution, it will usually be possible for them to present themselves weekly to the doctor who has undertaken their treatment for purposes of medical benefit, and for him to examine them and give such certificates as they may require. If, however, the circumstances of the case are such that the patient cannot be examined by that doctor, it must be left to the insured person to make such special arrangements as the circumstances permit for obtaining the necessary certificate from a doctor who has examined him, and is therefore in a position to certify.

Certificates in cases where Benefit is not claimed.

40. With regard to insured persons who, although incapable of work, are for some reason not entitled to or not claiming sickness benefit, it has already been pointed out that a First Certificate and Notice of Sickness may nevertheless be required. Subsequent certificates and declarations by the insured person are also required under the Rules of most Societies, and in cases in which they are not required the insured person will be so informed by his Society. The doctor, therefore, need not concern himself to discriminate between these two kinds of cases; the only difference so far as he is concerned will be that in some cases he will not be asked for all the Intermediate Certificates which in other cases he would be asked to give. A Final Certificate should be given in all cases.

Insured Persons not Members of Approved Societies.

41. Where an insured person is not a member of an Approved Society, but is a Deposit Contributor, or a member of the Navy and Army Insurance Fund, all notices which in the case of a member of a Society would be sent to the Society will be sent to the Insurance Committee for the area in which the insured person resides.

DESCRIPTION OF THE CAUSE OF INCAPACITY.

(a) Ordinary Cases.

42. Among the questions to which special prominence has always been given in conference with doctors is the necessity of requiring that the doctor should invariably enter in the certificate the name of the disease or injury which in the opinion of the doctor is the cause of the patient's incapacity for work. Many of the chief difficulties urged against the general proposition have been found to be due to misconceptions, and, after careful consideration of the question in all its bearings, the Commissioners have come to the conclusion, in which a considerable number of representative medical men have expressed their concurrence, that doctors can reasonably

be required to undertake the duty of making statements, with as much precision as is in each case possible, as to the specific disease or bodily or mental disablement by which the insured person is rendered incapable of work, in all cases other than those specifically excepted in Rule 11.

(b) Exceptional Cases.

43. The excepted cases for which the special procedure described in that Rule has been devised are those in which doctors have found difficulty in naming frankly on the certificate the particular disease which is the cause of the incapacity for work, because they believed that to do so would be gravely prejudicial to their patients. Two kinds of cases need consideration in this connection; they are:—(i.) cases in which there are medical grounds for believing that to communicate to the patient a precise statement as to the nature of his illness would be prejudicial to his health (as, for example, in certain cases of heart disease, cancer, or incipient insanity); and (ii.) cases in which unjustifiable distress or injury would, it is feared, be occasioned to the patient by giving to other parties information as to the cause of the incapacity; as, for instance, in the case of certain diseases peculiar to women, and in those cases of venereal disease in which the doctor has satisfied himself that the withholding of precise information from the Society will not result in the insured person obtaining benefit which, if the disease were due to his misconduct, he might not be entitled to receive.

44. The cases of venereal disease in which a doctor would be justified in adopting the special procedure are the following:—(a) cases in which the disease is congenital and, therefore, no question of the insured person's misconduct can arise; (b) cases in which the disease is acquired, but the doctor is able to satisfy himself, and can satisfy the Government Referee, that it was occasioned otherwise than by the patient's own misconduct; (c) cases in which the disease was acquired some considerable time before the application for the certificate; these last being cases in which no Society, if it were in possession of the facts, would (the Commissioners believe) suspend the member from benefit. As a definite period must, for practical purposes, be adopted, the limit taken is two years.*

45. The Commissioners are satisfied that in both the groups of cases dealt with in paragraph 43 (viz. those involving risk to the patient's health through disclosure of facts to him and those involving unwarrantable injury to the patient if the facts were disclosed to others) it is necessary to waive the otherwise invariable rule of precise nomenclature in order to secure a strict adherence to the general rule of precise certification in all other cases. Accordingly a special procedure is adopted for these exceptional cases, which, while relieving the doctor from the necessity of disclosing the true nature of the disease in his certificate, will also relieve the Society from the trouble and the insured person from the annoyance of unnecessary inquiries, and at the same time afford a safeguard against the use of the procedure in cases to which it does not properly apply. It is believed that this special procedure will sufficiently protect the interests of Societies, and that therefore they will be well advised to acquiesce in the further arrangement which is necessary for carrying it out satisfactorily, namely, that they should abstain from instituting any inquiries of their own in such cases, except by way of

---

* While the Commissioners are satisfied, as stated in the Memorandum, that Societies do not desire to inflict the penalty of suspension from benefit in respect of misconduct which has happened a long time before it comes under their notice, it is not possible to name any specific time limit as one which it is known that all Societies would regard as reasonable. In view, however, of the necessity of fixing some definite period for the guidance of the doctor (since the responsibility cannot properly be thrown upon him of deciding what is reasonable in each case) the Commissioners have experimentally fixed two years. This limit is open to revision after the system has been given a trial, and the Commissioners will be prepared to consider any representations which may be made to them on the subject.

reference to the Government Referee as explained in paragraph 47 below, although supervision by sick-visitors will still be required, to ensure due observance of the rules as to behaviour during sickness.

Special Procedure for Exceptional Cases.

46. The provision made for dealing with these exceptional cases is that, wherever a doctor advisedly uses in the certificate a description of the patient's condition which is less precise than his knowledge of the case enables him to give, he will, on the same day, send to the Society a notice in the form specified in Rule 11, informing them that he has given the member a certificate of this kind. This notice, and the particular expressions used by the doctor in the certificate, will be such as to convey to the Society no indication of the nature of the case, nor even to suggest into which of the two main groups it falls; the object is simply to assure the Society that the absence of definite details in the particular certificate was of set purpose, the case being one of the excepted cases indicated in paragraph 43 above.

47. The doctor will in every such case, as required by the Rule, communicate confidentially to the Government Referee (or until such Referees have been appointed, to the Commissioners), a precise statement as to the exact nature of the illness or disablement, and the circumstances which justify a resort to this special procedure. It will be the duty of the Government Referee to make a selection of cases in which a conference with the doctor concerned, a further examination of the insured person, or some other special action appears desirable, and to furnish a report thereon to the Commissioners. The Commissioners will take such action as may be needed on receipt of the Referee's report, communicating where necessary with the Society. Societies, on their part, will have the right of communicating with the Government Referee in any cases where they have reasonable grounds (after receiving from the doctor the form above described) for doubting whether the case is really one intended to be covered by this procedure, or whether the insured person is in fact incapable of work.

48. The form to be used by the doctor in communicating with the Approved Society is appended to the Rules (*see* page 191), and the Commissioners suggest that the communication to the Government Referee (or until such Referees are appointed, to the Commissioners) should be in the form shown below.* To save the doctor from the labour of writing out the forms in full, the Commissioners will supply a number of printed copies of both forms upon application being made to them by any doctor.

Difficulties of Early Diagnosis.

49. The attention of the Commissioners has repeatedly been drawn, in conferences with representatives of the medical profession, to difficulties which have been found to arise, through misunderstandings on the part of Societies, in regard to certificates given in the early stages of incapacity in certain cases. The difficulty is due to the fact, which has not been sufficiently

---

* Sir,
    I have to inform you that I have this day given to
of   (Address), being Member No.
of   Society,   Branch, a certificate
in which the cause of incapacity is not stated with full precision.

The precise diagnosis of the disabling condition according to my present knowledge is that this person is suffering from
    I have given a less precise certificate for the following reasons :—

I am,
Yours faithfully,
Address.
Date.   *Insurance Committee Area.*

appreciated by Society officials, that the precision with which even the most skilled and careful doctor can diagnose and describe the nature of the disease or injury from which a patient is suffering differs very widely, in different cases, in the initial stage of an illness. All that can reasonably be expected is that the doctor shall at each stage of an illness describe the condition and the cause of incapacity as exactly as the most careful examination of the case at that stage would enable him to do ; it must be realised that it is often impossible at an early stage for a doctor to name any more than the prominent symptoms, as the actual disease cannot then be determined. In many cases, therefore, of first certificates and occasionally even in second and later certificates, it is impossible for the doctor to make truthfully any more precise and specific entry as to the cause of the incapacity than some general term (e.g. " fever," or even in exceptional cases " debility ") indicating the condition of the patient when examined. On the other hand, Approved Societies cannot reasonably be expected to accept without question any certificates so drawn, even in the earliest stages of incapacity, unless they find that such use of general terms is resorted to by doctors in those cases only where they cannot yet reasonably satisfy their judgment as to a precise diagnosis, and that in those cases they will always put into the space for " other remarks " such explanatory information of the case as may be possible.

Precision in naming Cause of Incapacity.

50. It will be understood that the recognition of the fact that diagnosis of a patient's illness in the early stages cannot always be definite will not excuse or justify a doctor in using, then or at any stage, terms less precise than his knowledge of the case enables him to give. If, for example, first certificates only are considered, there can be but few cases in which a doctor is warranted in declaring a patient to be incapable of work, and yet is unable to ascertain some further facts as to the nature of the illness than are conveyed by such a vague term as " debility " standing alone. And if such further facts are ascertained, a more definite phrase than " debility " clearly can and ought to be employed. For instance, the doctor can certainly be expected in such a case to state, where he so finds, " debility with anæmia," or " debility with high temperature," or " debility with dyspepsia," and similarly in other conditions. An increasing degree of certitude and exactitude is, of course, always likely to be reached at each successive examination of a patient or as the disease develops ; and the Commissioners desire to call the attention of Societies to the fact that for a doctor to give at different stages of a case a different description, in his successive certificates, as to the cause of the patient's incapacity from that given at earlier dates in the same case, is not necessarily, as some officials of Societies have appeared to imagine, evidence of carelessness or incompetence in the doctor, but may rather be a proof of the skill and attention which he gives to his work.

51. For similar reasons, it is necessary that the condition of the patient, as known to the doctor at the time of giving a certificate, should on each occasion be stated explicitly, and not in terms involving reference to previous certificates. No provision, therefore, is made (as in the model forms of certificate previously issued by the Commissioners, which are now wholly superseded) for the use of the expression " the disease named in my last certificate," or any equivalent phrase ; and the use of such expressions will not be in conformity with the Rules.

52. This opportunity is taken of reminding doctors that, as explained in a recent circular : (i.) no distinction is to be drawn between incapacity due to pregnancy and that due to other causes, as affecting claims for sickness benefit ; (ii.) a certificate should, therefore, not be withheld on the ground, merely, that incapacity is due to, or accompanied by, pregnancy ; (iii.) where incapacity is believed to be due, directly or indirectly to pregnancy, pregnancy should be mentioned (with or without other conditions, as the case may be) in naming the cause of the incapacity ; (iv.) in these

as in all other cases a certificate can only be given where the doctor is satisfied that the insured person is incapable of work.

GENERAL CONSIDERATIONS.

53. The Commissioners hope that the scheme of certification set out in paragraphs 21 to 34 above, under which the vast majority of certificates will be given, will commend itself to insured persons, Approved Societies, and doctors as an advance towards simplicity and economy in working and a means of arriving at a better understanding between all concerned as to their rights and duties under the Acts.

54. Both the general scheme and the special arrangements proposed for dealing with exceptional cases (*see* paragraphs 35 to 48 above) will depend for their satisfactory operation on a general appreciation of their main features. The Commissioners have therefore arranged to reprint the Medical Certification Rules in each book of certificates issued to doctors, so that, apart from other steps which will be taken to inform insured persons and Approved Societies, every doctor will be in a position to explain to his patients or to Society officials in any case of difficulty, or where requests are made to which he cannot properly accede, the course of action which in particular circumstances is incumbent upon him under the terms of his agreement.

55. Special attention has been given to securing not only that the forms of certificates to be given by doctors should be uniform, but also that the procedure affecting the doctor should, as far as possible, be uniform, simple, and such as calls for no exercise of discretion on his part except what properly pertains to his professional capacity.

56. Thus, as regards First Certificates, he is not called upon to consider whether the member is or is not likely to desire to claim benefit nor to take into account any technical points such as the question of "linked-up," illnesses, or arrears, and so forth. If, in the course of his attendance upon a patient, he becomes satisfied that the patient is incapable of work, it will be his duty as a medical man to inform the patient to that effect, and he will then furnish the patient, if so desired, with a First Certificate of incapacity for work. As regards Intermediate Certificates, again, he has only to consider week by week, in the ordinary case, whether it is still necessary for the proper medical or surgical treatment of the patient with a view to speedy recovery that he should abstain from work. If he is satisfied of this and does not expect that the incapacity will cease before a further certificate would in the ordinary course be given, he will give an Intermediate Certificate in the ordinary form. If he thinks that the patient should not resume work immediately but will be fit in a few days he will give an Intermediate Certificate, and insert in the certificate the day when the patient should see him again. If he is satisfied that the patient can safely return to work on the next day, he will forthwith give a Final Certificate. If, lastly, the patient comes to the doctor on a day on which it is obvious that he had become fit for work before being seen, the doctor can only refuse the certificate, since the certificate requires that he should be able to certify from his own examination that the patient was in his view incapable of work up to the time of being seen.

57. It is not suggested that this procedure, or any procedure, will relieve a doctor of all the difficulties necessarily involved in some cases in deciding as to whether the patient's condition is or is not such as to render him incapable of work, any more than any system can relieve him of difficulties of diagnosis, and of decision as to proper treatment of a patient in other respects. These difficulties are inherent in the discharge of his professional responsibilities; but when he has discharged his medical duty to the best of his ability the system will, it is believed, make as easy as possible for him the giving of the kind of certificate which is proper in each case, in view of his diagnosis of the patient's condition. It is believed that the system will also strengthen the position of the doctor in dealing with patients who may be dissatisfied with his action with regard to giving or

withholding a certificate of any particular kind. While, as regards his professional judgment, as to whether the patient is on a particular occasion incapable of work or not, as on other questions of diagnosis or treatment, no system can protect him against occasional dissatisfaction on the part of his patients, on the other hand, on all questions of procedure consequent upon that judgment he has a conclusive answer so far as his responsibility is concerned, namely, that he is complying with the requirements of the Commissioners, as set out in the Rules which he has in his hand and can show to the patient. It may also be well for the doctor to bear in mind that the actual decision as to giving or withholding benefit depends, not upon him, but on the Society, and that, although the certificate constitutes a very important part of the evidence upon which the Society have to base their decision, it is not the only factor that they may have to take into account.

NATIONAL HEALTH INSURANCE COMMISSION (ENGLAND),
London, S.W.
NATIONAL HEALTH INSURANCE COMMISSION (SCOTLAND),
Edinburgh.
NATIONAL HEALTH INSURANCE COMMISSION (WALES),
Cardiff.

December 1914.

RULES AS DETERMINED BY THE INSURANCE COMMISSIONERS, THE SCOTTISH INSURANCE COMMISSIONERS, AND THE WELSH INSURANCE COMMISSIONERS, FOR THE GIVING OF CERTIFICATES TO INSURED PERSONS BY MEDICAL PRACTITIONERS WHO ARE ATTENDING THEM UNDER AGREEMENT WITH INSURANCE COMMITTEES.

WHEREAS it is a condition of a Parliamentary Grant to an Insurance Committee towards the cost of medical attendance and treatment amongst other things that certificates shall be furnished to every insured person, where he so desires and requests, in such form, on such occasions, and generally in such manner as the Commissioners may determine, for the purposes of any claim made by him for sickness or disablement benefit or for the purpose of determining or calculating the period during which sickness benefit is or would, but for any section of the principal Act disentitling him, have been payable, or of calculating arrears, and that unless and until the Commissioners so determine, such certificates shall be furnished for the purposes aforesaid as are required to be furnished in pursuance of the rules of the Society of which the insured person is a member or of the Committee, as the case may be :

Now THEREFORE the Insurance Commissioners, the Scottish Insurance Commissioners, and the Welsh Insurance Commissioners hereby determine as follows :

The form in which, the occasions on which, and the manner in which certificates shall be so furnished shall be the form, occasions, and manner set out in the following Rules.

Certificates.

1. Certificates shall be given by medical practitioners who are attending insured persons who are incapable of work, in the forms, on the occasions, and in the manner, required by these Rules, which may be referred to as the Medical Certification Rules.

Forms of Certificates.

2. The certificate shall be in each case in the appropriate form appended to these Rules.

First Certificates.

3. When first the practitioner, in the course of attendance upon the insured person, is of opinion that the insured person has become incapable of work by reason of some specific disease or bodily or mental disablement, he shall, if so desired by the insured person, give him a First Certificate.

Second Certificates (Intermediate or Final).

4. The practitioner shall, if so desired by the insured person, give to him, if still incapable of work, a Second Certificate within eight days of the First Certificate. If, on examining the insured person for the purpose of the Second Certificate, the practitioner is of opinion that he is fit to resume work immediately after the date of such examination, the certificate shall be a Final Certificate, and otherwise it shall be an Intermediate Certificate.

Further Intermediate Certificates.

5. If incapacity continues beyond eight days from the date of the First Certificate, further Intermediate Certificates shall be given by the practitioner, if so desired by the insured person, week by week, during the continuance of incapacity.

Final Certificates.

6. If at any time the practitioner finds, upon examination of the insured person, that he, having been up to the date of such examination incapable of work, is fit to resume work immediately thereafter, he shall forthwith give the insured person a Final Certificate.

Arrangements for examining Convalescent Patients.

7. If the practitioner, when giving a First or Intermediate Certificate, is of opinion that the insured person, although not fit to resume work immediately, may reasonably be expected to become fit to resume work before the date on which an Intermediate Certificate would next ordinarily be given, the practitioner shall insert in the appropriate space in the certificate a date on which the insured person, if his condition permits, is to come to see him, and the date so inserted shall be the day which the practitioner expects to be the last day of the insured person's incapacity for work; but nothing in this Rule shall debar the practitioner from making use of the space in other cases where he thinks it desirable that the insured person should see him on some particular day.

Special Final Certificates in certain Rural Areas.

8. If, upon examining an insured person who resides at a distance of more than two miles from the practitioner's residence, in a rural area approved for this purpose by the Commissioners, the practitioner is of opinion that the insured person, although not fit to resume work immediately after the date of such examination, will become fit to resume work on a date not more than three days after the date of examination, he may, instead of arranging to see the insured person again, give him a Special Final Certificate.

Particulars to be inserted in Certificates.

9. (i.) Every practitioner who gives a certificate under these Rules shall insert, in the appropriate spaces in the form, the name of the insured person, and a concise statement of the specific disease or bodily or mental disablement by which, in his opinion, the insured person is at the time rendered incapable of work.

(ii.) The practitioner shall sign the certificate and append the date on which he signs it; and, where this date is not the date on which he examined the insured person, he shall so alter the wording of the certificate as to show both the date on which the examination was made and the date of signing.

Time at which Certificates are to be given.

10. The practitioner shall, wherever practicable, give the certificate to the insured person at the time of the examination to which the certificate relates; where he is precluded from so doing he shall give the certificate at the first opportunity thereafter.

Statement of Cause of Incapacity.

11. The statement of the incapacitating disease or disablement in the certificate shall specify the cause of incapacity as precisely as the practitioner's knowledge of the insured person's condition at the time of the examination permits; provided that, in any case where a precise statement would, in the practitioner's opinion, be prejudicial to the health of the patient, or where it would inflict on him unwarrantable injury, the practitioner may describe the incapacitating disease or disablement in less precise terms; but in every such case he shall send, on the day on which such certificate is signed, to the Approved Society * of which the insured person is a member, a notice in the form appended to these Rules, and shall also forward to the Government Referee appointed for the purpose (or, if there be no such Referee, to the Commissioners) a precise description of the disabling condition and a statement of the reasons for which a certificate less precise than is possible has been given.

Dated this third day of December in the year one thousand nine hundred and fourteen.

John Anderson,
Secretary to the Insurance Commissioners.

John Jeffrey,
Secretary to the Scottish Insurance Commissioners.

Thomas Jones,
Secretary to the Welsh Insurance Commissioners.

NOTICE TO APPROVED SOCIETY.

(*See Rule* 11.)

I hereby declare that in the certificate of incapacity for work which I have to-day given to   , of   (address), being Member No.   of   Society,   Branch, I have stated the cause of the incapacity with less precision than my present knowledge of the insured person's condition makes possible, for good and sufficient reasons which I have this day communicated to the Medical Referee.†

---

* Where the insured person is a Deposit Contributor or a member of the Navy and Army Insurance Fund, the notice shall be sent to the Insurance Committee for the area in which the insured person resides.

† Substitute "Commissioners" for "Medical Referee," if under the Rule the notice is sent to the Commissioners.

Form Med. 40.

NATIONAL HEALTH INSURANCE.

NOTE.—For convenience, all the three kinds of files are been find on one slip; but no slip is to be used on more than one oc can. Every file, her First, or In ate, or Final, must be given on a separate slip.

FIRST CERTIFICATE AND NOTICE OF SICKNESS.

TO BE FILLED IN BY THE DOCTOR. | FOR USE BY INSURED PERSON.

Confidential.

First Certificate of Incapacity for Work.

To _____

I   dy certify that I have to-day examined you, and that in my opinion you are rendered incapable of work by reason of * _____

§ You should come to see me again on _____ day next.

Doctor's signature _____

Date of signing _____

Any other remarks } by Doctor _____

§ To be filled up at Doctor's discretion, where not obligatory under Rules.

Notice of Sickness.

FOR USE BY INSURED PERSON.

I hereby give notice that I was rendered incapable of work from _____ o'clock a.m./p.m. on _____ day, the _____ day of _____ 191 , by**_____
and I have since then not been at work.
† I enclose my Insurance Book.
‡ (Signed by or on behalf of)

Name _____

Present Address _____

Membership No. _____ Date _____

** Here insert either the word Illness or the word Accident; and in the case of accident state on a separate paper where and how it happened.
† Strike these words out if the Society already has the Book.
‡ If the insured person is unable to sign, the person signing on his behalf must indicate the fact.

FOR USE BY SOCIETY.

Member qualified for benefit?	
Member under 21?	
Member in Hospital?	
Section 8 (5)?	
Section 11?	
Section 47 or 53?	
Section 48?	
Late Entrant (Section 9 (4))?	
Arrears reduction?	
Benefit payable from?	

IMPORTANT.—This form must be completed by the insured person and sent on the day on which it is received from the Doctor to the Approved Society of which he or she is a member, or to the Insurance Committee in the case of a Deposit Contributor or of a member of the Navy and Army Insurance Fund. If not sent on that day a written explanation of the delay must be given.

* Here insert the name of the specific disease or accidental disablement which renders the insured person incapable of work.

NATIONAL HEALTH INSURANCE.

Form Med. 40.

Confidential. **INTERMEDIATE CERTIFICATE AND DECLARATION.**

TO BE FILLED IN BY THE DOCTOR.

To _____

I hereby certify that I have to-day examined you, and that in my opinion you have remained incapable of work, up to and including to-day, by reason of *_____

§ You should come to see me again on ____ day next.

Doctor's signature _____
Date of signing _____
Any other remarks }
by Doctor

§ To be filled up at Doctor's discretion, where not obligatory under Rules.

FOR USE BY INSURED PERSON.

I hereby apply for benefit and declare that in consequence of incapacity through sickness I have not been at work since the date of the last certificate forwarded to you. I have received no compensation or damages in respect of my sickness.

‡ (Signed by or on behalf of)
Name _____
Present address _____
Membership No. _____ Date _____

‡ If the insured person is unable to sign, the person signing on his behalf must indicate the fact.

Confidential. **FINAL CERTIFICATE AND DECLARATION.**

TO BE FILLED IN BY THE DOCTOR.

To _____

I hereby certify that I have to-day examined you, and that in my opinion you have remained incapable of work, up to and including to-day, by reason of *_____

and are fit to resume work after to-day.

Doctor's signature _____
Date of signing _____
Any other remarks }
by Doctor

FOR USE BY INSURED PERSON.

I hereby apply for benefit and declare that in consequence of incapacity through sickness I have not been at work since the date of the last certificate forwarded to you, up to and including to-day, and I hereby declare off as from to-morrow. I have received no compensation or damages in respect of my sickness.

‡ (Signed by or on behalf of)
Name _____
Present address _____
Membership No. _____ Date _____

‡ If the insured person is unable to sign, the person signing on his behalf must indicate the fact.

---

* Here insert the name of the specific disease or bodily or mental disablement which renders the insured person incapable of work.

IMPORTANT.—This form must be completed by the insured person and sent on the day on which it is received from the Doctor to the Approved Society of which he or she is a member, or to the Insurance Committee in the case of a Deposit Contributor or of a member of the Navy and Army Insurance Fund. If not sent on that day a written explanation of the delay must be given.

NATIONAL HEALTH INSURANCE.   Form Med. 40A.

SPECIAL FINAL CERTIFICATE AND DECLARATION to be used only in certain rural cases (a).

Confidential. TO BE FILLED IN BY THE DOCTOR.

To _____

I hereby certify that I have to-day examined you, and that in my opinion you have remained incapable of work, up to and including to-day, by reason of *_____, and that in my opinion you will be fit to resume work on _____ (b).

Doctor's signature _____

Date of signing _____

Any other remarks } _____
by Doctor

(a) This Form is issued for use only in the case of insured persons who reside at a distance of more than two miles from the Practitioner's residence in a rural area approved for this purpose by the Commissioners.

(b) The date here inserted must not be more than three days after the date of the certificate—e.g. if the certificate is given on October 2nd, this form of certificate must not be issued unless the Practitioner expects the insured person to be able to resume work at latest on the 5th. In any other case he should see the insured person again before giving a Final Certificate.

* Here insert the name of the specific disease or bodily or mental disablement which renders the insured person incapable of work.

FOR USE BY INSURED PERSON.

I hereby apply for benefit and declare that in consequence of incapacity through sickness I have not been at work since the date of the last certificate forwarded to you. I expect to be again capable of work on _____, and I hereby declare off as from that date.§ I have received no compensation or damages in respect of my sickness.

† (Signed by or on behalf of)

Name _____

Present address _____

Membership No. _____ Date _____

‡ If the insured person is unable to sign, the person signing on his behalf must indicate the fact.

§ Insured persons must remember that whilst still on the Funds they must not go to work.

IMPORTANT.—This form must be completed by the insured person and sent on the day on which it is received from the Doctor to the Approved Society of which he or she is a member, or to the Insurance Committee in the case of a Deposit Contributor or of a member of the Navy and Army Insurance Fund. If not sent on that day a written explanation of the delay must be given.

Dated this third day of December in the year one thousand nine hundred and fourteen.

JOHN ANDERSON,
Secretary to the Insurance Commissioners.

JOHN JEFFREY,
Secretary to the Scottish Insurance Commissioners.

THOMAS JONES,
Secretary to the Welsh Insurance Commissioners.

APPENDIX XI.

INSURANCE COMMITTEE AREAS FOR WHICH THE POST OFFICE MEDICAL SYSTEM HAS BEEN APPROVED UNDER SECTION 15 (4) OF THE NATIONAL INSURANCE ACT, 1911.

(See Cap. IV., Section (I.), paragraph (186).)

COUNTY COMMITTEES.

Aberdeen.	Dumfries.	Midlothian.
Argyll.	Elgin and Nairn.	Orkney.
Ayr.	Fife.	Peebles.
Banff.	Forfar.	Renfrew.
Berwick.	Haddington.	Ross and Cromarty.
Bute.	Inverness.	Roxburgh.
Caithness.	Kincardine.	Selkirk.
Clackmannan and Kinross.	Kirkcudbright.	Stirling.
	Linlithgow.	Zetland.

BURGH COMMITTEES.

Aberdeen.	Dumfries and Maxwelltown.	Kilmarnock.
Airdrie.		Kirkcaldy.
Arbroath.	Dundee.	Leith.
Ayr.	Dunfermline.	Motherwell.
Clydebank.	Falkirk.	Perth.
Coatbridge.	Greenock.	Rutherglen.
Dumbarton.	Hamilton.	Wishaw.
	Inverness.	

APPENDIX XII.

AGREEMENT BETWEEN PERSON UNDERTAKING TO SUPPLY DRUGS AND APPLIANCES AND INSURANCE COMMITTEE.

Form Med. 23
(Scotland.)

See (Cap. IV., Section (II.), paragraph (191).)

Note.—A modified Form (Med. 25 (Scotland)) is to be used where the Agreement is with a person undertaking to supply only (a) drugs other than scheduled poisons and medicines which require to be dispensed, and (b) for appliances.

AGREEMENT between the Insurance Committee for the   of
             (hereinafter called the "Committee") of the one
part and   of

(hereinafter called the "Chemist") of the other part, whereby it is agreed as follows :

1. The National Insurance Acts, 1911 to 1913, and the National Health Insurance (Medical Benefit) Regulations (Scotland), 1913 (hereinafter called "the Regulations"), and the National Health Insurance (Medical Benefit) Regulations (Scotland), 1914, or other Regulations for the administration of medical benefit in force for the time being in the area of the Committee are incorporated in and form part of this agreement.

2. (i.) The Chemist shall as from the date of the commencement of this agreement undertake the supply of drugs and appliances to insured persons on the terms of this agreement at the place or places of business mentioned in the First Schedule hereto, and at such hours as have been or may be specified in any scheme made by the Committee and the Pharmaceutical Committee in accordance with the Regulations.*

(ii.) The Chemist may, with consent of the Committee, which shall not be unreasonably withheld, alter the place or places of business; and he may, with consent of the Committee, reduce or increase the number of such places.

3. The Chemist shall, with reasonable promptness, supply to any person presenting an order for drugs or appliances on a form provided by the Committee for the purpose, and signed by any practitioner on the panel or his deputy, such drugs or appliances as are so ordered, and shall so far as practicable keep in stock for that purpose the drugs and medical and surgical appliances mentioned or referred to in the Second Schedule hereto.

4. All drugs and appliances shall be of good quality, and shall be supplied at the prices mentioned or referred to in the Second Schedule hereto together with a fee for dispensing (where dispensing is required) calculated in the manner mentioned or referred to in the said Schedule.

5. In the case of any drug, the price of which is not mentioned or referred to in the Second Schedule hereto, the price shall be calculated by reference to the scale mentioned or referred to in the said Schedule together with a dispensing fee calculated as aforesaid where dispensing is required.

6. The Chemist shall provide, free of charge to a person presenting such order as aforesaid, proper bottles or other vessels for any substances to which Section 5 of the Poisons and Pharmacy Act, 1908, or the Regulations made under Section 1 of the Pharmacy Act, 1868, relate.

7. Where a person upon presenting an order for any drug or appliance (not being a substance to which the last preceding clause hereof relates) for which a bottle or other vessel is requisite, deposits with the Chemist the price of the bottle or other vessel, the Chemist shall upon the return of the said bottle or other vessel in a clean condition pay back the sum so deposited.

8. The dispensing of medicines shall be performed either by or under the direct supervision of a registered pharmacist or by a person who for three years immediately prior to the 16th December 1911 has acted as a dispenser to a duly qualified medical pra it one or a public institution.

9. All drugs and appliances shall cbe supplied to the person presenting such order as aforesaid free of charge to that person.

10. (i.) If, owing to any breach on the part of the Chemist of this agreement, any expenses have been reasonably and necessarily incurred by the Committee or by any insured person, or the Committee are deprived of any sum which would otherwise have been payable towards the cost of providing medical benefit, the Committee shall be entitled to recover from the Chemist or his legal personal representative, either by deduction from any moneys payable under this agreement or otherwise, the amount of the expenses so incurred and of the sum of which the Committee have been so deprived.

(ii.) Before taking action on any matter under the provisions of this clause, the Committee shall, unless the matter has previously been dealt with by the Pharmaceutical Service Sub-Committee or Joint Services Sub-

---

* Regulation 10 (3) requires the Committee to make arrangements with the Pharmaceutical Committee for securing that in each area, so far as practicable, one or more of the places of business of persons supplying drugs or appliances shall at all reasonable times be open to insured persons.

Committee, refer it to the Pharmaceutical Service Sub-Committee which shall deal with the matter in accordance with the Regulations relating to the powers and duties of that Sub-Committee.

(iii.) The Chemist or his legal personal representative shall be entitled to appeal to the Commissioners against any decision of the Committee under this clause within fourteen days after receiving notice of the decision.

11. Any dispute or question (other than a question which under the provisions of the Regulations or of the last preceding clause hereof is referred to the Pharmaceutical Service Sub-Committee) arising between the Committee and the Chemist or his legal personal representative relating to the construction of this agreement or the rights and liabilities of the Committee or the Chemist or his legal personal representative hereunder shall be referred to the Commissioners.

12. In the event of the Commissioners exercising any of the powers conferred on them by the proviso to sub-section (2) of section 15 of the principal Act, or by proviso (i.) to sub-section (5) of that section, or by section 11 of the amending Act, in respect of the area of the Committee or any portion of that area, the Committee may, if the Commissioners so require, by giving not less than seven days' notice to the Chemist, determine this agreement, but save as aforesaid, this agreement shall not be varied or determined otherwise than in accordance with the provisions of Part II. of the Regulations,* as amended by the said National Health Insurance (Medical Benefit) Regulations (Scotland), 1914, or in the special circumstances to which Regulation 83 (2) applies, in accordance with said Regulation.

13. This agreement shall come into operation on the 1st day of January 1915, or on the date of the agreement, whichever date is the later.

14. Except where the context otherwise requires words and expressions used herein shall have the same meaning as in the Regulations.

IN WITNESS Whereof the parties hereto have executed this agreement together with the said Schedules hereto as follows :—

Sealed with the Common Seal of the Committee and subscribed on their behalf at
the   day of
One thousand nine hundred and
in presence of

Name ....⎫
Address ....⎬ Witness.
Designation ....⎭

Signatures⎤
on
behalf ⎬ ....
of
Committee.⎦

Name ....⎫
Address...,.................⎬ Witness.
Designation.................⎭

Signed and Delivered by the Chemist at   the
                                        day of
One thousand nine hundred and
in presence of

* Under Regulation 19 (2) a person supplying drugs or appliances may determine his agreement at the end of a year, as fixed by the Commissioners, by giving notice to the Committee, not later than four weeks before the commencement of the succeeding year, and may with the consent of the Committee determine his agreement at any other time.

Name ....⎫
Address ....⎬ Witness.
Designation ....⎭

Signature.....................

Name..........................⎫
Address ....⎬ Witness.
Designation ....⎭

THE FIRST SCHEDULE.

PLACES OF BUSINESS.

....

....

THE SECOND SCHEDULE.

(I.) Payment shall be made for drugs and appliances supplied on the basis of the prices mentioned or referred to herein, and shall be calculated in accordance with the following provisions of the Regulation, viz. :—

39.—(1) Every person supplying drugs or appliances (including a practitioner, other than a practitioner to whom capitation fees are paid in respect of the supply of drugs and appliances) shall, on dates to be appointed by the Commissioners, furnish to the Committee accounts on forms provided by the Committee, containing particulars of drugs and appliances supplied by him to insured persons and of the prices of those drugs and appliances, calculated in accordance with the method contained in his agreement with the Committee.

(2) The Committee shall, if the Pharmaceutical Committee so require, submit such accounts for the examination of the Pharmaceutical Committee, and the Pharmaceutical Committee shall make a report to the Committee stating which items in each account ought in the opinion of the Pharmaceutical Committee to be accepted and which, if any, ought to be reduced or disallowed, and any account as adjusted in accordance with the recommendations, if any, of the Pharmaceutical Committee made thereon shall be binding on the person furnishing the account as if it were an account stated.

(3) The Committee shall, if the Panel Committee so require, submit to that Committee the accounts and the report, if any, made thereon by the Pharmaceutical Committee, and, if the Panel Committee take any objection to any item in any account or to any recommendation contained in the report, the Committee shall decide as to the validity of such objection.

(4) The Panel Committee may, if they think fit, either with or without a previous examination of the accounts, inform the Committee that they are willing to accept all or any of the accounts or any part of any account as furnished to the Committee, or where they have been submitted to the Pharmaceutical Committee as adjusted in accordance with the recommendations, if any, made by that Committee, and, in so far as the accounts are accepted by the Panel Committee, they shall be binding on all the practitioners on the panel, and the Committee shall be entitled to credit sums to persons supplying drugs or appliances in accordance with those accounts.

(5) The Committee shall credit to each person furnishing an account the amount agreed under the foregoing provisions of this Regulation or where no agreement has been arrived at, the amount which the Committee may ascertain to be proper, and shall pay to each such person the amount so credited to him, or an amount bearing the same proportion to the sum so

credited to him as the amount remaining in the Drug Fund (after deducting any sums payable out of that fund to the Central Medical Benefit Fund and any sums appropriated under the last preceding Regulation) bears to the aggregate amounts so credited to all those persons, whichever is the less.

* * * * * * *

(8) As soon as may be after the receipt of an account from a person supplying drugs or appliances the Committee shall pay to the person furnishing the account such sum as may be agreed between the Committee and the Pharmaceutical Committee in advance of the amount due to him, and shall pay the balance of the amount so due as soon as may be after the expiration of the year.

(II.) The drugs and medical and surgical appliances which shall be kept in stock by the Chemist, and the prices fixed therefor, including a scale of dispensing fees, shall be as set forth in the Drug Tariff, as authenticated by the Seal of the Committee and the Signature of the Chairman or Vice-Chairman, and the Signature of the Chairman or Clerk of the Pharmaceutical Committee and deposited with the Clerk to the Committee.

(III.) The method of calculating the price of drugs not included in the said Drug Tariff shall be as follows :—

(a) In the case of such of said drugs as are included in the ordinary printed price lists of* Wholesale Druggists, in accordance with the principles set forth on page 1 of the Drug Tariff on the basis of the prices listed in said price lists ; and

(b) In the case of all other such drugs in accordance with said principles (so far as reasonably applicable) on the basis of the actual cost to the chemist ; and where such principles are not reasonably applicable on the basis of the actual cost to the chemist plus one-third thereof ;

together with in each case such dispensing charges, if any, as are payable in accordance with the dispensing charges contained in said Drug Tariff.

....

....

Note.—So as to simplify the execution of this Agreement by the parties thereto, and dispense with signatures on each page, the whole document should be printed on one sheet of paper only, although it may extend to four pages.

---

* Insert here name of any wholesale druggist.

[CARD.

APPENDIX XIII.
MEDICAL CARD.
(See Cap. IV., Section (IV.), paragraph (221).)
PAGE 1.

MEDICAL CARD

ISSUED BY THE INSURANCE COMMITTEE,

To (*Full Name*) —————
(*Address*) —————
(*Society and Branch*) —————
(*No. in Insurance Book*) —————

For Use of Insurance Committee only.

The above-named is on the list of :—
[*Dr.*] —————

{ This reference should always be quoted by the insured person in any correspondence as to Medical Benefit.

Committee's Stamp.

1

PAGE 2.

INSTRUCTIONS.

PLEASE READ CAREFULLY.

1. This Medical Card must be carefully kept and must be produced when treatment is required. If it is lost you may have difficulty in getting another. If you lose it you should at once give notice to the Insurance Committee.

2. If any other person than the person to whom this Medical Card is issued uses or attempts to use it for the purpose of obtaining benefit for himself, or if the person to whom it is issued uses it or attempts to use it after he has ceased to be entitled to Medical Benefit, he is liable to serious penalties.

3. If you have not chosen a doctor you must do so without delay by filling up Part A on the opposite page and presenting this Card to any doctor on the panel. If you are accepted, the doctor will retain the Card and send it to the Insurance Committee, from whom you will receive the Card with the name of the doctor entered in the space at the foot of the first page.

4. If owing to flitting or removal to a new address you cannot obtain treatment from the doctor named in this Card, you should at once make a fresh choice by filling up Part B on the opposite page and presenting the Card to any doctor on the panel. If you are accepted, the doctor will retain the Medical Card, and forward it to the Insurance Committee, from whom you will receive a new Card with the name of the doctor entered therein.

5. If you require treatment when away from home you may present this Card to any doctor on the panel or institution, after filling in Part C on page 4. If you are accepted, the doctor or institution will retain the Card and send it to the Insurance Committee, who will stamp the Card and return it to you for the purpose of obtaining treatment.

6. A list of available doctors and institutions for any district can be seen at the Post Offices in that district. If you have difficulty in getting accepted, you should write to the Clerk to the Insurance Committee at the address given in the Post Office list, enclosing this Medical Card.

7. A member of an Approved Society is under an obligation to notify any changes of address to his Society, and to inform it when he ceases to be insured. Women members must also notify their Society when they marry.

8. If the insured person desires to change his doctor at the end of the year, he must give notice to that effect before 1st December to the Clerk to the Committee, enclosing this Card. Except in special circumstances, or on removal, he can change his doctor during the year only with the consent of his doctor, by means of a form obtainable from the Committee.

9. Any enquiry or complaint by the insured person with regard to his Medical Benefit should be addressed to the Clerk to the Insurance Committee at the address named on the first page.

10. Postage must be prepaid on all communications to Insurance Committees.

This Card is the property of the Scottish Insurance Commissioners, to whom it should be returned if found.

PAGE 3.

	For use by County doctors only.
Part A. To be filled in when insured person is **not** on list of doctor and wishes to choose a doctor.	
I, (signature)_____, of	If doctor claims to supply drugs he should enter DR.
(present address)_____, wish to be placed	
on list of [Dr.]_____	Doctors may enter mileage distance
The above-named is accepted.	
(Signature of doctor)_____	M............
Part B. To be filled in when insured person has **flitted or removed** to a new address, and cannot therefore get treatment from doctor named on front page.	
I, (signature)_____, of	If doctor claims to supply drugs he should enter DR.
(present address)_____, wish to be placed	
on list of [Dr.]_____	Doctors may enter mileage distance
The above-named is accepted.	
(Signature of doctor)_____	M............

The insured person must sign here immediately he receives this Card.

3

NOTICE.

The Committee require an insured person in receipt of Medical Benefit to comply with the following Rules as to Conduct:—

(a) He shall obey the instructions of the practitioner attending him:
(b) He shall not conduct himself in a manner which is likely to retard his recovery:
(c) He shall not make unreasonable demands upon the professional services of the practitioner attending him:
(d) He shall, whenever his condition permits, attend at the surgery or place of residence of the practitioner attending him on such days and at such hours as may be appointed by the practitioner:
(e) He shall not summon the practitioner to visit him between the hours of 8 p.m. and 8 a.m., except in cases of serious emergency:
(f) He shall, when his condition requires a home visit, give notice to the practitioner, if the circumstances of the case permit, before 9.30 a.m. on the day on which the visit is required, except in cases of accident or emergency:
(g) He shall not attend at the surgery nor summon the practitioner to visit him on Sundays, except in cases of accident or emergency.

The Rules of the Committee also provide that any complaint by an insured person which is adjudged by them to be frivolous or vexatious, shall be regarded as a breach of their Rules.

Failure to observe the Rules may entail penalties of a fine (not exceeding 10s. or in the case of repeated failure 20s.) or of suspension from benefit for a period not exceeding one year.

These Rules are liable to alteration, due notice of which will be given in the public Press.

Part C. FOR USE IN TEMPORARY RESIDENCE.

I hereby declare that I am only temporarily residing in the locality of the address which I have given below and that I do not intend or expect to remain in the locality for as long as 3 months from the date of my arrival.

(Signature) _____

(Temporary Address) _____

_____ *(Date)* _____

Signature of doctor accepting : | Committee's Stamp.

This Card can only be used for obtaining treatment during one period of absence from home not exceeding 3 months. **When the above space has been used another Card must be applied for from the Insurance Committee at the address shown on the first page.**

APPENDIX XIV.

LIST OF SANATORIA, ETC., IN SCOTLAND, APPROVED BY THE LOCAL GOVERNMENT BOARD FOR SCOTLAND FOR THE INSTITUTIONAL TREATMENT OF TUBERCULOSIS UNDER THE NATIONAL INSURANCE ACTS.

(See Cap. V., Section (I.) (ii.), paragraph (286).)

	No. of Beds.	Addresses of Secretaries.
Aberdeen County—		
Aberdeen City Fever Hospital (Tuberculosis Wards)	122	The Town Clerk, Aberdeen.
Aberdeen City Tuberculosis Dispensary (at City Hospital)	—	Do. do.
Mrs. Smith's Convalescent Home and Sanatorium, Newbills	24	S. M. Chrystall, 21 Bridge Street, Aberdeen.
Thos. Walker Hospital, Fraserburgh	24	J. D. M'Intosh, Secretary, Fraserburgh.
Royal Aberdeen Hospital for Sick Children—Temporary premises at Kepplestone	—	D. M. M. Milligan, 12 Dee Street, Aberdeen.
Aberdeen County Tuberculosis Dispensary, 16 Golden Square, Aberdeen	—	The County Clerk, Aberdeen.
Peterhead Burgh Infectious Diseases Hospital (Observation Block)	—	The Town Clerk, Peterhead.
Argyll County—		
Argyll County Sanatorium, Oban	30	The County Clerk, Lochgilphead.
Campbeltown and Kintyre District Combination Hospital	7	The Town Clerk, Campbeltown.
West Highland Cottage Hospital, Oban (non-pulmonary)	—	The Clerk, Oban.
Ayr County—		
Ayrshire Sanatorium (Glenafton)	88	R. Welsh, Clerk, 42 Sandgate, Ayr.
Heathfield Hospital; Ayr (Tuberculosis Pavilions)	10	The Town Clerk, Ayr.
Ayr Burgh Tuberculosis Dispensary, 70 High Street	—	Do. do.
Kaimshill Cholera and Smallpox Hospital, Kilmarnock	12	The Town Clerk, Kilmarnock.
Kilmarnock Burgh Dispensary	9	Do. do.
Kilmarnock Royal Infirmary (non-pulmonary)	—	W. Austin, Secretary. Kilmarnock.
Biggart Memorial Hospital Home for Children, Prestwick (non-pulmonary)	—	A. M'Cracken, 81 Mitchell Street, Glasgow.
Ayr County Hospital	—	J. H. Goudie, Wellington Chambers, Ayr.
Banff County—		
Chalmers Hospital, Banff (pulmonary)	8	G. L. Cumming, Secretary to Chalmers Hospital, Banff.
(Non-pulmonary)	48	
Turner Memorial Hospital, Keith	—	John Pirie, 53 Moss Street, Keith.
Berwick County—		
Gordon Hospital (2 wards)	4	G. Rankin, W.S., Lauder.

	No. of Beds.	Addresses of Secretaries.
Bute County—		
Victoria Hospital, Rothesay (non-pulmonary)	—	A. D. MacBeth, 28 Castle Street, Rothesay.
Caithness County—		
Wick Joint Fever Hospital (Tuberculosis Shelter)	1	The County Clerk, Thurso.
Clackmannan County—		
Clackmannan County Hospital (non-pulmonary)	—	C. Thomson, Royal Bank Buildings, Alloa.
Dunbarton County—		
Helensburgh Burgh Smallpox Hospital	10	The Town Clerk, Helensburgh
Lanfine Home, Kirkintilloch	44	H. M'Leod, 101 St. Vincent Street, Glasgow.
Helensburgh Burgh Infectious Diseases Hospital (Tuberculosis Wards)	5	The Town Clerk, Helensburgh.
Broomhill Home, Kirkintilloch (non-pulmonary)	—	H. M'Leod, 101 St. Vincent Street, Glasgow.
Dumbarton Joint Hospital	18	The Town Clerk, Dumbarton.
Dumfries County—		
Dumfries Burgh Smallpox Hospital	8	The Town Clerk, Dumfries.
Lochmaben Joint Hospital (Tuberculosis Wards)	12	D. Cormack, Clerk to Lochmaben Joint Hospital, Lockerbie.
Thornhill Infectious Diseases Hospital (Tuberculosis Wards)	4	R. Wilson, Thornhill, District Clerk, Sanquhar.
Dumfries and Galloway Royal Infirmary (non-pulmonary)	—	J. Symons, 84 Irish Street, Dumfries.
Westmoreland Consumption Hospital, Grange-over-Sands	—	W. R. Parker, M.D., Stricklandgate, Kendal.
Elgin County—		
Elgin Sanatorium	8	The County Clerk, Elgin.
Dr. Gray's Hospital, Elgin (non-pulmonary)	—	Stewart & M'Isaac, Royal Bank Buildings, Elgin.
Fife County—		
Kirkcaldy Burgh Sanatorium	16	The Town Clerk, Kirkcaldy.
St. Michael's Hospital, near Leuchars (Tuberculosis Wards)	14	J. L. Macpherson, Clerk to St. Michael's Joint Hospital, St. Andrews.
Ovenstone Infectious Diseases Hospital, Pittenweem (Shelter)	12	J. L. Macpherson, District Clerk, St. Andrews.
Thornton Smallpox Hospital	18	A. & D. Beveridge, 220 High Street, Kirkcaldy.
Cameron Infectious Diseases Hospital, Buckhaven (1 Pavilion)	4	The Town Clerk, Buckhaven.
Forfar County—		
Dundee Municipal Tuberculosis Dispensary	—	The Town Clerk, Dundee.
Sidlaw Sanatorium, Auchterhouse	44	G. B. Brough, Royal Infirmary, Dundee.

	No. of Beds.	Addresses of Secretaries.
Forfar County—(continued).		
Forfar Infirmary (non-pulmonary)	—	A. MacHardy, Secretary, Forfar.
King's Cross Hospital, Dundee	90	The Town Clerk, City Chambers, Dundee.
Montrose Royal Infirmary (non-pulmonary)	—	A. Lyell, Secretary, Montrose.
Arbroath Joint Infectious Diseases Hospital (1 pavilion)	8	W. K. MacDonald, Clerk to Joint Hospital Committee, Arbroath.
Arbroath Infirmary, Greenbank House (non-pulmonary)	11	W. K. MacDonald, Hon. Secretary, Arbroath.
Arbroath Infirmary Convalescent House (non-pulmonary)	—	Do. do.
Noranside Sanatorium	60	The County Clerk, Forfar.
Haddington County—		
Haddington County Combination Smallpox Hospital	16	The County Clerk, Haddington.
Inverness County—		
Grampian Sanatorium, Kingussie	18	Dr. de Watteville, Medical Superintendent, Kingussie.
Inverness Burgh Tuberculosis Dispensary	—	The Town Clerk, Inverness.
Northern Infirmary, Inverness (Tuberculosis Wards)	8	D. Shaw, The Northern Infirmary, Inverness.
Do. do. (General Wards)	—	
Inverness-shire Sanatorium, Bridge of Oich	28	Mrs. Angelo, Cullachy, Fort-Augustus.
Kinross County—		
Coppins Green Sanatorium, Milnathort	47	Thomas Hart, Jun., C.A., 144 St. Vincent Street, Glasgow.
Ochil Hills Sanatorium	40	Do. do.
Lanark County—		
Dispensary at Blantyre Fever Hospital	—	W. E. Whyte, District Offices, Hamilton.
Tuberculosis Hospital, Uppertown, Longriggend	38	Do. do.
Hairmyres Sanatorium	10	Do. do.
Hairmyres Sanatorium Open Air School Pavilion (Children)	24	Do. do.
Tuberculosis Hospital, Stonehouse	52	Do. do.
Tuberculosis Hospital, Shotts	48	Do. do.
Tuberculosis Dispensary, Cambuslang	—	Do. do.
County Infectious Diseases Hospital, near Motherwell	32	Do. do.
County Infectious Tuberculosis Dispensary	—	Do. do.
Dalserf Infectious Diseases Hospital	—	Do. do.
Lightburn Joint Infectious Diseases Hospital (Tuberculosis Wards)	30	Jas. A. M'Callum, 15 West George Street, Glasgow.

	No. of Beds.	Addresses of Secretaries.
Lanark County—(continued).		
Upper Ward District Hospital, Carluke	12	A. W. Paterson, District Offices, Lanark.
Bellefield Sanatorium, Lanark	52	The Town Clerk, Glasgow.
Glasgow Corporation Dispensaries— Granville Street; Govan Chambers; Black Street; 128 Adelphi Street; Brown Street; 37 Elmbank Crescent, Glasgow	—	Do. do.
Knightswood Infectious Diseases Hospital, Anniesland (Tuberculosis Pavilion)	20	Do. do.
Shieldhall Infectious Diseases Hospital, Govan (Tuberculosis Pavilion)	24	Do. do.
Ruchill Infectious Diseases Hospital, Glasgow (five Pavilions)	170	Do. do.
Airdrie Burgh Reception House	7	The Town Clerk, Airdrie.
Coathill Infectious Diseases Hospital, Coatbridge—		The Town Clerk, Coatbridge.
Tuberculosis Block	28	
South Pavilion	20	
Tuberculosis Dispensary	—	
Hamilton Burgh Tuberculosis Dispensary, Oak Lodge	—	The Town Clerk, Hamilton.
Motherwell Burgh Infectious Diseases Hospital (Tuberculosis Ward Block)	18	The Town Clerk, Motherwell.
Wishaw Burgh Infectious Diseases Hospital (Tuberculosis Pavilion)	14	The Town Clerk, Wishaw.
Wishaw Tuberculosis Dispensary	—	Do. do.
Douglas Cottage Hospital (Non-Pulmonary)	—	Mrs. J. P. Baird, Castle Mains, Douglas, Lanarkshire.
Linlithgow County—		
Tippethill Smallpox Hospital, near Armadale	12	W. Allan, Town Clerk's Office, Bathgate.
Midlothian County—		
Edinburgh City Fever Hospital (Tuberculosis Pavilions)	231	The Town Clerk, Edinburgh.
Royal Victoria Dispensary, Edinburgh	—	Do. do.
Royal Victoria Hospital Farm Colony, Lasswade	23	Do. do.
Leith Dispensary (South Fort Street)	—	The Town Clerk, Leith.
Leith, East Pilton Hospital (Tuberculosis Pavilions)	75	Do. do.
Edinburgh Hospital for Women and Children (non-pulmonary)	—	Miss E. M'Laren, LL.B., 62 Frederick Street, Edinburgh.
Woodburn Sanatorium, Edinburgh	43	Dr. Isabella Mears, Woodburn, Morningside, Edinburgh.
Peebles County—		
Manor Valley Sanatorium, Peebles	30	A. J. Simpson, 8 Commercial Street, Leith.
Perth County—		
Dunblane Consumption Hospital	8	Dr. T. W. Dewar, Kincairn, Dunblane.

	No. of Beds.	Addresses of Secretaries.
Perth County—(continued).		
Hillside Homes (and 2 cottages)	49	S. T. Ellison, Clerk to Hillside Homes, Perth.
Perth Burgh Isolation Hospital (Tuberculosis Pavilion)	8	The Town Clerk, Perth.
Perth Royal Infirmary (non-pulmonary)	—	R. M. Bates, Secretary, 44 Tay Street, Perth.
Crieff and District Cottage Hospital (non-pulmonary)	—	C. E. Colville, Hon. Secretary, Crieff.
Renfrew County—		
Bridge of Weir Sanatorium	147	Miss Quarrier, Orphan Homes, Bridge of Weir.
Gockston Smallpox Hospital, Paisley	30	The Town Clerk, Paisley.
Paisley Burgh Fever Hospital (Tuberculosis Pavilion)	8	Do. do.
Paisley Municipal Dispensary	—	Do. do.
Greenock and District Combination Hospital (Gateside) (Tuberculosis Pavilion)	15	The Town Clerk, Greenock.
Greenock Corporation Tuberculosis Dispensary	—	Do. do.
Johnstone Combination Hospital Kilbarchan (Tuberculosis Pavilion and Chalets)	54	H. W. MacGregor, Clydesdale Bank, Johnstone.
Tuberculosis Dispensary, King Street, Port-Glasgow.	—	The Town Clerk, Port-Glasgow.
West Renfrewshire Combination Smallpox Hospital	17	The County Clerk, Paisley.
Blawarthill Fever Hospital (2 Tuberculosis Wards)	16	J. Hepburn, Burgh Chambers, Clydebank.
Darnley Joint Fever Hospital (Tuberculosis Pavilion)	36	Jas. A. MacCallum, 15 West George Street, Glasgow.
Roxburgh County—		
Anderson Sanatorium, Hawick	10	J. R. Purdom, Solicitor, Hawick.
Hawick Cottage Hospital (non-pulmonary)	—	R. Purdom, Hawick Cottage Hospital.
Selkirk County—		
Meigle Sanatorium, Galashiels	10	D. G. Stalker, Hon. Secy., Galashiels.
Stirling County—		
Falkirk Infirmary (non-pulmonary)	—	T. C. Wade, King's Court, Falkirk.
Stirling Royal Infirmary (non-pulmonary)	—	J. Dobbie, 3 Port Street, Stirling.
Stirling Royal Infirmary Convalescent Home (non-pulmonary)	—	Do. do.
Tuberculosis Dispensary, Melville Street, Falkirk	—	The Town Clerk, Falkirk.
Temporary Dispensary, 1 Viewfield Place, Stirling	—	The Town Clerk, Stirling.
Zetland County—		
Gilbert Bain Memorial Hospital, Lerwick (non-pulmonary)	—	G. W. Russell, Burgh Chambers, Lerwick.

APPENDIX XV.

MODEL SCHEME OF ARRANGEMENTS FOR THE DOMICILIARY TREATMENT OF TUBERCULOSIS, WITH RELATIVE CIRCULAR.

(*See Cap. V., Section (I.) (iv.), paragraph* (300).)

(1) CIRCULAR.

Memo. No. 602.

Under the provisions of Section 16 (1) of the National Insurance Act, 1911, one of the duties of an Insurance Committee is the making of arrangements for the treatment of tuberculosis otherwise than in sanatoria or other institutions—which treatment has come to be known as Domiciliary Treatment.

Such arrangements are to be made with persons and Local Authorities (other than Poor Law Authorities) undertaking treatment in a manner approved by the Local Government Board. The manner approved by the Board has been laid down by them in their Circular Public Health No. VI., 1913, in which it is made known that Insurance Committees who have made arrangements for the treatment of cases in conformity with the general lines approval of which is expressed by the Circular are relieved of the obligation to apply to the Board for approval of individual cases.

The arrangements are also to be to the satisfaction of the Insurance Commissioners. Arrangements hitherto considered by the Commissioners have been those put forward by Committees for, and with special reference to the needs of, individual cases; and the Commissioners have not been disposed to raise with Committees the question of general lines of procedure until sufficient time had elapsed to enable experience to be gained of the working of Sanatorium Benefit. The Commissioners, however, consider that Committees are now in a position to adopt and give effect to a General Scheme of arrangements.

A model form of such General Scheme—Form No. 603—accompanies this circular. It is suggested that Committees should obtain the advice of their Medical Adviser as to the medical comforts which should be made available for supply to patients in receipts of domiciliary treatment, should adopt the Scheme with the names of these substances entered in Section (4) thereof, other blanks, where necessary, duly filled in, and such modifications, if any, made as local or other circumstances may require, and should submit the Scheme, so completed, for the approval of the Commissioners. In submitting Schemes, it is requested that Committees will employ the model print herewith.

After adoption and approval of the general arrangements individual cases will require to be reported to the Commissioners as indicated in Section 22 of the Scheme, in order to enable the Commissioners to transmit to the Local Government Board the information required by the Board's Circular already referred to. While all cases must be *reported* by Committees to the Commissioners, *approval* need not be asked if the arrangements made are in accordance with the General Scheme. If, however, in any case for special reasons it is desired to depart from or modify the General Scheme special sanction must be secured by the Committee from the Commissioners in order to conform with the terms of the Act.

The Scheme will in general apply to arrangements proposed to be made in terms of Section 16 (1) (*b*) of the National Insurance Act, 1911, whether with persons or Local Authorities.

The medicines and appliances which may be ordered under the Scheme are dealt with in Section (4) of Form No. 603. Any medicines or appliances as defined in Section 8 (1) (*a*) of the National Insurance Act, 1911, and the Medical Benefit Regulations, as part of Medical Benefit may, when appropriate to the treatment of tuberculosis, be ordered for domiciliary treatment under the Scheme. When so ordered, however, they must be charged to the Sanatorium Benefit Fund, not to the Drug Fund.

It should be noted that where a patient who is receiving domiciliary treatment for tuberculosis under the Scheme suffers concurrently from a disease or injury not arising out of his tuberculosis, any medicines or appliances ordered by his panel doctor for the treatment of the concurrent disease or injury should be charged to the Drug Fund, since the patient, in respect of the concurrent disease or injury, would be under Medical Benefit.

The expression " medical comforts " as employed under the Scheme is intended to refer to substances other than medicines which may be regarded as essential to treatment. Where the substance is one which is often or habitually used for the purpose of subsistence or for a purpose other than the treatment of disease, the quantity allowed as part of treatment ought to be only the excess beyond the amount needed for ordinary use. It is impracticable owing to individual differences to define by rule the amount required for ordinary use; but so as to give effect to the principle, the total amount allowed as part of treatment, including medicines, appliances, and medical comforts, should be so limited that the inclusive cost shall not exceed 5s. weekly. It should, however, be borne in mind that none of these articles should be ordered as a matter of routine; they should be given if and so far as required for the individual needs of separate cases.

Medical comforts must always be charged to the Sanatorium Benefit Fund.

NATIONAL HEALTH INSURANCE COMMISSION (SCOTLAND),
83 PRINCES STREET, EDINBURGH,
31st *July* 1915.

(2) SCHEME.

Form No. 603.

I. CONDITIONS.

(1) The general arrangements made by the Committee for the purpose of administering Sanatorium Benefit shall be such as to secure that adequate medical treatment and supervision shall be provided for each case of domiciliary treatment (that is to say, treatment otherwise than in a sanatorium or other institution).

(2) In the case of an insured person, such treatment shall be undertaken by the medical practitioner by whom he is attended under Medical Benefit.

(3) In the case of a dependant of an insured person, the rate of remuneration for such treatment to the practitioner in attendance under arrangements made by the Committee for affording domiciliary treatment to dependants shall not exceed   per week.

(4) Subject as hereinafter provided, an insured person, or the dependant of an insured person, recommended for Sanatorium Benefit and in receipt of domiciliary treatment (hereinafter called a " patient ") may be supplied under arrangements made by the Committee with the following articles :—

(a) *Medicines and Appliances* * as defined in Section 8 (1) (a) of the National Insurance Act, 1911.

(b) *Medical Comforts :* † viz.

provided always that a patient shall not be supplied, under arrangements made by the Committee, with any medicines, appliances, or medical comforts other than those specified in this Section.

---

* Any medicines or appliances which are allowed under Medical Benefit may, when appropriate to the treatment of tuberculosis, be ordered for domiciliary treatment under the Scheme. When so ordered, they must be charged to the Sanatorium Benefit Fund, not to the Drug Fund.

† Medical comforts are substances other than medicines which may be regarded as essential to treatment. They must always be charged to the Sanatorium Benefit Fund.

(5) Subject as hereinafter provided, no medicines, appliances, or medical comforts specified in the foregoing Section shall be supplied under arrangements made by the Committee unless certified by the medical practitioner in attendance as required for the treatment of the tuberculosis from which the patient is suffering, and approved by the Medical Adviser of the Committee.

(6) The total inclusive cost of medicines, appliances, and medical comforts shall not exceed 5s. weekly.

(7) Save as hereinbefore provided, a patient shall not be supplied under arrangements made by the Committee with any food or other article of diet.

(8) Subject as hereinafter provided, arrangements may be made by the Committee with a person or Local Authority (other than a Poor Law Authority) undertaking treatment in a manner approved by the Local Government Board with a view to the carrying out of the treatment of the patient, including the supervision or control thereof (excepting in so far as any part of such treatment may be otherwise arranged for under this Scheme), and the provision, if considered by the Medical Adviser of the Committee to be required for the proper treatment of the patient, of a shelter, provided always that where the patient is unable himself to provide bed, bedding, or bedclothes, other than body clothes, for the due equipment of the shelter, such bed, bedding, or bedclothes, other than body clothes, may be provided as part of the arrangements made by the Committee.

(9) The charges payable by the Committee in respect of arrangements made under the foregoing section, in so far as including the provision of a shelter, shall not exceed 1s. 6d. per week; in so far as including the provision of a shelter with bed and mattress, shall not exceed 2s. per week; and in so far as including the provision of a shelter with bed, bedding (including mattress), and bedclothes, shall not exceed 2s. 6d. per week, provided that these charges in each case shall be held to include the cost of transport and erection.

(10) Save as hereinbefore provided, a patient shall not be supplied under arrangements made by the Committee with bed, bedding, or bed-clothes.

(11) A patient shall not be supplied under arrangements made by the Committee with foot-gear, under-clothing, or other wearing apparel.

(12) Save as hereinbefore provided, the rent, or any part of the rent, of premises occupied by a patient or of any part of such premises, shall not be defrayed under arrangements made by the Committee.

(13) The Medical Adviser of the Committee shall once in each inform the Committee as to the progress of the patient.

(14) A patient, either himself or through his representative, shall not be supplied by the Committee with any money to be disbursed on his behalf, but the Committee shall make arrangements with a view to the supply by purveyors to the patient of medicines, appliances, and medical comforts.

(15) Orders for medicines and appliances to be provided under arrangements made by the Committee shall, if given on the Medical Benefit Order Form of the Committee, be distinguished by an Index Mark appropriate to Domiciliary Treatment under Sanatorium Benefit.

(16) Orders for medical comforts to be provided under arrangements made by the Committee shall be given to purveyors in the Form D (o) (herewith), which shall be supplied by the Committee for this purpose to the practitioner in attendance on the patient.

(17) The general conditions for the domiciliary treatment of tuberculosis set forth in the Circular Public Health No. VI., 1913, of the Local Government Board shall be observed.*

---

* The general conditions of the Local Government Board are as follows:—

"(1) *That the name of every case recommended for domiciliary treatment, together with the address at which such treatment is to be carried out, shall be intimated by the Insurance Committee, through their Medical Adviser or otherwise to the Medical Officer of Health of the district where the patient is to be treated.*

II. Procedure.

(18) Domiciliary treatment shall be for a specified period, but such period shall not in any case exceed three months, provided that the Committee may at the close of any period, if they think fit, extend such treatment for a further period not exceeding three months.

(19) As soon as may be after the Committee has decided to grant domiciliary treatment, including any extension thereof, the Clerk to the Committee, in the case of an insured person, shall inform the practitioner on the panel from whom the insured person is entitled to obtain treatment that he has been granted domiciliary treatment, and in the case of a dependant of an insured person shall make arrangements for his treatment by a practitioner.

(20) As soon as may be after the Committee has decided to grant domiciliary treatment, including any extension thereof, if it is proposed that the patient shall be provided with any of the articles specified in Section (4) hereof, an estimate of the weekly cost of the articles shall be drawn up.

(21) Such estimate shall be in the Form D (e) (herewith), which shall be supplied by the Committee to the practitioner in attendance. The practitioner shall, in giving treatment, adhere as far as practicable to the terms of the estimate; but if during the currency of the treatment he considers it to be in the interest of the patient to depart from the terms of the estimate he shall be at liberty to do so, provided always that any articles ordered shall be among those specified in Section (4) hereof, and that the total weekly cost, unless in any grave emergency, shall not exceed that stated in the estimate. Any excess expenditure incurred in grave emergency shall without delay be intimated by the practitioner to the Committee, who shall, at such times and in such form as the Commissioners may require, report to the Commissioners regarding such excess expenditure.

III. Intimation to Commission.

(22) As soon as may be after the Committee has decided to grant domiciliary treatment, including any extension thereof, but not more than one week thereafter, the Clerk to the Committee shall transmit to the Commissioners in duplicate one or other of the forms herewith—in the case of an insured person Form D (1), and in the case of a dependant of an insured person, Form D (2)—duly filled in.

" (2) *That regular medical attendance and supervision are provided.*

" (3) *That the Medical Adviser of the Insurance Committee shall inform the Medical Officer of Health of any change either in the patient's condition or in his surroundings that may render the house or other place in which the treatment is being carried out unsatisfactory for the purpose.*

" (4) *That the Medical Adviser of the Insurance Committee shall inform the Medical Officer of Health when in his opinion continued residence of a patient at home might endanger the health of others, and when a patient has been removed to an institution.*

" (5) *That the treatment of the patient and the circumstances under which the treatment is conducted shall be in conformity with the provisions of the Public Health (Scotland) Act, 1897.*"

"The conditions above set forth apply to treatment undertaken by persons. Where a *local authority* propose to carry out such treatment, application should be made (1) for the Board's authority under Section 16 (1) (b) of the National Insurance Act, 1911, or (2) for their consent under Section 66 (1) (d) of the Public Health (Scotland) Act, 1897, if a Local Authority under the latter Act—or a County Council by virtue of their powers under Section 41 (3) of the National Insurance Act, 1913—prefer to proceed in terms of that Section. In such cases, the application for the Board's authority or consent as the case may be should be accompanied by a report by the Medical Officer of Health giving full details of the scheme of treatment proposed."

[Circular Public Health No. VI., 1913, Local Government Board].

Form D (1).

Insurance Committee for the............of.............. ....

INSURED PERSON.

* Recommendation
* Extension of Recommendation } for Sanatorium Benefit.

DOMICILIARY TREATMENT.

I hereby intimate the following arrangements
  † and apply for approval.
- (i.) Name of Insured Person......................
  Address..
  Age ....
- (ii.) Period of treatment is for................ending on..............
- (iii.) Form of Tuberculosis ....
- (iv.) Name of practitioner on panel from whom insured person is to obtain treatment..............................
- (v.) Are arrangements fully conform to general conditions for domiciliary treatment of tuberculosis set forth in Circular Public Health No. VI., 1913, of Local Government Board ? If not, the facts should be stated....................................
- (vi.) Have other conditions and the procedure laid down in General Scheme been adhered to ? If not, the facts and reasons should be stated......................
- (vii.) Is it proposed that a shelter should be provided ? If so, state name of person or Local Authority providing shelter, extent of equipment, and charge payable, if any ....
- (viii.) Is it proposed that medicines, appliances, or medical comforts according to Form D (*e*) should be provided ? If so, enter hereunder.

	Name of Article.	Estimated Quantity per week.	Estimated Cost per week.
Medical Comforts			
Medicines and Appliances			
Total estimated cost per week			

........................Clerk.
  Date....................

* Delete word or words inapplicable. In the case of an *extension of recommendation*, answers (iii.) to (viii.) inclusive, if the same as before, may be left blank.
  † Delete if answers to (v.) and vi.) are " Yes."

Form D (2).

Insurance Committee for the............of ....

DEPENDANT.

* Recommendation
* Extension of Recommendation } for Sanatorium Benefit.

DOMICILIARY TREATMENT.

I hereby intimate the following arrangements † and apply for approval.

(i.) Name of Dependant..........................
    Address....................................
    Age......................
    Relation to insured person.......................
    Name of insured person.........................
    Address of insured person.....................
(ii.) Period of treatment is for.................ending on............
(iii.) Form of Tuberculosis..........................
(iv.) Name of Practitioner with whom arrangements have been made for the medical attendance of the dependant, together with amount of fees proposed to be paid to such practitioner....................
(v.) Are arrangements fully conform to general conditions for domiciliary treatment of tuberculosis set forth in Circular Public Health No. VI., 1913, of Local Government Board? If not, the facts should be stated.
(vi.) Have other conditions and the procedure laid down in General Scheme been adhered to? If not, the facts and reasons should be stated........................
(vii.) Is it proposed that a shelter should be provided? If so, state name of person or Local Authority providing shelter, extent of equipment, and charge payable, if any...............................
(viii.) Is it proposed that medicines, appliances, or medical comforts according to Form D (e) should be provided? If so, enter hereunder.

	Name of Article.	Estimated Quantity per week.	Estimated Cost per week.
Medical comforts .			*
Medicines and Appliances . . .			
Total estimated cost per week			

...............................Clerk.

Date........................

    * Delete word or words inapplicable. In the case of an *extension of recommendation*, answers (iii.) to (viii.) inclusive, if the same as before, may be left blank.

    † Delete if answers to (v.) and (vi.) are " Yes."

Form (e)

Insurance Committee for the............of ....

DOMICILIARY TREATMENT.
ESTIMATE.

Name of Patient........................
I certify the following to be required for the treatment of the tuberculosis from which the above patient is suffering:

	Name of Article.	Estimated Quantity per week.	Estimated Cost per week.
Medical comforts			
Medicines and Appliances			
Total estimated cost per week			

....
Medical Practitioner in attendance.

Date........................

Note.—Medical comforts may only be ordered in so far as in excess of the amount required for ordinary maintenance. In the case of medical comforts, state name of article, estimated quantity per week, and estimated cost per week.

The medicines and appliances which may be ordered are the same as in Medical Benefit. In the case of medicines and appliances, state only estimated cost per week.

The total estimated cost per week must not exceed 5s.

APPROVED.

Date........................
....
Medical Adviser of the Committee.

Form D (o.)

Insurance Committee for the............of ....

DOMICILIARY TREATMENT.
Order for
MEDICAL COMFORTS.

Name of Patient................................

Address................................

To........................
Kindly supply for treatment of the above patient—

....
Medical Practitioner in attendance.

Date........................

To the Clerk

    Insurance Committee for the ....of ....

    I have supplied the above article....as ordered, and enclose my account herewith.

                                         ....
                                                Purveyor.

Date.............................

APPENDIX XVI.

COPY OF THE LETTER OF THE CHANCELLOR OF THE EXCHEQUER TO MR. HENRY HOBHOUSE.

(See *Introduction and Cap. V., Section (III.) (ii.), paragraph* (345).)

Dear Mr. Hobhouse,—

    The President of the Local Government Board and I have considered the representations which were submitted to us yesterday on behalf of the County Councils' Association with reference to the financial arrangements for defraying the cost of schemes for treatment of tuberculosis.

    As regards capital expenditure, the Government have provided a sum of £1,500,000 to aid the provision of sanatoria and other institutions, and in their circular letter of the 14th of May last * the Local Government Board announced that, subject to certain limitations, they would provide three-fifths of the outlay on sanatoria and four-fifths of the outlay on dispensaries out of this fund. We understand that local authorities are satisfied with these arrangements, and that their main anxiety is in regard to the annual cost of maintenance. I gathered that local authorities are prepared to bear 25 per cent. of the annual cost of schemes, if the remainder were provided from other sources; and that their request is that this should be paid to them direct by the Local Government Board. We have submitted your views to our colleagues, and the Government are prepared to go a long way towards meeting your requests.

    Before setting out what further arrangements the Government are prepared to make it may be well to recapitulate the present position. Under the Insurance Act an annual sum of about one million is provided for the treatment of insured persons. While the Bill was passing through Parliament provisions were inserted for extending sanatorium benefit to dependants of insured, and in view of this the Government consented to bear one half of any deficit in regard to sanatorium benefit where local authorities undertook the other half. It is now urged that schemes for the treatment of tuberculosis should relate to the whole community, and that generally they should be organised and carried out by the councils of counties and county boroughs. This extension involves additional outlay, and in view of this the Government have decided to place at the disposal of the Local Government Boards of the three kingdoms annually a sum of money which will represent approximately half the total estimated cost of treating the non-insured persons as well as the dependants of insured persons. This money will be distributed by the Local Government Boards, in pursuance of regulations to be made by those Departments, to local authorities which undertake schemes, to be approved by the Departments, for the general treatment of tuberculosis in their areas: and provision will

---

* This refers to the Circular of the English Local Government Board. The corresponding Circular of the Local Government Board for Scotland is that of 29th May 1912.

be made accordingly for these grants in the Estimates of the three Departments.

As regards the cost of treating insured persons, the sum already provided under the Insurance Act, which, as I have already stated, is about one million pounds, can only pass to local authorities in pursuance of agreements made between them and Insurance Committees. But I have no doubt that Insurance Committees generally will be anxious to deal with the Local Authority of their area, and the Association may rest assured that the Government will do all in their power to secure this.

I should like to take this opportunity of expressing my great appreciation of the way in which county councils and county borough councils have taken up this important work, and I feel sure that, in view of the additional grants I have herein described, they will proceed without delay to formulate and carry out their schemes.

Yours sincerely,
(Sgd.) D. LLOYD GEORGE.
31st *July* 1912.

APPENDIX XVII.

MODEL RULES FOR DEPOSIT CONTRIBUTORS.

(SUGGESTED FOR ADOPTION BY SCOTTISH INSURANCE COMMITTEES.)

(*See Cap. VI., Section (III.), paragraph* (365).)

1. GENERAL.

In these rules, unless the context otherwise requires or admits—

(1) "The Act" means Parts I. and III. of the National Insurance Act, 1911, and the National Insurance Act, 1913, and all regulations, orders, and special orders lawfully made thereunder and in force for the time being which shall be deemed to be incorporated in these rules, and anything in these rules inconsistent with any provision of the Act shall be void of and no effect.

(2) "Deposit Contributor" means any person contributing for or entitled to benefits under the Act who has not joined an Approved Society within the prescribed time, or who, having been a member of an Approved Society, has been expelled or has resigned therefrom, and has not within the prescribed time joined another Approved Society.

(3) "Committee" means the Insurance Committee for the County [Burgh] of

(4) "The Clerk" means the Clerk or the Acting Clerk of the Committee.

2. RESIDENCE.

(1) Except as otherwise provided in these rules no deposit contributor shall apply to the Committee for the payment to him of sickness or maternity benefit by the Committee unless he is resident in the County [Burgh] of

(2) Where a deposit contributor becomes temporarily resident in some place outside the area of the Committee but in the United Kingdom, or in the Isle of Man or the Channel Islands, the Committee, if satisfied that his residence outside the area of the Committee is temporary only, may take into consideration any application made by him for the payment of any sickness or maternity benefit.

(3) A deposit contributor who changes his place of residence shall notify the full postal address of his new place of residence to the Scottish Insurance Commissioners, and shall state whether he intends to reside in that place permanently or not.

3. SICKNESS BENEFIT.

(1) (a) A deposit contributor who desires to claim sickness benefit may do so by sending an application to the Committee at the end of the period during which he has been rendered incapable of work, or at the expiration of one week from the commencement of the disease or disablement whichever is the earlier.

(b) The application must be made on a form supplied to him for the purpose and must be accompanied by a declaration that he has been rendered incapable of work and that he has not recovered, is not in receipt of, and is not entitled to receive or recover, any compensation or damages such as are mentioned in Section 11 of the Act, by a certificate signed by a medical practitioner stating the cause of his incapacity, and by his contribution card. The Committee may in special circumstances require or allow a deposit contributor to furnish other evidence of his incapacity and require him to furnish a statement in writing of such other particulars as the Committee may think fit :

Provided that the Committee may take into consideration any application, notwithstanding that it is not made in accordance with the foregoing requirements.

(2) Every application for sickness benefit shall be taken into consideration within   days from the receipt of the application.

(3) At the end of every week after the first during which the incapacity continues the deposit contributor shall, for the purpose of receiving sickness benefit, send to the Committee such evidence as the Committee may by standing orders or otherwise require of the continuance of the incapacity.

(4) Any deposit contributor who—

(a) makes any false declaration as to incapacity for work ; or

(b) attempts by any means improperly to procure a payment to be made to him out of the Deposit Contributors' Fund ;

shall be liable to be suspended from sickness benefit for a period not exceeding one month or to a fine not exceeding   , or in the case of repeated breaches of this rule,

(5) A deposit contributor in receipt of sickness benefit—

(a) shall obey instructions of the doctor attending him ;

(b) shall not in any case be absent from home between the hours of 9 p.m. and 7 a.m. from 1st April to 30th September, and 7 p.m. and 9 a.m. from 1st October to 31st March, and shall not, except with the consent of, and subject to such conditions as may be imposed by, the Committee, be absent from home at any time without leaving word where he may be found ;

(c) shall not conduct himself in a manner which is likely to retard his recovery.

(6) The Committee may suspend payment of sickness benefit to a deposit contributor whose disease or disablement has been caused by his own misconduct.

(7) Any sickness benefit payable to a deposit contributor shall be paid by means of a postal order payable at such Post Office, and to himself or such other person, as he may specify in the form of application.

(8) Where a married woman who was at the date of her marriage a deposit contributor is by virtue of Section 44 of the Act suspended from ordinary benefits under Part I. of the Act, the following provisions shall have effect with respect to the payments to be made to her during any period of sickness or distress by way of benefits under Part III. of the Fourth Schedule to the Act :—

Any such married woman who is sick or in distress may make application in writing to the Committee for the payment to her during the sickness or distress of benefits under Part III. of the said Fourth Schedule, and the Committee may during the sickness or distress make to her towards such benefits weekly payments of such amounts as having regard to the circumstances of the case the Committee think fit, not exceeding in the whole two-thirds of the amount standing to her credit in the Deposit Contributors' Fund at the date of her suspension.

(9) If any deposit contributor is entitled to receive or recover any such compensation or damages as are mentioned in Section 11 of the Act he shall, prior to entering into any agreement in respect thereof, give notice of his intention to the Insurance Committee, and shall furnish such particulars thereof, and such information in connection therewith as the Committee may require; and any deposit contributor who has received or recovered or has made any agreement in respect of any such compensation or damages shall within three days after receiving or recovering the compensation or damages or after entering into the agreement, as the case may be, give notice in writing to the Committee setting out the amount of the compensation or damages.

(10) Any deposit contributor may make an application for sickness benefit by way of advance pending the settlement of a claim for any such compensation or damages as are mentioned in Section 11 of the Act, and the Committee, subject to the provisions of sub-section (3) of Section 11 of the Act, shall take the application into consideration and may pay benefit accordingly.

4. Maternity Benefit.

(1) Where a claim for maternity benefit arises in respect of a deposit contributor, notice of the confinement shall be given by or on behalf of the deposit contributor, or in the case of his being the husband by or on behalf of his wife, and that within 7 days after the confinement, and there shall also be produced if required a certificate signed by the doctor or midwife by whom the mother of the child was attended during the confinement, or such other sufficient evidence of the confinement; and where the claim for maternity benefit is in respect of the husband, a copy of his marriage certificate or such other evidence of the marriage as the Committee may think fit.

(2) For the purposes of these rules, "confinement" means labour resulting in the issue of a living child, or labour after 28 weeks of pregnancy resulting in the issue of a child whether alive or dead.

(3) The benefit shall be administered in the interests of the mother and child in cash or otherwise, at the discretion of the Committee, and any part thereof may, in the discretion of the Committee, be paid direct to the doctor or midwife attending at the confinement; all payments shall be made by means of a postal order payable at such Post Office as the recipient may specify, or, failing specification, as the Committee may determine.

(4) Maternity benefit being in every case the mother's benefit, the wife's receipt or the husband's receipt on her behalf, if authorised by her, shall be a sufficient discharge to the Committee, and where the benefit is paid to the husband he shall pay it to the wife.

(5) A woman who is an employed contributor and in respect of whose husband's insurance no maternity benefit, or a sum less than the full maternity benefit, is payable, shall on her confinement be entitled to receive in respect of her own insurance such sum as, with the sum, if any, payable in respect of her husband's insurance, is equal to the sum she would have been entitled to receive if he had not been an insured person.

(6) An insured woman in respect of whom a Maternity Benefit is payable in virtue of sub-section (3) of Section 14 of the National Insurance Act, 1913, shall abstain from remunerative work during a period of four weeks after her confinement, provided that any penalties imposed for breaches of this rule in the period of four weeks shall not exceed, in the aggregate, the sum payable in respect of the Maternity Benefit.

5. Payment to Dependants.

Where any sum is to be paid or applied under sub-section (2) (*a*) of Section 12 of the Act for the relief or maintenance of the dependants of a deposit contributor, the Committee may require the contributor to furnish them with the names and addresses of the dependants and such other information or such evidence relating to them as the Committee may think fit, and payment shall be made by means of a postal order payable at such Post Office as may be specified by the contributor in his form of application, or by the dependants, as the case may be.

6. Visitors.

The Committee may appoint visitors to visit and report upon deposit contributors in receipt of sickness benefit and deposit contributors or wives of deposit contributors to or in respect of whom maternity benefit is or may be payable :

Provided that no woman shall be visited otherwise than by a woman.

7. Offences.

(1) In the case of the breach of any of these Rules for which no penalty is assigned, the Committee may in their discretion inflict a fine or suspension of benefits :

Provided that :

(a) a deposit contributor shall not be fined a sum exceeding   or in the case of repeated breaches of Rules   , and shall not be suspended from any of the benefits under Part I. of the Act for more than one month, and

(b) maternity benefit shall not be suspended in respect of the confinement of the wife of a deposit contributor where the wife has not herself been guilty of any breach of rules, imposition or attempted imposition.

(2) A deposit contributor who has been fined and has failed to pay the fine within four weeks, shall be suspended from benefit until the expiration of one month, or until the fine is paid, whichever first happens.

(3) Before inflicting any penalty upon a deposit contributor the Committee shall give notice to him of their intention, and if within seven days from the receipt of the notice he gives notice to the Clerk that he desires to be heard in explanation of his conduct, the Committee shall fix a date for the hearing by the Committee of his explanation, and not less than seven days' notice shall be given to the deposit contributor of the date so fixed.

8. Notices of Marriage, etc.

(1) Where any deposit contributor being a woman marries, she shall, within fourteen days after the date of marriage, give notice thereof to the Clerk, and shall also if she continues to be employed within the meaning of the Act after her marriage state that she so continues.

(2) A deposit contributor, whose husband dies or whose marriage has been dissolved or annulled, shall give notice of the death of her husband or of the decree dissolving or annulling the marriage within fourteen days from the date of the death or decree, as the case may be.

(3) A deposit contributor giving any such notice or making any such statement as aforesaid shall, if and when required, produce satisfactory evidence of the facts appearing in the notice or statement.

APPENDIX XVIII

SEE CAP. VII. SECTION (I) I (e) paragraph (457).

ASSAGE OF MEDICAL BENEFIT MONEYS THROUGH THE

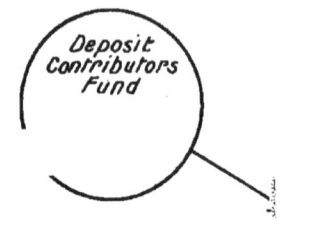

Deposit Contributors Fund

Societies' Credits in Nat. Health Insurance Fund

Treasury

General Medical Benefit Fund

Medical Benefit Fund Account

Domicilia

Domiciliar Sixpence

wed nts

Central Medical Benefit Fund

dents F

Res

APPENDIX XIX.

(*See Cap. VII., Section (I.), paragraph* (459).)

Scheme framed by the Scottish Insurance Commissioners and approved by the National Health Insurance Joint Committee and by the Lords Commissioners of His Majesty's Treasury for the Distribution of the Parliamentary Grant in Aid of Mileage in Sparsely-Populated Districts in Scotland, exclusive of the Highlands and Islands for the Year 1914.

CONDITIONS.

1. The Grant for the year 1914 shall be distributed in aid of mileage in sparsely populated districts of Scotland other than the Highlands and Islands as defined in the Highlands and Islands (Medical Service) Grant Act, 1913.

2. (1) The amount of the grant applicable to each County or portion of a County containing sparsely populated districts shall be determined by the Scottish Insurance Commissioners (hereinafter referred to as "the Commissioners") having regard to, *inter alia* :—

   (a) the amounts of the Mileage Grants paid in respect of each County or portion of a County for the year 1913–14;
   (b) such adjustments as the Commissioners may consider necessary in consequence of any change of circumstances in the case of any County or portion of a County including any change in the area of the sparsely populated districts;
   (c) any sum which the Commissioners may determine to be payable out of the funds for mileage in respect of members of the Seamen's National Insurance Society resident in those districts of Scotland to which the grant applies—such sum, if any, being payable to the Society in instalments or otherwise as the Commissioners think fit.

   (2) In making adjustments in consequence of change of circumstances, no account shall be taken by the Commissioners of insured persons resident within three miles by land of the residence of any medical practitioner on the Insurance Committee's List.

3. The sums determined as aforesaid shall be intimated by the Commissioners to the respective Insurance Committees and shall be paid to them in instalments or otherwise, and subject to such conditions as the Commissioners may think fit.

4. All sums so paid by the Commissioners shall be carried by the Insurance Committee to a special Mileage Fund which shall be audited by the Auditors appointed by the Treasury.

5. Subject, as hereinafter provided, the Insurance Committee shall distribute the Mileage Fund for the year 1914 among the practitioners on the panel who may be deemed by the Committee to be entitled to participate therein on the basis of one unit for every mile of "normal mileage," and two and a half units for every mile of "special mileage," and four units for every mile of "water mileage" respectively.

6. "Normal mileage" shall be the distance along a driving road between the residence of an insured person and that of the nearest practitioner on the Insurance Committee's List. "Special Mileage" shall be the like distance along a path or road not used for vehicular traffic or across moorland. "Water mileage" shall be the whole distance by sea or loch measured between the points of embarkation and landing, having regard to the length of an average voyage.

7. In making such distribution and in determining the sum, if any, payable to each practitioner on the panel, the Insurance Committee may take into account any special circumstances of their area, or any representations made by any of such practitioners or by the Local Medical

Committee or by the Panel Committee in regard thereto, and may vary the scheme of distribution accordingly.

8. The scheme of distribution adopted by the Committee, including any allowance for special circumstances, shall be such as to secure that the *cumulo* sum to be distributed by the Committee to the practitioners on the panel as aforesaid shall not in any area exceed the total sum payable to the Committee by the Commissioners in respect of mileage.

9. The Committee shall distribute the sum payable to each practitioner in such instalments as to secure that a practitioner who is on the panel for only part of the year shall not receive more than the share proportionate to the length of his service.

APPENDIX XX.

LIST OF OFFICIALS, Etc.

(See Cap. VIII., paragraph (532).)

(A.) COMMISSIONERS AND THEIR HEAD OFFICE STAFF.

Principal Office	83 Princes Street, Edinburgh (Tel. No. 8820-3 Central).
Accounts Branch	39 Buckingham Terrace, Edinburgh (Tel. No. 8920 Central).
Approved Society and Exemption Branches	42 Frederick Street, Edinburgh (Tel. No. 8924 Central).
Chairman	Sir JAMES LEISHMAN.
Deputy Chairman	Dr. J. C. M'VAIL.
Commissioners	{ Mr. JOHN M'NICOL. Miss MARY M. PATERSON.
Secretary	Mr. JOHN JEFFREY.
Assistant Secretaries	{ Mr. H. L. F. FRASER. Mr. WILLIAM LEITCH.
Legal Adviser	Mr. JOHN M. VALLANCE.
Accountant	Mr. J. STEWART SEGGIE.
Medical Officers	{ Dr. J. R. CURRIE. Dr. G. MATHESON CULLEN.
Actuary (on Joint Committee Staff)	Mr. J. W. THOMSON.
For all above Offices	Telegrams: "Benefits," Edinburgh.

(B.) SCOTTISH STAFF OF NATIONAL INSURANCE AUDIT DEPARTMENT.

Inspector of Audit—Mr. W. G. TWORT, 56 Castle Street, Edinburgh (Tel. No. 7751 Central).

District.	Auditor.	Address.
S1. (Aberdeen	Mr. J. D. Gardiner	25 Union Terrace, Aberdeen.
Sub-Office (Dundee)	Mr. J. D. Gardiner	29 Bank Street, Dundee.
S2. (Glasgow)	Mr. J. Davies	} 50 Wellington Street, Glasgow (Tel. No. 5428 Central).
S3. (Glasgow)	Mr. A. C. Aitken	
S4. (Glasgow)	Mr. W. M'Auslin	
S5. (Edinburgh)	Mr. D. Drysdale	56 Castle Street, Edinburgh (Tel. No. 7751 Central).

APPENDIX XX (*Continued*).

(C.) INSPECTORAL DISTRICTS AND STAFF.

(*See Cap. VIII., paragraph* (532).)

Chief Inspector—Mr. J. W. PECK, 83 Princes Street, Edinburgh, Tel. 8820-3.
Deputy Chief Inspectors—Mr. S. H. TURNER, Baltic Chambers, 50 Wellington Street, Glasgow, Tel. 5426-9.
Mr. A. NEWLANDS, 41¼ Union Street, Aberdeen, Tel. 2307.

District.	Headquarters.	Inspector.	Area.
1. South-Eastern	Edinburgh— 42 Frederick Street. Tel. 8820-3, Central.	Mr. J. W. Herries.	Edinburgh, Linlithgow, Haddington, Berwick, Roxburgh, Selkirk, and Peebles.
2. Western	Glasgow— Baltic Chambers, 50 Wellington Street, Tel. 5426-9, Central.	Mr. J. E. Highton.	Glasgow, Dunbarton, S. Argyll (Mid, Cowall, Kintyre, Islay), and Stirling.
3. South-Western	Glasgow— Baltic Chambers, 50 Wellington Street, Tel. 5426-9, Central.	Mr. A. Arneil.	Lanark (other than Glasgow), Renfrew (other than Glasgow), Ayr, Wigtown, Kirkcudbright, Dumfries, and Bute.
4. Eastern	Dundee— Eagle Buildings, Trades Lane. Tel. 2013.	Miss D. S. Allan.	Forfar, Fife, Kinross, Clackmannan, and Perth.
5. North-Eastern	Aberdeen— 41¼ Union Street. Tel. 2307.	Mr. A. Newlands.	Aberdeen, Kincardine, Banff, and Shetland.
6. Northern	Inverness— 20 Church Street. Tel. 232.	Mr. M. Beaton.	Nairn, Elgin, Inverness, Ross and Cromarty, Sutherland, Caithness, Orkney, and N. Argyll (Ardnamurchan, Mull, Lorn).

APPENDIX XXI.

(1) INSURANCE COMMITTEES IN SCOTLAND, WITH NAMES AND ADDRESSES OF CLERKS AND TELEPHONE NUMBERS.

(*See Cap. VIII., paragraph* (533).)

COUNTIES.

ABERDEEN.—Alexander Clark, 183A Union Street, Aberdeen (288 Central).
ARGYLL.—Malcolm Sinclair, County Offices, Lochgilphead (8 Lochgilphead).
AYR.—James D. Wyllie, 37 Bank Street, Kilmarnock (251 Kilmarnock).
BANFF.—J. D. Paterson, Solicitor, 5 Back Path, Banff (5x5 Banff).
BERWICK.—Thomas Agnew, 25 Market Square, Duns.
BUTE.—A. W. Herbert, County Office, Rothesay (54 Rothesay).
CAITHNESS.—A. B. Campbell, British Linen Bank Buildings, 18 Bridge Street, Wick.
CLACKMANNAN AND KINROSS.—James W. Moir, County Buildings, Alloa (15 Alloa).
DUNBARTON.—James Brown, 43 Church Street, Dumbarton (44 Dunbarton (office), 16 Alexandria (house)).
DUMFRIES.—John Robson, County Buildings, Dumfries (400 Dumfries).
ELGIN AND NAIRN.—E. D. Jameson, County Clerk's Office, Elgin (21 Elgin).
FIFE.—W. T. Duncan, Whytescauseway, Kirkcaldy (429 Kirkcaldy).
FORFAR.—Thomas Hani_k, Town House, Forfar (89 Forfar).
HADDINGTON.—W. B. Lawrie, Chambers, Bank of Scotland, Haddington (37 Haddington).
INVERNESS.—Duncan Shaw, County Clerk's and Treasurer's Office, Inverness (2 Inverness).
KINCARDINE.—J. Falconer, County Clerk's Office, Stonehaven (19 Stonehaven).
KIRKCUDBRIGHT.—Adam Brown, County Clerk's Office, Kirkcudbright (26 Kirkcudbright).
LANARK.—W. M. Marshall, 3 Merry Street, Motherwell (82 Motherwell).
LINLITHGOW.—J. G. B. Henderson, W.S., 61 High Street, Linlithgow (10B Linlithgow).
MIDLOTHIAN.—R. T. Wishart, 24 Hill Street, Edinburgh (6847 Central).
ORKNEY.—Peter Brass, 3 East Road, Kirkwall.
PEEBLES.—W. H. Williamson, High Street, Peebles (76 Peebles).
PERTH.—T. B. Marshall, Solicitor, 38 Tay Street, Perth (329 Perth).
RENFREW.—D. A. Morrison, Writer, 23 Moss Street, Paisley (675 Paisley).
ROSS AND CROMARTY.—W. J. Duncan, County Clerk's Office, Dingwall (14 Dingwall).
ROXBURGH.—A. Douglas Haddon, Royal Bank Buildings, Hawick (69 Hawick).
SELKIRK.—D. G. Stalker, Solicitor, Galashiels (92 Galashiels).
STIRLING.—James Learmonth, County Offices, Stirling (115 Stirling).
SUTHERLAND.—A. Argo, Solicitor, Golspie.
WIGTOWN.—Thomas M. Hunter, Union Bank Buildings, Stranraer (40 Stranraer).
ZETLAND.—William Williamson, St. Olaf Street, Lerwick.

BURGHS.

ABERDEEN.—Alexander M. Craig, Crown Mansions, 41½ Union Street, Aberdeen (67 Central).
AIRDRIE.—John A. Chapman, 13 Bank Street, Airdrie (97 Airdrie (office), 67 Airdrie (house)).
ARBROATH.—Rollo S. Black, London House, 7 Hill Street, Arbroath (87 Arbroath).
AYR.—John Boyd, Winton Buildings, 79 High Street, Ayr (268 Ayr).
CLYDEBANK.—George J. Miller, Solicitor, Municipal Buildings, Clydebank (11 Clydebank).
COATBRIDGE.—Robert Denholm, 17 Academy Street, Coatbridge (148 Coatbridge).

BURGHS (*Continued*).

DUMBARTON.—Kenneth S. Mackenzie, 80 Church Street, Dumbarton.
DUMFRIES AND MAXWELLTOWN.—R. A. Grierson, Town Hall Buildings, Dumfries (287 Dumfries).
DUNDEE.—D. Duncan, 2 Union Street, Dundee (637 Dundee).
DUNFERMLINE.—Robert Irvine, 39 Bridge Street, Dunfermline (376 Dunfermline).
EDINBURGH.—Jas. Russell, 18 Melville Street, Edinburgh (7812 Central).
FALKIRK.—John Wilson, Solicitor, Manse Place, Falkirk (327 Falkirk).
GLASGOW.—William Jones, 59 Bell Street, Glasgow (767 and 768 Bell).
GREENOCK.—R. W. Robertson, 4 Brymner Street, Greenock (294 Greenock).
HAMILTON.—Francis Cassells, 47 Cadzow Street, Hamilton (194 Hamilton).
INVERNESS.—William Michie, 28 High Street, Inverness (30 Inverness).
KILMARNOCK.—Thomas Johnstone, 1 St. Marnock Place, Kilmarnock.
KIRKCALDY.—James M. Lumsden, Solicitor, 288 High Street, Kirkcaldy (121 Kirkcaldy).
LEITH.—J. Kinghorn Miles, S.S.C., 46 Constitution Street, Leith (1031 Leith).
MOTHERWELL.—William Ballantyne, Commercial Bank, Motherwell (54 Motherwell).
PAISLEY.—Thomas Hunter, 94 High Street, Paisley (480 Paisley).
PERTH.—Wm. C. Burt, 36 High Street, Perth (394 Perth).
RUTHERGLEN.—John Henderson, 264 Main Street, Rutherglen.
STIRLING.—John Brown, Solicitor, 20 Barnton Street, Stirling (341 Stirling).
WISHAW.—Thomas S. Haran, Writer, Clyde Chambers, Wishaw (101 Wishaw).

(2) LIST OF ADDRESSES OF INSURANCE COMMITTEES IN ENGLAND, IRELAND, AND WALES.

(REVISED TO MARCH 1915.)

(*a*) ENGLAND.

Counties.

Committee. Address.

BEDFORDSHIRE.—The Clerk, Bedfordshire Insurance Committee, 1, 2, 3, & 4 Association Buildings, Harpur Street, Bedford.
BERKSHIRE.—The Clerk, Berkshire Insurance Committee, 2 Abbot's Walk, Reading.
BUCKINGHAMSHIRE.—The Clerk, Buckinghamshire Insurance Committee, 65 Buckingham Street, Aylesbury.
CAMBRIDGESHIRE.—The Clerk, Cambridgeshire Insurance Committee, 24 St. Andrew's Street, Cambridge.
CHESHIRE.—The Clerk, Cheshire Insurance Committee, 28 Nicholas Street, Chester.
CORNWALL.—The Clerk, Cornwall Insurance Committee, Lloyds Bank Chambers, Boscawen Street, Truro.
CUMBERLAND.—The Clerk, Cumberland Insurance Committee, 1 Lonsdale Street, Carlisle.
DERBYSHIRE.—The Clerk, Derbyshire Insurance Committee, 3 Market Place, Derby.
DEVONSHIRE.—The Clerk, Devonshire Insurance Committee, 60 High Street, Exeter.
DORSETSHIRE.—The Clerk, Dorsetshire Insurance Committee, 22 High East Street, Dorchester.
DURHAM.—The Clerk, Durham Insurance Committee, 20 New Elvet, Durham.
ESSEX.—The Clerk, Essex Insurance Committee, 58 Fillebrook Road, Leytonstone, N.E.
GLOUCESTERSHIRE.—The Clerk, Gloucestershire Insurance Committee, Shire Hall Chambers, Gloucester.
HAMPSHIRE.—The Clerk, Hampshire Insurance Committee, 39 Southgate Street, Winchester.

Committee.   Address.

HEREFORDSHIRE.—The Clerk, Herefordshire Insurance Committee, St Peter's House, St. Peter's Street, Hereford.
HERTFORDSHIRE.—The Clerk, Hertfordshire Insurance Committee, 12 Market Place, Hertford.
HUNTINGDONSHIRE.—The Clerk, Huntingdonshire Insurance Committee, 38 High Street, Huntingdon.
ISLE OF ELY.—The Clerk, Isle of Ely Insurance Committee, Station Road, March.
ISLE OF WIGHT.—The Clerk, Isle of Wight Insurance Committee, 113 Pyle Street, Newport, Isle of Wight.
ISLES OF SCILLY.—The Clerk, Isles of Scilly Insurance Committee, Council Offices, St. Mary's, Isles of Scilly.
KENT.—The Clerk, Kent Insurance Committee, Station Road, Maidstone.
LANCASHIRE.—The Clerk, Lancashire Insurance Committee, 1 Fishergate Hill, Preston.
LEICESTERSHIRE.—The Clerk, Leicestershire Insurance Committee, 144 London Road, Leicester.
LINCS. (HOLLAND).—The Clerk, Lincs. (Holland) Insurance Committee, Spalding.
LINCS. (KESTEVEN).—The Clerk, Lincs. (Kesteven) Insurance Committee, 16 Finkin Street, Grantham.
LINCS. (LINDSEY).—The Joint Clerks, Lincs. (Lindsey) Insurance Committee, Stonebow, Lincoln.
LONDON.—The Clerk, London Insurance Committee, 5 Chancery Lane, W.C.
MIDDLESEX.—The Clerk, Middlesex Insurance Committee, 13 Victoria Street, Westminster, S.W.
NORFOLK.—The Clerk, Norfolk Insurance Committee, 54 Prince of Wales Road, Norwich.
NORTHAMPTONSHIRE.—The Clerk, Northamptonshire Insurance Committee, 30 Market Square, Northampton.
NORTHUMBERLAND.—The Clerk, Northumberland Insurance Committee, 3 Royal Arcade, Pilgrim Street, Newcastle-upon-Tyne.
NOTTINGHAMSHIRE.—The Clerk, Nottinghamshire Insurance Committee, Clumber Buildings, Clumber Street, Nottingham.
OXFORDSHIRE.—The Clerk, Oxfordshire Insurance Committee (County Insurance Office), New Road, Oxford.
RUTLANDSHIRE.—The Clerk, Rutlandshire Insurance Committee, Church Passage, Oakham.
SALOP.—The Clerk, Salop Insurance Committee, Talbot Chambers, Shrewsbury.
SOKE OF PETERBOROUGH.—The Clerk, Soke of Peterborough Insurance Committee, 45 Priestgate, Peterborough.
SOMERSET.—The Clerk, Somerset Insurance Committee, Frome, Somerset.
STAFFORDSHIRE.—The Clerk, Staffordshire Insurance Committee, Market Square, Stafford.
SUFFOLK, EAST.—The Clerk, Suffolk, East, Insurance Committee, 62 Carr Street, Ipswich.
SUFFOLK, WEST.—The Clerk, Suffolk, West, Insurance Committee, 4 Lower Baxter Street, Bury St. Edmunds.
SURREY.—The Clerk, Surrey Insurance Committee, County Insurance Office, Penrhyn Road, Kingston-on-Thames.
SUSSEX, EAST.—The Clerk, Sussex, East, Insurance Committee, 81 High Street, Lewes.
SUSSEX, WEST.—The Clerk, Sussex, West, Insurance Committee, County Insurance Offices, Arundel.
WARWICKSHIRE.—The Clerk, Warwickshire Insurance Committee, 15 Waterloo Place, Leamington.
WESTMORLAND.—The Clerk, Westmorland Insurance Committee, Central Chambers, Lowther Street, Kendal.
WILTSHIRE.—The Clerk, Wiltshire Insurance Committee, Clerk's Office, Trowbridge.

Committee.	Address.

WORCESTERSHIRE.—The Clerk, Worcestershire Insurance Committee, Bank House, Shaw Street, Worcester.

YORKSHIRE, EAST RIDING.—The Clerk, East Riding Insurance Committee, County Hall, Beverley.

YORKSHIRE, NORTH RIDING.—The Clerk, North Riding Insurance Committee, White House, High Street, Northallerton.

YORKSHIRE, WEST RIDING.—The Clerk, West Riding Insurance Committee. County Hall, Wakefield.

County Boroughs.

BARNSLEY.—The Clerk, Barnsley Insurance Committee, Market Place, Barnsley.

BARROW-IN-FURNESS.—The Clerk, Barrow-in-Furness Insurance Committee, 92 Duke Street, Barrow-in-Furness.

BATH.—The Clerk, Bath Insurance Committee, 2 Quiet Street, Bath.

BIRKENHEAD.—The Clerk, Birkenhead Insurance Committee, Hamilton Chambers, Hamilton Street, Birkenhead.

BIRMINGHAM.—The Clerk, Birmingham Insurance Committee, 191 Corporation Street, Birmingham.

BLACKBURN.—The Clerk, Blackburn Insurance Committee, 44 Ainsworth Street, Blackburn.

BLACKPOOL.—The Clerk, Blackpool Insurance Committee, Town Hall, Blackpool.

BOLTON.—The Clerk, Bolton Insurance Committee, Central Hall, 9 Acresfield, Bolton.

BOOTLE.—The Clerk, Bootle Insurance Committee, Central Library, Oriel Road, Bootle.

BOURNEMOUTH.—The Clerk, Bournemouth Insurance Committee, 200 Old Christchurch Road, Bournemouth.

BRADFORD.—The Clerk, Bradford Insurance Committee, 38 King's Arcade, Market Street, Bradford.

BRIGHTON.—The Clerk, Brighton Insurance Committee, 82 Grand Parade, Brighton.

BRISTOL.—The Clerk, Bristol Insurance Committee, Sun Buildings, 1 Clare Street, Bristol.

BURNLEY.—The Clerk, Burnley Insurance Committee, Old Technical School Elizabeth Street, Burnley.

BURTON-UPON-TRENT.—The Clerk, Burton-upon-Trent Insurance Committee, 31 Union Street, Burton-upon-Trent.

BURY.—The Clerk, Bury Insurance Committee, 17 Manchester Road, Bury.

CANTERBURY.—The Clerk, Canterbury Insurance Committee, 30 Watling Street, Canterbury.

CARLISLE.—The Clerk, Carlisle Insurance Committee, Midland Bank Chambers, Carlisle.

CHESTER.—The Clerk, Chester Insurance Committee, 21 Old Bank Buildings, Chester.

COVENTRY.—The Clerk, Coventry Insurance Committee, Grey Friars Chambers, Hertford Street, Coventry.

CROYDON.—The Clerk, Croydon Insurance Committee, 14 Katharine Street, Croydon.

DERBY.—The Clerk, Derby Insurance Committee, Old Bank Chambers, Iron Gate, Derby.

DEWSBURY.—The Clerk, Dewsbury Insurance Committee, Church Street, Dewsbury.

DUDLEY.—The Clerk, Dudley Insurance Committee, Labour Exchange Room, 15 Holloway Chambers, Priory Street, Dudley.

EASTBOURNE.—The Clerk, Eastbourne Insurance Committee, 5 Pevensey Road, Eastbourne.

EXETER.—The Clerk, Exeter Insurance Committee, The Court House, Exeter.

Committee.   Address.

GATESHEAD.—The Clerk, Gateshead Insurance Committee, Savings Bank Buildings, West Street, Gateshead.

GLOUCESTER.—The Clerk, Gloucester Insurance Committee, Westgate Chambers, Berkeley Street, Gloucester.

GREAT YARMOUTH.—The Clerk, Great Yarmouth Insurance Committee, Fastolff House, Regent Street, Great Yarmouth.

GRIMSBY.—The Clerk, Grimsby Insurance Committee, Victoria Street, Great Grimsby.

HALIFAX.—The Clerk, Halifax Insurance Committee, 15 King Cross Street, Halifax.

HASTINGS.—The Clerk, Hastings Insurance Committee, Queen's Chambers, Harold Place, Hastings.

HUDDERSFIELD.—The Clerk, Huddersfield Insurance Committee, 4 Byram Street, Huddersfield.

IPSWICH.—The Clerk, Ipswich Insurance Committee, Town Hall, Ipswich.

KINGSTON-UPON-HULL.—The Clerk, Kingston-upon-Hull Insurance Committee, 6 Wright Street, Hull.

LEEDS.—The Clerk, Leeds Insurance Committee, 74 New Briggate, Leeds.

LEICESTER.—The Clerk, Leicester Insurance Committee, 58 London Road, Leicester.

LINCOLN.—The Clerk, Lincoln Insurance Committee, Silver Street, Lincoln.

LIVERPOOL.—The Clerk, Liverpool Insurance Committee, Alexandra Buildings, 55 Dale Street, Liverpool.

MANCHESTER.—The Clerk, Manchester Insurance Committee, Union Bank Buildings, Piccadilly, Manchester.

MIDDLESBROUGH.—The Clerk, Middlesbrough Insurance Committee, 79 Grange Road West, Middlesbrough.

NEWCASTLE-UPON-TYNE.—The Clerk, Newcastle-upon-Tyne Insurance Committee, 26 Ellison Place, Newcastle-upon-Tyne.

NORTHAMPTON.—The Clerk, Northampton Insurance Committee, 31 Market Square, Northampton.

NORWICH.—The Clerk, Norwich Insurance Committee, 17 Haymarket, Norwich.

NOTTINGHAM.—The Clerk, Nottingham Insurance Committee, 12 Victoria Street, Nottingham.

OLDHAM.—The Clerk, Oldham Insurance Committee, Union Bank Chambers, Church Lane, Oldham.

OXFORD.—The Clerk, Oxford Insurance Committee, 38 Queen Street, Oxford.

PLYMOUTH.—The Clerk, Plymouth Insurance Committee, 7 Sussex Terrace, Princess Square, Plymouth.

PORTSMOUTH.—The Clerk, Portsmouth Insurance Committee, Town Hall, Portsmouth.

PRESTON.—The Clerk, Preston Insurance Committee, 11 Market Street, Preston.

READING.—The Clerk, Reading Insurance Committee, Broadway Buildings, Station Road, Reading.

ROCHDALE.—The Clerk, Rochdale Insurance Committee, 33 Oldham Road, Rochdale.

ROTHERHAM.—The Clerk, Rotherham Insurance Committee, Empire Chambers, High Street, Rotherham.

ST. HELENS.—The Clerk, St. Helens Insurance Committee, 11 Hardshaw Street, St. Helens.

SALFORD.—The Clerk, Salford Insurance Committee, 241 Chapel Street, Salford.

SHEFFIELD.—The Clerk, Sheffield Insurance Committee, Overend Chambers, 41 Church Street, Sheffield.

SMETHWICK.—The Clerk, Smethwick Insurance Committee, 120 High Street, Smethwick.

SOUTHAMPTON.—The Clerk, Southampton Insurance Committee, 17 Hanover Buildings, Southampton.

Committee. | Address.

SOUTHEND-ON-SEA.—The Clerk, Southend-on-Sea Insurance Committee, Coronation Chambers, 51 High Street, Southend-on-Sea.
SOUTHPORT.—The Clerk, Southport Insurance Committee, Town Hall, Southport.
SOUTH SHIELDS.—The Clerk, South Shields Insurance Committee, Edinburgh Buildings, 34 King Street, South Shields.
STOCKPORT.—The Clerk, Stockport Insurance Committee, Central Buildings, St. Petersgate, Stockport.
STOKE-ON-TRENT.—The Clerk, Stoke-on-Trent Insurance Committee, 6 Glebe Street, Stoke-on-Trent.
SUNDERLAND.—The Clerk, Sunderland Insurance Committee, Baliol Chambers, West Sunniside, Sunderland.
TYNEMOUTH.—The Clerk, Tynemouth Insurance Committee, 7 Northumberland Square, North Shields.
WALLASEY.—The Clerk, Wallasey Insurance Committee, 4A Church Street, Egremont.
WALSALL.—The Clerk, Walsall Insurance Committee, 40 Bradford Street, Walsall.
WARRINGTON.—The Clerk, Warrington Insurance Committee, Trinity Chambers, Market Gate, Warrington.
WEST BROMWICH.—The Clerk, West Bromwich Insurance Committee, 2 Lodge Road, West Bromwich.
WEST HAM.—The Clerk, West Ham Insurance Committee, 399 and 401 High Street, Stratford, E.
WEST HARTLEPOOL.—The Clerk, West Hartlepool Insurance Committee, "Magdala," York Road, West Hartlepool.
WIGAN.—The Clerk, Wigan Insurance Committee, 23 Market Place, Wigan.
WOLVERHAMPTON.—The Clerk, Wolverhampton Insurance Committee, 62 Dudley Street, Wolverhampton.
WORCESTER.—The Clerk, Worcester Insurance Committee, 6 Shaw Street, Worcester.
YORK.—The Clerk, York Insurance Committee, 11 Castlegate, York.

(b) IRELAND.

Counties.

ANTRIM.—The Clerk, Antrim Insurance Committee, County Courthouse, Belfast.
ARMAGH.—The Clerk, Armagh Insurance Committee, Courthouse, Armagh.
CARLOW.—The Clerk, Carlow Insurance Committee, 30 Dublin Street, Carlow.
CAVAN.—The Clerk, Cavan Insurance Committee, Courthouse, Cavan.
CLARE.—The Clerk, Clare Insurance Committee, Courthouse, Ennis.
CORK COUNTY.—The Clerk, Cork County Insurance Committee, 10 Grand Parade, Cork.
DONEGAL.—The Clerk, Donegal Insurance Committee, Courthouse, Lifford.
DOWN.—The Clerk, Down Insurance Committee, Courthouse, Downpatrick.
DUBLIN COUNTY.—The Clerk, Dublin County Insurance Committee, Cavendish House, Rutland Square, Dublin.
FERMANAGH.—The Clerk, Fermanagh Insurance Committee, The Orchard, Enniskillen.
GALWAY.—The Clerk, Galway Insurance Committee, 12 Dominick Street, Galway.
KERRY.—The Clerk, Kerry Insurance Committee, County Hall, Tralee.
KILDARE.—The Clerk, Kildare Insurance Committee, Courthouse, Naas.
KILKENNY.—The Clerk, Kilkenny Insurance Committee, 1 William Street, Kilkenny.
KING'S.—The Clerk, King's County Insurance Committee, Courthouse, Tullamore.
LEITRIM.—The Clerk, Leitrim Insurance Committee, Cloonaghmore, Glenfarne, Enniskillen.

Committee.   Address.

LIMERICK COUNTY.—The Clerk, Limerick County Insurance Committee, 82 O'Connell Street, Limerick.
LONDONDERRY COUNTY.—The Clerk, Londonderry County Insurance Committee, County Courthouse, Londonderry.
LONGFORD.—The Clerk, Longford Insurance Committee, Courthouse, Longford.
LOUTH.—The Clerk, Louth Insurance Committee, 90 Clanbrassil Street, Dundalk.
MAYO.—The Clerk, Mayo Insurance Committee, Spencer Street, Castlebar.
MEATH.—The Clerk, Meath Insurance Committee, Courthouse, Navan.
MONAGHAN.—The Clerk, Monaghan Insurance Committee, Courthouse, Monaghan.
QUEEN'S.—The Clerk, Queen's County Insurance Committee, 2 Church Street, Maryborough.
ROSCOMMON.—The Clerk, Roscommon Insurance Committee, Abbey Street, Roscommon.
SLIGO.—The Clerk, Sligo Insurance Committee, 13 Castle Street, Sligo.
TIPPERARY (N.R.).—The Clerk, Tipperary (N.R.) Insurance Committee, Courthouse, Nenagh.
TIPPERARY (S.R.).—The Clerk, Tipperary (S.R.) Insurance Committee, Courthouse, Clonmel.
TYRONE.—The Clerk, Tyrone Insurance Committee, 4 Castle Street, Omagh.
WATERFORD COUNTY.—The Clerk, Waterford County Insurance Committee, County Offices, Dungarvan.
WESTMEATH.—The Clerk, Westmeath Insurance Committee, County Chambers, Mullingar.
WEXFORD.—The Clerk, Wexford Insurance Committee, 87 North Main Street, Wexford.
WICKLOW.—The Clerk, Wicklow Insurance Committee, Kilmullen, Newtownmountkennedy.

County Boroughs.

BELFAST.—The Clerk, Belfast Insurance Committee, 64 Royal Avenue, Belfast.
CORK.—The Clerk, Cork Insurance Committee, City Hall, Cork.
DUBLIN.—The Clerk, Dublin Insurance Committee, 1 College Street, Dublin.
LIMERICK.—The Clerk, Limerick Insurance Committee, 40 O'Connell Street, Limerick.
LONDONDERRY.—The Clerk, Londonderry Insurance Committee, Guildhall, Londonderry.
WATERFORD.—The Clerk, Waterford Insurance Committee, 10 John's Hill, Waterford.

(c) WALES.

Counties.

ANGLESEY.—The Clerk, Anglesey Insurance Committee, Shire Hall, Llangefni.
BRECON.—The Clerk, Brecon Insurance Committee, 16 Bridge Street, Brecon.
CARDIGANSHIRE.—The Clerk, Cardigan Insurance Committee, Cambrian Chambers, Terrace Road, Aberystwyth.
CARMARTHENSHIRE.—The Clerk, Carmarthenshire Insurance Committee, County Insurance Offices, Carmarthen.
CARNARVONSHIRE.—The Clerk, Carnarvonshire Insurance Committee, 22 Castle Square, Carnarvon.
DENBIGHSHIRE.—The Clerk, Denbighshire Insurance Committee, 25 Bridge Street, Wrexham.
FLINT.—The Clerk, Flint Insurance Committee, Bank Chambers, Mold.
GLAMORGAN.—The Clerk, Glamorgan Insurance Committee, Glamorgan Buildings, Frederick Street, Cardiff.
MERIONETHSHIRE.—The Clerk, Merioneth Insurance Committee, Finsbury Square, Dolgelley.

Committee.   Address.

MONMOUTHSHIRE.—The Clerk, Monmouthshire Insurance Committee, Skinner Street, Newport, Mon.
MONTGOMERYSHIRE.—The Clerk, Montgomeryshire Insurance Committee, Montgomery.
PEMBROKESHIRE.—The Clerk, Pembrokeshire Insurance Committee, Shire Hall, Haverfordwest.
RADNOR.—The Clerk, Radnor Insurance Committee, County Buildings, Llandrindod Wells.

County Boroughs.

CARDIFF.—The Clerk, Cardiff Insurance Committee, City Hall, Cardiff.
MERTHYR TYDFIL.—The Clerk, Merthyr Tydfil Insurance Committee, 34 Victoria Street, Merthyr Tydfil.
NEWPORT.—The Clerk, Newport Insurance Committee, 35 Commercial Street, Newport, Mon.
SWANSEA.—The Clerk, Swansea Insurance Committee, 18 Castle Street, Swansea.

APPENDIX XXII.

REFERENCE CIPHERS OF INSURANCE COMMITTEES (UNITED KINGDOM).

(*See Cap. VIII., paragraph* (533).)

The ciphers contained in the following lists are officially recognised for use in reference to Insurance Committees in the United Kingdom.

(1) SCOTLAND.

Counties.

Ad—Aberdeenshire.
Al—Argyll.
Ar—Ayrshire.
Ba—Banff.
Bk—Berwick.
Bt—Bute.
Cn—Caithness.
CK—Clackmannan and Kinross.
Df—Dumfriesshire.
Db—Dunbarton.
EN—Elgin and Nairn.
Ff—Fife.
Fr—Forfar.
Ha—Haddington.
In—Inverness-shire.
Kd—Kincardine.

Ku—Kirkcudbright.
Lr—Lanark.
Li—Linlithgow.
Ml—Midlothian.
Or—Orkney.
Pb—Peebles.
Pr—Perthshire.
Rn—Renfrew.
RC—Ross and Cromarty.
Rx—Roxburgh.
Se—Selkirk.
Sg—Stirlingshire.
Sd—Sutherland.
Wg—Wigtown.
Zt—Zetland.

Burghs.

Abd—Aberdeen.
Ard—Airdrie.
Arb—Arbroath.
Ayr—Ayr.
Cbk—Clydebank.
Ctb—Coatbridge.
Dbt—Dumbarton.
DMt—Dumfries and Maxwelltown.
Dee—Dundee.
Dfn—Dunfermline.
Edb—Edinburgh.
Flk—Falkirk.
Glw—Glasgow.

Gnk—Greenock.
Htn—Hamilton.
Inv—Inverness.
Kmk—Kilmarnock.
Kdy—Kirkcaldy.
Lth—Leith.
Mtl—Motherwell.
Psy—Paisley.
Pth—Perth.
Rgn—Rutherglen.
Stg—Stirling.
Whw—Wishaw.

(2) ENGLAND.

Counties.

Bd—Bedford.
Be—Berkshire.
Bu—Buckinghamshire.
Cb—Cambridgeshire.
Ch—Cheshire.
Cr—Cornwall.
Cu—Cumberland.
De—Derbyshire.
Dn—Devonshire.
Do—Dorsetshire.
Dr—Durham.
Ex—Essex.
Gl—Gloucestershire.
Hr—Herefordshire.
Ht—Hertfordshire.
Hu—Huntingdonshire.
Ie—Isle of Ely.
Iw—Isle of Wight.
Is—Isles of Scilly.
Ke—Kent.
La—Lancashire.
Le—Leicestershire.
Lh—Lincs., Holland.
Lk—Lincs, Kesteven.
Ll—Lincs., Lindsey.
Ln—London.
Mx—Middlesex.
Nf—Norfolk.
No—Northamptonshire.
Nr—Northumberland.
Nt—Nottinghamshire.
Ox—Oxfordshire.
Ru—Rutlandshire.
Sa—Salop.
Sk—Soke of Peterborough.
Sm—Somerset.
So—Southampton.
St—Staffordshire.
Su—Suffolk, East.
Sw—Suffolk, West.
Sy—Surrey.
Te—Sussex, East.
Tw—Sussex, West.
Wa—Warwick.
Ws—Westmorland.
Wl—Wiltshire.
Wr—Worcestershire.
Ye—Yorks., E. Riding.
Yn—Yorks., N. Riding.
Yw—Yorks., W. Riding.

County Boroughs.

Baa—Barnsley.
Bar—Barrow-in-Furness.
Bat—Bath, City of.
Bik—Birkenhead.
Bir—Birmingham, City of.
Blb—Blackburn.
Blp—Blackpool.
Bol—Bolton.
Boo—Bootle.
Bou—Bournemouth.
Bra—Bradford, City of.
Bri—Brighton.
Brs—Bristol, City of.
Bry—Burnley.
Bun—Burton-upon-Trent.
Buy—Bury.
Can—Canterbury, City of.
Cal—Carlisle.
Che—Chester, City of.
Cov—Coventry, City of.
Cro—Croydon.
Deb—Derby.
Dey—Dewsbury.
Dud—Dudley.
Est—Eastbourne.
Exe—Exeter, City of.
Gat—Gateshead.
Glo—Gloucester, City of.
Gry—Great Yarmouth.
Gyy—Grimsby.
Hal—Halifax.
Has—Hastings.
Hud—Huddersfield.
Ips—Ipswich.
Khu—Kingston upon-Hull, City of.
Lds—Leeds, City of.
Lec—Leicester.
Lin—Lincoln, City of.
Lip—Liverpool, City of.
Man—Manchester, City of.
Mid—Middlesborough.
New—Newcastle-upon-Tyne, City of.
Noh—Northampton.
Nor—Norwich, City of.
Not—Nottingham, City of.
Old—Oldham.
Oxr—Oxford, City of.
Ply—Plymouth.
Por—Portsmouth.
Pre—Preston.
Red—Reading.
Roc—Rochdale.
Rot—Rotherham.
Sai—St. Helens.
Sal—Salford.
She—Sheffield, City of.
Sme—Smethwick.
Soh—Southampton.
Sth—Southend-on-Sea.
Sop—Southport.
Sos—South Shields.
Spt—Stockport.
Sto—Stoke-on-Trent.
Sun—Sunderland.

County Boroughs—(continued).

Tyn—Tynemouth.
Waa—Wallasey.
Wal—Walsall.
War—Warrington.
Wbn—West Bromwich.
Wea—West Ham.

Weh—West Hartlepool.
Wig—Wigan.
Wom—Wolverhampton.
Wos—Worcester, City of.
Yor—York, City of.

(3) IRELAND.

Counties.

An—Antrim.
Ah—Armagh.
Cw—Carlow.
Cv—Cavan.
Cl—Clare.
Co—Cork.
Dg—Donegal.
Dw—Down.
Dl—Dublin County.
Fm—Fermanagh.
Gw—Galway.
Ky—Kerry.
Ki—Kildare.
Kk—Kilkenny.
Kc—King's.
Lt—Leitrim.
Lm—Limerick County.

Ld—Londonderry County.
Lf—Longford.
Lo—Louth.
Ma—Mayo.
Me—Meath.
Mh—Monaghan.
Qc—Queen's.
Rm—Roscommon.
Sl—Sligo.
Tn—Tipperary (N.R.).
Ts—Tipperary (S.R.).
Ty—Tyrone.
Wf—Waterford.
Wm—Westmeath.
Wx—Wexford.
Wk—Wicklow.

County Boroughs.

Bel—Belfast.
Crk—Cork.
Dbl—Dublin.

Lmk—Limerick.
Ldd—Londonderry.
Wfd—Waterford.

(4) WALES.

Counties.

As—Anglesey.
Br—Brecon.
Cd—Cardigan.
Cm—Carmarthen.
Ca—Carnarvon.
Dh—Denbigh.
Fl—Flint.

Ga—Glamorgan.
Mr—Merioneth.
Mt—Monmouth.
My—Montgomery.
Pk—Pembroke.
Ra—Radnor.

County Boroughs.

Cdf—Cardiff.
Mer—Merthyr Tydvil.

Npt—Newport.
Swa—Swansea.

APPENDIX XXIII.

FAIR WAGES CLAUSE IN CONTRACTS.

(*See Cap. VIII., paragraph* (534).)

NATIONAL HEALTH INSURANCE COMMISSION (SCOTLAND),
83 PRINCES STREET,
EDINBURGH, 14th *April* 1913.

SIR,—

I am directed by the National Health Insurance Commission (Scotland) to draw the attention of Insurance Committees to the accompanying memorandum embodying the Resolution passed by the House of Commons on the

10th March 1909, on the subject of Fair Wage Clauses in Government Contracts, and the recommendations made by the Advisory Committee of representatives of Government Departments which has been established as suggested in paragraph 124 of the Report of the Fair Wages Committee of 1908 (Cd. 4422).

It will be seen that the Advisory Committee recommend that clauses such as those inserted in Government contracts should also be introduced into contracts which are not entered into by Government Departments, but which involve the expenditure of public money or other consideration granted by a Government Department.

In view of the terms of this recommendation the Commissioners consider it desirable that the policy adopted in the case of Government contracts should be followed in the cases of all contracts for the execution of works or supply of materials entered into by Insurance Committees; and I am accordingly to suggest that your Committee should give the matter careful consideration with a view to the introduction in their contracts of clauses on the lines of those inserted in Government contracts.

I am, Sir,
Your obedient Servant,
JOHN JEFFREY.
To the Clerk to the Insurance Committee.   *Secretary.*

Memorandum referred to.

FAIR WAGES CLAUSES IN GOVERNMENT CONTRACTS.

The following clauses recommended by the Fair Wages Advisory Committee for general use in Government contracts, with a view to carrying out the objects of the Fair Wages Resolutions of the House of Commons, have been generally adopted by the contracting Departments:—

FOR INCLUSION IN ALL CONTRACTS.

1. **Fair Wages Clause.**—The Contractor shall, in the execution of this contract observe and fulfil the obligations upon contractors specified in the Resolution passed by the House of Commons on the 10th March 1909, namely:—" The Contractor shall pay rates of wages and observe hours of labour not less favourable than those commonly recognised by employers and trade societies (or, in the absence of such recognised wages and hours, those which in practice prevail amongst good employers) in the trade in the district where the work is carried out. Where there are no such wages and hours recognised or prevailing in the district, those recognised or prevailing in the nearest district in which the general industrial circumstances are similar shall be adopted. Further, the conditions of employment generally accepted in the district in the trade concerned shall be taken into account in considering how far the terms of the Fair Wages clauses are being observed. The Contractor shall be prohibited from transferring or assigning, directly or indirectly, to any person or persons whatever, any portion of his contract without the written permission of the Department. Sub-letting, other than that which may be customary in the trade concerned, shall be prohibited. The Contractor shall be responsible for the observance of the Fair Wages clauses by the Sub-Contractor."

2. **Exhibition of Notice at Works.**—The Contractor shall cause the preceding condition to be prominently exhibited, for the information of his workpeople, on the premises where work is being executed under the contract.

3. **Inspection of Wages Books, etc.**—The Contractor shall keep proper wages books and time sheets, showing the wages paid and (so far as practicable) the time worked by the workpeople in his employ in and about the execution of the contract, and such wages books and time sheets shall be produced whenever required for the inspection of any Officer authorised by the Department.*

---

* Specify the Department.

FOR INCLUSION IN CONTRACTS IN CERTAIN TRADES.

4. **Factory Clause.**—All work executed under the contract shall be carried out at the Contractor's own factory or workshop at.............., or other place approved by the Department,* and no work under the contract shall be done in the homes of the workpeople.

5. **Direct Payment of Wages.**—All wages earned by workers engaged on work under the contract shall be paid directly to them and not through a foreman or others supervising, or taking part in, the operations on which the workers are engaged.

SEMI-GOVERNMENT CONTRACTS.

The Fair Wages Advisory Committee have recommended, that in the case of contracts which are not entered into by a Government Department but which involve the expenditure of public money or other consideration granted by the Department, or which have to be approved by a Government Department, the Department concerned should adopt the principle already followed in some instances, and should require the insertion in such contracts of Fair Wages clauses on the lines of those inserted in Government contracts, with such modifications as may be necessary in particular cases.

March 1911.

APPENDIX XXIV.

CONTRACTS WITH MEMBERS.

(*See Cap. VIII., paragraph* (535).)

No. 427.

NATIONAL HEALTH INSURANCE COMMISSION (SCOTLAND).
83 PRINCES STREET,
EDINBURGH, *September* 1913.

SIR,—
I am directed to inform you that the Scottish Insurance Commissioners have had several enquiries as to the position of an Insurance Committee in entering into contracts with one of its members.

Town Councils, County Councils, and Parish Councils are, by express provisions in the respective Acts under which they carry on their administration, debarred from entering into contracts with one of their members, and a member may not, except in certain limited cases,—such as being a shareholder of a Railway or other Company, etc.,†—either directly or indirectly share any consideration derived from any contract or employment by the Council.

The attention of the Commissioners has also been directed to an Opinion given in the year 1878 by the Scottish Law Officers (afterwards Lord Gordon and Lord Watson) regarding the power of a School Board to enter into a contract with one of its members, to the effect that such contracts were in law not void, but were voidable at the instance of the Board, and that it was manifestly expedient in general cases that such contracts should not be entered into.

The Commissioners appreciate that the position of Insurance Service Practitioners and Chemists, who are members of Insurance Committees, is special, and contracts between them and the Committee for service on the panel must be entered into. In these cases the individual representatives on the Committee can secure no better terms for themselves than for the general body of practitioners or chemists, and have no special *individual* interest in the contracts.

---

* Specify the Department.
† See Sec. (220) of the Local Government (Scotland) Act, 1894.

As regards other contracts, however, where the effect of the Committee contracting with a member is to exclude a contract with other persons carrying on business, and where the member may thereby obtain personal advantage, it would appear that an Insurance Committee may, by such action, render themselves liable to criticism, and the Commissioners would urge upon Committees the desirability of passing a resolution that in such cases no member of the Committee should be allowed either to contract with the Committee or to share in any consideration derived from such a contract.—I am, Sir, your obedient servant,

JOHN JEFFREY,
Secretary.

The Clerk to the Insurance Committee.

APPENDIX XXV.

(*See Cap. VIII., paragraph* (540).)

No. 382.

NATIONAL HEALTH INSURANCE COMMISSION (SCOTLAND),
83 PRINCES STREET,
EDINBURGH, July 1913.

Ref. I.C. 41,752.

SIR,—

ADMISSION OF PRESS TO MEETINGS.

I am directed by the Scottish Insurance Commissioners to say that representations have recently been made to them as to the desirability of the Press being admitted to meetings of Insurance Committees.

It has been pointed out that Insurance Committees are important Local Authorities, representative of varied interests and entrusted with the administration of public moneys contributed by insured persons, employers, and the State, and that it is desirable that their proceedings should receive due publicity.

The Commissioners acquiesce in the views presented to them and recognise the importance of the question, and while they are advised that the Local Authorities (Admission of the Press to Meetings) Act, 1908, does not apply to an Insurance Committee in view of the definition of a Local Authority in Scotland therein contained, there would appear to be no reason to believe that, had Insurance Committees been in existence at the passing of the Act, Parliament would have regarded the Committees as being in any less responsible position than Distress Committees and similar bodies to whom the Act was applied. The Commissioners accordingly suggest that Insurance Committees should voluntarily apply by resolution the principles of Section 1 of the Admission of the Press Act to their meetings.

Under such application, representatives of the Press will be granted admission to the meetings of every Insurance Committee. The Committee, however, may temporarily exclude such representatives from a meeting as often as may be desirable at any meeting when, in the opinion of a majority of the members of the Committee present at such meeting, expressed by resolution, in view of the special nature of the business then being dealt with or about to be dealt with, such exclusion is advisable in the public interest.

The Commissioners are advised that there is no legal prohibition against a Committee admitting representatives of the Press to its meetings.

I am, Sir,
Your obedient Servant,
JOHN JEFFREY,
Secretary.

The Clerk, Insurance Committee.

INDEX.

Numbers refer to Paragraphs.

	Paragraphs
Accounting . . .	489–531

Accounts—
Alternative 530
Bank, entries in . . . 491
  „ safeguards for operating on 531
Entering up of . . . 489–530
Of Chemists—
  See **Drug Accounts.**
Of Deposit Contributors, kept by Commissioners . . 429
  „ Doctors, for Temporary Residents . . 450–456

Administration—
Income for . . . 476–481

Administration Fund—
Accounting . . 490, 501, 526, 527
Payments into, from Sanatorium Benefit Fund . . 464, 523

Admiralty and Army Council—
Duties in regard to National Health Insurance . Introduction

Advances—
To Chemists, to be agreed upon by Pharmaceutical Committee and Insurance Committee . . . 159
  „ Doctors, to be agreed upon by Panel Committee and Insurance Committee . . 142
  „ Insurance Committees, for Medical Benefit, from the Scottish National Health Insurance Fund . . 443

Advisory Committee—
Purposes of . Introduction

Agreements—
Entered into by Insurance Committees, register of . . 490

Agreements—Insurance Committees and Chemists—
Alterations in . . . 203
Breach of . . . 264
Conditions of . . . 191, 192
Disputes as to . . . 192
Period of . . . 204
Preparation and approval of . 191

Agreements—Insurance Committees and Doctors—
Alterations in . . 137, 171

	Paragraphs
Application by Doctor to enter into	165
Approval of . . .	167
Breach of . . . 171, 262
Period of . . .	173
Places and Hours of Attendance to be stated in . .	168
Preparation of . . 137, 167
Terms of . 137, 167, 168, 171, 172

Agreements — Insurance Committees and Local Authorities—
For purposes of Sanatorium Benefit 282, 293, 299, 314, 346, 347

Alien Enemies—
Deposit Contributors, no refund to be made to . . . 353

Aliens—
Maternity Benefit of . . 408
Sickness „ „ . . 392
State Grants not payable in respect of . . . 437, 461

Allocation to Doctors of Insured Persons—
Duties of Panel Committee in regard to . . . 143
Who have not exercised choice . 163

Appeals—
By Chemists to Commissioners . 264
  „ Doctors to Commissioners . 260

Appliances—
Emergency 196
Loan of 197
Supply of, under Medical Benefit 161, 197, 198
  „ „ Sanatorium Benefit . 302, 305, 307, 324–326

Approved Dispensaries—
For treatment of Tuberculosis 294–297, 348

Approved Institutions—
Application and conditions for approval . . . 185, 186
Financial arrangements in regard to 511–515
Issue of lists of persons choosing 169
  „ „ medical cards to persons choosing . . 235
Right of insured persons to treatment in 237

287

Paragraphs
Right of insured persons to treatment in, during temporary absence from home . 229
Withdrawal of approval, right of insured persons to select another method of treatment . 242
For treatment of Tuberculosis—
See **Institutions for Treatment of Tuberculosis.**

Approved Societies—
Contributions of, to General Administration Expenses of Insurance Committees . . 476
Contributions of, to cost of Medical Benefit . 436–440
Contributions of, to cost of Administration of Medical Benefit 476, 478
Contributions of, to cost of Sanatorium Benefit . . . 461
General Duties of . Introduction
Grouping of, for Valuation . 77
Issue of Medical Card to members of 223
Members over 70 — title to benefits 207
Powers of Insurance Committees in regard to the administration of grouped societies . 77
Register of members of 205–215, 218
Right of, to represent member at hearing of complaint . 270

Approved Societies—Representation on Insurance Committees . 9–12, 14–25, 27–46
Allocation of Representatives to "A" Societies . . 14, 16–24
Allocation of Representatives to "B" Societies . 14, 15, 19–24
Appointment of Representatives of "A" Societies . . 25, 27
Appointment of Representatives of "B" Societies . . 25, 28–36
Count of members in connection with 11
Default and technical errors in Election . . . 39, 45
Disqualification of Representatives 41, 42
Election entrusted to the Clerk to the Committee . . . 9, 10
Electoral Unit, determination of 12
Notices to Societies in regard to appointment of Representatives 25
Numbers of Representatives of various Societies . . 14–20
Publication of names of Representatives . . . 37
Regulations governing Election 9
Representation of Women . 46
Representatives on more than one Insurance Committee . 38
Return showing allocation of Representatives . . 21–25
Term of Office of Representatives 40
Vacancies 38, 43, 44

Paragraphs
Approved Systems . 185, 186
See also **Approved Institutions.**
Approved Tuberculosis Dispensaries 294–297, 348
Areas of Insurance Committees 3
Army—
See **Soldiers.**
Association of Deposit Contributors . . 26, 252
Association of Insurance Committees in Scotland—
Authority for . Introduction
Attendance by Doctor—
Places and hours of, arrangements for alterations in . 168
Places and hours of, to be specified in agreement . . 168
Audit Department . . . 532
Bandages—
Supplied under Medical Benefit 197
Bank Accounts of Insurance Committees—
Entries in 491
Must be in name of Committee, safeguards for operating on . 531
Bedding—
Provision of, under Domiciliary treatment . . 304, 310
Benefits—
See also **Disablement Benefit, Maternity Benefit, Sickness Benefit**, etc.
Administration of, by Insurance Committees (general) . . 72
Income of Insurance Committees for administration of . . 476
Of Deposit Contributors . 366–428
" " " rules for administration of . . . 365
Postal Orders for payment of . 496
Suspension of, in case of Deposit Contributors . . 367–372
Suspension of, on Marriage . 397
Books—
Account.
See **Accounts**, also **Ledger, General Cash Book**, etc.
Insurance.
See **Insurance Books.**
Breach—
Of Chemists' Agreements . 192, 264
" " Chemists liable to refund expenses incurred as result of . . 264
" Chemists' Agreements, Chemists liable to refund amount of Parliamentary Grant withheld on account of 264
" Doctors' Agreements . 171, 262
" Doctors' Agreements, Doctors liable to refund expenses incurred as result of. 171, 262

	Paragraphs
Of Doctors' Agreements, Doctors liable to refund amount of Parliamentary Grant withheld on account of	262
,, rules for administration of Medical Benefit .	245–247, 259, 264
,, rules in regard to Maternity Benefit	410

Burial—
Of insured persons dying in Sanatorium . . . 292, 333

Cards—
See **Contribution Cards, Medical Cards,** etc.

Case Values—
In connection with Medical Benefit 447, 448
In connection with Sanatorium Benefit . . 464, 466, 469, 474

Cash Book—
See **General Cash Book.**

Central Drug Fund—
Distribution of, to Chemists . 455
,, ,, to Insurance Committees . . . 452
Establishment of . . . 449

Central Medical Benefit Fund—
Accounting . . . 453, 505
Constitution of . . . 445–449
Distribution of, to Chemists and Doctors . . . 454–456
Distribution of, to Insurance Committees . . 450–453
Purposes of 445

Central Panel Fund—
Distribution of, to Doctors 453, 454, 456
,, ,, to Insurance Committees . . . 453
Establishment of . . . 449

Central Sanatorium Benefit Fund—
Payments into . . . 318
,, from . . 318–320

Centralisation—
Of Index and Suspense Registers 219
,, Orange Slips . . . 219

Certificates—
For payment of Maternity Benefit . . . 422–428
Of Incapacity . 82, 184, 255, 402, 403
,, Marriage . . . 421, 423

Change of Address—
Affecting title of Doctor to dispense 175
Alterations in Index Register and Medical Index on account of . . 215, 217, 228, 430, 431
Of Deposit Contributors, procedure in regard to Index Slip, Medical Card, etc. . 351, 353–356, 430, 431

	Paragraphs
Of Deposit Contributors, Exempt persons, procedure in regard to Index Slip, Medical Card, etc. . .	217
,, Own Arrangers .	234, 257, 518
Temporary, procedure regarding Medical Benefit during	215, 219–233
To be notified to Insurance Committees by Approved Societies if prior to 11th January 1914 . . .	215

Change of Status—
Alterations in Index Register, etc., on account of . 213, 216

Chemists—
Accounts.
See **Drug Accounts.**
Admission of, to Panel, inquiries as to . . . 177
Agreements.
See **Agreements—Insurance Committees and Chemists.**
Conditions of Service of 187, 191, 192, 203
Continuance on Panel, representations by Insurance Committees in regard to . . 264
Continuance on Panel, procedure at inquiries as to . 277
See also **Inquiry as to Admission to or Continuance on Panel of Chemist.**
Definition of 187
Dispensing by 187
Exhibition of Notice by . . 190
Lists of—
See **Panel Lists (Chemists).**

Choice of Doctor—
Right of Insured Persons as to 236–244

Claims—
By Deposit Contributors for Maternity Benefit . . 421–428
,, Deposit Contributors for Sickness Benefit . . 401–405

Classified Cash Book. . . 522

Clothing—
Provision of, for Domiciliary Cases 303
Provision of, for Sanatorium Cases 288

Combination of Insurance Committees—
For establishment of Drug Accounts Committee . . 61
General 59, 60

Commissioners—
Accounts of Deposit Contributors kept by . . 429, 433
Appeal to, by chemist in regard to breach of agreement . 264
Appeal to, by doctor in regard to breach of agreement 171, 260
Appointment of medical referees by 178

	Paragraphs
Approval of Institutions by, under Section 15 (4) of 1911 Act	185
Approval of necessary, in case of alteration in conditions of service of doctors and chemists	172, 203
Approval of rules by, for administration of Medical Benefit	245
Approval of schemes by, for issue of emergency drugs and appliances	196
Certificates, contribution cards, and insurance books to be forwarded to, in connection with Sickness Benefit of Deposit Contributors	402, 404, 405
Certificates in connection with Maternity Benefit of Deposit Contributors to be forwarded to	423, 426, 427
Claims of Deposit Contributors for Maternity Benefit to be forwarded to	423, 424
Consent of, to increase in number of members of Medical Service Sub-Committee	79
Consideration by, of representations of Panel and Pharmaceutical Committees before approval of schemes for Medical Benefit	138, 157
Current Accounts of Insurance Committees with	490, 491, 493, 501–503, 526
Financial arrangements of Insurance Committees with Institutions for the treatment of Tuberculosis to be to the satisfaction of	287, 289
General Powers of	Introduction
Joint Committee	Introduction
Offices and Staff of	532
Power of, to constitute Inquiry Committee	269, 277
Power of, to hold inquiry as to continuance of doctor on Panel	266
Power of, to hold inquiry as to admission to or continuance on Panel of chemist	266, 277
Power of, to postpone inquiry as to admission to or continuance on Panel of chemist	267, 277
Power of, to postpone inquiry as to continuance of doctor on Panel	267
Powers and duties of, in regard to establishment of General Medical Benefit Fund	436–440
Recognition of Local Medical Committees by	120
Recognition of Local Medical Committees by, conditions of	122, 123

	Paragraphs
Representations to, by Insurance Committees in serious cases of complaint against doctors or chemists	261, 264
Representatives of, on Insurance Committees	7, 58
Retrospective sanction by, of arrangements of Insurance Committees for Sanatorium Benefit	328
Sanction by, of arrangements for provision of Sanatorium Benefit	280
Sanction by, of arrangements of Insurance Committees for Dispensary treatment of Tuberculosis	295, 296
Sanction by, of arrangements of Insurance Committees for Domiciliary treatment of Tuberculosis	299, 301
Sanction by, of arrangements of Insurance Committees for Institutional treatment of Tuberculosis	287
To prescribe reports to be made by Insurance Committees	73

Commissioners of Inland Revenue—

Duties in regard to National Health Insurance	Introduction

Committee of Inquiry—

Into question of admission to or continuance on Panel of chemist	277
Into question of continuance of doctor on Panel	269

Compensation—

For loss of remunerative time by members of Insurance Committee	483, 485, 486
Payment of, under Workmen's Compensation Act and Employers' Liability Act, effect on Sickness and Disablement Benefits	376–382
Under Workmen's Compensation Act and Employers' Liability Act, title of Territorials and Special Reservists to	382

Complaints by or against Chemists—

Duty of Pharmaceutical Committee to consider	156
Procedure at Hearings by Joint Services Sub-Committee in connection with	95, 96
Procedure at Hearings by Pharmaceutical Service Sub-Committee in connection with	91, 263
Proceedings at Hearings to be reported to Insurance Committee	92, 98, 264
Referred to Joint Services Sub-Committee	97, 265

	Paragraphs
Referred to Pharmaceutical Service Sub-Committee	92, 263, 264
Removal of chemist from Panel, following	277
Report of Joint Services Sub-Committee	98
Report of Pharmaceutical Service Sub-Committee	92
Representations of Insurance Committee to Commissioners, following	264, 277

Complaints by or against Doctors—

Duty of Local Medical Committee to consider	126
Procedure at Hearings by Joint Services Sub-Committee in connection with	95, 96
Procedure at Hearings by Medical Service Sub-Committee in connection with	79–88, 259
Procedure following report of Medical Service Sub-Committee to Insurance Committee	259–262
Proceedings to be reported to Insurance Committee	86, 98, 259, 265
Referred to Joint Services Sub-Committee	97, 265
Referred to Medical Service Sub-Committee	82, 259
Removal of doctor from Panel, following	266–276
Report of Joint Services Sub-Committee to Insurance Committee	98
Report of Medical Service Sub-Committee to Insurance Committee	86
Representation by Insurance Committee to Commissioners, following	261
Right of Panel Committee in regard to conduct of inquiry into	144

Comptroller and Auditor-General—

Duties in regard to National Health Insurance . Introduction

Conditions of Service of Chemists . 187, 191, 192, 203

Conditions of Service of Doctors . 167, 168, 171, 172

Confinement—

Arrangements by Insurance Committee for attendance of midwife or doctor at, in the case of Deposit Contributors	419, 420
Insured person has no title to Medical Benefit during	177
Notice of, in connection with the payment of Maternity Benefit	422

	Paragraphs
Payment of Sickness Benefit during	398

Constitution of Insurance Committees . . . 4–8

Contracts—

Entered into by Insurance Committees	534, 535

Contribution Cards—

Of Deposit Contributors, despatch to Commissioners on death of Contributor	364
Of Deposit Contributors, despatch to Commissioners in connection with claims for Maternity Benefit	423
Of Deposit Contributors, despatch to Insurance Committee in connection with claims for Sickness Benefit	401, 404

Contributions—

Rates of, for different classes of contributors	350, 352

Contributions to Hospitals—

Powers of Insurance Committees in regard to	75

Conveyance of Insured Persons—

In connection with Sanatorium Benefit	329–333

County Councils—

Arrangements for Sanatorium Benefit to dependants	340, 342–344
Representatives of, on Insurance Committees	47–49
Schemes for treatment of Tuberculosis	344, 348

Current Account—Insurance Committee and Commissioners—

Entries in	491, 493, 501–503, 526
To be entered in Ledger	490

Damages—

Effect of payment of, on Sickness and Disablement Benefits	376–382

Day Books—

Medical Day Books	181, 182

Death—

Of Deposit Contributor—Refund in case of	357–363
„ Deposit Contributor, procedure in regard to Index Slip	217, 433
„ Doctor, arrangements consequent on	238, 241
„ Insured Person, amendment of Index Register, etc.	213, 214
„ Insured Person in Sanatorium	292, 333

Deficit—

In funds of Insurance Committee for Sanatorium Benefit	335, 336

	Paragraphs
Dependants—	
Domiciliary treatment of	306, 338
Extension of Sanatorium Benefit to	306, 307, 334–348
Deposit Contributors—	
Accounts of	429, 432
Association of	26, 252
Change of Address of	216, 351
Classification of	73
Contributions, Rates of	350, 352
Disablement Benefit of	397, 406
See also **Disablement Benefit (Deposit Contributors.)**	
Duties of Insurance Committees in regard to classification of	73
Income of Insurance Committees for payment of benefits to	476
Index Slips of	205, 207, 214, 216,
,, ,, Medical Cards, etc., procedure in regard to	429–433
Joining an Approved Society	432–433
Maternity Benefit of	369, 407–428
See also **Maternity Benefit (Deposit Contributors).**	
Medical Benefit of	366–372
Over 70—title to Benefits	207, 372
Position of, as regards payment of Benefits (general)	349
Postal Orders for payment of Benefits of	496
Powers of Insurance Committees in regard to administration of benefits of	72
Register of	205, 206, 351
Rules for administration of benefits of	365
Sanatorium Benefit of	366–372
Sickness Benefit of	369, 373–405
See also **Sickness Benefit (Deposit Contributors).**	
Suspension from Benefits	368–371, 375, 415
Deposit Contributors Benefits Account—	
Insurance Committee to keep	490
Purposes of	528
Deposit Contributors Fund—	
Payments from	367, 370, 371, 397
Deposit Contributors—Representation on Insurance Committees	9–13, 21–26, 37–46
Allocation of Representatives	13
Appointment of ,,	26
Count of Deposit Contributors in connection with	11
Default and technical errors in Election	39, 45
Disqualification of Representatives	42
Electoral Unit, determination of	12
Number of Representatives, calculation of	13

	Paragraphs
Publication of Names of Representatives	37
Regulations governing Election	9
Representation of Women	46
Representatives on more than one Insurance Committee	38
Return showing allocation of Representatives	21–25
Vacancies	43, 44
Deposit Contributors Sub-Committee	99
See also under **Sub-Committees of Insurance Committees.**	
Deputies—	
Of Doctors, arrangements for	170, 174
,, members at Meetings of Insurance Committees	536
Diagram—	
Illustrating Medical Benefit Accounts	457
Diligence—	
Protection of insured persons against	78
Disablement Benefit (Deposit Contributors)—	
Qualifications for	406
Suspension of, on Marriage	397
Dispensaries for Treatment of Tuberculosis	294–297, 348
Dispensary Treatment of Tuberculosis	282, 294–297
Approval by Local Government Board	282, 295
Charges for	296
Conveyance of insured persons in connection with	332
Poor Law Authorities, arrangements not to be made with	282
Dispensing—	
By Chemists	187
,, Doctors	137, 154, 175, 176
District Insurance Committees	111–118
Doctors—	
Accounts of, for Temporary Residents	450–456
Advances to	142
Agreements.	
See **Agreements—Insurance Committees and Doctors.**	
Allocation of insured persons to	143, 163
See also under **Allocation.**	
Arrangements by Insurance Committee for attendance of, at confinement, in the case of Deposit Contributors	419, 420
Choice of, right of insured persons in regard to	163, 236–244
Continuance on Panel, procedure at inquiries as to	266–276

	Paragraphs
Continuance on Panel, representations of Insurance Committees in regard to	261
See also **Inquiry as to Continuance of Doctor on Panel.**	
Death of, arrangements consequent on	241
Death of, transfer of insured persons from lists of	238
Deputies, arrangements for	170, 174
Dispensing by	137, 154, 175, 176
Lists of insured persons who have chosen	169, 236–244
Places and hours of attendance of, to be specified in agreement	168
Removal from Panel	126, 174, 238–240
Remuneration of (general)	180
" for Domiciliary treatment	316
Representation on Insurance Committees	50–57
See also under **Doctors— Representation on Insurance Committees.**	
Right of Choice of, by insured person	163, 236–244
Withdrawal from Panel	173, 174

Doctors — Representation on Insurance Committees.

Disqualification of Representatives	56
Election by association of duly qualified medical practitioners	50
Election of Representatives	50–57
Initial appointment of Representatives	50–55
Meeting for election of Representatives may be convened by Commissioners	55
Meeting for election of Representatives, procedure at	54
Meeting for election of Representatives, quorum at	53
Meeting for election of Representatives, report of	54
Meeting for election of Representatives, summoning of	51, 52
Number of Representatives	7, 50
Term of Office of "	56
Vacancies	57

Doctors' Lists—

Preparation and issue of	169
Transfers of names of insured persons from	236–244

Domiciliary Sixpence Accounting . 436, 457

For remuneration of doctors for treating Domiciliary cases of Tuberculosis 316

	Paragraphs
Domiciliary Treatment of Tuberculosis—	
Approval by Local Government Board of manner of treatment	282, 312, 313
Arrangements for	299–314
" with Local Authorities	306, 314
Bedding, provision of	304, 310
By doctors	177
Clothing, provision of	303
Conditions for	299
Dependants, treatment of	306, 307, 338
Meaning of	298
Medicines, etc., provision of	302, 305, 307, 324–326
Parish Councils, arrangements not to be made with	282, 299, 314
Payments to patients during	307
Poor Law Authorities, arrangements not to be made with	282, 299, 314
Recommendations for, by Insurance Committee	322, 323, 327, 328
Rent, extra	308
Sanction by Commissioners of arrangements for	299, 301
Scheme for	300
Shelters, provision of	304, 309–311

Drug Accounts—

For Temporary Residents	450–456
Power of Panel Committee to disallow	139
Power of Pharmaceutical Committee to disallow	155
Powers and duties of Drug Accounts Committee in regard to	62, 63
Submission to Panel Committee	139
" " Pharmaceutical Committee	155

Drug Accounts Committee 61–69

Authority for	61
Constitution and election of members	64–67
Expenditure, defrayment of	69
Proceedings of	68
Purposes of	62, 63
Qualifications for membership	64, 66
Quorum of	68
Reports by, to Insurance Committees	62, 63, 69
Term of Office of	67
Vacancies	67

Drug Fund—

Accounting	510
Payments from, in error in respect of Domiciliary cases of Tuberculosis	199
Payments from, in error in respect of temporary residents	200
Payments from, in respect of treatment of diseases concurrent with Tuberculosis	325

	Paragraphs
Drug Grant, Special Parliamentary—	
Accounting in connection with	521
Administration of	460
Amount of	460
Available to Insurance Committees	458
Origin and purpose of	460
Drug Tariff—	
Consultation by Insurance Committee with Panel Committee in regard to	137
Consultation by Insurance Committee with Pharmaceutical Committee in regard to	154
Definition of	193
Model Form of	193
To be sanctioned by Commissioners	193
Drugs—	
Emergency	196
Not on Tariff	198
Price of	193–195, 201
Proper and sufficient	195
"Starred"	194, 203
Supply of, affected by war	195, 201
„ „ to insured persons, provision for, by Insurance Committees (general)	161
Supply of, to insured persons, arrangements with chemists for	187–192
Supply of, to insured persons, arrangements with doctors for	137, 154, 175, 176
Supply of, under Sanatorium Benefit	302, 305, 307, 324–326
Duplicate Index Slips	218, 219
Election of Members of Insurance Committees—	
Representatives of Approved Societies	9–12, 14–25, 27–46
See also **Approved Societies**—Representation on Insurance Committees.	
Representatives of Chemists	58
Representatives of Commissioners	58
Representatives of County and Town Councils	47–49
Representatives of Deposit Contributors	9–13, 21–26, 37–46
See also **Deposit Contributors**—Representation on Insurance Committees.	
Representatives of Doctors	50–57
See also **Doctors**—Representation on Insurance Committees.	
Representation of Women	46
Emergency Drugs and Appliances	196
Employers' Liability Act—	
Payment of compensation under, effect on Sickness and Disablement Benefits	376–382

	Paragraphs
Epidemics—	
Provision of Drugs for	458, 460
Excessive Prescribing—	
Investigation of, by Panel Committee	140
Representation of Pharmaceutical Committee to Panel Committee in regard to	155
Excessive Sickness—	
Powers of Insurance Committees in regard to	76
Exempt Persons—	
Index Slips of	205, 207, 214, 217
Medical Cards, issue to	223, 235
Sanatorium Benefit, financial arrangements for	461
Suspension from Benefits, procedure in regard to Index Slips	217
Exempt Persons Fund—	
Payments to General Sanatorium Benefit Fund	461
Extension of Sanatorium Benefit to Dependants	334–348
Arrangements with Local Authorities	340–348
Classification of dependants	339
Domiciliary treatment	338
Finance and Accounting of Insurance Committees	434–531
Diagram of	457
Regulations for	434
Finance and General Sub-Committee	99
See also under **Sub-Committees**.	
Fines—	
See **Penalties**.	
Form Med., 50—	
Issue of Medical Card on receipt of	218
Gauzes—	
Supplied under Medical Benefit	197
General Administration Fund—	
Payments into and distribution of	477
General Cash Book—	
Entries in	491–500, 502, 509, 510, 515, 519, 522, 524, 527
Insurance Committees to keep	490
General Medical Benefit Fund—	
Advances to Insurance Committees	443
Distribution to Insurance Committees	441–443
Payments into	436–440
General Purposes Fund—	
Account to be kept in Ledger	490
Payments into	487
Payments out of	529

	Paragraphs
General Purposes Fund Account—	
Expenditure chargeable against	529
Income to be credited to	487
General Purposes Rate	344
General Sanatorium Benefit Fund—	
Constitution of	461–463
Distribution to Insurance Committees	464
Health Lectures—	
Powers and duties of Insurance Committees in regard to	74
Hearings—	
By Joint Services Sub-Committee	95–96
By Medical Service Sub-Committee	81, 83, 85, 86
„ Pharmaceutical Service Sub-Committee	91
In regard to admission to or continuance on Panel of chemist	277
In regard to continuance of doctor on Panel	266–276
Highlands and Islands (Medical Service) Board	
Purposes of (general)	Introduction
Hobhouse Letter	345, 347
Hospitals, etc.	
Payment of Maternity Benefit when mother in	416–418
Payment of Sickness Benefit while contributor in	383–387
Housing—	
Inadequate, causing excessive sickness	76
Inadequate, in connection with Domiciliary treatment of Tuberculosis	308
Incapacity Certificates	82, 184, 402, 403
Income Limit	137, 141, 155, 158, 251, 252
Index Register—	
Arrangement of	209
Centralisation of	219
Preparation and Maintenance of	205–207, 208–218
Purposes of	205
Index Slips—	
Centralisation of	219
Classes of	207
Comparison with Suspense Slips	218
Definition of	207
Despatch of, by Societies to Insurance Committees	211–215
Duplicates	218, 219
Of Deposit Contributors, procedure in regard to	216, 429–433
Of exempt persons, procedure in regard to	217
Of members of Approved Societies, procedure in regard to	210–215

	Paragraphs
Of soldiers, sailors, and marines	210
Of Travellers, procedure in regard to	248
Receipt of, by Committees, procedure following	218
Removals, procedure in case of	215, 217, 228, 430, 431
Inquiry as to Admission to or Continuance on Panel of Chemist	277
See also under **Inquiry as to Continuance of Doctor on Panel.**	
Inquiry as to Continuance of Doctor on Panel	266–276
Adjournment of	272
Amendment or withdrawal of representation to hold	268
Appearance at, by proxy	270
Committee of Inquiry	269
Conditions for holding	266
Forms in connection with	271
May be held at instance of Commissioners without representation from Insurance Committee	273
May be stopped temporarily by Commissioners	275
Notices of	267, 270, 273, 276
Parties who may be present at	270
Regulations governing	266
Report of Inquiry Committee	274
Representations to hold	266
Rules for procedure at	272
Verification of allegations by complainer	266
Inquiry Committee—	
Into question of admission to or continuance on Panel of chemist	277
Into question of continuance of doctor on Panel	269
Inspectorate—	532
Institutional Treatment of Tuberculosis	282–293, 297
Approval by Local Government Board	282, 285–287
Charges for	287, 289, 290, 292
Conveyance of insured persons in connection with	329–331
Local Authorities, arrangements with	292, 293
Poor Law Authorities, arrangements not to be made with	282, 293
Recommendation for	322, 323, 327, 328
Institution—	
Payment of Maternity Benefit when mother in	416–418
Payment of Sickness Benefit when contributor in	383–387
Institutions—	
Approved for purposes of Medical Benefit	185, 186
See also under **Approved Institutions.**	

	Paragraphs
Institutions for Treatment of Tuberculosis—	
Approval by Local Government Board	282, 285–287
Available	283, 284, 286
Conveyance of insured persons to or from	329–331
Detention in	291
Erection of, by Local Authorities	348
Institutions Fund—	
Accounting	490, 511–515
Payments from, to Sanatorium Benefit Fund	514, 515
Insurance Books—	
Despatch to Commissioners in connection with claims for Maternity Benefit	423
Despatch to Commissioners in connection with claims for Sickness Benefit	401, 404, 405
Despatch to Commissioners on death of Deposit Contributor	364
Insurance Commissioners—	
See under **Commissioners.**	
Insurance Committees—	
Areas of	3
Association of	Introduction
Bank account of	491, 531
Bodies corporate	2
Business, motions, voting, signing of deeds, etc.	70
Chairman, appointment of	70
Clerks to, names and addresses of	533
Clerks to, question of holding paid appointments under Approved Societies	539
Combination of, for establishment of Drug Accounts Committee	61
Combination of (general)	59, 60
Constitution of	4–8
Definition of	1
Disqualification of representatives of insured persons on	41
Employment of Officers	70
Expenditure of	489
Finance and Accounting	434–531
Income of, for administration	476–485
See also under **Administration.**	
Income of (general)	435
„ for General Purposes	487
„ to defray cost of Medical Benefit	435–460
Income of, to defray cost of Sanatorium Benefit	461–457
Inventory of property of	490
Meetings of, absence of members from	42
Meetings of, admission of Press to	539
Meetings of, arrangements for	70
„ „ attendance of members in person	535

	Paragraphs
Meetings of, outwith area of Committee	71
Meetings of, procedure at	70
„ „ arrangements for	70
Office accommodation of	71
Powers and duties of (general)	1, 2, 72–78
See **Powers and Duties of Insurance Committees.**	
Qualifications for membership	537, 538
Quorum of	70
Standing Orders for procedure of	70
Subsistence allowance to members of	483, 484, 486
Term of office of	40
Travelling expenses of	481, 482
Vice-Chairman, appointment of	70
Insurance Committees— Election of Members—	
Representatives of Approved Societies	9–12, 14–25, 27–46
See also under **Approved Societies — Representation on Insurance Committees**	
Representatives of Chemists	58
„ „ County and Town Councils	47–49
Representatives of Deposit Contributors	9–13, 21–26, 37–46
See also **Deposit Contributors — Representation on Insurance Committees.**	
Representatives of Doctors	50–57
See also **Doctors—Representation on Insurance Committees.**	
Representation of Women	46
Inventory—	
Of property of Insurance Committees	490
Itinerants—	
In connection with Post Office Medical System	186
Joint Advisory Committee—	
Purposes of	Introduction
Joint Commitee—	
National Health Insurance Joint Committee, general powers and duties of	Introduction
Of Insurance Committees	59, 60
Joint Services Sub-Committee	93–98
Chairman, election of	94
Constitution of	93
Hearings, admission to, procedure, reports, etc.	95, 96
Powers and duties of	97, 98
Questions referable to	97, 265
Quorum of	96
Report of	98
Term of office of	96

	Paragraphs
Vice-Chairman, election, powers and duties of	94

Journal—
Keeping of, by Insurance Committee 498

Late Entrants—
Contributions, rates of . . 352
Sickness Benefit of . . 388–390

Ledger—
Accounts in . 490, 491, 498–528
Proving of 499

Lints—
Supplied under Medical Benefit 197

Lists of Chemists—
See Panel Lists (Chemists).

Lists of Doctors—
See Panel Lists (Doctors).

Local Authorities—
Arrangements with, for Domiciliary treatment . . 314
Arrangements with, for Institutional treatment . . 293
Arrangements with, for treatment of dependants . 340–348
Definition of 71

Local Government Board—
Dispensary treatment, approval of 282, 296
Domiciliary treatment, approval of . . . 282, 312, 313
Excessive sickness, power of, to decide action to be taken . 76
Excessive sickness, power of, to order payment of expenses incurred 76
General powers and duties of, in regard to National Health Insurance . . Introduction
Institutional treatment, approval of . . 282, 285–287
Power of, to appoint diseases to be treated under Sanatorium Benefit 278

Local Medical Committees—
Constitution of . . . 123, 124
Decisions of . . . 128, 178
Powers and duties of . 125–128, 178
Procedure in cases of failure to agree with Insurance Committee . . . 128, 178
Purposes of (general). Introduction, 119
Questions referable to . . 87, 125–127, 178
Recognition of . . . 120, 121
„ „ conditions for 122, 123
„ „ Panel Committees as . . 122, 136
Statutory provision for . . 119
Term of office of . . 120

Marines—
Index Slips of . . . 210
Procedure in regard to claims for Maternity Benefit . . 428

	Paragraphs
Sanatorium Benefit of	320, 475
Sickness Benefit of	400

Marriage—
Suspension of Benefits on . 397

Marriage Certificates . 421, 423

Married Women Voluntary Contributors—
Index Slips of 207
See also Pink Slips.
Title to Benefits . . . 207

Maternity Benefit (Deposit Contributors)—
Amount of . . . 408, 410
Claims for . . . 421–428
Conditions modifying payment of 415–420
Definition of 407
Mother's Benefit . . . 411
Of Aliens 408
Payable in respect of husband's insurance 409
Payment when mother in hospital, etc. . . . 416–418
Penalty for breach of rules in regard to 410
Provision of Midwife or Doctor 419, 420
Qualifications for payment of . 412
„ „ (residential) . . . 413, 414
Suspension of . . 368–370
„ „ on marriage . 397

Mauve Slips—
Purpose of 207

Med. 50—
See Form, Med. 50.

Medical Benefit—
Administration of, consideration by Insurance Committee of representations of Panel Committee 138
Administration of, consideration by Insurance Committee of representations of Pharmaceutical Committee . . 157
Administration of, Income of Insurance Committees for 476, 478–480
Administration of, Powers and Duties of Insurance Committees in regard to (general) 72, 160–163
See also Powers and Duties of Insurance Committees.
Administration of, Powers and Duties of Panel Committees in regard to . . 136–138
Administration of, Powers and Duties of Pharmaceutical Committees in regard to . 154–159
Administration of, Regulations governing . . . 162–163
Administration of, Rules for . 83, 245–247
Administration of, to old and disabled members of Societies 163

	Paragraphs
Arrangements by Insurance Committee with doctors and chemists (general)	161
Definition of	160
Defrayment of cost of	436–440
Deposit Contributors, administration to	366–372
Deposit Contributors over 70	207, 372
During confinement	177
Finance and Accounting in connection with	435–460, 476, 478–480, 489–521
General Scheme of	163
Income of Insurance Committees for	435–460
Persons over 70, title to	207
Standard of treatment to be to the satisfaction of the Commissioners	179
Suspension of, on marriage	397
,, ,, in case of Deposit Contributors	368–371
Temporary residents, financial arrangements in respect of	445–456
Title of insured persons to, in connection with Income Limit	141, 158, 207
Travellers, financial arrangements in respect of	445–456
Travellers, special arrangements for administration to	248, 249
Voluntary Contributors, title to	207

Medical Benefit Drug Fund—

Payments from, in error, in respect of domiciliary cases of tuberculosis	199
Payments from, in error, in respect of temporary residents	200
Payments from, in respect of treatment of diseases concurrent with tuberculosis	325

Medical Benefit Fund—

Accounting	444, 490, 501, 504
Payments into Panel Service Fund	506
Payments into Institutions Fund	512

Medical Benefit Fund Account—

Payments into	444, 501, 504
,, out of	504
To be kept in Ledger	490

Medical Benefit Sub-Committee . . . 99

See also under **Sub-Committees.**

Medical Card—

Application for	223
Change of doctor, procedure in regard to	226
Deposit Contributors, procedure in regard to	430
Form of	221, 222

	Paragraphs
Issue of, on receipt of Index Slip (general)	218, 223
Issue of, to exempt persons	235
,, ,, to members of Approved Societies	211
Issue of, to persons receiving Medical Benefit through the Post Office System	235
Issue of, to Own Arrangers	233, 234, 256
Lost Medical Card	227
Presentation of, to doctor	224
Procedure in regard to temporary residence	229–232
Purposes of	221, 222
Removals, procedure in regard to	217, 228–234, 430
Return of, to insured person	225

Medical Card System—
See Medical Card.

Medical Certificates . 82, 184, 402, 403

Medical Comforts—

Supply of, under Sanatorium Benefit	302, 305, 307, 324–326

Medical Day Books . 181, 182

Medical Index—

Additions to, on receipt of Medical Card signed by doctor	218
Alterations in, on suspension of insured persons from Medical Benefit	214
Alterations in, on change of address of insured persons	228
Alterations in, on insured persons obtaining travellers' voucher	248

Medical Practitioners—
See Doctors.

Medical Records—

General	181–183
Own Arrangers	255
Travellers	249

Medical Record Cards 181, 183

Medical Referees—

Appointment of	128, 178
Decisions binding on Medical Service Sub-Committee	87
Powers and Duties of, in regard to decisions	178

Medical Research Fund—

Payments into	317

Medical Service—

Conditions of	167, 168, 171, 172
Consultation with Panel Committees in regard to terms of	137
Range of	177, 178
,, ,, settlement of questions as to	87, 127, 128, 178
Standard of treatment to be to the satisfaction of the Commissioners	179

	Paragraphs
Medical Service Sub-Committee	79–88
Appointment of	79
Chairman, election of	80
Constitution of	79, 80
Hearings, admission to	81, 84
,, procedure at	83, 85
,, reports on	86
Jurisdiction of	82, 87, 259
Meetings of	83
Procedure for raising question for hearing	83
Questions to be referred to Local Medical Committee	87
Quorum of	85
Report of	86, 259, 266
Term of office of	85
Vice-Chairman, appointment, powers and duties of	80

Medical Year—
Quarters of . . 164

Medicines—
See also under **Drugs**.
Dispensing of, by chemists	187
Dispensing of, by doctors	137, 154, 175, 176
Proper and sufficient	195
Supply of, to temporary residents	200
Supply of, under Sanatorium Benefit	302, 305, 307, 324–326

Meetings of Insurance Committees—
Absence of members from	42
Admission of Press to	540
Arrangements for	70
Attendance of members in person	536
Outwith area of Committee	71
Procedure at	70

Membership of Insurance Committees—
Appointment of representatives of Commissioners . . 58
Appointment of representatives of County and Town Councils 47–49
Election of representatives of Approved Societies.
    See also under **Approved Societies — Representation on Insurance Committees.**
Election of representatives of Deposit Contributors.
    See also under **Deposit Contributors — Representation on Insurance Committees.**
Election of representatives of Medical Practitioners . 50–57
    See also under **Doctors— Representation on Insurance Committees.**
General	4–8
Representation of Women	46
Representatives of Chemists	58

Mercantile Marine—
Contributions, rates of	352
Sickness Benefit of	395, 396

Midwife—
Arrangements by Insurance Committee for services of, at confinement, in case of . 419, 420

Migrants—
Medical Benefit of Deposit Contributor, financial arrangements	445–456
Own Arrangers, title to Medical Benefit	233
Payments from Drug Fund in error on account of	200
Procedure in regard to Index Slips of	215
Procedure in regard to Medical Cards of	229–233
Sanatorium Benefit of	318, 465–474
Special, in connection with Post Office Medical System	186

Mileage Fund—
Accounting . . . 444

Mileage Grants for Highland and Lowland Areas—
Accounting	444, 521
Amount and distribution of Lowlands Grant	458, 459
Distribution of Highlands and Islands Grant	459

Minors—
Unmarried, sickness Benefit of . 391

Minute Book—
Of Insurance Committee . . 490

Misconduct of Patient—
Penalties for . . 245, 259

National Health Insurance Fund—
Advances to Insurance Committees from . . 443

National Health Insurance Joint Committee—
General Powers and Duties of   Introduction

Navy—
See **Sailors**.

Navy and Army Insurance Fund—
Benefits of Members of	400
Management of	Introduction
Payments from, for Sanatorium Benefit of members of	320
Purposes of, general	Introduction

Notice—
By Approved Society to Insurance Committee Clerk naming representatives elected to be members of Committee	27
,, chemist to Insurance Committee regarding termination of agreement	204

	Paragraphs
By doctor to Insurance Committee regarding transfer of patient during year	243
„ doctor to insured persons and Insurance Committee of transfer of patients on removal of name from panel	239
„ doctor to Insurance Committee in regard to withdrawal from Panel	173
„ exempt person to Insurance Committee, of his duty to make own arrangements	253
„ Insurance Committee Clerk to Approved Society showing number of members of Insurance Committee allocated to it	25
„ Insurance Committee Clerk to Commissioners, naming representatives of insured persons elected to be members of Insurance Committee	37
„ Insurance Committee Clerk to Commissioners, of death of Deposit Contributor	358
„ Insurance Committee Clerk to delegates, of meeting to elect representatives of " B " Societies on Insurance Committee	28
„ Insurance Committee, of intention to fix Income Limit	251
„ Insurance Committee to chemists, of alteration in agreements	203
„ Insurance Committees to Commissioners, of alterations in Panel List	166
„ Insurance Committees to Commissioners, of cases of Domiciliary treatment of Tuberculosis	287
„ Insurance Committees to doctors, of alteration of conditions of service	172
„ Insurance Committees to insured persons, of death of doctor	241
„ Insurance Committees to Local Authorities, as to exhaustion of funds available for Sanatorium Benefit	322
„ iusured person to Insurance Committee, of desire to change method of treatment	237
„ insured person to Insurance Committee, of desire to transfer to list of another doctor	236, 243
„ insured person to Insurance Committee, of objection to transfer to list of another doctor	239
„ Local Government Board to Commissioners, of changes in list of Institutions approved for treatment of Tuberculosis.	286

	Paragraphs
Failure to give proper, in connection with election of representatives of insured persons on Insurance Committees	45
In connection with inquiry regarding admission to or continuance on Panel of chemist	267, 270, 271, 273
„ connection with inquiry regarding continuance of doctor on Panel	267, 270, 271, 273
„ Press, specifying representatives of insured persons elected to be members of Insurance Committee	23
„ regard to representatives of Approved Societies ceasing to be members of Insurance Committees	41
Of Confinement in connection with claim for Maternity Benefit	422
„ objection of insured persons to transfer to list of another doctor	239
„ question to be raised for hearing of Medical Service Sub-Committee	83
„ question to be raised for hearing of Pharmaceutical Service Sub-Committee	91
Summoning meeting for appointment of representatives of medical practitioners on Insurance Committees	51, 52, 55, 57
Summoning meeting for filling vacancy among representatives of insured persons on Insurance Committee	43
Summoning meeting of doctors to adopt form of constitution of Local Medical Committee	123
Summoning meetings of Insurance Committees	70 (4)
To chemist, of decision of Insurance Committee regarding complaint	264
„ doctor, of decision of Insurance Committee regarding complaint	260

Notice as to Supply of Drugs and Appliances—
Exhibition of, by chemists	190

Office Buildings of Insurance Committees . 71

Operations—
Range of, under Medical Benefit	177–178
Range of, under Medical Benefit, settlement of questions as to,	87, 127, 128, 178

Orange Slips—
Centralisation of	219
Procedure, in case of Deposit Contributors	216, 431
Procedure, in case of exempt persons	217

	Paragraphs
Procedure, in case of members of Approved Societies	214
Purposes of	213

Outworkers—
Contributions, rates of	352

Own Arrangements—
Accounting and Finance in respect of persons making	516–519
See also **Special Arrangements Fund.**	
Allowance to make	250, 254
Conditions for making	250–253, 255
Exemptions from requirements to make	251, 252

Own Arrangers—
Absence from home, right to Medical Benefit	233, 517, 518
Classes of	516
Issue of Medical Cards to	233, 234, 256
Medical Records of	255
Removal of	233, 234, 257, 518

Panel—
Admission to or continuance of chemist on, representation of Insurance Committee in regard to.	264
Admission to or continuance of chemist on, procedure at inquiries as to	277
Continuance of doctor on, representation of Insurance Committee as to	261
Continuance of doctor on, procedure at inquiries in regard to	266–276
Removal of doctor from	126, 174, 238–240
Withdrawal of chemist from	204
„„ doctor from	173, 174

Panel Committees—
Advances to doctors, a matter for arrangement with Insurance Committee	142
Authority for	129
Complaints, hearing of	144
Constitution of	131–133
Disqualifications for membership of	133
Drug Accounts, examination of, and power to disallow	139, 140
Election of members of	130
Excessive prescribing, hearings, and reports in regard to	140
Expenditure of, arrangements for defrayment of	145, 146
Income limit, power to dispute right of insured person to Medical Benefit on account of	141
Inquiry into complaint against doctor, rights as to	144
Insurance Committees to consult	137
Powers and duties of	136–144
Prescriptions, scrutiny of	194

	Paragraphs
Purposes of (general)	Introduction
Quorum of	134
Recognition as Local Medical Committees	122, 136
Secretary, appointment of	135
Term of office of members of	132
Vacancies	132, 133

Panel Lists—Chemists—
Preparation, approval, and issue of	188, 189
Removal of Chemist's name from	156
Right of Chemists to have name included in	163, 187
Withdrawal of Chemist's name from	204

Panel Lists—Doctors—
Alterations in, to be notified to the Commissioners	166
Authorised by Regulations	163
Exhibition of	166
Preparation of	165, 166
Reference to partnerships may appear in	166
Removal of Doctor's name from	126, 174, 238–240
Right of Doctors to be included in	163, 165
Submission to Pharmaceutical Committee	157
Withdrawal of Doctor's name from	173, 174

Panel Service Fund—
Accounting	490, 506–508

Parish Councils—
Arrangements with, for domiciliary treatment of tuberculosis	314

Parliamentary Drug Grant
458, 460, 521

Parliamentary Grant—
For defraying cost of Administration of Medical Benefit	478–480

Parliamentary Grant (of 2/6d. per Insured Person)—
Accounting	444, 521
Conditions for Payment of	177, 179, 181, 184
Deductions from, accounting	521
Deductions from, liability of doctor or chemist to refund to Insurance Committee	262, 264
Payment of, in case of Own Arrangers	256

Parliamentary Special Mileage Grants—
See **Mileage Grants.**

Partnerships—
Reference to, in Panel Lists	166

Payments to Chemists—
Accounting	509, 510
Advances to be agreed upon by Pharmaceutical Committee and Insurance Committee	159

	Paragraphs
In respect of temporary residents	455
Payments to Doctors—	
Accounting	509
Advances to be agreed upon by Panel Committee and Insurance Committee	142
Doctor not to accept fees other than in terms of Agreement	180
For domiciliary treatment of tuberculosis	316
For temporary residents	456
Penalties—	
For breach of rules for Administration of Medical Benefit	245, 259
„ breach of rules in regard to Maternity Benefit	410
Pharmaceutical Committees—	
Authority for	147
Complaints, hearing of	156
Constitution of	149
Drug Accounts, examination of, and power to disallow	155
Election of, etc.	148
Insurance Committees to consult	154
Powers and duties of	154–159
Purpose of (general). Introduction	
Qualifications for membership of	149
Quorum of	152
Recognition of	147
Representations of, to Panel Committees in regard to excessive prescribing	155
Secretary, appointment of	153
Term of office of members of	150
Vacancies	150, 151
Pharmaceutical Service Sub-Committee	89–92
Appointment of	89
Chairman, election of	91
Constitution of	90
Hearings, admission to, proceedings, reports on, etc.	91
Powers and duties of	92
Questions referable to	263
Quorum of	91
Report of	92
Term of office of members of	91
Vice-Chairman, election, powers and duties of	91
Pharmacy Act, 1868	192, 204
Pink Slips—	
Procedure in connection with	214
Purposes of	207, 213
Poisons and Pharmacy Act, 1908	192, 204
Poor Law Authority—	
Dispensary treatment, arrangements with, for	282
Domiciliary treatment, arrangements with, for	282, 299, 314
Institutional treatment, arrangements with, for	282, 293, 346, 347

	Paragraphs
Sanatorium Benefit, general arrangements for	282, 346
Poor Law Institutions	293
Poorhouse, etc.—	
Payment of Maternity Benefit when mother in	416–418
Payment of Sickness Benefit while contributor in	383–387
Post Office—	
Duties in regard to National Health Insurance Introduction	
Post Office Medical System	186, 514
Postal Orders—	
For payment of Benefits of Deposit Contributors	496
Powers and Duties of Insurance Committees—	
Accounts	490, 531
Administration of Benefits (general)	Introduction, 72
Agreements with Chemists	191, 203
„ „ Doctors	137, 165, 167, 168, 171, 172
Business, Motions, Voting, Signing of Deeds, etc.	70
Collection of information for purpose of classifying Deposit Contributors	73
Consultation with Panel Committees	136, 137
Consultation with Pharmaceutical Committees	154
Contributions to Hospitals	75
Conveyance of Insured Persons in connection with Sanatorium Benefit	329–333
Delegation of powers and duties to Sub-Committees	104–109
Drug Accounts Committee, establishment of	61
Drugs, supply of	202
Employment of Officers	70
Excessive sickness	76
Grouping of Approved Societies for valuation	77
Health Lectures, etc.	74
Income limit	251, 252
Index Register	205–218
Medical Benefit—Administration of	161–164
Medical Service Sub-Committee, appointment of	79
Office accommodation	71
Own Arrangements	250–258
Panel Lists (Chemists)	188, 189
„ „ (Doctors)	165, 166, 169
Protection of Insured Persons against diligence	78
Removal of Chemist from Panel	204
„ „ Doctor from Panel	173, 174, 238–240
Reports and Returns	73
Sanatorium Benefit, administration of	279–282, 322

	Paragraphs
To acquire and hold land	2
To sue and be sued	2
Transfers between Funds	488

Practitioners—
See **Doctors.**

Practitioners Fund—
Accounting	509
Payments into, from Drug Fund	509

Pregnancy—
Payment of Sickness Benefit during	398

Prescriptions—
Scrutiny of	195
Specially marked for domiciliary cases	324, 326
Specially marked for temporary residents	200

Public Health Acts—
Tuberculosis, treatment of, under	343

Quarters of Medical Year . 164

Range of Medical Service
	177, 178
Settlement of questions as to	87, 127, 128, 178

Recommendation for Sanatorium Benefit—
By Insurance Committees	322, 323, 327, 328
Intimation of, to Doctor	327
Period of	323

Record Cards—
Medical Record Cards	181, 183

Records—
Medical Records (general)	181–183
,, ,, own arrangers	255
,, ,, travellers	249

Referees—
Appointment of	128, 178

Refunds—
By Chemist, of expenses incurred as a result of breach of agreement	264
By Chemist, of Parliamentary Grant withheld as result of breach of agreement	264
By Doctor, of expenses incurred as a result of breach of agreement	171, 262
By Doctor, of amount of Parliamentary Grant withheld as result of breach of agreement	262
In respect of death of Deposit Contributors	357–363
To Deposit Contributors on ceasing to reside in United Kingdom	353–356

Register—
Of Instruments, Agreements, etc., entered into by Insurance Committees	490
Of medical certificates for purpose of protecting insured persons against diligence	78

	Paragraphs
Of payments for Benefits of Deposit Contributors	490
Of payments for drugs	490
Of payments to Approved Institutions	490
Of payments to Doctors	490
Of payments to Own Arrangers	490

Registers—
See **Index Register, Medical Index, Suspense Register,** etc.

Registrar of Friendly Societies . Introduction

Reinstatement to Benefits—
Of Deposit Contributors	216
Of exempt persons	217

Reinstatement List . 216

Removal—
Of Chemists from Panel	156, 204
Of Doctors from Panel	126, 173, 174, 238–240

Removal Cases—
Provision of Sanatorium Benefit to—financial arrangements	466–475

Removal Slips—
Procedure, in case of members of Approved Societies	215
Procedure, Deposit Contributors	217, 430–432

Removals—
Abroad	213, 353–356
Affecting title of Doctor to dispense	175
Alterations in Index Register and Medical Index on account of	215, 217, 228, 233, 430, 431
Of Deposit Contributors	351, 353–356, 430, 431
Of Own Arrangers	233, 257, 518
Temporary, procedure regarding Index Slips	215
Temporary, procedure regarding Medical Cards	229–233
To be notified to Insurance Committees by Societies if prior to 11th January 1914	215
To Ireland	215

Remuneration of Doctors—
See also **Payments to Doctors.**
For Domiciliary treatment	316
General	180

Remunerative Time—
Of members of Insurance Committees, compensation for loss of	483, 485, 486

Rent—
Extra, in connection with Domiciliary treatment	308

Reports and Returns—
To be made by Insurance Committees	73

Research—
Medical Research Fund	317

	Paragraphs
Reservists (Navy or Army)—	
See also under **Sailors and Soldiers**.	
Procedure in regard to claims for Maternity Benefit	428
Residence—	
Outwith area of Insurance Committee, effect on payment of Sickness Benefit	374
Outwith United Kingdom, refunds to Deposit Contributors on account of	353–356
Qualifications for payment of Maternity Benefit	413, 414
Temporary, in area of other Committee, procedure in regard to Medical Benefit	229–234
Right of Insured Person to choose Doctor	163
Rules—	
For administration of benefits of Deposit Contributors	365
For administration of Medical Benefit	83, 245–247, 259, 264
Sailors—	
Index Slips of	210
Procedure in regard to claims for Maternity Benefit	428
Sanatorium Benefit, administration of	320
Sanatorium Benefit, administration of (financial) arrangements	475
Sickness Benefit of	399
Sanatoria—	
Approval by Local Government Board	282, 285–287
Available	283, 284, 286
Conveyance of insured persons to or from	329–331
Detention in	291
Erection of, by Local Authorities	348
Sanatorium Benefit—	
Burial of insured persons dying while in receipt of	292, 333
Conveyance of insured persons in connection with	329, 333
Definition of	278
Delegation to Sub-Committees of powers in regard to	104–109
Dependants, extension to	306, 307, 334–348
Deposit Contributors over 70, title to	207, 372
Dispensary treatment	282, 294–297
See also **Dispensary Treatment of Tuberculosis**.	
Domiciliary treatment	177, 282, 298–314
See also **Domiciliary treatment of Tuberculosis**.	
Exempt persons, financial arrangements	461
Finance and accounting	461–475, 522–525
Financial arrangements in regard to	315–322

	Paragraphs
Institutional treatment	282–293, 297
See also **Institutional treatment of Tuberculosis**.	
Local Authorities, arrangements with	293, 314, 340–348
Medicines, etc., provision of	302, 305, 307, 324–326
Migrants	318
See also **Strays**.	
Navy and Army Fund, payments from, in respect of	320
Of Deposit Contributors	366–372
Poor Law Authorities, arrangements not to be made with	282, 293, 299, 314
Powers of Insurance Committees to administer	72, 104–109, 279
Powers and duties of Sub-Committees in regard to	104–109
Prescriptions to be specially marked	324–326
Recommendation for	322, 323, 327, 328
See also **Recommendation for Sanatorium Benefit**.	
Research, funds for	317
Sailors, provision to	320, 475
Sickness Benefit, payment of, while in receipt of	321
Soldiers, provision to	320–475
Strays, financial arrangements in respect of	318, 464–473
Suspension of, on marriage	397
Travellers, provision to	319, 474
Sanatorium Benefit Account—	
Payments from, for Domiciliary treatment	444
Sanatorium Benefit Fund—	
Accounting	490, 501, 522–525
Payments into, from Institutional Fund	514, 515
Payments from, to Administration Fund	464, 488, 523
Payments from, to Central Sanatorium Benefit Fund	464
Sanatorium Benefit Register	490
Sanatorium Benefit Sub-Committee	99
See also under **Sub-Committees**.	
Seamen—	
Index Slips of	210
Procedure in regard to claims for Maternity Benefit	428
Sanatorium Benefit of	320, 475
Sickness Benefit of	399
Seamen's National Insurance Society	Introduction
Secretary for Scotland	Introduction
Section 11—	
Effect of, on payment of Sickness and Disablement Benefits	376–382

	Paragraphs
Section 47—	
Rates of contributions in respect of contributors insured under	352
Sickness Benefit of contributors insured under	393
Section 53—	
Rates of contributions in respect of contributors insured under	352
Sickness Benefit of contributors insured under	394
Service by Chemists—	
Conditions of	187, 191, 192, 203
Service by Doctors—	
Conditions of	167, 168, 171, 172
Range of	177, 178
,, ,, settlement of questions as to	87, 127, 128, 178
Standard of treatment to be to the satisfaction of the Commissioners	179
Shelters—	
Cost of	311
Provision of, under Domiciliary treatment	304, 309–311
Sickness Benefit (Deposit Contributors)—	
Aliens	392
Claims for	401–405
Circumstances by which suspended or modified	375
Late Entrants	388–390
Mercantile Marine	395, 396
Minors, unmarried	391
Payment of, during confinement	398
Payment of, where compensation recoverable	376–382
Payment of, while outwith area of Committee	374
Payment of, while in hospital, etc.	383–387
Payment of, to members of Approved Societies while in Sanatorium	321
Qualifications for payment of	373
Seamen, Marines, and Soldiers	399
Suspension of	369, 370, 375
,, ,, on marriage	397
To contributors insured under Section 47	393
,, contributors insured under Section 53	394
Waiting period	400
Slips—	
See under **Index Slips**, **Orange Slips**, **Suspense Slips**, etc.	
Soldiers—	
Index Slips of	210
Procedure in regard to claim for Maternity Benefit	428
Sanatorium Benefit, administration of	320
Sanatorium Benefit, administration of (financial)	475
Sickness Benefit of	400

	Paragraphs
Special Arrangements Fund—	
Accounting	516–519
Special Drug Grant—	
Accounting in connection with	521
Administration of	460
Amount of	460
Available to Insurance Committees	458
Origin and purpose of	460
Special Married Women Voluntary Contributors—	
Index Slips of	207
See also **Pink Slips**.	
Title to Benefits	207
Special Mileage Grants—	
See **Mileage Grants**.	
Special Parliamentary Drug Grant	458, 460, 521
Special Parliamentary Grant—	
For defraying cost of administration of Medical Benefit	478–480
Special Parliamentary Grant (of 2/6d. per insured person)	
Accounting	444–521
Conditions for payment of	177, 179, 181, 184
Deductions from, accounting	521
,, ,, liability of doctor or chemist to refund to Insurance Committee	262, 264
Payment of, in case of Own Arrangers	256
Special Reservists—	
See also **Soldiers**.	
Compensation, title to	382
Procedure in regard to claims for Maternity Benefit	428
Strays—	
Provision of Sanatorium Benefit to, financial arrangements	318, 464–473
Sub-Committees of Insurance Committees	99–110
Appointment and Constitution of	100–102
Expenditure, sanction of	104
Powers and duties of	104–110
Proceedings, regulation of	103
Reports of	110
Sub-Committees established by Insurance Committees	99
Subsistence Allowance—	
To members of Insurance Committees	483, 484, 486
Sundries—	
Column of General Cash Book	495
Suspense Register—	
Centralisation of	219
Preparation of	208
Suspense Slips—	
Centralisation of	219

	Paragraphs
Comparison with Index Slips	218
Deposit Contributors	433

Suspension from Benefits—
Alterations in Index Register, etc., on account of. 213, 214, 216, 431
Conditions for . See under **Medical Benefit**, etc.

Systems—
Approved for purposes of Medical Benefit . . . 185, 186

Temporary Residents—
Definition of . . . 445
Medical Benefit of, financial arrangements . . 445–456
Own Arrangers, title to Medical Benefit 233
Payments from Drug Fund in error, on account of . . 200
Procedure in regard to Index Slips of 215
Procedure in regard to Medical Cards of . . 229–233
Sanatorium Benefit of . . 318

Temporary Residents Fund—
Accounting . . 453, 490, 520, 521

Terms of Service of Chemists
187, 191, 192, 203

Terms of Service of Doctors
167, 168, 171, 172

Territorials—
See also **Soldiers.**
Compensation, title to . . 382
Procedure in regard to claims for Maternity Benefit . 428

Town Councils—
Arrangements with, for Sanatorium Benefit to dependants . . . 340, 342, 343
Representatives, of on Insurance Committees . . . 47–49

Transfers—
Between Societies, adjustments regarding cost of, Medical Benefit 440
Between Societies, notification of, on Index Slips . 212, 214
Between various Funds . . 488
From Doctors' Lists . 236–244, 259
Of Deposit Contributors to Approved Societies and *vice versa*, adjustments regarding cost of Medical Benefit 440
Of Deposit Contributors to Approved Societies, changes in Index Register, etc., on account of 216, 432

Travellers—
Medical Benefit of, accounting . 445–456
Medical Benefit of . 218, 249
Medical Records of . . 249
Prescriptions of, to be specially marked. . . 219
Sanatorium Benefit of . 319
„   „   „ (finance) . 474

	Paragraphs
Supply of drugs to	249
Vouchers	249

Travelling Expenses—
Of members of Insurance Committees . . . 481, 482

Treasury—
Powers and duties of, in regard to National Health Insurance Introduction

Tuberculosis Dispensaries
294–297, 348

Tuberculosis, Treatment of—
Agreements between Insurance Committees and Local Authorities . . . 292, 293
Approval of Institutions by Local Government Board . 282, 285, 286, 287
Arrangements for, by Insurance Committees . . 279–280
Delegation to Sub-Committees of powers in regard to . 104–109
Dispensary . . 282, 294–297
See also **Dispensary treatment of Tuberculosis.**
Domiciliary . . 282, 298–314
See also **Domiciliary treatment of Tuberculosis.**
Institutional . . 282–293, 297
See also **Institutional treatment of Tuberculosis.**
Local Authorities, arrangements with . 293, 314, 340–348
Non-pulmonary . . 281, 284
Payments from Drug Fund in error on account of . . 199
Persons outwith area of Insurance Committee . . . 297
Pulmonary . . . 281, 283

Unmarried Minors—
Sickness Benefit of . . . 391

Valuation of Approved Societies—
Powers and duties of Insurance Committees in regard to 77

Voluntary Contributors—
Contributions, rates of . 352
Medical Benefit, title to 207

Waiting Period—
For payment of Sickness Benefit 399–400

Water Supply—
Contaminated, causing excessive sickness . . . 76

Withdrawal of Doctor from Panel . . . 173, 174

Wool—
Cotton, Wood, Supply of, under Medical Benefit . . . 197

Workmen's Compensation Act—
Payment of compensation under, effect on Sickness and Disablement Benefits . 376–238

Lightning Source UK Ltd.
Milton Keynes UK
UKHW012214301118
333276UK00011B/1207/P